D0926506

THE MIND'S STAIRCASE

Exploring the Conceptual Underpinnings of Children's Thought and Knowledge

THE MIND'S STAIRCASE

Exploring the Conceptual Underpinnings of Children's Thought and Knowledge

ROBBIE CASE

in collaboration with

Marta Bruchkowsky
Alessandra M. Capodilupo
Joanna Crammond
Sonja Dennis
Thomas A. Fiati
Jill Goldberg-Reitman
Sharon Griffin

Zopito Marini
Anne McKeough
Yukari Okamoto
Marion Porath
Denise T. Reid
Robert Sandieson

LEA LAWRENCE ERLBAUM ASSOCIATES, PUBLISHERS
1992 Hillsdale, New Jersey   Hove and London

Lawrence Erlbaum Associates, Inc., Publishers
365 Broadway
Hillsdale, New Jersey 07642

Library of Congress Cataloging-in-Publication Data

Case, Robbie.
    The Mind's staircase : exploring the conceptual underpinnings of
children's thought and knowledge / Robbie Case in collaboration with
Marta Bruchkowsky . . . [et al.].
        p.   cm.
    Includes bibliographical references and index.
    ISBN 0-8058-0324-6 (c). ISBN 0-8058-1190-7 (pbk.)
    1. Human information processing in children.   2. Cognition in
children.   I. Title.
    BF723.I63C37   199
    155.4'13—dc20   91-24819
                                                        CIP

Printed in the United States of America

10   9   8   7   6   5   4   3   2   1

Contents

PART I
INTRODUCTION

PART II
THE ROLE OF CENTRAL CONCEPTUAL STRUCTURES IN
THE DEVELOPMENT OF CHILDREN'S LOGICO—
MATHEMATICAL THOUGHT

PART III
THE ROLE OF CENTRAL CONCEPTUAL STRUCTURES
IN THE DEVELOPMENT OF CHILDREN'S SOCIAL AND
EMOTIONAL THOUGHT

PART IV
THE ROLE OF CENTRAL CONCEPTUAL STRUCTURES
IN THE DEVELOPMENT OF CHILREN'S SPATIAL THOUGHT

PART V
CROSS-DOMAIN SYNCHRONY AND ASYNCHRONY
IN THE ACQUISITION OF DIFFERENT CENTRAL
CONCEPTUAL STRUCTURES

PART VI
CONCLUSION

List of Contributors

Marta Bruchkowsky
Department of Psychology
Credit Valley Hospital
2200 Eglinton Ave. West
Mississauga, Ontario
CANADA L5M 2N1

Alessandra M. Capodilupo
Department of Child Studies
Brock University
St. Catharines, Ontario
CANADA L2S 3A1

Robbie Case
Center for Educational Research
  at Stanford
Stanford University
Stanford, CA
U.S.A. 94305

Joanna Crammond
Laboratory for Applied Cognitive
  Science
Department of Educational
  Psychology
Faculty of Education
McGill University
Montreal, Quebec
CANADA H3R 1Y2

Sonja Dennis
Department of Psychology
Winthrop College
Rock Hill, SC
U.S.A. 29733

Thomas Ata Fiati
(Deceased)

ix

Jill Goldberg-Reitman
Department of Psychology
North York General Hospital
4001 Leslie Street
Willowdale, Ontario
CANADA M2K 1E1

Sharon Griffin
Department of Education
Clark University
Worcester, MA
U.S.A.

Zopito Marini
Department of Child Studies
Brock University
St. Catharines, Ontario
CANADA L2S 3A1

Anne McKeough
Department of Educational
    Psychology
University of Calgary
Calgary, Alberta
CANADA T2N 1N4

Denise T. Reid
Department of Rehabilitation
    Medicine
University of Toronto
Toronto, Ontario
CANADA M5T 1W5

Marion Porath
Department of Educational
    Psychology & Special Education
Faculty of Education
University of British Columbia
Vancouver, British Columbia
CANADA V6T 1Z5

Robert Sandieson
Faculty of Education
University of Western Ontario
London, Ontario
CANADA N6A 5C2

Preface

This volume had its origin in two theoretical developments, both of which took place in the early 1980s. The first of these was the attempt on the part of a number of psychologists with an interest in Piaget's theory of intellectual development, to rework his classic system in the light of recent developments in learning theory and information science (e.g., Case, 1985; Fischer, 1982; Halford, 1982; Pascual-Leone & Goodman, 1979). The second was the attempt on the part of a number of psychologists with an interest in Chomsky's theory of language, to rework the same classic Piagetian system in terms of recent developments in linguistics and in neuroscience (Carey 1986; Feldman, 1983; Fodor, 1982; Gardner, 1983; Keil, 1984).

As might be expected, the new theories that resulted from these two endeavors were quite different. The view of the mind that resulted from the first enterprise was that of a general or all-purpose computing device, whose basic capacities undergo periodic changes in the course of development. According to this view, as these basic capacities change, the mind acquires the potential for acquiring new and more sophisticated control structures, as well as new data structures and skills of increasing complexity. The second endeavor gave rise to another view, which also utilized the computational metaphor. However, in this case the mind was seen as a *modular* computing device, each of whose modules has its own unique capacities and structures. The theory was that, as these various capacities change, each of the structures to which it gives rise changes as well. However, because each of the capacities is seen as modular, each set of structures is hypothesized to change in its

xi

own unique way and to follow its own unique developmental course (Carey, 1985; Gardner, 1983; Keil, 1986).

During the early 1980s, these two research programs proceeded independently, with relatively little contact between them. As the decade wore on, however, it became apparent that each program was making important conceptual progress. Thus, a number of attempts were made to bring the two programs closer together, and to stimulate some sort of productive exchange between them. The first of these took place at Tel Aviv University in 1984, and gave rise to a volume entitled "Stage and Structure: Reopening the Debate" (Levin, 1986). The second took place at the biennial meeting of the Society for Research on Child Development (SRCD) in Toronto some 2 years later. The dialogue continued at similar scientific gatherings in the years that followed, in East Lansing, Madison, Philadelphia, Sydney, and Palo Alto.

The project that is reported in this volume was an indirect result of these encounters. As a participant in several of these meetings, I had the opportunity to become familiar with the modular viewpoint and the sort of data it was generating. Moreover, as I did so, I became more and more convinced of its merit. At the same time, as a long-time member of the "general-system" or "neo-Piagetian" group of theoriests, I was reluctant to give up the notion of system-wide change completely. As a result, it occurred to me that both positions might, conceivably, be valid. There might indeed be several aspects of children's intellectual functioning that were modular, each of which followed its own unique developmental trajectory. At the same time, however, there might also be general systemic changes, ones that were so broad in their scope as to affect children's ability to deploy *any* basic capacity in a real-world context, even those that were, in all other respects, completely modular.

In thinking about how one might test such an idea, it occurred to me that the methodology that had been used up until that time had been theory-specific. Each group of theorists had tended to study subtly different phenomena, using research methods that were subtly different also. By and large, general systems theorists had tended to study children's intellectual *processes,* using constructs such as encoding, retrieval, working memory, executive control, and the like. They had also tended to study these processes using reasonably large groups of children, in laboratory settings where tight control could be exercised over such extraneous variables as children's background knowledge, social sophistication, and linguistic skill.

By contrast, modular theorists had tended to investigate the *products* of children's intellectual processing, that is, their specific knowledge. Moreover, they had shown a particular interest in exploring this knowledge in precisely the real-world contexts where this knowledge was acquired, and in the "modular" domains that the first group of theorists had avoided. Finally, far from trying to escape the influence of background knowledge and other such factors, they had actively focused on them, thereby elucidating their action, and often doing detailed case studies of individual subjects whose background knowledge, interests, and talents could be chronicled in great detail.

Given this close association between theory and method, it seemed possible that one way to break out of the theoretical impasse might be to address the methodological one. Accordingly, I resolved to expand my interest in children's executive control structures and working memory, and to begin examining the knowledge that resulted from, or that supported the use of, these processes in real world contexts. I also decided to investigate a broader range of domains, especially those that modular theorists had suggested were "informationally encapsulated." Finally, I decided to expand my purview to include children exhibiting atypical as well as typical development.

I began my collaboration with the individuals who are the co-authors of this volume. At the time this project was initiated, all but one of these co-authors were graduate students at The Ontario Institute for Studies in Education (OISE), where I was a professor. Like many graduate schools of education, OISE is extremely fortunate in the diversity of the student body it attracts. It is particularly fortunate to attract a number of students who have already had extensive professional or personal experience with some particular aspect of children's development, and who return to graduate school with an interest in placing their knowledge on a broader and more academic footing. Each of the authors whose work appears in the volume had some particular expertise of this sort. As I began to develop an interest in children's domain-specific knowledge, they began to develop an interest in neo-Piagetian theory and the possibility it offered for elucidating the developmental phenomena with which they were already familiar. It was the melding of our interests and expertise, then, that led to the research that is reported in this volume.

The joint venture on which we embarked was intended to be a very straightforward one. Our plan was to investigate several different strands of development simultaneously and then search for any commonalities across these strands that neo-Piagetian theory might reveal. In effect, we planned to examine each strand of children's development separately, but to be on the alert for any sign that each of these strands was part of some more general tapestry. Unfortunately, like many who had trod this path before us, we soon found that we had underestimated the difficulty of such an endeavor. One of the most stubborn of the problems we encountered stemmed from the diversity of operations that children employ in the various domains that we studied, and the resultant diversity of their knowledge. The dilemma here was how to model children's specific knowledge in each domain in a fashion that would do justice to its uniqueness, yet still permit some sort of meaningful comparison to be made from one domain to the next. While neo-Piagetian theory provided a set of formalisms for analyzing children's intellectual *processes* across domains, it offered virtually no guidance as to how to analyze the knowledge or other products to which these processes might lead. Thus, each time we entered a new domain of knowledge, we had to grapple with the same dilemma anew: How to analyze the specific data that we had gathered about children's knowledge, in a way that would permit us to apply the general systemic constructs that neo-Piagetian theory provides.

A second and ultimately more formidable problem was that the sort of results neo-Piagetian theory had led us to *expect* in various domains of development were not always what we discovered. In their place we often found phenomena that at first appeared completely different, yet on closer inspection were not so completely different as to warrant a rejection of the neo-Piagetian framework entirely. What we often had to do, then, was to recover from our original surprise, revise our conceptualization of the phenomena in question, and test our revised expectations with further experiments.

Whether we were justified in revising—rather than rejecting—our original theoretical framework, is a question the reader will have to judge. Some may object that, rather like Columbus, we would have done better simply to map the territory in each new domain that we entered, and to give up hope that our exploration would lead us somewhere else. Others might maintain that the new territories we discovered were, in fact, not new at all, and that we would have done better to obtain a map from their original inhabitants. Still others might maintain that we were right in conserving our original goal of constructing a cross-domain map of children's development, but we chose the wrong theoretical tools to do so.

These possible objections notwithstanding, this volume is an attempt to elucidate the reason we elected to pursue the particular goal that we did at the outset, the way in which our understanding of this goal evolved as we pursued it, and the methods and results to which this evolving understanding led. The book is organized in six parts. In the first, I trace the history of the theoretical question in which we became interested, and the methods that we elected to use at the outset of the project. In the next three parts, we describe the way in which these methods evolved, and the new data and conceptions to which they led, as we explored children's evolving knowledge and skills in three broad domains: logico-mathematical, socioemotional, and visual motor functioning. In Part Five, we describe our studies of special populations, and the way in which their cognitive processes and knowledge differs from those of other children. Finally, in Part Six we summarize the revised view of development to which we were led as a result of our various studies, and the constructs we evolved for bridging the gap between the modular and the general-systems perspectives.

Before launching directly into an account of our scientific methods and findings, a word is in order about the social process by which they were arrived at. For a number of years in succession, the authors of this volume participated in the same research enterprise, and met with other members of the research group on a weekly basis. Although the group's membership varied considerably from year to year, the general topic remained the same, as did the modus operandi: In the course of their time in the group, each one of the participants conceived, executed, and reported at least one (and often several) empirical studies in his or her own area of expertise, that he or she felt would help illuminate the general issues in which we all were interested. At certain points in the development of each project, the members of the group also met with me privately on an individual basis, in order to work out the details of their tasks and task analyses in a mutually satisfactory fashion. Finally, at regular intervals during the 7-year period that our research group was "in session," each member also took some particular aspect of his or her ongoing investigation, and developed it into a doctoral or master's thesis.

Although the perspective presented in the pages that follow had its most direct origins in the crucible of our weekly meetings, it was of course also affected by the more general intellectual environment in which these meetings took place, and that was provided first by the Centre for Applied Cognitive Science at the OISE, and later by the Center for Educational Research at Stanford. The work also profited from the seriousness with which the other faculty in these centers took our project, and the specific suggestions that they made with regard to the various studies we initiated. In this regard, we would like to express our particular gratitude to Carl Bereiter, Andrew Bielmiller, James Greeno, Daniel Keating, Peter Lindsay, David Olson, Bill Postl, Linda Siegel, Ross Traub, and Otto Weininger, all of whom served in an advisory capacity on at least one of the dissertations that were produced. We would also like to thank the external readers of the various theses, especially John Berry, Jack Canfield, David Feldman, Carl Fredrikson, E. Tory Higgins, Dennis Newman, Sydney Strauss, and Esther Thelen.

Throughout the project, our work profited not just from the input of the faculty at OISE and Stanford, but also from the input of other students. In this regard, I would like to express thanks to Sonja Masciuch, Karen Leitner, Marc Lewis, and Hal White at OISE, whose primary interest was in other topics, but who participated in our weekly discussions nonetheless, and were instrumental in shaping many of the concepts and experiments that resulted. I would also like to thank Deborah Baranyi, Rick Berg, Charles Bleiker, and Barbara Henderson, who played a similar role at Stanford, and also gathered the data that are reported in chapter 15.

To Cheryl Williams at OISE, for her efforts in organizing our meetings during the first 5 years of the project, and for preparing the first drafts of our chapters, I owe a special and very personal debt. For their organizational assistance at Stanford, I am also indebted to Sharon Griffin, Anne McKeough and Yukari Okamoto. Finally, we would like to extend our thanks to Frances Tolnai, David Ray and Andrea Evans for helping prepare the final draft of the manuscript, and also to Rick Berg, Charles Bleiker, Barbara Henderson, Beverly Bushey, Nancy Beth Garrett, Kim Marra, Yukari Okamoto, and Christina Tsai, for proofreading the galleys and preparing the author index.

The actual production of any academic book is always a collaborative effort to at least some degree. However, I feel that in the present case this was particularly true. The project on which the book was based was a collaborative one to begin with, and much of the writing was done collaboratively as well. Each author or group of authors also had the opportunity to comment on the entire manuscript, not just the chapter of which they were the authors. These comments were then scrutinized very carefully before the final drafts of each chapter were prepared. In a very real sense, then, the book should be considered a multiply—rather than a singly—edited volume.

On behalf of the entire group, I would like to conclude by expressing our gratitude to Harry Beilin, Howard Gardner, and Chava Casper for the criticism, encouragement, and assistance they offered us in the editorial process. I would also like to thank Michael Cole and Richard Snow for their comments on the final chapter. Finally, I would also like to express my thanks to the Ontario Ministry of Education, the Social Sciences and Humanities Research Council of Canada, the McDonnell Foundation, and the Spencer Foundation, without whose combined resources neither the original project nor this volume would have been possible. Of course, neither the project nor the volume would have been possible without the support of our many friends and loved ones, either. It is to them that this volume is dedicated.

—Robbie Case

INTRODUCTION

In the present section, three contemporary views of intellectual development are presented, and placed in historical context. Each one of these views constitutes a different response to the same historical dilemma, namely, the one that was created when Piaget's theory of intellectual development was confronted with massive evidence of exceptions to the monolithic pattern of development he had hypothesized. Notwithstanding the similarity in their origins, the three theories nonetheless differ in a number of fundamental respects, particularly with regard to the stance they take on the degree of generality that should be imputed to the human cognitive system and the process by which this system develops. After a detailed presentation of the theory out of which the present project evolved, we show that—notwithstanding its other attractive features—the theory does not do full justice to the most recent data on the modularity of the human mind and its development. The conclusion is that the theory's assumptions must somehow be altered or expanded if a satisfactory position on this issue is to be reached. A research strategy for working toward such an objective is then proposed, and its relationship to subsequent sections of the volume explicated.

General and Specific Views of the Mind, Its Structure and Its Development

Robbie Case
Stanford University

With the emergence of cognitive science, a new form has been given to an old question. In its original form, the question was whether differences in intellectual capability were best thought of as stemming from differences in a single, underlying intellectual factor, or whether they were better thought of as stemming from the differential development of a number of more discrete mental faculties. In its modern form, the question has been phrased in more technical terms: Is the mind better thought of as a general, all-purpose computing device, whose particular forte is general problem solving? Or is it better thought of as a modular device, each of whose modules has evolved to serve a unique biological function that it performs in its own unique and specialized way?

As in the past, advocates can be found for each position. There are those who see the mind's power as stemming from its modularity (Fodor, 1982; Gardner, 1983), and those who see its power as residing in its more general problem-solving capabilities (Newell & Simon, 1972). In recent years, there has been an acknowledgement that the truth very probably lies in between (Cecci, 1989; Sternberg, 1989). As yet, however, the conceptual apparatus for explicating this position has not been fully developed.

There does appear to be considerable agreement that the mind has conceptual or computational capabilities that are general, as well as those that are specific. There also appears to be considerable agreement that each sort of capability is vital in our daily lives, and that each is shaped by a variety of external and internal forces. Exactly how these different types of capability interact, however, has not as yet been specified. Nor has much thought been given to the way in which they might combine to influence the overall course of our intellectual growth, or how they might be impacted by the twin forces of maturation and enculturation.

This monograph is an attempt to lay the groundwork for answering some of these questions. Although the various chapters have different authors, the common theme that unites them is the interaction between system-wide and modular capabilities in shaping children's mastery of the concepts and skills that are their cultural heritage. Since this issue is by its nature developmental, I begin with a brief history of recent attempts to conceptualize children's general and specific capabilities in the field of intellectual development.

PIAGET'S THEORY OF INTELLECTUAL DEVELOPMENT

Without question, the notion of a "generalized intellectual competence" found its strongest expression in the writings of Jean Piaget. In keeping with his roots in the rationalist tradition, Piaget viewed the child as a young intellectual, constructing ever more powerful theories of the world as a result of applying a set of logical tools of increasing generality and power. Beginning with his wartime lectures, and continuing for the next 15 or 20 years, Piaget attempted to specify the nature of these general tools, the process by which they are acquired, and the knowledge of the world to which they give rise.

The tools in question were construed as logico-mathematical operations that were universal in nature, and remained invariant across considerable differences in the content to which they were applied. It was by actively applying these operations, according to Piaget, that children were able to make sense of their world. Thus, their understanding at any point in time was a reflection—not just of the external properties of the world itself, or their experience with it—but of the properties of the operations that they had applied in order to make sense of this experience.

Certain very basic and discrete cognitive operations were acknowledged to be present from birth. Even these pre-wired and relatively reflexive operations, however, were not seen as remaining independent for very long. Rather, with experience, they were seen as gradually becoming differentiated and coordinated into systems of increasing complexity and coherence. Piaget believed that, at several points in development, these systems became particularly stable, and acquired a number of organizational properties that could be described via symbolic logic (commutativity, associativity, reversibility, etc.). One of these points was at the age of about 2 years, after the development of children's earliest sensory and motor capabilities was complete. Another was at the age of 7 to 10 years, after the emergence and development of a higher-order set of operations that were "representational" in nature. The third point was at the end of adolescence, after the emergence and development of a class of representations that were more abstract or "formal."

Because Piaget saw these stable systems as playing a fundamental role in shaping children's views of the world around them, he divided children's cognitive development into four general stages, defined as a function of the attainment (or non-attainment) of the thought that these systems permitted. He termed the four stages the *sensorimotor* stage (0 to 2 years), the *pre-operational* stage (2 to 7 years), the *concrete operational* stage (7 to 10 years) and the *formal operational* stage (11 to adulthood). With development divided into these four general stages, he went on to address the question of how children make the transition from one of these stages to the next. The answer he proposed was that children's active reflection on the products of their current mental activity plays a key role in the stage-transition process, as does their attempt to deal with the inherent contradictions that this reflection reveals.

In summary, while Piaget acknowledged that reality could be parsed into various domains (his own favorites being the Kantian ones of space, time, causality, etc.), he nevertheless saw children's understanding in each of these domains as being determined, to a major extent, not just by their domain specific experience, but by the general set of operations that they brought to their experience, and the general set of auto-regulative processes by which these operations were assembled into stable systems or groups.

RESPONSES TO PIAGET'S THEORY

One of the most important features of Piaget's theory was that it focused investigators' attention on the active role of the individual in the construction of his or her own knowledge. Another was that it stressed the general organization of knowledge during an historical epoch in which human knowledge was more often viewed in an extremely atomistic fashion. Perhaps the most important feature of Piaget's theory with regard to the topic of the present volume, however, was that it led to the discovery of a wide range of empirical phenomena for which it also provided a coherent and parsimonious explanation. Among the data that were explained by the theory were the following: (a) A great many sequences of intellectual development appear to be universal, both within and across cultures; (b) children are unable to solve a wide variety of logical problems, no matter how "rationally oriented" or "logical" their culture, until a remarkably late age; (c) training children to solve these problems is a very difficult endeavor, when it is possible at all; and (d) a wide variety of these problems appear to be solved spontaneously (i.e., without training) during middle childhood.

In spite of its broad explanatory power, Piaget's theory had a number of shortcomings, which became apparent as it was examined from the perspective of other theoretical systems. Some of these problems were largely rational in nature, such as the inherent difficulty of explaining how a cognitive system could be open to cultural innovation when it is only equipped with a universal and closed set of logico-mathematical operations (Keating, 1980). Another was the difficulty of accounting for human cognition that was *not* logical or mathematical, when the underlying theory asserted that logico-mathematical structures were paramount (Broughton, 1984). Yet another difficulty was the lack of correspondence between the form in which Piaget's structures were articulated (i.e., symbolic logic) and the form in which they were represented in children's minds: It seemed that Piaget's theory was better equipped for representing the structure in the mind of logicians than the structure in the minds of young children. The fourth, and perhaps most serious, problem was that the theory provided little or no explanation for *exceptions* to the general pattern of development. In this regard, the following data were particularly problematic:

1. *Cross-Task Correlations.* For Piagetian measures that were passed at the same age, it was often the case the intertask correlations were low or insignificant. Why this should be the case, if the underlying factor postulated to account for all of them was the acquisition of a single underlying structure, was not apparent (Pascual-Leone, 1969; Pinard & Laurendeau, 1969).

2. *Decalages.* Although certain Piagetian measures were passed at the same age, it was more often the case that different measures of the same underlying construct were passed at very different ages. When conservation of weight was used as the assessment tool, for example, children appeared to have reached the stage of concrete operations by the age of 8 or 9 years. By contrast, when conservation of number was used, they appeared to reach that stage by age 5 or 6 (Piaget & Inhelder, 1974). Why the acquisition of one general underlying structure should lead to this sort of asynchronous pattern of cross-task performance was not clear (Pinard & Laurendeau, 1969; Fischer, 1980; DiRibeaupierre & Rieben, 1985).

3. *Instruction.* According to Piaget's theory, one would expect that purely external manipulations—especially manipulations of a didactic sort—would not have much impact on children's performance on tests that assessed the presence or absence of an underlying logico-mathematical structure. To the extent that instruction did have any impact, though, one would also expect a broad pattern of transfer to structurally similar tasks in other domains. In fact, the pattern was the reverse: Quite a number of training studies produced significant gains in children's performance on measures such as conservation, as a result of instruction that was strongly didactic in nature (Gelman, 1969; Beilin, 1971a). Although children showed broad transfer to other variants of these same problems, however, they almost never showed transfer to tests of different concepts that were supposed to be structurally equivalent (e.g., classification or seriation).

4. *Development in Other Cultures.* A fourth set of data came from cross-cultural investigations. Here the anomaly was that, in many cultures, success did not appear to be achieved on Piagetian tests of formal operations even in adulthood (Dasen, 1972). Because the achievement of formal operations was supposed to be universal, this was difficult to explain. Piaget's position in this matter was that the measurement devices were at fault (Piaget, 1972): Were measures developed that were better suited for use in other cultures, and that contained content with which the culture was thoroughly familiar, the logico-mathematical structures of formal thought would be found to be truly universal.

THE RISE OF TASK-SPECIFIC THEORIES AND THE BEGINNINGS OF "COGNITIVE SCIENCE"

As data like those just cited began to accumulate, many investigators in North America, especially those with roots in the empiricist tradition, began to reject Piaget's notion of general logical structures (Brainerd, 1978; Flavell, 1963, 1982; Gelman, 1969, 1972) and turned their attention to three lines of research that they felt Piaget had neglected. The first was the investigation of intellectual competence in early childhood (Gelman, 1972; Meltzoff, 1981; Shatz & Gelman, 1973); the second was the investigation of children's linguistic competence (Bates, 1976; A. L. Brown, 1973; C. Chomsky, 1970; E. Clark, 1973; Gentner, 1975; Slobin, 1973); and the third was the investigation of children's social cognition (Damon, 1977; Flavell, Bolkin, Fry, Wright, & Jarvis, 1968; Selman, 1980; Turiel, 1975). At the same time that investigators were branching out into these new substantive fields, they began pursuing new theoretical directions as well. On the one hand, they became interested in Chomskian linguistics; on the other, they became interested in the newly emerging discipline of information science (Newell, Shaw, & Simon, 1958). These two strands of thought ultimately merged into the discipline that became known as "cognitive science." However, during the 1970s they remained at least relatively distinct, and led to different sorts of theoretical renewal.

As Klahr (1988) has pointed out, the number of investigators who developed detailed "information processing" models of children's cognition during this period was quite small. However, a substantial number of investigators began to adopt the general metaphor on which information processing theory was based. That is to say, they began to accept the utility of thinking of the mind as a device for processing information from a variety of modalities, encoding it symbolically in some sort of working buffer, accessing additional relevant information from long-term memory, and executing series of transformations on the resultant content. One consequence of this trend was that investigators began to study developmental changes in the capacities of the various sensory stores and buffers (Case, 1972b; Pascual-Leone, 1970; L. S. Siegel, 1968). Another was that they began to study children's strategies for managing the control of information flow, and for circumventing memorial difficulties (Belmont & Butterfield, 1971; A. L. Brown, 1974; Case, 1970, 1974; Chi, 1976; Flavell, 1971). In addition, they began to look at changes in children's ability to represent and relate various items of information in an integrated fashion, via such devices as scripts, rules, semantic networks, and production systems (Gentner, 1975; Klahr & Wallace, 1976; Nelson, 1978; Siegler, 1976).

There was one further trend that went unnoticed at first, but that in the end turned out to be just as important. With the exception of those who embraced Chomsky's original view of language acquisition—and held to this view in the face of the semantic, pragmatic, and contextual challenges that were mounted against it—there was an implicit resurgence in the field of the empiricist epistemology on which earlier investigations and theories in North America had been based: According to this view, learning could profitably be understood as the acquisition of a set of relatively specific competencies, and development could be seen as the result of cumulative learning. One of the most common features of research that was done in North America during the 1970s and 1980s, then, was that it attempted to model the development of children's competencies on a wide variety of "tasks" without regard to how the various models or competencies might be related to each other. The nature of these models was far more sophisticated then earlier models of the stimulus-response (or S–R) variety, but the underlying epistemology was the same.

PROBLEMS WITH THE EARLY
POST-PIAGETIAN MODELS

As a dialectical historian might have predicted, the assumption that children's cognitive processes could be viewed in such a highly atomistic fashion eventually began to encounter its own problems—ones that were directly the opposite of those entailed by Piaget's overly monolithic system. These difficulties may be understood by re-examining the general classes of data that were mentioned earlier.

1. *Intertask Correlations.* Although it was true that many tasks that one would have expected to correlate on the basis of Piaget's theory did not do so, it was also true that reliable clusters of correlations *did* emerge among many subgroups of Piagetian test items (Pascual-Leone, 1969; Toussaint, 1974). Given that this sort of "horizontal structure" was present in the developmental data, it seemed clear that development in different areas could not be conceptualized as proceeding in a totally isolated fashion. Rather, the many "trees" of development had to be seen as part of some smaller set of "forests" (Carey, 1985; Case, 1985).

2. *Decalages.* As investigators explored the competencies of younger children, the strategy they adopted was one of seeing how low on the developmental or phylogenetic scale they could go and still find evidence of the logical competencies that had been held by Piaget to be characteristic of concrete operational thought. As the conservation studies of Mounoud and Bower (1974) and the number studies of Starkey, Spelke, and Gelman (1983) made apparent, the answer was very low indeed. Both sets of investigators ultimately found evidence of the logical competencies with which they were concerned in early infancy.

While these findings demolished the old basis for inferring qualitative differences in children's performance (or at least the popular interpretation of that basis) they simultaneously raised the question of what to replace it with. To say that young infants possess a set of logical competencies that had once been thought to be unique to 7- and 8-year-olds was to tell only half of the story. The other half was that they could only reveal these competencies under extremely constrained testing conditions (A. L. Brown, Bransford, Ferrera, & Campione, 1983; Chi, 1988; Gelman, 1978).

Of even greater significance was the fact that—at first blush, at least—the tasks on which children could reveal such competencies in infancy appeared to share a number of features in common that made them quite unlike the tasks on which they revealed these competencies during the preschool years. Similarly, the tasks on which they revealed such competencies during the preschool years appeared to share certain characteristics that made them quite unlike those that were appropriate for children aged 5 to 10. The new problem that was raised, then, was how to account for this sort of "vertical structure" in the data without getting trapped in the problems that had plagued Piaget's general-structural theory.

3. *Instruction.* Although children did not show the pattern of learning and transfer that would be expected on the basis of Piaget's general-structural theory, there was one aspect of their performance that was not well explained by specific process-models of development. This was that, below a certain age, there was very little evidence of success. For example, considerable evidence was obtained that many children could be trained on tests of liquid conservation at age 5 or 6. Prior to that age, however, there was massive failure (Halford, 1989). While such failure did not establish the *impossibility* of earlier training, it did at least demonstrate the far greater *difficulty* of such training. And, once again, this finding needed some sort of explanation.

4. *Development in Other Cultures.* The final data that were problematic came from the cross-cultural arena. These had to do with universality of children's success on the first three classes of tasks invented by Piaget, namely, tests of sensorimotor, preoperational, and concrete operational intelligence. Given the apparent *lack* of cultural universality in children's experience, especially as regards logic and mathematics, these cultural universals also appeared to require some new form of explanation.

In summary, while Piagetian theory tended to paint a picture of children's cognitive development that was too monolithic, universal, and "endogenous," the early reactions to this theory presented a view that was too atomistic, context-specific, and focused on external experience. Thus, what a number of investigators began to suggest was that a new body of theory was called for, one that somehow did justice to the more general features of children's cognition to which Piaget's research had drawn attention *and* the more specific and contextually sensitive features on which subsequent research had focused (Beilin, 1971b; Carey, 1985; Cecci, 1989; Chi, 1988; Inhelder, Sinclair, & Bouvet, 1974; Kuhn, 1983; Pascual-Leone, 1976; Stone, 1976).

Although a number of attempts to integrate these two perspectives were made, three are of particular relevance to the work reported here.

CONTEMPORARY SOLUTIONS TO THE
POST-PIAGETIAN DILEMMA

Neo-Piagetian Theory: Renewing the Search
for System-Wide Constraints and Structural Potentials

In the late 1970s and early 1980s, a number of neo-Piagetian theories were proposed, in which general and specific characterizations of cognitive development were combined (Biggs & Collis, 1982; Case, 1978, 1985; Demetriou & Efklides, 1988; Fischer, 1980; Fischer & Pipp, 1984; Halford, 1982, 1988; Mounoud, 1986). These theories drew on the early neo-Piagetian proposals by Pascual-Leone (1969) and McLaughlin (1963) concerning the general systemic limitations to which all children's cognitive processes must be subject. In addition, they re-incorporated a number of structural notions from Piaget's theory, while adding a number of new notions from elsewhere. As might be expected, the theories that were proposed also differed from each other in a number of important ways (see Case, 1988, for a review). Nevertheless, with regard to certain core postulates, they were essentially identical. These postulates may be summarized as follows:

1. Three or four levels of structure may be identified in the course of children's cognitive development (Case, 1978; 1985; Demetriou & Efklides, 1988; Fischer, 1980; Halford, 1982; Mounoud, 1986).

2. Higher structures include lower ones, and are assembled by their coordination (Case, 1978, 1985; Fischer & Ferrar, 1988; Halford, 1982, 1988; Pascual-Leone, 1970, 1988).

3. Notwithstanding any commonalities in their general form, each structure at any level is assembled independently from each other structure, in a fashion that is highly dependent both on the context in which this assembly takes place, and the child's previous experience within that context (Case, 1978, 1985; Fischer, 1980; Halford, 1982).

4. There are important differences, both within and between individuals, in the way in which individual structures are assembled and the rate at which they are acquired (Demetriou & Efklides, 1988; Fischer & Canfield, 1986; Pascual-Leone, 1969, 1988).

5. Even under optimal environmental and organismic conditions, there is an "upper bound" to the level of structure that children can assemble at any age. This upper bound can give rise to a stage-like "evenness of functioning" across different tasks, under conditions where experiential and individual differences are controlled (Case,

1985; Fischer & Canfield, 1986; Halford, 1988; Pascual-Leone, 1988).

6. Among the factors that play an important role in determining the upper bound of children's functioning are the size of their working memory (Case, 1974, 1978, 1985; Fischer, 1980; Halford, 1982; Pascual-Leone, 1970), and/or the speed of the basic operations they can execute within this memory (Case, 1985; Halford, 1988).

Neo-Nativist Theory: Biologically Based Modules, Constraints, and Conceptual Structures

During the same period, a second group of theorists developed a very different solution to the problem of modeling the general and specific aspects of human development within one theoretical system. This group also re-introduced a structural perspective on the process of cognitive change. However, the particular form of structuralism they proposed derived from Chomsky's work in linguistics rather than Piaget's work in cognition. At the risk of oversimplifying a very dynamic research program, the general set of propositions to which this second group of theorists subscribed may be characterized as follows:

1. At birth, human infants come equipped with a primitive set of modular structures that predispose them to attend to certain particular classes of stimuli, and to expect certain kinds of patterns in them (Carey, 1988; Keil, 1981; Spelke, 1988; Starkey et al., 1988).

2. What happens with the passage of time is that children's maps or "theories" of each domain undergo periodic restructuring (Carey, 1988; Keil, 1986).

3. Some of these restructurings are relatively minor, and can be thought of as involving the addition and/or merging of local structures into more general ones. Others, however, are truly major, and involve a fundamental change in (a) the nature of children's concepts, (b) the relationships among these concepts, and (c) the phenomena that these concepts are viewed as explaining (Carey, 1985, 1988; Wiser, 1988).

4. Because the structure of each module is innately specified, the possibility of a biological timetable for development cannot be overlooked (Gardner, 1983; Keil, 1986).

5. To the extent that such a timetable does exist, it is unlikely to be the same across different modules (Gardner, 1983; Keil, 1986).

The above propositions should not be construed as implying that the human mind contains no more general machinery for coordinating the results of its modular computations. Clearly it does, and neo-nativist theorists acknowledged this. However, these propositions do imply an acceptance of Fodor's (1982) position on individual and developmental differences in children's knowledge. Such differences are not seen as being primarily a function of differences in the central machinery of cognition, but rather are seen as being due to differences that are module-specific.

The New Learning Theory: Changes in the Structure of Children's Representations as They Move from Universal Novicehood to Domain-Specific Expertise

At the same time that the neo-nativist view of young children's cognition was being developed, a new learning framework for viewing children's intellectual development was being worked out as well. This view began with the attempts of Herbert Simon and his colleagues to characterize the difference between the problem-solving processes of "novices" and "experts" in various domains of knowledge (D. P. Simon & H. A. Simon, 1978). However, it gathered its real momentum as the notion of a novice–expert continuum was taken over by educational and developmental psychologists, who adopted the notion as a metaphor for characterizing the cognitive differences between children and adults (Anderson, 1983; Chi, 1978, 1988; Chi & Rees, 1983; Larkin, 1983; McClelland, 1989). Once again, the superordinate view of cognition that united the new learning theories was not formalized. Nevertheless, with regard to the following general principles, there did appear to be a considerable degree of agreement.

1. In any given culture, a number of internally coherent bodies of knowledge are built up over generations, for dealing with various discrete classes of problem that the culture encounters and deems to be of lasting significance. Examples in our own culture would include the knowledge that is of relevance to such scholastic domains as mathematics, chemistry, biology, or physics (Chi & Rees, 1983; Larkin, 1983; D. P. Simon & H. A. Simon, 1978).

2. The sort of external "world-relationships" that these bodies of knowledge represent vary widely from domain to domain, as does the method by which children are initiated into any given domain by their culture (Chi & Rees, 1983; D. P. Simon & H. A. Simon, 1978).

3. One of the most important ways in which children's knowledge in any domain changes with age is that, as children acquire more experience in the domain, they begin to form new connections (whether conceptual, procedural, or purely associationistic) among the basic elements of which the domain is comprised. These new connections lead to the integration of knowledge structures that were previously discrete (Chi, 1988).

4. Once integrated, new knowledge structures or networks, in turn, lead to new *strategies* for approaching problems in the domain and to new *memorial capabilities* (Chi, 1985).

5. The different sorts of intellectual development that are observed in different domains are the result of this cumulative learning process, as are the apparent changes in underlying memorial capacities (Chi, 1976; Chi & Rees, 1983).

Relationships Among These Positions

In terms of their epistemological assumptions, the closest relationship among the three bodies of theory that have just been reviewed is between neo-Piagetian and neo-nativist theory. Both of these theories have their roots in the rationalist tradition, and share a similar view of knowledge and the knowing process. In terms of their position on the generality–specificity issue, however, it is the new learning theory and neo-nativist theory that bear the closest resemblance to each other, because both of those theories locate the generality in children's cognitive structures within domains, rather than across them.

SUMMARY

On the issue of whether children's cognitive development is general or specific, a dialectical tension may be identified that has both an historical and a contemporary aspect. From an historical point of view, there has been a clear dialectical progression: from an original structural theory where cognitive development was viewed as monolithic, universal, and endogenous, to a subsequent empiricist view in which development was seen as atomistic, contextually specific, and exogenous, and then to a contemporary set of views where a balance has been struck between these two positions.

Even within these theories, however, a similar though less pronounced tension may be identified. This tension is between the class of theories in which the generality in children's cognition is localized *within* domains (whether of the "hard"- or "soft"-wired variety), and the class of theories that ascribe generality to the more general cognitive system. It is this tension with which the present volume is concerned, and for which it suggests a provisional remedy. In order to understand the nature of the proposed remedy, however, it is necessary to have a slightly more detailed understanding of the research program from which it originated, and of the dilemma that this program faced at the time the present project was initiated. Such a description is presented in the next two chapters.

A Neo-Piagetian Approach to the Issue of Cognitive Generality and Specificity

Robbie Case
Stanford University

As was mentioned in the previous chapter, neo-Piagetian theory had its roots in the attempt to build a model of intellectual development that would preserve the strengths of Piaget's theory, while eliminating its weaknesses. More specifically, the goal was to build a model that would account for the many exceptions to the pattern of development that Piaget had described without losing the power to account for this pattern itself.

Two core notions underpinned the first generation of neo-Piagetian theories. The first was that the process of structural change is a local, not a general, one. That is to say, each cognitive structure is assembled independently of each other structure, in a fashion that is sensitive both to the context in which the child currently finds him- or herself, and to his or her previous learning history (Pascual-Leone, 1969). The second core notion was that the process of structural assembly is subject to a general developmental constraint. This constraint was construed as a limitation in a hidden, quantitative parameter (called M in Pascual-Leone's theory), which changes very gradually with age, and which limits the maximum amount of information to which a child can attend at any one moment (Pascual-Leone, 1969).

Most of the more recent neo-Piagetian theories that have been proposed have preserved these two original notions. In addition, however, they have attempted to provide more detail with regard to the process by which individual structures are modified in a context-sensitive fashion (Case, 1978, 1985; Fischer, 1980; Halford, 1980, 1982; Pascual-Leone, 1988), and to provide a better characterization of the general structural

17

sequence that results (Case, 1985; Fischer, 1980; Halford, 1988; Demetriou & Efklides, 1988; Mounoud, 1986). Two additional concerns have been to explain why the general quantitative limitation on children's thought changes in the first place (Case, 1985; Fischer & Pipp, 1984; Mounoud, 1986; Pascual-Leone, 1989), and how it is that different individual children appear to follow such different developmental paths, when subject to the same general cognitive-developmental limitations (Demetriou & Efklides, 1988; Fischer & Silvern, 1985; Hoppe-Graffe, 1989; Pascual-Leone & Goodman, 1979).

One effect of the neo-Piagetian movement has been to reduce the historic tension between monolithic, structural-developmental characterizations of intellectual development, and more atomistic, learning-oriented views. Another effect, however, has been to open up a whole new set of questions and challenges with regard to the issue of cognitive generality and specificity. In the present chapter, I present a brief summary of the particular neo-Piagetian theory that I developed during the 1980s, and the solution it implied with regard to the generality–specificity issue. In the next chapter, I describe the new problems to which this theory gave rise, and the research strategy that we decided to pursue in the present project, in order to overcome them.

A NEO-PIAGETIAN THEORY OF INTELLECTUAL DEVELOPMENT

Children's Thinking at Different Stages of Development

The general view of children's development that was proposed is illustrated in Chapter 19 (see pg. 348). Four major stages of development stages were hypothesized. Each of these was believed to have its own distinctive type of cognitive operation and structure. Within each of these four general stages, three substages were also proposed. At the first, a new type of structure is assembled, but can only be applied in isolation; at the second stage, two such units can be applied in succession, but cannot be integrated in a definitive fashion; and at the third, two or more such structures can be applied simultaneously and integrated into a coherent system. As a result of this integration, the system acquires the general set of properties that Piaget referred to with such terms as "reversibility" and "compensation." Another result is that the system can now serve as the building block for further progress at the next stage. As a consequence, development "recycles," in the recursive fashion indicated in the figure.

Developments During the First Few Months of Life

The representation in Fig. 19.1 (pg. 346) is an abstract one; thus, in principle, the letters A and B could be instantiated by many different sorts of mental units. In fact, the particular sorts of mental units that were hypothesized were control structures for solving the elementary problems that children encounter, universally, in their daily lives. In order to understand the nature of these structures, it is useful to examine a concrete example. Consider, for example, the developmental changes in children's responses to a simple piece of physical apparatus whose operation they find inherently interesting. When seated in their mothers' laps and confronted with the apparatus illustrated in Fig. 2.1, infants of 2 or 3 months of age react in a characteristic fashion to any rocking motion of the balance armature: As the beam is set in motion, their eyebrows go up and their eyes widen. They then track the side that is directly in front of them as it goes up and down, sometimes moving their entire head in order to do so (Case & Hayward, 1984).

In and of itself, this is hardly surprising. However, since babies who are younger than this often *fail* to track the beam as it moves out of their field of focal vision, the phenomenon suggests that an important change has taken place in the infants' sensory orienting capabilities, even by this early age. In effect, infants have learned how to solve the problem of maintaining their gaze on an interesting object as the object leaves their field of focal vision. The internal *program* or *executive control structure* by which they do so might be represented as follows.

PROBLEM SITUATION ⟶ OBJECTIVE
Interesting object moving out of view in upward (or downward) direction.

Return pattern of stimulation to its original focal state.

STRATEGY
Move head and eyes in an upward (or downward) direction, using peripheral input as a guide.

At the same time as they consolidate structures for directing their eyes in a voluntary fashion, babies also consolidate structures for directing their hands in voluntary fashion: for example, for getting their thumb back to their mouth, when it is removed for some reason by their caretaker. The structure by which this second problem is solved might be represented as follows:

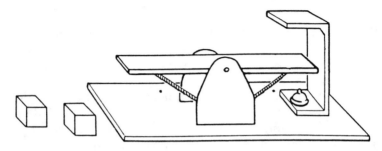

FIG. 2.1.   Apparatus used for investigating preschoolers' understanding
of a balance beam.

PROBLEM SITUATION ————→ OBJECTIVE
Pleasant stimulation from mouth   Return pattern of oral stimula-
ended, by removal of hand in a   tion to its original pleasant state.
lateral direction.

                                      STRATEGY
                                      Move arm and hand back
                                      toward mouth, perhaps using
                                      input from the mouth
                                      as a directional guide.

As is no doubt apparent, these two control structures have a great
deal in common: Each one contains (a) a representation of the infant's
current sensory state, (b) a representation of some other, more desirable,
sensory state that has just previously been experienced, and (c) a representation of a simple motor strategy for effecting a change from one of
these states to the other. It is these sorts of simple structure, then, that
are represented in the bottom panel of Fig. 19.1 (pg. 348) by the letters
"A" or "B."

Developments During the Sensorimotor Stage

Substage 1: 4–8 months.   At about the age of 4 months, children's
disposition toward a moving balance undergoes a marked change.
Rather than passively watching the beam as one of its ends goes up and
down and gradually comes to rest, infants reach out and actively engage
the apparatus in a variety of ways. In effect, they begin to treat the beam
as an exciting toy that they can bring into motion at will. The control
structure by which they re-produce some particularly interesting action
of the toy (such as the ringing of a bell that is placed under the beam) is

spelled out in the top panel of Table 2.1. An assumption behind this description is that there has been a subtle *differentiation* and *interleaving* of the two control structures that have just been described, plus the creation of a higher order structure in which one of these two structures serves as the goal, and the other serves as the means to achieving it. It is this *hierarchical integration* of two existing control structures—one of which controls the fine-motor orienting activity of a sensory system, and one of which controls the gross-motor orienting activity of the child's limbs—that is presumed to herald the infant's arrival at the sensorimotor stage proper. In Fig. 19.1 (see pg. 348) this integration is represented as A—B. In this notation, the two letters stand for the two structures that were originally discrete, and the solid line indicates the (means–end) relationship that the infant now sees between them.

Substage 2: 8–12 months.   Between approximately 4 and 8 months, infants' visual activity during exploration of an object appears to be relatively localized in space; thus, on the balance beam, they appear to be concerned primarily with exploring the reaction of the part of the beam that is nearest to them. At about 8 to 12 months, however, they begin to be interested in effects that are less proximal. Thus, they now begin to split their attention, and to examine the actions and reactions that take place at the *other* end of the beam, in response to the actions and reactions that they produce at the end that is nearest. During this period, babies will actively try to ring a bell that is placed over the other end of a balance beam, by pushing down on the end that is closest to them (Case & Hayward, 1984. The full control structure they use to do so is spelled out in the middle of Table 2.1. It may also be represented in more abstract form in the third panel from the bottom in Fig. 19.1 (see pg. 348), namely,

$$A_1–B_1$$
$$\vdots$$
$$A_1–B_2$$

In this notation, the two A–B pairs represent the action and reaction at each end of the beam, and the dotted line indicates the child's global apprehension that some sort of causal connection exists between them.

Substage 3: 12–18 months.   Between the ages of 12 and 18 months, further developments take place in infants' sensorimotor behavior. Infants now begin to explore the reversible relationship between pairs of actions and reactions whose global relationship they have already

TABLE 2.1
Infant Control Structures for Making Balance Beam move as Desired

	PROBLEM SITUATION	OBJECTIVE
4–8 Mos.	• Balance beam exhibits interesting change in movement (plus sound).	• Re-initiate pattern of movement.
	• Experimenter's hand made contact with beam at X.	• Move own hand to balance beam at X.

STRATEGY
1.   Move arm from current
     position (Y) to X.
2a. Strike or touch beam
     with hand.
2b. Monitor change in beam
     that results.

	PROBLEM SITUATION	OBJECTIVE
8–13 Mos.	• Bell rings at other end of balance beam.	• Ring bell at other end.
	• Ring produced by movement of beam.	• Re-initiate beam movement.
	• Experimenter's hand made contact with beam at position X.	• Move hand to beam, at X.

STRATEGY
1.   Move arm from current
     position (Y) to X,
     monitoring its approach.
2a. As hand approaches or
     touches beam, turn head
     and look at other end.
2b. Strike or push beam as
     hand makes contact.
3.   Monitor results at other
     end

	PROBLEM SITUATION	OBJECTIVE
13–20 Mos.	• Bell rings at other end of balance beam.	• Ring bell at other end.
	• Ring produced by downward movement of beam at other end.	• Make beam go down at other end.
	• Experimenter pulled this side of beam up.	• Pull this side of beam up.
	• Experimenter made contact with beam (or handle) at lX	• Move hand to beam at X.

STRATEGY
1. Move arm from current position (Y) to X, monitoring its approach.
2a. As hand approaches beam, turn head and monitor other end.
2b. Move the beam up, after hand makes contact.
3. Monitor direction of beam. (If it is not going in desired direction, reverse.)
4. Monitor contact of beam with bell; if it does not ring, repeat 2b with vigor.

apprehended. With the balance beam, for example, babies can now differentiate between a push on the beam and an upward pull. In fact, they will occasionally execute each action in succession, watching the different re-actions that take place at other end of the beam as they do so. Situations where the position of a bell is changed from above to below the beam—after a habit has first been established to the first position— thus no longer give them any serious difficulty. The full control structure that is responsible for generating this sort of flexible behavior may be represented in the elaborate fashion indicated in the bottom panel of Table 2.1. Alternatively, it may be represented in the more schematic fashion indicated in Fig. 19.1 (see pg. 348), namely,

$$A_1–B_1$$
$$X$$
$$A_2–B_2$$

The above sort of control structure, with the attendant capability that it produces for operational reversibility, marks the pinnacle of Piaget's sensorimotor thought. In structural terms, the achievement indicates that two action–reaction units on which the child was able to focus during the second substage of the period have become sufficiently well differentiated and coordinated for the child to apprehend the reversible relationship that exists between them. In process terms, the achievement indicates that children are now capable of solving sensorimotor problems in which several different subgoals must be established and pursued, en route to obtaining a major goal. In subsequent years, children go on to higher and qualitatively different forms of thought. At least in the present framework, however, all of the subsequent changes that take place are seen as having the same general form as those that have just been described.

Developments During the Interrelational Stage

As just mentioned, by the end of the sensorimotor stage (about 20 months) children fully understand the relationship that obtains between two action–reaction action units. What happens at the end of this stage is a bit similar to what happened during the first few months of life. Just as children consolidated their basic structures for monitoring sensory input and generating goal-oriented motor responses during the first few months of life, so they now begin to consolidate relational control structures, such as those just described in Substage 3 of the sensory motor stage (i.e., structures in which the specific relationship between two objects is apprehended and manipulated in a reversible fashion). Then, just as they began to coordinate two qualitatively different forms of orienting structure in making their transition into the first substage of the sensorimotor period at 4 months, so at 20 months they begin to coordinate two different forms of relational structure, in making a second major transition in their thought. This change can be observed on the balance beam in two different ways. First, children can now be given the task by verbal instruction (thus demonstrating the ability to coordinate verbal and non-verbal relationships). Second, their nonverbal structures can now be seen to involve two different types of component relation: an enabling or *instrumental* relationship, and a preventive or *blocking* relationship. As a consequence, children can now solve problems that involve the beam and a support on which the beam rests. For example, they can now remove a pair of blocks under the beam in order to test the beam's reversible or rocking motion. After children have made the transition to this new form of thought, they make two more advances, which are also parallel to those that were made earlier, during the sensorimotor stage. Midway through the interrelational stage (27 to 42 months) their focus of attention expands to include two rather than one interrelational unit. Then, as they near the end of the stage (3½ to 5 years) further elaborations are introduced, with the result that the workings of a reversible system of interrelations can be apprehended. This means that children can now understand a system of relations such as that indicated in Fig. 2.2.a, and make the correct prediction that the action of a heavy weight on one side of the balance will override or reverse the action of a light weight on the other. They can also apprehend systems of relations of the same general complexity in other domains, such as those inherent in the act of counting. These relations are illustrated in Fig. 2.2.b.

(a)

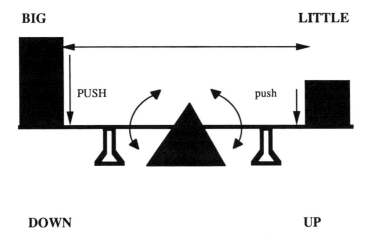

BIG　　　　　　　　　　　　　　　　LITTLE

PUSH　　　　　　　push

DOWN　　　　　　　　　　　　　　　UP

(b)

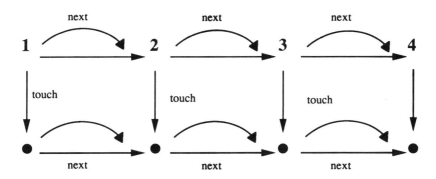

FIG. 2.2. Systems of conceptual relations understood by 4-year-olds, as indicated by their ability (a) to manipulate a balance successfully, and (b) to count without errors of omission or "double-tagging."

The hypothesized sequence of control structures that underlies further progression on the balance beam is indicated in Table 2.2. Once again, one may describe the new developments in two different ways. In structural terms, one could say that children come to differentiate and integrate two of the sorts of interrelational pairs that they first assembled at the beginning of the interrelational period, with the result that they

TABLE 2.2
Preschool Structures for Making Balance Beam Move as Desired

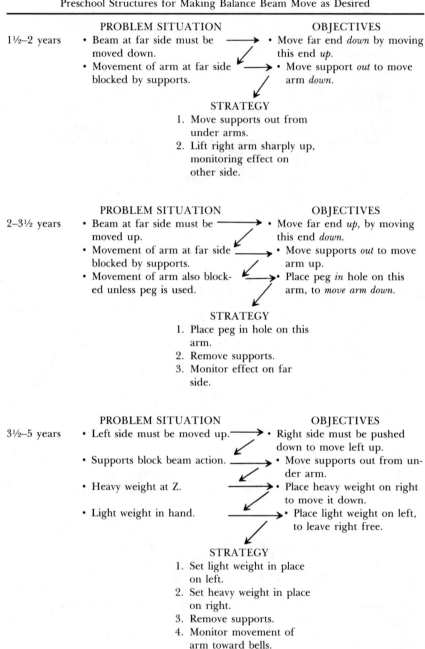

1½–2 years

PROBLEM SITUATION
• Beam at far side must be moved down.
• Movement of arm at far side blocked by supports.

OBJECTIVES
• Move far end *down* by moving this end *up*.
• Move support *out* to move arm *down*.

STRATEGY
1. Move supports out from under arms.
2. Lift right arm sharply up, monitoring effect on other side.

2–3½ years

PROBLEM SITUATION
• Beam at far side must be moved up.
• Movement of arm at far side blocked by supports.
• Movement of arm also blocked unless peg is used.

OBJECTIVES
• Move far end *up,* by moving this end *down.*
• Move supports *out* to move arm up.
• Place peg *in* hole on this arm, to *move arm down.*

STRATEGY
1. Place peg in hole on this arm.
2. Remove supports.
3. Monitor effect on far side.

3½–5 years

PROBLEM SITUATION
• Left side must be moved up.

• Supports block beam action.

• Heavy weight at Z.

• Light weight in hand.

OBJECTIVES
• Right side must be pushed down to move left up.
• Move supports out from under arm.
• Place heavy weight on right to move it down.
• Place light weight on left, to leave right free.

STRATEGY
1. Set light weight in place on left.
2. Set heavy weight in place on right.
3. Remove supports.
4. Monitor movement of arm toward bells.

can eventually solve a number of problems involving some form of reversibility or compensation. In process terms, one could say that they can, by the end of the stage, establish a sequence of relational goals as a means to achieving a terminal goal that is itself relational in nature.

Developments During the Dimensional Stage

As indicated in Fig. 19.1 (see pg. 348), this entire process recycles at two further points in children's development. At the age of 5 or 6, children for the first time coordinate their structures for dealing with spatio-causal systems such as a balance beam, with their structures for dealing with spatio-temporal systems such as those inherent in the act of enumeration. As a consequence, they now begin to conceptualize variables such as weight in a quantitative rather than a qualitative fashion. If asked which side of a balance will go down when two sets of weights that differ only slightly in size are placed on it, they now focus on the *number* of weights in each set, and make an intelligent "rule-based" prediction (Siegler, 1978). This major shift in their thought is followed by two other developments that appear to be more minor. In the first (at 7 to 8 years), children's attentional focus expands to include the dimension of distance from the fulcrum as well as weight. In the second (at 9 to 11 years), children elaborate on this bifocal structure until they understand the higher order relationships that exist among these dimensions (e.g., quantitative compensation). As a consequence, they now begin to solve balance problems where the dimensions of weight and distance are put into conflict, and where a correct answer cannot be obtained unless the global magnitude of the *difference* in any dimension is noticed, and the dimension with the greater difference is used for making a decision. The control structures that are presumed to underlie this further sequence of developments are indicated in Table 2.3.

Developments During the Vectorial Stage

The last major qualitative shift in children's thinking prior to adulthood takes place at about the age of 11 or 12. At that time, children for the first time begin to coordinate the sort of dimensional-compensation structure that they assembled for dealing with the tradeoff between weight and distance with other formally similar structures, such as those for comparing two fractions or ratios. Once again, this leads to a qualitative shift in their thought. And, once again, after this shift has taken place, there is a subsequent expansion of focus (at 13 to 16 years), which is then followed by a further elaboration (at 16 to 19 years). This last elaboration permits children to understand abstract *systems* of dimensions in which there is no concrete referent for any pair of items that

TABLE 2.3

PROBLEM SITUATION		OBJECTIVE
4 years	• Balance beam with an object ⟶ on each arm. ↙	• Determine which side will go down.

STRATEGY
1. Look at each side. Predict that the one which looks *heavy* will go down, the *light* one up.

PROBLEM SITUATION		OBJECTIVES
6 years	• Balance with stack of objects ⟶ on each arm. ↙	• Predict which side will go down.
	• Each stack composed of a ⟶ number of identical units ↙	• Determine which side has larger number of units.

STRATEGY
1. Count each set of units; note which side has the bigger number.
2. Pick side with bigger number as the one will weigh more (and there-fore go down).

PROBLEM SITUATION		OBJECTIVE
8 years	• Balance beam with stack of ⟶ objects on each side ↙	• Predict which side will go down.
	• Each object stack composed of ⟶ a number identical units. ↙	• Determine side with greater number of objects.
	• Each object at a specifiable ⟶ distance from fulcrum. ↙	• Determine side with weight at greater distance.

STRATEGY
1. Count each set of weights; note which side has greater number.
2. Repeat 1 for distance pegs.
3. If the weights are about equal, predict that the side with the greater dis-tance will go down. Otherwise predict that the side with greater weight will go down.

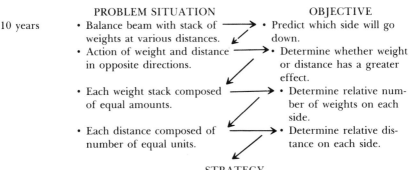

10 years

PROBLEM SITUATION
- Balance beam with stack of weights at various distances.
- Action of weight and distance in opposite directions.

- Each weight stack composed of equal amounts.

- Each distance composed of number of equal units.

OBJECTIVE
- Predict which side will go down.
- Determine whether weight or distance has a greater effect.

- Determine relative number of weights on each side.

- Determine relative distance on each side.

STRATEGY
1. Count each distance; note size as well as direction of difference.
2. Repeat step 1 for weight.
3. Compare the magnitude of the results in steps 1 and 2. Notice which is bigger.
4. Focus on dimension of greater difference. Pick side with higher value as one which will go down.

might be compared, as when the ratios of weights and distances are first converted to two new ratios having a common term, and these new ratios are then compared to decide which side will go down (Furman, 1981). The control structures that are presumed to underlie this last progression are indicated in Table 2.4. Note that the component operations in this last table, such as the calculation of ratios, are no longer cultural universals. Moreover, even in cultures in which operations such as ratio are used, the operations are not normally internalized (i.e., reconstructed by children) without some form of direct instruction. In the context of the present theory, therefore, the content of children's intellectual structures at higher ages is presumed to become less culturally universal and more dependent on some form of formal schooling.

The Process of Stage Transition

Assuming for the moment that the foregoing characterization of children's development is adequate, what sort of underlying mechanism or process should be hypothesized to account for it? A number of formal requirements must be met by any system that can coordinate two existing structures into a higher order structure in the recursive fashion that has just been described. The first of these requirements is that two lower order units must somehow be activated by the system at the same time or

TABLE 2.4
Preadolescent and Adolescent Control Structures for Predicting Action
of Balance Beam

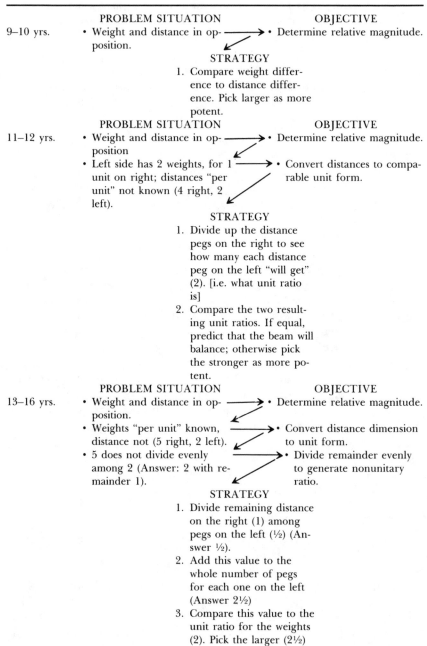

9–10 yrs.

PROBLEM SITUATION
• Weight and distance in opposition.

OBJECTIVE
• Determine relative magnitude.

STRATEGY
1. Compare weight differ-
ence to distance differ-
ence. Pick larger as more
potent.

11–12 yrs.

PROBLEM SITUATION
• Weight and distance in opposition
• Left side has 2 weights, for 1
unit on right; distances "per
unit" not known (4 right, 2
left).

OBJECTIVE
• Determine relative magnitude.
• Convert distances to compa-
rable unit form.

STRATEGY
1. Divide up the distance
pegs on the right to see
how many each distance
peg on the left "will get"
(2). [i.e. what unit ratio
is]
2. Compare the two resulting unit ratios. If equal,
predict that the beam will
balance; otherwise pick
the stronger as more po-
tent.

13–16 yrs.

PROBLEM SITUATION
• Weight and distance in opposition.
• Weights "per unit" known,
distance not (5 right, 2 left).
• 5 does not divide evenly
among 2 (Answer: 2 with remainder 1).

OBJECTIVE
• Determine relative magnitude.
• Convert distance dimension
to unit form.
• Divide remainder evenly
to generate nonunitary
ratio.

STRATEGY
1. Divide remaining distance
on the right (1) among
pegs on the left (½) (An-
swer ½).
2. Add this value to the
whole number of pegs
for each one on the left
(Answer 2½)
3. Compare this value to the
unit ratio for the weights
(2). Pick the larger (2½)
as more potent.

PROBLEM SITUATION
- Weight and distance in opposition
- Neither dimension in unit form.
- Values on weight dimension are 7 left, 3 right.
- 7 does not divide among 3 evenly (Answer: 2 with remainder 1).

OBJECTIVE
- Determine relative magnitude.
- Convert each ratio to unit form.
- Convert weight dimension to unit form.
- Divide remainder evenly as well.

STRATEGY

1. Divide remainder (1) among other number (3)(Answer ⅓).
2. Add to answer from whole number division (2) (Answer 2⅓).
3. Repeat division for other dimension, that is,
3a. Divide 5 among 2 (2 remainder: 1).
3b. Divide 1 among 2 (½).
3c. Add fraction to answer from whole number division (2) (Answer 2½).
4. Compare results from 2 divisions; pick large ratio (2½) as more potent.

in immediate sequence. In information processing terms, this means that some sort of *schematic search* for a second control structure must be conducted, while the first one remains active. Next, the utility of the combination must be apprehended, which, in information processing terms, requires some sort of *schematic evaluation*. Next the two schemes must be reorganized or "interleaved," so that they can be reactivated as a pair in the future. In information processing terms, this requires some sort of *re-tagging* of the two structures in question. Finally, the reorganized pair must somehow be changed into a smoothly running unit in its own right, which presumably requires some sort of *schematic consolidation*.

According to the present theory, these four information processes are extremely common ones, occurring in many of the activities in which children engage spontaneously in their daily lives. In particular, they are activated in the course of activities that are pursued independently, such as exploration and problem solving, and those that are more socially directed, such as imitation and mutual regulation. Both of these general activities are thus seen as being ones that can strongly shape the course of children's cognitive growth.

As I have already mentioned, there is one form of mutual regulation that is of particular importance for higher order forms of development in this system, namely, *instruction*. Although children are rarely, if ever, instructed in the sorts of problem solving or logical activities that Piaget studied, in certain cultures they are frequently exposed to models for the executing components of these activities, such as procedures for determining fractional equivalence. Moreover, in cultures where such modeling or instruction is not present, they fail to show development into and through the higher stages that Piaget described on tasks that involve these component operations (Dasen, 1972). As children grow older, then, the culture is increasingly seen not just as presenting children with the *opportunity* for development, but as providing direct *assistance* in the developmental process by facilitating the construction of the tools necessary to solve the higher order problems children will encounter "independently" at later points in their lives.[1]

Constraints to Which All Transition Processes are Subject

There is one final set of theoretical assumptions that are important to mention, namely, those that are concerned with explaining why intellectual development occurs at such a relatively slow rate, and across such a broad range of fronts at more or less the same time. As the reader may have noticed, children's progression through the sensorimotor period was accompanied by an increase in the size of the "goal stack" that they had to maintain as they worked on the problems that are characteristic of this stage. The present position is that the number of goals children can maintain (and hence the complexity of problem they can solve) is determined by the size of their short-term memory for the particular class of operations in question. As was indicated in Fig. 19.1 (see pg. 348), a further assumption is that this Short-Term Storage Space (STSS) can hold 1, 2, 3, and 4 items at the preliminary, first, second, and third substage of each period, respectively. A final assumption is that this increase in STSS occurs as the result of two factors: maturation and experience.

Maturation.   It is presumed that, corresponding to each of the four levels of control that have been specified there is a corresponding level of neurological control, which involves some form of "hard-wired" system that takes input from lower order systems, and executes further

---

[1] In this suggestion, the present theory is closer to that of Vygotsky (1962) or Bruner (1964) than to that of Piaget.

processing on it (Case, 1985, chapter 17). The first assumption, then, is that there is a limit on the efficiency of any operation, which is set by the degree of maturation of the relevant neurological system. Until this system reaches some critical level of maturation, it cannot coordinate the input from two lower level systems, even if the structures that are indicated have been well consolidated. Continued maturation permits this system to perform this function more efficiently and eventually to deal with input from 3 and then 4 well automated structures (hence, the increase in STSS).

Exactly what sort of maturation is entailed is not clear. However, myelinization of major nerve fibers, particularly fibers connecting one topographical area with another, is one possibility.

Experience. The second factor is experiential. In order to take advantage of whatever degree of neurological maturation is present, it is presumed that a certain degree of practice with any operation is necessary, and that this practice will have the effect of automatizing the operation in question, up to some asymptotic level that is maturationally dependent.

APPLICATION OF THE THEORY TO THE PROBLEM OF DEVELOPMENTAL GENERALITY VERSUS SPECIFICITY

As was mentioned at the beginning of the chapter, neo-Piagetian theory had its roots in an attempt to account for the many exceptions to the pattern of development that Piaget had described, without losing the power to account for this pattern itself. Before concluding the present chapter, it is worthwhile to pause and to indicate exactly how the neo-Piagetian theory that has just been described fulfilled each of these dual functions.

Aspects of Development Presumed Universal and General

The aspects of children's development that were presumed to be general, and to give it the universal character that Piaget originally postulated, may be summarized as follows:

1. Although each executive control structure represents a device for dealing with a different, specific problem situation, all executive control structures undergo a similar set of transformations with time, and pass through a universal sequence of four major stages: those of

sensorimotor, interrelational, dimensional, and vectorial thought. What differentiates these stages is the level of relationship that the child must represent and manipulate. Structures at higher stages are assembled by the intercoordination of two well consolidated but qualitatively different structures from the previous stage.

2. Within each major stage, a universal sequence of three substages may also be identified: the substages of *unifocal, bifocal,* and *elaborated* coordination. What differentiates these substages is the number of elements that children must represent and the way in which these elements must be organized.

3. Under conditions where adequate problem-specific experience is provided, each stage of development is traversed during a characteristic time period, across a broad range of content domains. What gives development this natural time-course is that each successive stage of development entails operations that are controlled by a higher level neurological system, and there is a biological limit to how fast each progressively higher system can come "on-line" to perform the integrative function it is designed to serve.

4. Under conditions where adequate domain-specific experience is provided, each substage is also traversed during a characteristic time period. Substage development is also limited by how fast further maturation of each higher level system can take place. The rate of this maturation sets an upper bound on the *efficiency* with which the operations of that level can be executed and this, in turn, sets an upper bound on subjects' working memory for the products of these operations. Except in highly controlled instructional settings, more complex structures cannot normally be assembled without placing a higher load on the working memory system.

Aspects of Development That are Presumed to be Specific

The aspects of development that are presumed to be specific, and to account for the considerable variability that is observed from one child, task, or context to the next, are as follows:

1. The intellectual operations that children construct, especially at higher stages of development, are entities that are cultural inventions, such as ratio-comparison, not universal logico-mathematical operations. Accordingly, the course of children's intellectual development must vary as a function of the *culture* in which they are raised, and the *historical epoch* within that culture's life.

2. As they grow older, children must depend increasingly on some form of instruction, either formal or informal, in order to acquire the

high-level operations that the culture values, and that are used in its communal "work." It follows that children's intellectual development will vary as a function of the social group within a culture in which they are raised, and the access that this group provides to educational resources of this sort (Case, 1975).

3. The control structures children develop at any age are devices for dealing with specific problem situations. Moreover, it is by the integration of existing specific structures that individuals progress from one stage or substage of development to the next. It follows that development will vary to a considerable extent, both in its overall course and in its rate, as a function of children's individual learning history within their social group (Case, 1978).

4. Because control structures have three specific components, it follows that children's individual learning histories can vary as a function of factors that relate to any one of them:

(a) Because the first component is a representation of a particular situation, it follows that children's development can vary as a function of the *particular contexts* in which they receive their initial exposure to particular problems, and the match of these contexts to those in which these problems are encountered at subsequent points in their lives.

(b) The second component is a representation of the goal to be achieved in the particular class of situations. It follows that children's intellectual development can, thus, vary as a function of affective and motivational features in their own makeup or in the world around them, which predispose them to pursue or to avoid particular sorts of goals (Case, Hayward, Hurst, & Lewis, 1987).

(c) Finally, the third component is a set of operations that children apply in order to reach the goals they elect to pursue in a particular situation. Therefore children's intellectual development can vary as a function of the match between whatever endogenous operational capabilities they may possess, and the operations that turn out to be most important for solving the particular problems that the culture renders most salient.

In summary, it may be seen that the neo-Piagetian theory described in this chapter preserves the general structure of Piaget's theory, but modifies those aspects of the theory that suggest that children's development is impervious to the physical or cultural environment around them. The advantages and disadvantages of this general view—and of its embodiment in the particular theory that has just been described—are taken up in the next chapter.

Advantages and Limitations of the Neo-Piagetian Position

Robbie Case
Stanford University

In the present chapter, the advantages and disadvantages of the neo-Piagetian theory described in the previous chapter are discussed. A solution for remedying the weaknesses is then proposed, together with a research strategy for implementing it. Finally, a description is provided of the way in which this strategy was realized, in the research that is reported in the rest of the present volume.

COMPARISON OF NEO-PIAGETIAN THEORY WITH PREVIOUS THEORETICAL SYSTEMS

One of the first hopes for any new theory is that it should be able to deal with the major classes of problems identified, but not resolved, by its predecessors. As the reader may recall, there were actually two classes of theory in existence at the time the present neo-Piagetian theory was proposed. Piaget's structural theory hypothesized four broad levels of structure, to which all logico-mathematical tasks are assimilated. The new "process" theories modeled children's cognitive processes on each logico-mathematical task in isolation from all others. In order to see the advantage of the present theory in comparison to these two previous sorts of theory, it is worthwhile to revisit the four classes of data that were mentioned in chapter 1.

Synchrony and Asynchrony in Cognitive Development. For classic Piagetian theory, one of the major problems was how to explain the fact that logically equivalent tasks are often passed at very different points in children's development. For the first generation post-Piagetian "process" theories, the challenge was precisely the opposite: how to account for instances where logically equivalent tasks are passed at the same point in children's development, even though they do not appear to share any specific component processes. Within the context of neo-Piagetian theory, neither of these data are particularly problematic. All things being equal, the first outcome is expected whenever two tasks require control structures or skills of differing levels of complexity. Similarly, the second outcome is expected whenever two tasks require control structures or skills of the same level and complexity.

Of course, it is one thing to explain two contrasting sets of data in a post hoc fashion, and quite another to use this sort of explanation to make predictions about new task situations. However, empirical tests of the present theory indicated that, when the operational level and working memory demands of two tasks were systematically varied, and the appropriate experiential controls introduced, asynchrony and synchrony in cognitive development could be differentially predicted (Case, 1985; Khanna, 1985; Liu, 1981; Marini, 1984, chapters 7–10).

Effects of Training on Specific Developmental Competencies. A second major problem was how to explain the success of task training that did not appear to be aimed at inducing a major reorganization of children's underlying logico-mathematical structures. For the newer process theories, the problem was once again the opposite: how to explain instances of training *failure*, particularly when the children who were trained already demonstrated all the specific skills and concepts that had been hypothesized as prerequisites for training. Once again, in the context of neo-Piagetian theory, neither of these data are problematic. It is expected that some direct interventions will be successful and others unsuccessful, and that this will vary as a function of whether or not they overload the child's working memory system. In order to test this explanation, a variety of new training studies were conducted in which children were assigned to conditions where the training either was or was not consonant with their available working memory. And, once again, it was found that both general forms of data—both success and failure—could be predicted (Case, 1985, chapter 15).

Individual Differences in Cognitive Development. A third class of data that was problematic for previous developmental theories had to do with intra- and inter-individual differences in cognitive development. From the structural perspective of Piaget's theory, the problem was how to explain the many instances in which performance on two logically related tasks is not correlated. From the local process perspective, the problem was how to explain the equally numerous cases where clusters of logically related tasks are strongly correlated in the absence of any specific process commonality.

Within the context of the neo-Piagetian theory described in the previous chapter, the first sort of data could be explained by appeal to the particular operations that the different tasks entail, and the situations in which these operations are acquired and elicited: Because individual control structures are presumed to be assembled in specific contexts in response to the specific problems that these contexts pose, modest to weak correlations between many developmental tasks are expected under normal testing conditions. Under circumstances where these latter variables are controlled, however, the size of children's working memory is expected to exert a common ceiling effect, and thus, cross-task correlations of considerable magnitude are expected.

As with the previous explanations, the foregoing account was submitted to a variety of experimental tests. And, once again, these tests were, by and large, successful (Marini, 1984, cited in Case, 1985, chapters 10 and 18; Rich, 1979, 1982).[1]

Cross-Cultural Studies of Cognitive Development.   The final set of data that had to be addressed were those that emerged from cross-cultural studies of development. From the classic structural perspective, the problem was how to explain the absence of abstract or "formal" operations, at least as assessed by Piaget's tasks, in certain individuals or in certain cultures. From the newer process perspective, the problem was how to explain the apparent universality of lower order operations, such as those indexed by conservation, even in cultures where there was no obvious environmental emphasis on the underlying concepts.

The neo-Piagetian explanation for these phenomena has already been alluded to. Given that the context of children's high-level structures is culturally specific and that social interaction plays a stronger role in fostering stage transition at higher age levels, one would expect increasing variability in the course and rate of children's intellectual growth as a function both of the general culture in which children are raised, and each child's unique developmental history.

Of all the explanations that have been considered, this final one was subjected to the least empirical scrutiny, for the simple reason that the resources for effective cross-cultural research are not easy to come by. In those few studies where the theory *was* tested, however (for example, by

---

[1]In neo-Piagetian systems such as Pascual-Leone's, where individual differences in cognitive style are taken into consideration as well, the capability for predicting correlational patterns is even stronger (Pascual-Leone, 1969).

examining the interaction of social class and instruction on children's performance on various developmental measures), the results appeared to be quite promising (Case, 1975).

Position Accorded to Universal Logical Forms
in the Process of Intellectual Development

As was mentioned in the first chapter, classic Piagetian theory was beset by other problems that stemmed as much from its exclusive emphasis on the "logical" aspect of children's functioning as they did from any particular set of empirical data. Three of the most frequently cited examples in this category were (a) the lack of any obvious fit between the content of Piaget's logico-mathematical models and the actual thought processes that children appeared to utilize, (b) the lack of any obvious way in which logico-mathematical operations could be used to model children's performance in social or emotional situations, and (c) the difficulty of explaining how higher forms of thought could emerge in a culture across generations, in a cognitive system for which the endpoint of development was pre-determined.

In the present neo-Piagetian theory all three of these problems were reduced or eliminated. First, the new *executive control structures* that were hypothesized were designed to be congruent with the best available data on children's on-line cognitive processing. Second, because the content of these structures was not specified in logico-mathematical terms, they were, in principle, just as easy to formulate for problem situations with social and emotional content as for situations with scientific or mathematical content. In fact, in several instances they were used explicitly for this purpose (see Case, 1985, 1988; Case, Hayward, Lewis, & Hurst, 1987). Finally, the notion that higher order operations were cultural inventions that were passed on to succeeding generations via social processes was actually built into the structure of the new system. Thus, the criticism that the theory presented a static or "closed" picture of human cognitive development was not applicable.

If the problem of classic Piagetian theory was its excessive reliance on rationality and logical models, the problem with early information-processing models was their excessive reliance on specific learning. To many laymen and teachers, at least, the notion that development could be accounted for entirely in terms of learning seemed implausible. Given the many physical changes that occurred between birth and adolescence, it seemed implausible to suggest that there were no corresponding biologically facilitated changes in mental functioning. Here again, the present theory offered a potential middle ground. Although new structures were seen as being acquired via learning, this learning was seen as taking place under the biological constraints and potentials afforded by successively higher working memory systems.

Relevance of Developmental Theory to the Field of Education

A final set of problems that had beset previous theories was how to deal with the complex issues of education. Adherents of the classical Piagetian approach were able to articulate certain very general principles of "child-centered" instruction: ones that were congruent with Dewey's progressivism on the one hand, and Piaget's constructivism on the other (Elkind, 1976; Ginsburg & Opper, 1969; I. E. Sigel, 1969). What they were not able to do, however, was to indicate how this general set of principles could be used as a basis for providing explicit instruction in specific culturally valued skills. Adherents of the newer information-processing theories, on the other hand, were able to articulate a detailed set of guidelines for instructional programming on specific scholastic tasks (Glaser, 1976; Resnick, 1976). Their difficulty was in suggesting how to plan a fully rounded educational experience: one that would optimize the intellectual and social potential of the "whole child." A final difficulty was that *neither* of the classic approaches— either alone or in combination—provided a very successful means for dealing with certain educational problems that had a strong developmental component. Among these were the problems of children with general developmental delay and children who experienced a severe mismatch between the culture of their home and the culture of the school, with a consequent developmental disability of a more specific nature.

By combining the two previously opposed perspectives, the new theory offered a means for combining a concern for children's general development with a concern for the teaching of specific subject matter (Case & McKeough, 1990). Perhaps serendipitously, it also offered a new approach for tackling each of the specific problems cited above. In each case, the key to this approach lay in conducting a detailed developmental analysis of the control structures underlying successful and unsuccessful performance. On the basis of such analyses, it became possible to specify a new basis for assessing children's "entering competence" and for setting developmentally realistic goals. It also became possible to plan a more effective set of intervention strategies (Case & Griffin, 1989; Case, Sandieson, & Dennis, 1986).

EVALUATION OF NEO-PIAGETIAN THEORY AS A
TOOL FOR GENERATING NEW DISCOVERIES

If the first hope for any new theory is that it should offer some new
perspective on the problems inherited from previous generations, the
second hope is that is should possess a set of emergent properties of its
own, whose exploration leads to the creation of new paradigms and the
discovery of new classes of data. Of course, with the new paradigms and
data may come new problems as well. Nevertheless, the power to open
up such problems is a positive one, on which the progress of any field is
critically dependent. This being the case, it is appropriate to inquire as to
whether neo-Piagetian theories in general, and the particular theory
described in the previous chapter in particular, demonstrated this sort of
heuristic power. Although the *extent* of this power might be questioned,
the fact that some heuristic power was present seems undeniable, in light
of the following three features:

1. Recursive structural parallels in development. The first new property of the theory lay in the hypothesis that a precise structural
parallel could be identified within each developmental stage. A corollary of this hypothesis was that, at least in certain formal respects, the
thought of 4-month-old children should be more like that of 2-year-
olds and 5-year-olds than like that of immediately adjacent age
groups (Pascual-Leone, 1988), because these three age groups share
properties in common that are only found as a new stage is entered.
Although this hypothesis was the most counter-intuitive feature of the
new theory, it did, in fact, lead to the creation of quite a number of
new experimental hypotheses. Moreover, many of these hypotheses
were confirmed (Bruchkowsky, 1984, 1989; Case & Hayward, 1984;
Liu, 1981; Reid, 1987).

2. Recursive cycles of working memory growth. A second new property of the theory was the suggestion that there is a recursive growth
of working memory within each major stage of development. For the
dimensional stage, measurement paradigms were already well established. For other stages, however, they were not, and thus this
property also led to the creation of a number of new tasks and the
discovery of several new classes of data—not just on the growth of
working memory, but on the relationship between this growth and
the potential for new structural acquisitions (Case, 1985; chapters 14
& 15; Daneman & Case, 1981; Liu, 1981).

3. Factors controlling working memory growth. The third new fea-

ture of the theory was its attempt to specify the more basic factors that control the growth of working memory: in particular, the hypothesis that operational efficiency and working memory size should be directly related. Once again, this hypothesis led to the generation of new data. Although the interpretation of these data has been challenged (Hulme, Thomson, Muir, & Lawrence, 1984), it was clear that—at global level at least—the new set of predictions was confirmed (Case, 1985, chapters 7, 8, 14, 16, 17).

COMPARISON OF NEO-PIAGETIAN THEORY WITH OTHER CONTEMPORARY THEORIES

As Lakatos (1962) has pointed out, the evaluation of a new theory never hinges entirely on its ability to offer an explanation for the problems inherited from previous theoretical systems. Nor does it rest entirely on its ability to generate a novel set of paradigms, predictions, or applications. Rather, the evaluation of any theory depends is how it fares in each of these respects *relative to each of its potential competitors.*

As I mentioned in the first chapter, the neo-Piagetian position was not the only one that was developed in response to the historic confrontation between developmental theories of the monolithic and the atomistic varieties. At least two other classes of theory were developed, which also offered potential solutions. One of these was neo-nativist theory, which held that the structuring in children's thought was confined to a relatively small set of informatically encapsulated "modules." The other was a new form of learning theory, which contended that the structure in children's thought was produced by the structure of their knowledge, in domains where they became experts.

Both of these theories were also capable of solving many of the unresolved dilemmas posed by previous generations of theories. Both of these theories also possessed a set of emergent properties that gave them impressive heuristic and predictive power (Carey, 1985; Chi, 1988; Keil, 1986). The final question that must be examined, therefore, is how well the present neo-Piagetian theory fared in comparison to these other theories. Of particular interest is the question of whether these other theories brought to light any data that neo-Piagetian theory was incapable of explaining, or that it could only explain in a post-hoc fashion.

In examining this question, it is important to remember that the primary issue dividing neo-Piagetian theory from other contemporary theories was not the question of whether children's knowledge has a complex internal structure, or even whether major transformations take place in this structure in the course of children's development. Nor was it whether the human mind has some sort of general processing capability, in addition to its more specific modular units. Rather, the real issue was whether there was any *change* in the mind's general capabilities with age, of a sort that permits a parallel set of transformations in the structure of children's knowledge across a variety of domains at once.

It was on this critical issue that sharp differences between the various positions emerged, and it was from the exploration of those differences that data emerged which seemed problematic for each of the existing alternatives.

Data for Which Neo-Piagetian Theory Offered No Adequate Account

There were four classes of data that were particularly difficult to explain within the context of neo-Piagetian theory in general, and the theory described in the previous chapter in particular.

1. The first set of data came from studies that assessed children's performance in domains for which they possessed a rich knowledge-base (e.g., knowledge of dinosaurs or chess). The finding here was that children's performance on such tasks appeared to resemble that of adults quite closely even though, in all other aspects, their performance remained quite child-like (Chi, 1978; Chi & Koeske, 1983).

2. The second class of data came from the literature on child prodigies. Here, too, it appeared that children's performance resembled that of adults in the child's particular area of expertise—even on tests that appeared to tap intellectual processes or skills rather than specific knowledge (Feldman, 1986; Gardner, 1983).

3. When the literature on localized neurological injury was examined, it turned out that it contained numerous clinical examples of adults whose performance in one particular cognitive domain appeared to be little better than that of young children, while their performance in all other domains remained relatively unaffected (Gardner, 1983).

4. Finally, when tests of children's conceptual understanding were developed that went beyond the classical ones devised by Piaget, two parallel sets of data were obtained. First, correlational clusters emerged that appeared to be specific to particular neurologically defined modules. Second, on tests within these clusters children tended to show developmental spurts at the same point in development, while on tests across these clusters they did not (Carey, 1985; Demetriou, Shayer, & Pervez, 1988; Keil, 1986).

All of these types of data seemed more compatible with the view of intellectual development proposed by modular or stage-specific theorists (or for that matter culturally oriented psychologists) than with the view entailed by neo-Piagetian theory.

Data for Which Other Contemporary Theories Offered No
Adequate Account

Theories that were more domain-specific or modular also had their shortcomings, however.

1. On the sorts of working memory measures designed by neo-Piagetian theorists, the age norms that were found appeared to be constant across a remarkably wide range of content. The developmental trajectories of the different measures also appeared to be similar. (Case, 1985, chapter 14; Pascual-Leone, 1988). Theories that viewed development in a more specific or "locally situated" manner offered no principled explanation for this finding.

2. On the sorts of structural measures that were designed by neo-Piagetian theorists to assess the upper bound, or the optimum level, of children's performance, the same general pattern emerged: namely, that tests with different content also appeared to show the same general direction, and limits in rate of growth (Case, 1985, chapters 6–11; Fischer & Canfield, 1986; Johnson, Fabian, & Pascual-Leone, 1989).

3. Finally, in studies where working memory measures and structured measures were related, it appeared that the particular content underlying the measures was relatively unimportant. For example, if the working memory measure was spatial, and the structural measure was non-spatial, performance on the former measure could still serve as a reasonable predictor of performance on the latter (Case, 1985, chapter 16).

Although the contrast between the domain-specific and general/systemic positions was not as strong or as all-encompassing as that between Piaget and his more empirically or culturally oriented critics, it would appear that the general pattern was similar. Not only was there a similar theoretical tension, but this tension yielded a similar pattern of reciprocal anomalies. A similar conclusion thus appeared to be warranted: namely, that neither the general system position of neo-Piagetian theory nor the domain-specific positions of other contemporary theories could be completely correct. Rather, the truth had to lie somewhere in between. It was toward the search for an intermediate position, then, that the program of research reported in the rest of this volume was devoted.

TOWARD A RESOLUTION OF THE CURRENT CONFLICT

In attempting to forge a synthesis of structural and information processing theory during the late 1970s and early 1980s, the general approach I had employed was one of combining the methodologies that had previously been reserved exclusively for one approach or the other (Case, 1985). In essence this had meant developing a form of information-processing analysis that would be sufficiently fine-grained to specify at least some of the interesting components of children's strategies for solving particular problems in particular contexts, but sufficiently general that it applied across a broad range of such problems, and could thus be used as a vehicle for exposing their general structure. It was this synthesis of method that had led to the theoretical synthesis embodied in the version of neo-Piagetian theory that was discussed in the previous chapter.

Given that a methodological synthesis had served to precipitate a theoretical synthesis in the past, it seemed reasonable to assume that such an approach might once again be of some service. Stated in more concrete terms, it seemed reasonable to assume that it might once again be fruitful to specify some of the major methodological differences between the two currently polarized positions, and to launch a program of research that combined these features in some fashion.

The methodological features of modular and/or domain-specific theory that seemed most promising were the ones that led to the four classes of anomalous data already discussed:

- a focus on tasks for which children require a rich base of general knowledge, and the use of analytic techniques for modeling that knowledge (Chi & Koeske, 1983)
- a focus on individual children with unique interests, knowledge, talents, or abilities, in addition to the more standard groups of children with normative knowledge and capabilities (Chi, 1981; Feldman, 1986; Gardner, 1983)
- a focus on domains other than those tapped by traditional Piagetian tasks, especially those that have classically been regarded as involving different neurological substrates (Gardner, 1983)

- a focus on the conceptual rather than the strategic changes that take place in the course of children's approaches to cognitive tasks (Carey, 1985; Keil, 1986)

At the same time, it seemed that the features of neo-Piagetian theory from which it derived its greatest power were:

- Its investigations spanned a broad a range of tasks and domains, rather than being limited to just one.
- The level of analysis that it employed was an intermediate one, that permitted cross-task parallels to be noticed and modeled without neglecting meaningful cross-task differences.

The research strategy we decided to adopt then, was a "conjoint" one, which incorporated both of these sets of features. The present volume describes four general lines of research that we conducted, with the foregoing goals and methods in mind.

Section II contains data from a set of logical and mathematical tasks that were increasingly different from the one described in the second chapter (namely, the balance beam task), and more like the ones that children encounter in their everyday lives, where their previous knowledge and/or training is more extensively implicated. This sort of branching out forced three other sorts of change concurrently. The first was a change in the form of data that were gathered; the second was a change in the analysis to which these data were subjected; and the third and most important was a change in the concepts that were invoked to explain the data.

The two subsequent sections (III and IV) contain data from domains that entail different operations from those used in Piaget's classic logico-mathematical tasks, not merely different background knowledge. The two principal forms of operation that are explored in these sections are those involved in the regulation of children's socioemotional, spatial, and motor functioning. Once again, the ways in which the tasks are analyzed differ considerably from those described in the second chapter, and the constructs that are required to explain the patterns in these analyses differ considerably as well.

In the penultimate section (V), we report studies that examine the development of children with some distinctive form of ability or background experience in the domains that were explored in the preceding sections. Finally, in Section VI, a revised theory of children's intellectual development is proposed, that grows out of the findings of the previous sections.

SUMMARY

In the first chapter of the present section I suggested that an historical tension can be identified between theories of mental development that are general and those that are specific. Over the past 50 years, there has been a clear dialectical progression: The first theories that were proposed adopted a general perspective, according to which development was seen as monolithic, universal, and endogenous. The next generation of theories adopted a more specific viewpoint, according to which development was viewed as atomistic, contextually specific, and exogenous. Finally, a contemporary set of theories has emerged, in which a balance has been struck between these two opposing perspectives.

The precise nature of this balance still differs from theory to theory, however, and remains tilted at least slightly in one of the two classic directions. On the one hand, there is a class of theories in which much of children's development is viewed as stemming from changes in mental capacity that are system-wide in their nature. These theories are often referred to as "neo-Piagetian" because they retain many of Piaget's core assumptions, as well as his rationalist epistemological stance. On the other hand, there are two alternative classes of theory, one with a nativist and one with an empiricist bias. Within both of these theoretical frameworks, children's development is seen as taking place in a fashion that is domain-specific. While much cross-task generality is acknowledged, this generality is presumed to extend only to tasks that tap a particular neurological module or domain of knowledge, not to tasks that span the entire range of a child's interests and capabilities.

In the second chapter, I described a theory that falls into the former (neo-Piagetian) camp, and that constituted the starting point for the research that is reported in the rest of this volume. According to this theory, much of children's intellectual development stems from a change in the control structures they have available for solving specific intellectual problems. These control structures are tripartite entities that contain (a) a representation of the essential features of some particular problem, (b) a representation of the goals that this problem most frequently occasions, and (c) a representation of the sequence of operations that will bridge the gap between the problem's initial and terminal states. Because children's control structures are specific to particular classes of problems, and because these problems become increasingly culture-bound as they become more abstract, it is to be expected that children will show different patterns of development as a function of a variety of experiential factors, such as (a) the culture or subculture in which they are raised, (b) the specific problems they encounter most frequently within that culture. and (c) the models that the culture provides for successful problem solution. It is also to be expected that children's development will vary as a function of a variety of individual factors of a motivational or socioemotional nature, because such factors will determine the particular goals that children pursue most frequently, and the particular methods for achieving these goals that they find most attractive.

At the same time, a set of developmental changes were hypothesized that are general, and that serve to constrain the sorts of control structures children can assemble in any specific problem situation. These general changes are presumed to have a strong biological component and to set a limit on the highest level of intellectual operation that children can execute successfully, and their working memory for the products of such operations. As these upper limits shift, children's control structures are hypothesized to progress through a sequence of four recursive cycles or stages in each problem domain to which they have any long-term exposure, and in which they maintain a long-term interest. In each of these four stages, the following progression takes place: (a) As children enter the stage, they assemble a new class of operations for dealing with the problems with which they are familiar, by coordinating two well established operations that are already in their repertoire; (b) as their working memory grows, and as they practice these new operations, they enter a second substage in which they become capable of executing two such operations in sequence; (c) finally, with a further growth in working memory, and with further practice, they enter a substage in which they become capable of executing two or more operations of the new sort in parallel, and integrating the products of these operations into a coherent system. Once consolidated, these integrated systems can then function as the basic units from which the structures of the next stage are assembled.

In the present chapter, the implications of the foregoing theory were examined, to determine what sorts of solution they imply to the dilemmas posed by classical developmental theories of either the system-wide or context-specific sort. It was suggested that most of these classic dilemmas can be resolved in a satisfactory manner: that is, one that suggests testable explanations for data that would otherwise appear anomalous. It was also suggested that the theory contains certain elements that imply the existence of new developmental phenomena, phenomena that have not been previously understood as part of the normal developmental process, and that can be investigated in their own right. A number of such investigations have already been launched, and have shown promising results.

Notwithstanding these promising results, it was also suggested that the new theory has a number of problems, many of which still involve the classic dilemma of how to model general and specific developmental changes within a single theoretical framework. These problems become particularly clear when the theory is contrasted with the other contemporary theories that were mentioned in chapter 1: those that provide an account of development that is domain- or module-specific. Unlike these theories, there is an important class of data for which neo-Piagetian theory offers no obvious or simple interpretation. This class of data involves individual children who perform in a child-like fashion on most intellectual tasks, but in an adult-like manner on tasks from one particular problem class. Such data have been reported in the literature when one or more of the following conditions have obtained: (a) The particular problems or tasks have been ones that permit children to apply a rich and extensive knowledge base; (b) the children in question have had extensive exposure to this class of tasks and the time to develop such a knowledge base; and (c) the children are highly motivated, and have shown a particular talent for this class of tasks from an early age. If taken at their face value, these data would appear to support a domain specific view of intellectual development, and to violate the notion of a cross-domain upper limit to which all children's thought is subject.

While the foregoing data are certainly anomolous, it is important to realize there also exist data that seem to support a system-wide view of intellectual development, and that are difficult for domain- or module-specific theories to handle. All of these data involve some sort of cross-domain parallel in performance, or neo-Piagetian tests of working memory with very different sorts of content. Faced with this pattern of reciprocal anomalies, it would seem clear that the two sorts of data, and the research methods that generate them, can no longer be treated in isolation, but must somehow be combined, with a view to building a theory that is mote comprehensive.

Accordingly, an attempt has been made in this volume to combine the different sets of methods of the two classes of theory and to examine the two types of data in greater detail. The approach that has been taken comprises two major components. The first derives from the Piagetian and neo-Piagetian traditions and involves the examination of a wide range of tasks, using measures and analytic methods that permit specific developmental structures and more general capacities to be related to each other. The second component derives from modular and/or domain-specific theory, and involves applying these analytic and empirical methods to three separate sorts of data: data from tasks that tap the sort of knowledge and expertise that children accumulate in their everyday lives, and that can aid them in understanding particular logical or mathematical tasks (Section II); data involving similar knowledge-rich tasks, but ones whose content is drawn from domains that appear to involve different neurological and/or experiential substrates such as these (Sections III and IV); and data from children with some identified developmental exceptionality of a task or domain-specific sort (Section V). The final section (Section VI) is then devoted to a theoretical synthesis involved in socioemotional and spatial functioning of the data and concepts that are presented in previous sections.

II

THE ROLE OF CENTRAL CONCEPTUAL STRUCTURES IN THE DEVELOPMENT OF CHILDREN'S LOGICO-MATHEMATICAL THOUGHT

As was indicated in the previous section, the primary issue that divides modular from general-system theorists is not a question of whether children's knowledge has a complex internal structure, or whether major transformations take place in this structure in the course of children's development. Nor is it whether the human mind has some sort of general processing capability in addition to more specific modular units. Rather, it is whether there is any change in the mind's general capabilities with age, of a sort that permits a parallel set of transformations in the structure of children's knowledge across a variety of domains simultaneously.

In the present section, a number of studies are reported in which a preliminary attempt was made to investigate this issue. The basic goal of most of the studies was quite simple: to examine the development of children's thinking in one domain, and to see whether it bears any parallel to their development in some other. The general research strategy was also quite straightforward. In each study, the investigators began with a known developmental sequence in one domain, and then designed a new set of tasks in some other domain that would permit them to determine whether a parallel developmental sequence might be present there as well. In addition, one other feature was normally added to each study: the second domain was one for which, as a result of their daily experience, children possessed a richer knowledge base than they did in the domain for which a developmental sequence had already been established.

The results that were obtained using this approach were not exactly as predicted; however, they were extremely regular, and they led to a theoretical re-formulation of considerable potential significance.

Synchrony and Asynchrony in the Development of Children's Scientific Reasoning

Zopito Marini
Brock University

If one were to select two task domains that were equally valued by a particular culture, and to isolate an intellectual operation that was used with equal frequency in each, it would seem to be a trivial matter to demonstrate that children begin to utilize this operation in each domain at about the same point in their development. In fact, however, this sort of demonstration has proved quite elusive. As Fischer (1980) has pointed out, studies that have been designed with this intent have usually revealed a strong degree of asynchrony or *décalages* in children's development, not synchrony.

If these décalages were relatively small in magnitude, it might be possible to dismiss them. As a number of investigators have pointed out, however, they are often quite massive. The type of competence on which the acquisition of Piagetian conservation is dependent, for example, has been shown to emerge as early as 3 years of age on certain tasks (Gelman, 1978a) or as late as 10 or 11 on others (Elkind, 1961; Gelman, 1972). In fact, using ingenious experimental techniques, Mounoud and Bower (1974) and Starkey and Cooper (1980) have found evidence of this competence as early as the first year of life. A similar finding has emerged for tasks assessing children's ability to "decenter." According to classic Piagetian theory, this ability is not supposed to emerge until the acquisition of concrete operations. Once again, however, depending on the particular assessment device, decentration has been shown to emerge as early as 3 years in certain circumstances (Flavell, Shipstead, & Croft, 1978) or as late as 15 in others (Laurendeau & Pinard, 1970). Similar results have been reported for transitivity

(Bryant & Trabasso, 1971) and role taking (Borke, 1971; Flavell, 1974; Inhelder & Piaget, 1958; Shatz & Gelman, 1973).

When such data were first reported, they were interpreted by Piaget and his colleagues as being due to problems in measurement. Thus, for example, Piaget (1974) argued that tests that appeared to demonstrate an early grasp of conservation do not, in fact, tap "true" conservation. Other investigators made similar arguments for alternative measures of transitivity (Lunzer, 1965), and role taking (Chandler & Greenspan, 1972).

While there may well be some merit in these arguments, the fact remains that they were almost always made after the fact. Moreover, they rarely led to new experiments in which strong cross-task synchrony was demonstrated. At best, they led to studies showing that, if one uses exactly the same sort of task that Piaget used, one obtains roughly the same age norms. However, Piaget's own tasks showed strong décalages in certain areas. For example, conservation of number was usually acquired at 5 or 6 years of age, whereas conservation of weight was not acquired until 8 or 9 (Inhelder & Piaget, 1958). Thus, to most investigators who were not in the Piagetian tradition (and even to many who were), the data on décalages were recognized as posing a serious problem for the classic Piagetian position, one that could not be explained away by referring to problems of measurement (Beilin, 1971b; Gelman, 1978b; Pinard, 1975).

A second form of explanation for décalages hinges on the distinction between "competence," and "performance." According to this explanation the classical Piagetian theory was a theory of underlying "competence" (Flavell & Wohlwill, 1969; Overton, 1983; Pascual-Leone, 1988). What is needed in order to explain décalages is a theory that includes moderator variables to translate this competence into "performance." One such potential factor is task familiarity. For obvious reasons, it is difficult to equate children's prior familiarity with two different types of task. Moreover, it seems reasonable to suggest that it takes a certain amount of familiarity with a task before children can apply their underlying operative structure to it. A second factor is perceptual salience. Like familiarity, this is a factor that is difficult to equate across different tasks. And, once again, it seems reasonable to suggest that certain perceptual features might facilitate the activation of a particular operative structure, while other features might inhibit this activation. Unless these sorts of performance factors are controlled, it could be argued that one should expect at least some content-related difference in the difficulty of two structurally equivalent tasks, and some corresponding décalages as a consequence.

This second argument also has some merit. However, it becomes problematic when it is used to explain décalages of the magnitude that have been demonstrated. For if the underlying operational competence on which various logical concepts depend is actually present by 2 years of age, and it is only more extraneous "performance" factors that delay the utilization of this competence on other tasks until 3 to 15, then it must be these same "extraneous" factors that control children's cognitive development during this age range in the first place! In short, it must be these same performance factors that constitute the true motor of cognitive development.

In the context of neo-Piagetian theory, a third sort of explanation for décalages is offered. Virtually all neo-Piagetian theories make a distinction between the *type* of competence or concept that a task requires (conservation, transitivity, etc.), and the epistemic *level* of that competence. In effect, their claim is that any competence can be demonstrated to be present in some form at almost any age level, depending on the nature and complexity of the epistemic operations that are necessary to construct it. Since it is the level of these operations that changes most noticeably with development, any uncontrolled variation in the level that one requires in order to pass different tasks would be expected to result in a parallel variation in the age of acquisition.

It was this argument that was developed in chapter 2. As was mentioned there, one of the first sets of experiments that neo-Piagetian theorists conducted were designed to use this notion in a predictive fashion. Thus, for example, Fischer, Hand, Watson, VanParys, and Tucker (1984) demonstrated that they could predict the pattern of synchrony and asynchrony for a novel set of role-taking tasks using the concepts of optimal and functional level as defined in Fischer's (1980) theory. A similar demonstration was made for classification tasks by Pascual-Leone and Smith (1969), and for formal operational tasks by Scardamalia (1974), using Pascual-Leone's (1970) notions of M-demand and M-capacity.

Unfortunately, in order to support the sort of claim I was interested in exploring in the present project, none of these previous neo-Piagetian studies was completely adequate. To begin with, all the previous studies had used variants of neo-Piagetian theory that were somewhat different from the one in which I was interested (Case, 1985). More importantly however, none of the previous studies had distinguished, as sharply as I would have liked, between the operational structure required by a task and the content-domain to which this structure had to be applied. Although the studies had shown synchrony across different tasks when the level of task complexity was controlled, the content of the tasks had normally been drawn from the same content domain. But what I wished to determine was whether this pattern of synchrony would hold across *different* content domains.

For all of these reasons, I felt it would be desirable to design a set of tasks in which the operational level of the task, as defined by Case's (1985) theory, could be treated as one variable, and the domain from which the task was drawn could be treated as another. With the appropriate performance factors controlled, I hoped to show that the operational level of a task exerts a major impact on the age at which it is first mastered, whereas the content domain to which these operations must be applied exerts relatively little.

STUDY 1: SOCIAL AND NON-SOCIAL DEVELOPMENT: COMPARISON OF THE JUICE MIXING AND BIRTHDAY PARTY TASKS

The objective of the first study was to develop two formally equivalent tasks that could be understood at any of the operational levels specified by Case's (1985) theory for the "dimensional" stage, and to show that, at each of several successive age groups, children would display the level of understanding specified by the theory, regardless of the task content. Stated another way, the object was to show that children's progression through the dimensional stage on two different tasks would be in close temporal synchrony regardless of the domain of knowledge from which the two tasks were drawn.

Method

Tasks

The Juice Mixing Task. The first task was a modified version of Noelting's (1980a, 1980b) Juice Mixing Task. The experimenter explained that several tumblers of orange juice (represented by orange cups) and several tumblers of water (represented by white cups) were going to be poured into each pitcher. The subjects were asked to predict which mixture would taste more strongly of orange juice, and why. On the basis of Case's theory and Noelting's original data (Noelting, 1980a, 1980b), it was presumed that the control structures children applied to these tasks would vary with age, in the fashion indicated in chapter 2 (see Table 2.3).

The Birthday Party Task.   This task was designed so that its content would be from a different domain of knowledge, but would require the same underlying operational structures, and yield the same age-related progression in performance. In the Birthday Party Task, subjects were shown pictures of two boys, David and Bill, and told that each was going to have a birthday party. Before the party, they were told, each child wished for a certain number of hand-polished stones. (The number wished for by each boy was specified at this point.) At the party, each boy opened his presents, and found out how many polished stones he had actually received. (The stones actually received by each boy were then laid under the pictures.) The subjects were then asked which boy would be happier, and why. The combinations of orange juice and water, as well as the numbers of stones wished for and received are listed in Table 4.1.

This second task is formally equivalent to the juice mixing task in the sense that the experimenter asks a question about one variable (which boy is happier), in a context where that variable can potentially be affected by two others (number of stones wished for and number actually received). The particular content that is involved, however, differs substantially, because the second task draws on children's social rather than their physical knowledge.

Subjects

A total of 104 children were selected from a public school that served a predominantly middle-class neighborhood. The children ranged in age from 4½ to 11½ years, and were randomly drawn from the following grades: Junior Kindergarten (JK; 10 boys, 9 girls; mean age = 5.0 years, SD = .26 yr), Grade 1 (17 boys, 11 girls; mean age = 7.1 years, SD = .30 yr), Grade 3 (15 boys, 12 girls; mean age = 9.1 years, SD = .30 yr), and Grade 5 (13 boys, 17 girls; mean age = 11.0 years, SD = .41 yr).

Procedure

The children performed the Juice Mixing Task on one day, and the Birthday Party Task the next. Testing was done on an individual basis, in a quiet room supplied by the school for this purpose. Students' responses to each item were tape-recorded, and subsequently transcribed.

Scoring

Each answer, together with its attendant justification, was scored by two raters, as follows:

TABLE 4.1
Test Items Used in Sessions 1 and 2 of Study 1

Session 1

Juice Mixing Task

	Pitcher A		Pitcher B	
Trial	Juice	Water	Juice	Water
1	3	6	2	3
2	1	2	2	4
3	2	4	4	8
4	5	6	2	3
5	1	2	3	5
6	6	3	5	2
7	2	3	3	4
8	4	3	2	2
9	2	3	3	4
10	4	2	2	1
11	3	6	2	4
12	2	5	6	10
13	2	1	4	3
14	4	2	5	3
15	5	2	7	3

Session 2

Birthday Party Task

	David		Bill	
Trial	Received	Wanted	Received	Wanted
1	2	0	0	0
2	4	0	6	0
3	3	6	3	4
4	6	9	5	6
5	4	3	3	5

Level 0: Predimensional. To be classified at this level, answers had to focus only on global aspects of the task ("This one, because it has so many cups" or "This one, because there are lots of rocks"). The specific numbers could not be mentioned, and the only items passed had to be those where there was a very large difference on the most salient variable.

Level 1: Unidimensional. To be classified at this level, answers had to focus on one particular dimension and compare the numbers that were involved in a meaningful fashion (e.g., "A is juicier, because A has 3 orange juice and B only got 2" or "Bill, because Bill has 2 more rocks than David"). An additional criterion was that no mention could be made of the second dimension.

Level 2: Bidimensional. To be scored at this level, both variables had to be taken into account in a meaningful fashion (e.g., "The same, since there's more orange juice here but more water here" or "Bill, since David did not get what he wanted"). An additional criterion was that no explicit mention could be made of the magnitude of the difference on the second variable.

Level 3: Bidimensional, with Elaboration. At this last level, each variable had to be taken into account in a meaningful fashion. However, the size of the variation along each had to be noted, at least in an approximate fashion (e.g., "A will taste stronger, since there's 3 more water in A but 4 more water in B" or "Bill got almost what he wanted, but David is three short").

Both the answers and the justifications were taken into account in scoring the items at each level. Responses were never assigned a passing score simply because the answer given was correct. The children also had to demonstrate, via a relevant justification, that they had reached this answer by using one of the operational sequences indicated in chapter 2 (Table 2.3). After a child's answers and justifications had been classified in this fashion for each item, an overall structural level was computed in one of two ways. Using the constant number method, the second highest level at which the child had performed on at least two problems in the set was noted. By this criterion, the agreement between the two raters was 90% on the Juice Mixing Task and 87% on the Birthday Party Task. Using the constant ratio method, the child was assigned the second highest level at which at least 60% of the items on each scale was passed.

Results

Because the two scoring methods yielded results that were virtually identical, only those from the constant number method are reported. The mean scores are given in Table 4.2. The means for the two tasks were very close across tasks within any age group, but substantially different across age groups within any task. As might be expected under such circumstances, an analysis of variance (ANOVA) revealed a very strong effect due to age, $F(3, 100) = 42.50$, $p < 0.01$, but no significant effect due to task, $F(1, 100) = 1.04$, $p < 0.31$.

TABLE 4.2
Means (*M*) and Standard Deviations (*SD*) of
Performance on Juice Mixing and Birthday
Party Tasks, by Grade

Task	Grade			
	JK	*1*	*3*	*5*
Juice Mixing				
M	0.95	1.18	2.00	2.37
SD	0.71	0.48	0.73	0.67
Birthday Party				
M	0.95	1.29	2.19	2.43
SD	0.71	0.60	0.83	0.90

When the performance of individual subjects was examined, the correspondence between the two tasks was not as high. As is shown in Table 4.3, only about half the subjects (52%) in the younger two grades performed at the same level on both tasks. Of the remainder, 41% showed a discrepancy of one level and 7% showed a discrepancy of 2 levels. As a consequence, the correlation between the two tasks was only moderate ($r = 0.53$, $p < .001$), and was reduced to insignificance when age was partialled out statistically ($r = 0.19$, $p < .11$).

Discussion

Both the individual and the aggregate results were in good accordance with neo-Piagetian theory. The individual results support the notion that children construct their answers to each task independently, with

TABLE 4.3
Percentage of Subjects Showing Different Degrees of
Developmental Synchrony, by Grade (Study 1)

Grade	Perfect Synchrony (same level on both tasks)	Asynchrony of One Substage	Asynchrony of Two Substages
JK	47	42	11
1	57	39	4
3	30	63	7
5	33	47	20

the aid of whatever task-specific background knowledge and/or talent they may possess; the group results support the notion that this process is subject to strong age-related constraints, and that a common structural ceiling is reached when specific task and individual factors are controlled.

STUDY 2: SOCIAL AND NON-SOCIAL DEVELOPMENT: COMPARISON ACROSS A BROADER RANGE OF TASKS

Although the results from Study 1 were encouraging, a number of possible criticisms could be leveled at them. One is that, due to the presence of a ceiling effect, the degree of synchrony between the two tasks may have been overestimated in the highest age group. A second possible criticism is that, because only two tasks were used, the degree of agreement that was found may be unique to these particular task situations. A third objection is that, because the tasks did not have a unique item-type for each hypothesized structural level, the raters may have been forced to rely too heavily on the children's justifications. To the extent that children's linguistic sophistication remained constant across tasks and the raters were influenced by it, the degree of synchrony in children's thought may have been overestimated at all age levels.

All of the above features might cause one to overestimate the degree of synchrony in development across tasks that are drawn from different content domains. However, the tasks also contained several characteristics that might cause one to *under*estimate the degree of cross-task synchrony. One such factor was that the two tasks appeared to be differentially familiar to the younger subjects. While young children are very familiar with what goes on at a birthday party, and can predict the feelings of major participants (Borke, 1973; Nelson, 1978), they are not necessarily as familiar with the juice-mixing situation. Also, in the Juice Mixing Task there were perceptual clues that clearly indicated the magnitude of both variables, whereas in the Birthday Party Task one of the two variables (the number wished for) had to be remembered.

In order to control both kinds of factors, I decided to do a second study. The basic goal of the second study was the same as the first, as was the underlying experimental design. However, both the number and the nature of the tasks were different.

Method

Tasks

The Birthday Party Task. This version of the task was modified to take into account the problems just discussed. The most important modifications were as follows: The number of trials was increased from 5 to 10, in order to parallel the other tasks more closely; two items were constructed for each structural level, in such a way that a correct answer would not be possible if a lower level of thought was used (so as to ensure that the raters would not have to place undue reliance on the sophistication of children's justifications and/or language); an additional structural level was introduced at the "top end" of the test, in order to eliminate any possible ceiling effect (For this level, some form of simple proportional or multiplicative procedure was required in estimating which of the dimensions would be more powerful); and the procedure was changed so that the children saw physical representations of the gifts that were wished for, as well as those that were received (The sets that were wished for were represented by small cardboard pictures, placed in a bubble over each story character's head). Two final changes were introduced for motivational reasons: The story characters were changed from two boys to one boy and one girl, and the objects wished for were changed from polished stones to marbles.

The Reward Distribution Task. The second task was also designed to draw on background knowledge that children as young as 4 are known to possess. It was modeled on a set of problems developed by Demerssman (1976), which had been based on prior work by Damon (1973). In the version of the task used for the present study, the subjects were told a story about two children, John and Mary, who volunteered to stay after school to help the teacher by making drawings of bunny rabbits on postcards to be sent to children in hospital. The subjects were also told the number of days that John and Mary had come in to help, as well as the number of postcards each had made. A set of cards was placed in front of the children—with John's on the left and Mary's on the right—as a mnemonic. Finally, the subjects were told that the teacher wanted to give each of the children some candies for helping with the work, and a pile of real candies was displayed at this point. The questions were, "Who should get more?" and "Why?". Once again, ten problems were presented in succession, with each successive pair of problems requiring a higher level of thought to be solved. The specific number of objects in each problem was the same as in the corresponding problems on the Birthday Party Task, as illustrated in Table 4.4

The Balance Beam Task. The Balance Beam Task was a slightly modified version of one developed by Siegler (1976), which in turn was based on prior work by Inhelder and Piaget (1958). The central beam was 38″ in length. The center of the beam rested on a 5″ elevated support, permitting it to pivot freely at the fulcrum. Each side of the beam had 9 pegs, which were 1½″ high and spaced 2″ apart. The metal washers that were placed on the two sides were 1½″ in diameter, and ¼″ in thickness, with a center hole that was ¾″ in diameter. A wooden support was placed under each arm, to prevent the beam from moving when the washers were placed in their position (see Fig. 4.1).

In order to compensate for lack of familiarity with this sort of apparatus, the subjects were introduced to the beam without supports at the outset, and shown how it could pivot. They were then handed a washer so that they could get an idea of its weight, and were shown what happened when it was placed on one side of the beam (i.e., that it tilted in that direction). This same procedure was repeated for the other side.

TABLE 4.4
Test Items Used in The Four Tasks of Study 2

| Level | Trial | Left Side Dimensions | | Right Side Dimensions | | Relationship Between Dimensions | |
		1	2	1	2	1	2
0	1	6	2	2	2	Large difference	Equal
	2	4	3	7	3	Large difference	Equal
1	3	3	7	4	7	Small difference	Equal
	4	6	8	7	8	Small difference	Equal
2	5	4	6	4	7	Equal	Small difference
	6	5	4	5	5	Equal	Small difference
3	7	6	6	4	7	Small difference	Small difference
	8	2	5	5	2	Small difference	Small difference
4	9	1	2	3	1	Simple ratio	Simple ratio
	10	1	4	2	1	Simple ratio	Simple ratio

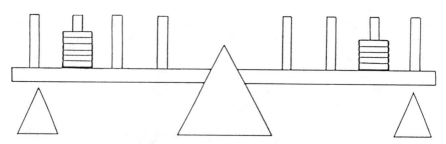

FIG. 4.1. Balance beam apparatus.

After that, the subjects were encouraged to take the weight, and to place it in several positions themselves. To prevent any possible misunderstanding, the subjects were told that this was a "fair" instrument, with no tricks to it. They were also told that the distance between the pegs was the same. At the end of the demonstration (which usually lasted at least 5 minutes), they were shown 10 configurations with the supports in place, and asked which side they thought would go down in each case, and why. Once again, the problems were constructed so that each successive pair tested for the availability of a higher structure, and so that the specific numbers employed were the same as those specified in Table 4.4.

The Projection of Shadows Task. Like the Balance Beam Task, this measure was adapted from a task developed by Siegler (1978), on the basis of prior work by Inhelder and Piaget (1958). The general appearance of the apparatus is illustrated in Fig. 4.2. Two 60-watt bulbs were used as light; the bars casting the shadows, and forming a "T," were made up of hollow 1″ tubes, mounted on vertical 8″ posts. The two bases in which the posts were mounted had 9 holes each in them, spaced at 2″ intervals. Each base was placed between the light and a screen, such that the distance from the light was 6″ and the distance from the screen was 8″.

Prior to the presentation of the test items, the children were introduced to the apparatus in a standardized fashion. First it was explained that all the tubes were of equal length, that the holes on the wooden bases were evenly spaced, and that the height of the T-bars was equal. Then two tubes were placed on the arm of a T-bar, which was in the middle of one of the bases, and the light was turned on to project a shadow. The same procedure was repeated on the other base, and the children were allowed to handle the apparatus themselves, varying both the distance from the screen and the number of tubes on the bars. After this familiarization period was over, 10 test items were presented, in which the subjects were asked to predict which of the two shadows would

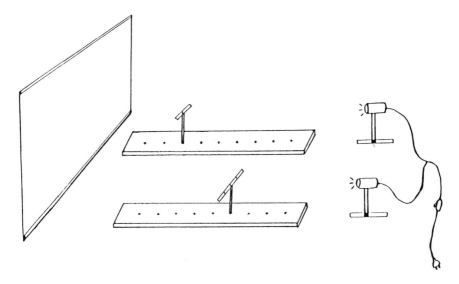

FIG. 4.2.   Projection of shadows apparatus.

be larger, and why. The length of the tubes and the distance from the screen were varied from trial to trial in exactly the same way as the dimensions on the other three tasks (see Table 4.1).

Subjects

The subject sample consisted of 80 elementary school students between the ages of 4 and 11, who were drawn from a public school serving a middle-class neighborhood. Twenty students were selected at random from each of the following grades: Junior Kindergarten (mean age = 4.4 years, SD = .37), Grade 1 (mean age = 6.8 years, SD = .27), Grade 3 (mean age = 9.0 years, SD = .53), and Grade 5 (mean age = 10.9 years, SD = .38).

Procedure

The study was carried out in two sessions, each involving the presentation of two tasks. In the first session, the Balance Beam and Birthday Party Tasks were presented. In the second session (usually administered the next day) the Projection of Shadows and Reward Distribution Tasks were presented. All tasks were administered individually, in a quiet room provided by the school. There was no specific time limit on the duration of a session. However, each task tended to take from 20 to 30 minutes, depending on the student. To prevent excessive fatigue, the children were given a 5-minute rest between the presentation of the two tasks each day. As an additional control on background experience related to the two physical tasks, the children received feedback at the end of the first item at each level: In the Balance Beam Task, this involved removing the blocks and showing subjects whether or not their predictions were confirmed. In the Projection of Shadows Task, it involved turning on the two lights. Testing was continued until a student failed all the items two full levels above his or her last single success. Students' predictions and justifications were written down verbatim at the end of each trial.

Scoring

The success criterion for the two physical tasks was a correct answer, coupled with a justification indicating that the answer had not been arrived at by guessing, but was the result of a genuine attempt to think about the problem at the level in question. An overall score was then assigned by examining the subject's total pattern of successes and failures on each task, and assigning the level of his or her second highest success. As was the case in the first study, the rationale for adopting this criterion was to avoid overestimating children's capabilities. Note that a child who got both items correct at his or her highest level (e.g., 3) would be assigned a final score at that level (in this case, 3). However, if a child got only one item correct at level 2 and one at level 3, he or she would be assigned an overall score corresponding to the second highest level at which he or she succeeded, in this case level 2.

For the two tasks with social content, there was no correct or incorrect answer in any absolute sense. However, in the Reward Distribution Task, children in general agreed that both dimensions cited by the experimenter were of relevance, and disagreed only in the direction of operation they ascribed to them. According to one line of thought (which was dubbed the "socialist" option) children were seen as deserving more candies if they had come in more frequently, even if they had not made any more cards, because this meant that they had "put in more time." According to the other line of thought (which was nicknamed the "capitalist" option) children were seen as deserving more candies if they had made the same number of cards in fewer days, because this meant that they had done a good job or "worked well." In the Birthday Party Task, all subjects treated both variables as relevant, and also saw them as exerting their effects in the same manner (i.e., more presents make for more happiness, unless you wished for even more than you receive, in which case wishing for more makes you less happy).

Given that the general thrust of students' reasoning was this straightforward, it was possible to use the same scoring criteria on the social tasks as on the physical tasks, with the single exception of having to make the award of a "correct" answer on the Reward Distribution Task contingent on the subject's particular way of looking at the problem (i.e., socialist vs. capitalist). Using the same general criteria as for the previous study, the percent of agreement of two raters on the four tasks was as follows: Birthday Party: 93%, Reward Distribution: 83%, Balance Beam: 89%, and Projection of Shadows: 80%. The interrater reliabilities were .95, .94, .95, and .90, respectively. In cases of disagreement between two raters, the difference was never more than one level. Disagreements were resolved by discussion.

Results

The mean scores on each task at each age level are given in Table 4.5. The scores were, once again, very close across tasks within each age level, and substantially different across age levels within each task. Although there appeared to be some tendency for the spread in mean scores to increase with age, neither the task nor the Task × Age interactions were

TABLE 4.5
Means and Standard Deviations on
the Four Tasks of Study 2,
by Grade

| Task | Grade | | | |
	JK	1	3	5
Balance Beam				
M	0.12	1.05	1.80	2.55
SD	0.52	0.22	0.70	0.69
Projection of Shadows				
M	0.12	1.05	1.75	2.45
SD	0.41	0.22	0.79	0.76
Birthday Party				
M	0.05	1.25	1.90	2.80
SD	0.61	0.55	0.72	0.70
Reward Distribution				
M	0.05	1.05	2.05	2.80
SD	0.69	0.22	0.76	0.52

significant, $F(3, 228) = 1.45$, $p < 0.23$, and $F(9, 228) = 1.31$, $p < 0.23$, respectively. The age effect was large and significant, $F(3, 76) = 135.30$, $p < 0.01$.

Once again, the correspondence among the four tasks was not as high when the performance of individual subjects was examined. Table 4.6a and Table 4.6b present relevant data, tabulated using two different methods. In the top panel, in order to permit a comparison to be made with the first study, all possible pairwise comparisons of tasks were considered, and the proportion of same-level performance was averaged, first within, and then across, subjects. As may be seen, the degree of synchrony across pairs of tasks was higher in Study 2 than in Study 1, averaging 73% in the two lower grades, and 50% in the two higher grades (the comparable figures for Study 1 were 52% and 32%). In the bottom panel the pattern is presented across all four tasks: The

TABLE 4.6a

Percentage of Subjects Showing Different Levels of Synchrony for Each Grade Averaged Across All Six Possible Pairs of Tasks

Grade	Perfect Synchrony (same level on two tasks)	Asynchrony of One Substage	Asynchrony of Two Substages
JK	60	39	1
1	85	14	1
3	46	46	8
5	53	42	5

TABLE 4.6b

Percentage of Subjects Showing Asynchrony of One level, Across the Four Tasks

Grade	Same Level on Three of Four Tasks, One Level Difference on the Other	Same Level on Two of Four Tasks, One Level Higher (or lower) on Both the Other Two Tasks	Same Level on Two of Four Tasks, One Level Higher on One Task, One Level Lower on the Other
JK	70	25	5
1	95	0	5
3	45	25	10[a]
5	65	25	5[b]

Note.[19] [a]Three subjects showed an asynchrony of two levels; [b]one subject showed an asynchrony of three levels.

modal pattern was not one of perfect synchrony across all four tasks, but rather scoring at one level on two or three tasks out of four, and at a level above or below that on the other(s). The raw correlation across tasks was .8. The corresponding age-partialed correlation was .28.

A final question was whether the experimental means obtained in this study were substantially different from the means that would be expected on the basis of the theory outlined in chapter 2. Figure 4.3 presents the data relevant to this question. It is clear that there was very little difference between the expected and the observed mean across the four tasks, except at the highest level. As a consequence, the ANOVA showed no significant difference between the predicted and observed grand means, $F(1, 72) = 1.52$, $p < 0.22$.

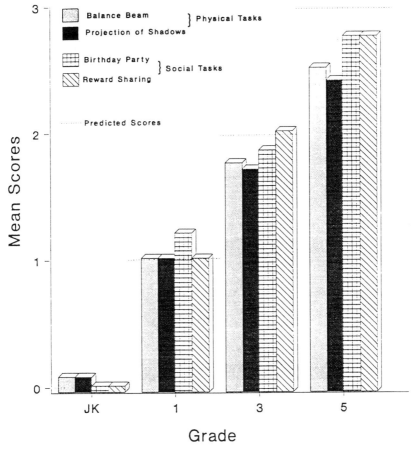

FIG. 4.3. Elementary school students' mean scores on measures of social and non-social cognition at four different grade levels.

Discussion

Both the individual and the aggregate results were in good agreement with neo-Piagetian theory in general, and with the version of that theory presented in chapter 2, in particular. The first finding, modest but significant cross-task asynchrony at the individual level, supports the notion that children construct their answer to each task independently, with the aid of whatever task-specific background knowledge and/or talent they may possess, and using whatever specific perceptual and/or contextual factors the task presents. The second finding, strong cross-task synchrony at the group level, supports the notion that this process is subject to strong age-related constraints, and that a common developmental ceiling is reached across different sorts of content, when task-specific and individual-specific factors are controlled.

GENERAL DISCUSSION AND CONCLUSION

In spite of the variation in task content, procedure, and scoring methods, the results across the two studies were remarkably consistent. Under conditions where the children were reasonably familiar with the general situations with which they were faced, the variables that were involved were reasonably salient, and the problem-questions and response-alternatives were parallel, cross-task décalage was weak, and cross-task consistency was strong. Children passed through the same developmental sequence: from predimensional to unidimensional to bidimensional to integrated (or elaborated) bidimensional thought. Moreover, at least at the group level, they did so at the same rate. That is to say, both their mean scores, and the distribution of these scores were statistically indistinguishable across all the tasks that were administered, regardless of the content domain from which the tasks were drawn or the children's general level of familiararity with that content.

This general pattern of results is not the one that has been found by other researchers. As was mentioned at the beginning of the chapter, strong task effects in developmental research are relatively common, except for those studies where neo-Piagetian theory has been used to establish levels and the task content has been drawn from within the same domain. The fact that no task effect was found in the present study, even when the content varied *across* domains, may be taken as an indication that the level and organization of children's cognitive operations are crucial factors in determining their task performance, across a broader range of content than might otherwise be expected.

ACKNOWLEDGMENTS

The preparation of this manuscript was supported, in part, by grant #410-82-0379 from the Social Sciences and Humanities Research Council of Canada. I would like to express my gratitude to the Scarborough Board of Education, and to the students and teachers in the schools in which the studies were conducted. I would also like to extend particular thanks to the following individuals: M. Wideman, D. Weir, D. Thompson, A. Kerr, and N. Bender. Special thanks are also due to Bill Postl for his assistance with computer work, and to Carl Bereiter, Andrew Biemiller, and Howard Russell for their comments on an earlier version of the manuscript.

5

Synchrony and Asynchrony in the Acquisition of Children's Everyday Mathematical Knowledge

Sharon Griffin,
Clark University
Robbie Case,
Standford University
Robert Sandieson
University of Western Ontario

The data that were reported in the previous chapter are not typical of those in the developmental literature. Thus, at first glance, they would appear to constitute a rather strong confirmation of the neo-Piagetian theory by which they were predicted, and to argue against the view that knowledge acquisition follows a unique developmental course in each domain. In fact, however, there exists a straightforward counter-interpretation that leaves the domain-specific position on development unscathed. This argument holds that the real reason no décalage was found was not that all the tasks make a common demand on the child's general system, but rather that all the task-specific performance variables responsible for décalages were held constant across tasks, while at the same time certain of these same variables were systematically *manipulated* across age levels. The variables that were held constant across tasks were:

1. Background experience. Massive experience had clearly been provided by the culture for the two social tasks. It was also ensured for the two physical tasks, by the warm-up play period and the practice trials.
2. Stimulus arrays. In each case two clear "sides" were present in the array, each of which contained two sets of countable objects.
3. Type of operation. The operation required by the tasks (counting) was identical.
4. Operational difficulty. The difficulty of executing the counting

75

operation was also controlled by using the same number of objects for each variable and for each trial, across the four tasks.

5. Question format. In each case the question format was similar, namely: "Will this side have the larger X (tilt, shadow, degree of happiness, number of candies) or will this side, or will they be the same?"

6. Response format. In each case the response format was identical: Children simply had to pick one of the three alternatives posed by the question, and then provide a simple quantitative justification.

7. Instruction. In no case were the children provided with any direct instruction on any of the tasks in question.

Given that virtually every variable that has been postulated as being of developmental relevance by task- or domain-specific theorists was held constant across the four tasks, while both informal and formal experience (i.e., schooling) was allowed to vary so widely across the four age groups, one could argue that what is remarkable is not that there was a strong age effect across tasks, and no task effect, but that there was any variability from task to task at all!

This argument clearly has some merit, and must somehow be addressed. In the present set of studies, therefore, we sought to move from laboratory tasks, in which children had little direct practice or training (i.e., in which they had only general background experience) and in which all relevant performance variables were controlled, to tasks that they encountered more frequently and directly in their everyday lives. By drawing from the universe of naturalistic tasks, we sought to assess children's intellectual development in the presence of task factors that varied in a less rigidly controlled fashion and for which background knowledge and other factors might, therefore, play a stronger role. The two general classes of tasks we sampled involved telling time and handling money.

STUDY 1: A DEVELOPMENTAL ANALYSIS OF CHILDREN'S ABILITY TO "TELL TIME"

Our first study was designed to assess the development of a basic functional skill, telling time, which poses a daily challenge to young children. Using the theory outlined in chapter 2, we reasoned that 4-year-olds would be able to solve time-telling problems requiring a global distinction within the time dimension, provided that the features to be distinguished were perceptually salient. Thus, for example, they should be able to recognize that certain events (e.g., driving to another town) take a long time and other events (e.g., blinking an eye) take a short time. They should also recognize that certain long events take "hours" whereas certain short events take "minutes." Finally, they should be able to recognize global differences in clock patterns and, when the numbers are small, identify changes in certain "hour" patterns on the clock (e.g., 1:00 becomes 3:00 when the hour hand is moved to 3).

At 6 years of age, we predicted that children would be able to solve time-telling problems that required them to seriate elements within a single time dimension. We reasoned that, if children were now able to coordinate their counting procedure with their procedure for making global time distinctions, they should be able to use this higher-level procedure to solve more complex time-telling problems. They should be able to compare two or three numerical values along one time dimension and recognize, for example, that 2:00 comes before 3:00 and that 7:00 is later than 4:00. They should also be able to identify most of the hour times on a clock and compare hour values, provided that the minute hand is straight up and presents no misleading cue.

We predicted that 8-year-olds would be able to seriate elements within *two* time dimensions, would be able to shift their focus from one dimension to another, and would be able to solve time-telling problems that required them to read "hours" and then "minutes" on a clock. Because a fully integrated use of two-dimensional procedures was not postulated until the final dimensional substage (i.e., 10 years), we expected that 8-year-olds would only be able to read hour *and* minute values on a clock if no compensation between these values was required. Thus, we predicted that 8-year-olds would be able to read clock times in which the minute hand approached half past the hour, but not those in which the minute hand moved toward the hour. The latter task requires that the child's hour reading be adjusted, in an on-line fashion, to accommodate the minute reading on the clock, and thus appeared to require a level of operational complexity consistent with that postulated for 10-year-old children.

The task of reading a digital clock poses no such computational requirements. Children need only note the colon separating the two numerical values and read "hours" and then "minutes." It was predicted, therefore, that 8-year-olds would be able to read digital times that displayed both hours and minutes (e.g., 9:16) and 6-year-olds would succeed only when just one of these dimensions was displayed (e.g., 9:00). Using the same reasoning, we predicted that 8-year-olds would be able to compare time values along two dimensions instead of one and recognize, for example, that two hours and one minute is a longer time to wait than is one hour and fifty-six minutes.

Finally, we predicted that 8-year-olds would be able to read analogue clock times requiring computation of two variables, "hours" and "minutes by five" (e.g., 4:15), whereas 10-year-olds would be able to read analogue clock times requiring computation of three variables, "hours," "minutes by five," and "minutes by one" (e.g., 4:18). When value comparison problems required children to focus on two dimensions *and* effect a compensation between these dimensions (e.g., Is one hour and thirty minutes longer than 90 minutes?), we predicted, likewise, that the triple demands of this sort of task could not be met until the age of 10.

Method

Procedures

To test these predictions, we assembled an assortment of time-telling problems that children in this age range could be expected to encounter in their everyday lives. These problems were then assigned to one of four developmental levels, on the basis of the theoretical analysis described above. The resulting battery of 38 "naturalistic" time-telling tasks is presented in Table 5.1

Note that, in contrast to the study reported in the previous chapter, task factors vary much more widely in this test battery, both across tasks within each level and across levels within tasks. Stimulus array, for example, varies from one item (#3) to three (#7), with the objects included in the sets varying as well. Question format varies from straightforward questions (e.g., What time is this?), to hypothetical questions presenting two values to be considered (#11), to questions that present a brief scenario and request an explanation (#37). Response format varies from an open-ended response choice requiring a justification (#37) to two-response alternatives (#5). The type of operation required on these tasks varies as well, with some requiring an "add-on" operation (#8); others requiring a comparison of two or three values (#10); and many others requiring a straight reading of time on an analogue or digital clock.

Because these factors fluctuate so widely across tasks, it was assumed that operational difficulty would vary as well. At the very least, it was assumed that tasks requiring a comparison of three sets as opposed to two, or an add-on operation with large numbers as opposed to small, would be procedurally more complex and thus present a greater chance for error. On the two final task factors, background experience and instruction, cross-task variations appeared likely, due to differences in children's exposure to these problems in their everyday life.

The battery of tasks described in Table 5.1 was administered, in-

TABLE 5.1
Percentage of Children Passing Developmental Time Test

Items	Age (years)			
	4	6	8	10
Level 0: Polar Dimensional (Global) Thought				
1. This says 7 o'clock (demonstrate). See the small hand is here and the big hand is here. Now I'm going to change it, now it's 5 o'clock. Can you tell me what time this is (4 o'clock)?*	73	92	100	100
2. What time is this (3 o'clock)?	73	100	100	100
3. Suppose I asked you to blink your eyes like this. Would that take a short time or a long time?	64	69	100	100
4. I'm going to make two marks with my pencil, watch. Which one took me a long time to make? Which one took a short time to make?	100	69	100	100
5. Suppose you're waiting for someone and you have to wait 7 hours. Is that a short time or a long time?	91	92	100	100
6. Suppose you have to wait one minute. Is that a short time or a long time?	91	92	100	100
Level 1: Unidimensional Thought				
7. Can you tell me which one of these times comes first? Which comes next? And which comes next? (Show 8, 4, and 3 o'clock analogue times all on one sheet.)	18	61	92	100
8. If you wait for one miniute, and then you wait for two more minutes, how many minutes have you waited all together?	9	92	100	100
9. This clock has only one hand (hour hand). See how it says 3 o'clock. If it moves one hour where will the hand be pointing?	36	61	85	100
10. Which of these times is later?, earlier? (show 6:00, 8:00 in digital)	64	77	92	100
11. Suppose I tell you I'll meet you at 6 o'clock and I get there at 5 o'clock. Am I early or late?	45	85	100	100
12. Suppose I tell you I'll meet you at 6 o'clock and I get there at 7 o'clock. Am I early or late?	55	85	92	100
13. Can you tell me what time this is (3:00—digital)?	36	100	100	100
14. Can you tell me what time this is (10:00—digital)?	18	85	100	100
15. Can you tell me what time this is (6:00—digital)?	36	100	100	100
16. Can you tell me what time this is (9:00—analogue)?	18	100	100	100
17. Can you tell me what time this is (2:00—analogue)?	45	100	100	100

(continued)

TABLE 5.1 (*continued*)

Items	Age (years)			
	4	6	8	10
Level 2: Bidimensional Thought				
18. Can you tell me what time this is (5:03)?	0	8	61	100
19. Can you tell me what time this is (2:34—digital)?	0	62	100	100
20. Can you tell me what time this is (3:20—digital)?	0	54	100	100
21. Can you tell me what time this is (12:41—digital)?	0	54	92	100
22. If the clock was here (12:00) and moved to here (12:02), how much time has passed?	0	0	77	100
23. If the clock was here (6:00) and moved to here (6:04) how much time has passed?	0	8	77	100
24. If the clock was here (9:00) and moved to here (9:07) how much time has passed?	0	0	69	100
25. Suppose I wait in line for 60 minutes then I wait for another 60 minutes. How long have I waited altogether?	0	8	77	89
26. Which is longer: 1 hour and 50 minutes or 2 hours and 1 minute?	0	15	61	94
27. Which of these two times is earlier in the afternoon: 3:35 or 2:55 (digital)?	0	38	100	100
28. Which of these two times is earlier in the afternoon 4:23 or 4:19 (digital)?	0	38	92	100
29. What time is this (9:10)?	0	0	61	100
30. What time is this (2:15)?	0	0	69	100
31. What time is this (6:20)?	0	0	69	94
Level 3: Elaborated Bidimensional Thought				
32. Can you tell me what time this is (11:37)?	0	0	38	83
33. Can you tell me what time this is (6:48)?	0	0	54	83
34. Can you tell me what time this is (3:43)?	0	0	38	67
35. Can you tell me what time this is (9:29)?	0	0	54	78
36. Suppose the clock was here (4:00) and moved over to here (5:10). How much time has passed?	0	0	54	94
37. I had a friend who walked to school and it took him 90 minutes. On the way back he said it only took him an hour and a half. Can you explain?	0	0	8	67
38. If I walk for 1 hour and 25 minutes and then I walk for 2 hours and 55 minutes, how long have I walked altogether?	0	0	15	50

*All times are analogue unless stated otherwise.

dividually, to 55 children from a middle-class, urban population. The sample contained 11 four-year-old children, and 13 children at each of 6, 8, and 10 years. A score of 1 was assigned for each item passed at each level, and a score of 0 for each item failed. Developmental scores were derived by computing the child's mean score for each level, summing across levels, and subtracting 1.0 from the resulting sum. Hence, a child passing all tasks at Level 0 and failing all tasks at higher levels $(1 + 0 + 0 + 0 = 1)$ would achieve a developmental score of $(1 - 1 = 0)$ 0.0; a child passing all tasks at Levels 0 and 1, and failing all tasks at Levels 2 and 3 would achieve a developmental level score of 1.0, and so on.

Results

The percentage of children passing each task at each of the four hypothesized levels is reported in Table 5.1 for the four age-groups. There was clearly more cross-task variability in these findings than in the studies reported by Marini in the previous chapter. However, it was also the case that a majority of children passed a majority of tasks at the predicted level. Moreover, the mean developmental level scores achieved by four age groups (Table 5.2) were strikingly similar to the pattern found by Marini (see Fig. 4.2) and conformed closely to theoretical expectations. A Guttman scale analysis also revealed the presence of a strong developmental progression. With the criterion for passing a level set at 60%, the coefficient of reproducability was 1.00, and the coefficient of scalability was .98.

Discussion

The strong developmental progression in these findings suggested that a "dimensional analysis" could be quite accurate in predicting age-related performance in a domain of knowledge (i.e., everyday time-telling) for which little prior data existed. This progression was maintained, moreover, in the presence of task factors that fluctuated across tasks in a naturalistic fashion. Although cross-task variability was present in the percentage of children passing tasks at each developmental level, the extent of this variability was contained to a modest range.

To obtain a more precise estimate of the proportion of variability that

TABLE 5.2
Actual and Predicted Mean Scores Achieved by Four Age
Groups on the Time-Telling Test (Standard Deviations are
in Brackets)

	Age (years)			
Mean Score	4	6	8	10
Actual	0.2 (.3)	1.0 (.3)	2.1 (.7)	2.7 (.3)
Predicted	0.0	1.0	2.0	3.0

could be attributed to task effects, as opposed to level effects, we needed to focus on each of these variables separately, and vary them in an independent fashion. Although this sort of factorial design had been precluded by our selection of a "naturalistic" task battery, we were able to produce such a design artificially by instigating a post-hoc analysis of the tasks included in the battery. In this analysis, we sought to identify sets of tasks that differed widely in task structure and conditions from each other, but that preserved the same internal structure and conditions across three or four developmental levels. This effort yielded three sets of tasks (see Table 5.3) that were distinct from each other in terms of stimulus array, task question, response format, and type of

TABLE 5.3
Time-Telling Task Sets*

Set 1:   Type of operation: Add-on; Stimulus array: 2 sets; Task Question: How much altogether?
           Level 1 (#8)   Wait 1 minute; then wait 2 more minutes.*
           Level 2 (#25) Wait 60 minutes; then wait another 60 minutes.
           Level 3 (#38) Walk 1 hour and 25 minutes; then walk 2 hours and 55 minutes.

Set 2:   Type of operation: Value comparison; Stimulus array: 1 or 2 sets; Task question: variable (in parentheses).
           Level 0 (#5)   Wait 7 hours. (Is that a short or long time?)
                (6)   Wait 1 minute. (Is that a short or long time?)
           Level 1 (#11) Say meet me at 6; arrive at 5. (Am I early or late?)
                (#12)   Say meet at 6; arrive at 7. (Am I early or late?)
           Level 2 (#26) 1 hr. and 50 min.; 2 hrs. and 1 min. (Which longer?)
           Level 3 (#37) It took 90 minutes to go; one hour and a half to come back. (Can you explain?)

Set 3:   Type of operation: Read time on an analogue clock; Stimulus array: 1 set; Task Question: What time is it?
           Level 0 (#1)   4:00 (Procedures demonstrated)
                (#2)   3:00 (Procedures demonstrated)
           Level 1 (#16)   9:00
                (#17)   2:00
           Level 2 (#18)   5:03
                (#29)   9:10
                (#30)   2:15
                (#31)   6:20
           Level 3 (#32) 11:37
                (#33)   6:48
                (#34)   3:43
                (#35)   9:29

*Note. All tasks are described in abbreviated form. For a full description see Table 5.1.

operation required. All tasks excluded failed to meet the specified criteria (i.e., they preserved their internal structure across only one or two developmental levels).

Because Sets 2 and 3 included more than one task at some developmental levels, we established as a criterion for passing a level, success on a majority of tasks at that level. Developmental level scores were assigned to children's performance on each set, on the basis of the highest level passed. A score of 0.0 was assigned to a pass performance at Level 0, a score of 1.0 was assigned to a pass performance at Level 1, and so on. This scoring procedure, using the highest level passed to assign scores, is somewhat different from the one used in the earlier analysis and was adopted to accommodate Set 1, which includes tasks at only three of the four developmental levels. Because Set 1 contained no tasks at Level 0, a score of 0 was automatically assigned if a child failed tasks at all higher levels.

The above scoring procedure enabled us to examine systematic variation across four age levels and across three sets of tasks with distinct task factors, in a 4 × 3 MANOVA. The mean scores achieved at each age level on the three sets of tasks are presented in Table 5.4. Note that the means are reasonably consistent across sets and, with the exception of the scores achieved by the 10-year-old group on Set 1, are consistent with theoretical expectations as well. The results of the MANOVA indicated a significant age-level effect, $F(3,51) = 87.9$; $p < .000$; a non-significant set effect, $F(2,102) = .29$; $p < .75$; and a non-significant interaction effect, $F(6,102) = 2.0$; $p < .07$. When the percentage of explained variance (ω^2) was computed, age-level was found to account for 82% of the variance, set for 1% of the variance, and Age-level × Set for 5% of the variance.

As might be expected, a Guttman scale analysis revealed the presence

TABLE 5.4
Mean Time-Telling Scores Achieved by Four Age Groups on Three Distinct Task Sets (Standard Deviations are in Brackets)

Set	Age (years)			
	4	6	8	10
1	0.1 (.3)	1.0 (.4)	1.9 (.7)	2.4 (.7)
2	0.2 (.4)	1.0 (.6)	1.6 (.8)	2.6 (.7)
3	0.2 (.3)	1.0 (.0)	2.0 (.9)	2.8 (.3)

of a strong developmental progression on each set, with reproducability coefficients of .99, 1.00, and 1.00 for Sets 1, 2, and 3, respectively, and scalability coefficients of .97, .98, and .99, respectively. These results confirm the interpretation offered earlier, on the basis of a visual inspection of the percentage of children passing tasks at four developmental levels. They allow us to assert, with greater assurance, that the dimensional complexity of an item accounts for more variance in children's time-telling performance than so-called performance factors, although each explains a portion of the variance. For the particular performance factors distinguished on these sets (i.e., type of operation, stimulus array, and response format), the portion of the variance that was explained was very small indeed.[1]

One final analysis of the sets was conducted in order to discover the extent to which the consistent level of performance across tasks, which was present in the group findings, was present in the performance of individual children as well. Cross-task synchrony was determined by computing the percentage of children who achieved: (a) an identical level score on all three sets; (b) an identical level score on two sets and a score one level removed on the third set; and (c) different level scores on all three sets. The results indicated that the most common pattern was one in which children performed at the same developmental level across two sets and at one level removed on the third set. Only one out of the 55 children performed at a different level on all three sets, and a majority of one group (i.e., the 6-year-olds) performed at an identical level on all three sets (see Table 5.5).

The results in Table 5.5 are once again parallel to those described by Marini in the previous chapter. What they indicate is that performance fluctuation across sets is confined to a very modest range, that is, to one developmental level. Further, there is a substantial amount of synchrony in the rate at which children master time-telling tasks with different task demands. These results can, we believe, best be explained by suggesting, once again, that the structural complexity of a task— and the sort of executive control structure it requires as a consequence —account, to a considerable degree, for children's performance on everyday time-telling problems. This factor appears to account for performance consistencies across tasks with fluctuating task requirements and formats, as well as for performance variations across four distinct age levels.

---

[1]It is, of course, possible that this variance might have been substantially higher had different factors been used.

TABLE 5.5
Percentage of Children with Cross-Task Synchrony
and Asynchrony on Three Time-Telling Task Sets

Synchrony/Asynchrony	Age (years)			
	4	6	8	10
Same level on 3 sets	45	54	23	33
Same level on 2 sets*	55	46	77	61
Different levels on 3 sets	0	0	0	6

*Performance on the third set was one level re-
moved, for all subjects.

STUDY 2: A DEVELOPMENTAL INVESTIGATION
OF CHILDREN'S SKILL IN HANDLING MONEY

Our second study was designed to assess the development of a second
basic functional skill—handling money—that also poses everyday challenges to young children. Following the same line of reasoning as for
time, we predicted that 4-year-olds would be able to solve money problems requiring them to make global distinctions within a monetary
dimension (e.g., cents or dollars), provided that the features to be distinguished were perceptually salient. Thus, for example, they should be
able to recognize that a quarter is worth more than a nickel, because a
quarter is bigger. Conversely, they should be likely to mistakenly identify
a nickel as worth more than a dime because the nickel is bigger. They
should be able to implement simple, automatic counting routines, by
starting at one and proceeding, in an overlearned sequence, to five.
They should also be able to use these routines to compute the quantity of
a small array of coins or bills (i.e., 5 or under). Hence, when one penny is
added to an array of two pennies, a child at this age should be able to
compute the correct total, simply by counting the new array.

At the 6-year-old level, we predicted that children would be able to
coordinate their counting routine with one for making global monetary
distinctions. Using this higher level procedure, they should be able to
solve money problems that required them to seriate elements along a
monetary dimension. Thus, they should now recognize that a dime is
worth more than a nickel, because ten is a larger number than five; that
a $1 bill is worth less than either a $5 bill or a $10 bill; and that one $5 bill
has a greater monetary value than two $1 bills.

An ability to seriate numbers along a dimension should also enable

6-year-olds to compute quantity without starting at one and counting the entire set of coins or bills. They should now recognize, in the absence of countable objects, that when one penny is added to a set of three pennies, the sum is four because four is the next number in the number sequence. Finally, they should now be able to handle numbers greater than five, providing the numbers are confined to one place value. Within this constraint, they should be able to add on to numbers greater than five, using numbers less than five, by counting up from the first set. A similar capability should emerge for subtraction.

At 8 years of age, we predicted that children would be able to seriate elements along two monetary dimensions, shift their focus from one dimension to another, and solve money problems that required them to deal with both dollars and cents. Thus, for example, they should be able to recognize that $5 and 1 penny is worth more than $1 and 20 pennies because, although there are more cents than dollars, dollars have a larger monetary value. It was predicted, as well, that an ability to handle two dimensions would enable children to deal with two place values and consequently, with numbers up to 100. Addition and subtraction with double-digit numbers should therefore be possible at this age level, provided that the addend and minuend numbers are sufficiently small for children to count up or down without having to set up a "double entry" system for either of the two dimensions.

At 10 years, we predicted that children would be able to seriate or quantify elements along two monetary dimensions and coordinate the products in an integrated fashion. Thus, for example, they should be able to compute the total of several combinations of dollars and cents by quantifying the dollar values, quantifying the cents values, and integrating the subtotals appropriately. They should also be able to solve problems in which dollars and cents are expressed in an integrated fashion (e.g., $9.34) and manage three place values. Finally, they should be able to handle numbers larger than 100, and add and subtract using double-digit numbers.

Procedures

To test these predictions we assembled an assortment of money-handling problems that children in this age range could be expected to encounter in their everyday lives. These problems were then assigned to one of four levels, on the basis of the theoretical analyses described above. The resulting battery of 25 "naturalistic" money-handling tasks is presented in Table 5.6. Note that again, in contrast to the study reported in the previous chapter, task factors vary quite widely in this test battery,

TABLE 5.6
Percentage of Children Passing the Developmental Money Test

	Age (years)			
Items	4	6	8	10

Level 0: Polar Dimensional (Global) Thought

Items	4	6	8	10

1. I have 2 piles of money here (pennies) ..Which is worth more (or is bigger)?
a. 0 0   b. 0 0 0 0 0 0 0 0 0
        0 0 0 0 0 0 0 0 0
        0 0 0 0 0 0 0 0 0
	92	100	100	100

2. Here are 2 piles of money. Which is worth less (or is smaller)? a. $1 $1 $1 $1 $1 $1 $1 b. $1 $1 $1 $1 $1 $1 $1 $1 $1	92	100	100	100
3. Here are two tapes. Which one do you think costs more?	83	100	100	100
4. Here are two chocolate bars. Which one do you think costs less (or costs the smallest amount)?	92	100	100	100
5. I'm going to give you 2 pennies (do so), count 1 penny, 2 pennies. Now if I give you 1 more (do so) how many pennies do you have?	83	100	100	100
6. I'm going to give you 3 pennies (do so). Now I'm going to take back 1 (do so). How many do you have now?	92	100	100	100
7. Here is a pile of coins. Now I'm going to take some (0 0 0), and I'm going to give you one (0). (a) Do we have the same amount? (b) Who did I give too much to?	92	100	100	100
8. Can you make your pile the same as mine?	92	100	100	100
9. Pretend I'm a storekeeper. My friend Joe wanted to buy a piece of bubble gum (show gum). It costs 2 cents, but he doesn't count his money when he pays. This is how much he gave me (show 3 cents). Is this right?	58	73	100	100

(continued)

TABLE 5.6 (*continued*)

Items	Age (years)			
	4	*6*	*8*	*10*
Level 1: Unidimensional Thought				
10. (continued from 9) What should I do? (prompt: Give him back money or ask for more? How much?)	17	60	100	100
11. Here are two amounts of money. a. $1 $1 b. $5 Which is worth more (or is the bigger amount)?	0	60	100	100
12. If I give you 1 cent and then I give you 2 more cents, how much did I give you altogether? (Question is verbal only.)	25	100	100	100
13. Here are 3 bills: $5 $1 $10 (Show picture.) Which one is worth the most (or is the biggest)? Now which one is the next largest amount?	17	80	100	100
14. I want you to pretend I'm a storekeeper and you want to buy this bear (Show picture.) It costs $4. You give me $5. What do I have to do?	0	40	93	100
Level 2: Bidimensional Thought				
15. Here are two amounts of money. (Show picture.) a. $1, 20 pennies B. $5, 1 penny Which is worth more?	0	33	87	100
16. If I give you 25 cents and then give you 6 more cents, how much have I given you?	0	0	87	100
17. You have $47. You give me 2 dollars. How much do you have left?	0	13	73	100
18. You want to buy a candy. It costs 19 cents. You give me 25 cents. What am I going to do? (Prompt: How much should you get back?)	0	0	60	93
19. You want to buy a chocolate bar. It costs 93 cents. You give me $1 (or 100 cents). What do I do? (Prompt: How much should you get back?)	0	0	53	80
20. Pretend I'm the storekeeper. This tape cost 100 cents or one dollar. You only have 98 cents. If you give me 98 cents, what am I going to say? (Prompt: How much more do you need?)	0	0	73	100
Level 3: Elaborated Bidimensional Thought				
21. How much money is this altogether? $1 $2 $5 25¢ 10¢ 2¢	0	0	40	87

22. Here are 3 amounts of money.
    a. $1 $1 $1 $1 $1 $1 $1   25¢ 25¢
    b. $5 $2   25¢ 10¢ 10¢ 10¢
    c. $1 $1 $1 $1 $1   25¢ 25¢ 25¢
    Which amount has the most money? Why? (must give
    correct justification) Which is the next largest amount of
    money?

23. Suppose you want to buy a clock? It costs $4.29. You
    give the storekeeper $10.00. What is he going to do?
    (Prompt: How much change will he give you back?)
    (Can use pencil and paper if they ask.)   0   0   6   60

24. You want to buy a tape recorder. It costs $100. You
    have only $19. If you give me $19 what am I going to
    do? (Prompt: How much more money do you need?)   0   0   26   80

25. A chocolate bar cost 56 cents. You give the storekeeper
    $1.00. What is he going to do? (Prompt: How much
    change do you get back?)   0   0   6   80

---

both across tasks and across levels. As was the case with the time-telling battery, cross-task variations are present in each of the seven factors enumerated at the beginning of the chapter.

The battery of tasks in the table was administered, individually, to 57 children from a middle-class, urban population. The sample contained 12 four-year-old children and 15 children at 6, 8, and 10 years of age. Scoring procedures were identical to those used in the time-telling test. A score of 1 was assigned for each task passed at each level, and developmental scores were derived by computing the child's mean score for each level, summing across levels, and subtracting 1.0.

Results

The percentage of children passing each task at each age is depicted in Table 5.6. The percentages are similar to those found in the time-telling study and indicate that a majority of children passed a majority of tasks at the predicted level. The mean scores achieved by the four age groups (Table 5.7) are also similar to those reported by Marini, and conform to theoretical expectations. Finally, a Guttman scale analysis revealed the presence of a strong developmental progression: With the criterion for passing a level set at 60%, the coefficients of reproducability and scalability were both 1.00. It should be noted, however, that the results indicated considerably more cross-task variability than was found in Marini's study, or the previous study reported in this chapter.

TABLE 5.7
Actual and Predicted Mean Scores Achieved by Four Age Groups
on the Money-Handling Test (Standard Deviations are
in Brackets)

Mean Score	Age (years)			
	4	6	8	10
Acutal	0.0 (2)	0.7 (.4)	2.0 (.3)	2.7 (.4)
Predicted	0.0	1.0	2.0	3.0

Discussion

The foregoing results suggest that a dimensional analysis can be quite useful for predicting age-related performance in another domain of everyday knowledge, money-handling. They also suggest that structural level accounts for more variability in the findings than task effects do. Although greater cross-task variability was apparent in these findings, the extent of this variability was still not greater than that predicted by neo-Piagetian theory; that is, it was contained to the range from 50 to 100% passing at the predicted age levels.

In order to examine the proportion of variability that could be attributed to task effects and age-level effects independently, we once again instigated a post hoc analysis of the task battery. Our effort to identify sets of tasks that preserved the postulated structure across three or four levels, and on which task conditions remained reasonably constant, yielded three problem sets. These sets (presented in Table 5.8) varied in question format, response format, and type of operation required, yet held the general type of operation constant across all four age levels. All tasks excluded from the sets failed to meet these criteria (e.g., they required a different operation at two different levels).

The criterion for passing a level differed slightly from the one used for the time-telling sets. In the case of the time-telling items, certain task factors (e.g., a forced-choice response format) gave children good odds for success. Thus, a pass was assigned to a level only if three of four tasks (or two of two tasks) included at that level were passed. By contrast, in the only money-handling set that included more than one task per level, the task factors gave children good odds for failure. A lower pass criterion was therefore adopted (namely, 50%). Note that this scoring difference was pertinent to only two levels of one set (i.e., Set 3). In all other respects, the scoring criteria adopted for these sets were identical to those used for time-telling.

As with the previous tasks, a Guttman scale analysis revealed the

TABLE 5.8
Money-Handling Task Sets

Set 1: Type of operation: Add-on; Response format: Open-ended response choice;
Task question: How much altogether?
Level 0 (#5)   Give 2 pennies; give 1 more (real objects)*.
Level 1 (#12) Give 1¢; give 2¢ more (presented verbally).
Level 2 (#16) Give 25¢; give 6¢ more (presented verbally).
Level 3 (#21) Show $1, $2, $5, 25¢, 10¢, 2¢.

Set 2: Type of operation: Value comparison; Response format: Choose one; Task
question: Which is worth more?
Level 0 (#1)   00 vs. 00000000
Level 1 (#13) $5 vs. $1 vs. $10
Level 2 (#15) $1, 20 pennies vs. $5, 1 penny
Level 3 (#22) Compare 3 sets, each with an array of dollars and cents

Set 3: Type of operation—Determine over- or under-payment (assisted by prompts)
and compute difference; Response format—Forced-choice on first operation
(assisted by prompts) and open-ended response choice on second operation;
Task question—What does the storekeeper have to do? (Prompt given on most
tasks, in the form of "How much do you get back?" or "How much more do you
need?")
Level 0 (#8)   Make your pile (0) the same as mine (000).
        (#9)   Cost 2¢; pays 3¢. (Is this right?)
        (Note: Task demands are reduced at this level)
Level 1 (#10)   Costs 2¢; pays 3¢.
        (#14)   Costs $4; pays $5.
Level 2 (#18)   Costs 19¢; pays 25¢.
        (#19)   Costs 93¢; pays 100¢.
        (#20)   Costs 100¢; pays 98¢.
Level 3 (#23)   Costs $4.29; pays $10.00.
        (#24)   Costs $100.00; pays $19.00.
        (#25)   Costs 56¢; pays $1.00.

---

*Note. All tasks are described in abbreviated form. For a full description of each, see
Table 5.6.

presence of a strong developmental progression on each set, with a
reproduceability coefficient of 1.00 found for each set and scalability
coefficients of 1.00, 1.00, and .98 for Sets 1, 2, and 3, respectively. When
mean level scores were computed for the four age groups, they were
found to conform to theoretical expectations on each set (see Table 5.9).
Note also that the scores of the 4- and 10-year-old groups were highly
consistent across sets, and the scores of the 6- and 8-year-old groups
were less consistent, although still within the general ranges predicted by
the theory.

The results of a MANOVA analysis indicated a significant age level
effect, $F(3,53) = 135.0$; $p < .000$, a significant set effect, $F(2,106) = 8.31$;

TABLE 5.9

Mean Money-Handling Scores Achieved by Four
Age Groups on Three Distinct Task Sets (Standard Deviations are in Brackets)

Set	Age (years)			
	4	6	8	10
1	0.1 (.5)	1.0 (.0)	2.3 (.6)	2.9 (.3)
2	0.1 (.4)	1.1 (.8)	2.4 (.7)	2.8 (.4)
3	0.1 (.3)	0.7 (.4)	1.7 (.5)	2.7 (.5)

$p < .000$, and a non-significant interaction effect $F(6,106) = 1.72; p >$
.10. When the size of these effects was computed, age level was found to
account for 87% of the variance, set for 11%, and Age level × Set for 3%
of the variance. Although task effects accounted for a larger proportion
of the variance in this study than in the time-telling study, in both studies
the proportion of the variance they explained was minor in relation to
the substantial age-level effects that were present.

Strong cross-task consistency was also found when the pattern of
performance of individual children was assessed. Table 5.10 presents
the percentage of children who achieved: (a) an identical score on all
three sets; (b) an identical score on two sets and a score one level
removed on the third set; and (c) different scores on all three sets. The
results are similar to the time-telling findings and indicate that the most
common pattern of performance was one in which children performed
at the same developmental level across two sets, and at one level removed on the third set. Only two subjects out of 57 performed at
different levels across the three sets.

GENERAL DISCUSSION

Given the findings we have described, it seems clear that the pattern
obtained in Marini's study (chapter 4) was not merely an artifact, resulting from the fact that so many performance variables of developmental
relevance were controlled. It is important to realize, however, that a
subtle change took place in the theoretical rationale for deriving the
developmental predictions in this study, as we moved from the precisely
specified problems posed by Marini to a more naturalistic set. In the
problems used by Marini, the predictions were made on the basis of: (a)
a precise specification of the "executive control structures" that children

TABLE 5.10
Percentage of Children with Cross-Task Synchrony
and Asynchrony on Three Money-Handling
Task Sets

	Age (years)			
Synchrony/Asynchrony	4	6	8	10
Same level on 3 sets	42	27	13	47
Same level on 2 sets*	50	73	80	53
Different levels on 3 sets	8	0	7	0

*Performance on the third set was one level re-
moved for most subjects, and two levels removed for
13% of the subjects in this category.

would need to assemble in order to pass each increasingly difficult
variant of the balance beam problem (See chapter 2, Table 2.3), and (b) a
corresponding analysis of the increase in working memory load associated with setting up an appropriate representation and "goal stack" in
each case. By contrast, in the present studies, the successful predictions
were made on the basis of a more global, "dimensional analysis" of each
problem. What was taken into account was the number of quantitative
dimensions the problem required children to focus on, in order to
achieve success. In fact, earlier attempts to focus exclusively on working
memory load for various subtle task features, while ignoring the overall
structure of the operations that were required, were not particularly
successful (Case & Sandieson, 1987). Of course, this does not mean that
working memory load and working memory growth are not important
variables. However, it does suggest that working memory may be of
importance primarily for its role in determining the overall structure of
children's performance, not for its more "procedural" or "bookkeeping"
functions.

What exactly does it mean to "determine the overall structure of
children's performance"? Two interpretations would seem possible within the context of the control theory that was outlined in chapter 2. The
first is that working memory is required to orchestrate the overall flow of
children's intellectual operations, because of the "goal stacks" that these
operations entail. According to this view, the developmental change in
children's quantitative operations might be represented in the manner
illustrated in Fig. 5.1. What this figure suggests is that predimensional
children are incapable of integrating quantitative comparisons into their
executive processes. By contrast, unidimensional children are capable of
making one quantitative comparison, bidimensional children are capa-

<u>4 YRS</u>   (predimensional strategy):

Classify Side A	w/r*	Weight
Classify Side B	w/r	Weight
If A (or B) Big	w/r	Weight

And Other Side Not,
   Predict That A or B Will Go Down (or vice versa)

(otherwise Guess)

<u>6 YRS</u>   (unidimensional strategy):
Count Weights on Side A → QWeight (A)
Count Weights on Side B → QWeight (B)
Compare Magnitude
IF   QWeight (A) > QWeight (B) (or vice versa)
       Predict That (A) Will Go Down (or vice versa)

(otherwise predict "balance)

<u>8 YRS</u>   (bidimensional strategy):
Count Weights on Side A → QWeight (A)
Count Weights on Side B → QWeight (B)
Compare Magnitude   •Store•
Count Distance on Side A → QDistance (A)
Count Distance on Side B → QDistance (B)
If   QWeight (A) ≈ QWeight (B)
And   QDistance (A) > QDistance (B) (or vice versa)
       Predict That A Will Go Down (or vice versa)

(otherwise proceed as at 6)

<u>10 YRS</u>   (integrated bidimensional strategy):
Count Weights on Side A → QWeight (A)
Count Weights on Side B → QWeight (B)
Compute Different • Store • →QDiff (weight)
Count Distance on Side A → QDistance (A)
Count Distance on Side B → QDistance (B)
Compute Difference   •Store• → QDiff (distance)
If QDiff (weight) > QDiff (distance)

Predict Side with Greater Weight Will Go Down
If QDiff (distance) > QDiff (weight)

Predict Side with Greater Distance Will Go Down

(otherwise predict balance)

FIG. 5.1. Procedures used by children at different ages for solving the balance beam problem.

*w/r = with regard to

ble of meeting two such comparisons in sequence (i.e., of making one such comparison while storing a "pointer" in working memory to a second), while children at the final substage are capable of making 3 or more such comparisons.

A second, rather different way of interpreting the same pattern is illustrated in Fig. 5.2. According to this second interpretation, what is important is how children *represent* a problem, i.e., their conceptual understanding of it.

As the figure indicates, it could be that 4-year-old children tend to represent each possible variable in a global or polar fashion, so that they can make mappings of the sort "Big things are worth more; little things are worth less." In contrast, 6-year-olds might tend to represent variables in a continuous fashion, i.e., as having two poles and a number of points in between. Moreover, they might realize that these points can be treated as lying along a mental number line, such that values that have a higher real value (e.g., move up) will also have a higher number associated with them. Eight-year-olds might think in terms of two independent quantitative variables (e.g., hours and minutes on a clock), but might not be able to make successful comparisons between variations along each. Finally, at 10, children might make these sorts of comparisons, by thinking in terms of the interaction between two quantitative variables.

Before proceeding, it must be emphasized that what is at issue is not whether it is mental representations or mental procedures that are more important for task success. Clearly, both are vital. Rather, what is at issue is which factor is of greater developmental significance. As a specific example, the question is whether 4-year-olds experience a problem with unidimensional tasks primarily because they cannot represent them in terms of a single continuous variable, or whether they experience a

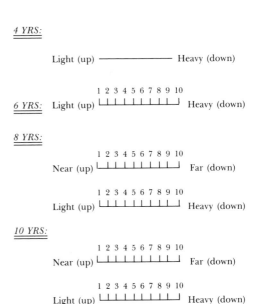

FIG. 5.2. Conceptual representation hypothesized to underlie children's procedures for solving the balance beam, at different ages.

problem primarily because they cannot execute a procedure of the sort
COUNT X, COUNT Y, COMPARE MAGNITUDE.

A tentative answer to this question may be suggested by examining
problems whose procedural requirements differ in complexity with at
least some degree of independence from their representational requirements. Consider the following Level 2 tasks drawn from the time-telling
battery. Task #7 asks which of three "hour" times (displayed on an
analogue clock) comes first, which comes next, and which comes next.
Task #8 asks for the sum of 1 minute plus 2 more minutes. From the
point of view of their representational requirements, the task demands
are equivalent: They both require children to think in terms of a single
continuous variable, or a single "mental number line."

The procedural requirements, however, seem quite different. In the
second problem one need only count two units up from one, and realize
that the answer is "3." In the first problem one must compute two
quantitative values (for the first two clocks), and compare their magnitude. One must then remember the smaller value, compute a third
quantitative value, and compare it to the one retained, ultimately picking
the smaller of these two numbers as the one that comes earliest. In terms
of procedural complexity, the second problem is more closely akin to
tasks that are normally solved at age 4 (i.e., Level 1), while the first
problem is more closely akin to tasks that are normally solved at age 8
(i.e., Level 3).

When the percentage of children passing each of these tasks is examined, one finds that a majority of 4-year-olds fail both tasks and a
majority of 6-year-olds pass both. At each age level the task that is more
complex procedurally is also more difficult; it is passed by 61% of the
6-year-old group, in contrast to the 92% who pass the procedurally less
complex task. Thus, procedural requirements do appear to have a
considerable impact on children's performance. However, at least on
these particular items, as well as in the findings already discussed, the
representational factor appears to be much more powerful. When the
tasks required a unidimensional representation, they were rarely passed
before the age of 6, no matter what their computational complexity.
Similarly, when the tasks required a bidimensional representation, they
were rarely passed before the age of 8, no matter what their computational complexity.

In view of the similar result reported in instructional studies (Case &
Sandieson, 1988; Dennis, 1981), we conclude that it may be relatively
easy for children to circumvent the working memory demands of a
complex procedure, as long as an age-appropriate representation is in
place to serve as a guide or mnemonic aid. However, it may be very
difficult for children to circumvent the working memory demands of

constructing an appropriate representation—even when procedural factors are very simple—because there is no corresponding "general sense" of the task to guide their mental activity.

In conclusion, then, we would like to suggest that a characterization of development that focuses on the way children represent problems at different ages may be of greater utility than a characterization that focuses on procedural complexity. It is not that procedural complexity has no effect. It is just that this effect seems considerably smaller, from a developmental perspective. Certain representational capacities seem to act as a constraint on the acquisition of particular procedures, in the sense that they must somehow be brought into place before these procedures can be assembled and employed with effectiveness and flexibility.

A Neo-Structural Analysis of Children's Response to Instruction in the Sight-Reading of Musical Notation

Alessandra M. Capodilupo
Brock University

In the previous studies reported in this volume, the competencies that were analyzed were not ones that are transmitted by our culture in any systematic fashion. Although most children eventually come to understand what makes a shadow shrink or grow, for example, or how much change to expect when something costs 4¢ and they pay 5¢, they rarely receive direct instruction in such matters.[1] A question that naturally arises, therefore, is whether the same general progression and age norms would be obtained for competencies in which direct instruction does take place.

Elsewhere, Case and Threadgill-Sowder (1990) have analyzed several basic competencies in elementary mathematics, and argued that they do follow the same general progression and age norms. There are two difficulties with this argument from the present perspective, however. The first is that the training children received took place in the context of their regular classroom schooling, and was therefore not open to experimental manipulation and control. The second was that the training was in aspects of mathematics that were related to the competencies that were assessed, but that did not focus on these competencies directly. In this respect, then, the Case and Threadgill-Sowder study was really quite similar to those reported in the two previous chapters, in that children were exposed to a great deal of experience that was indirectly

---

[1] The only possible exception to this generalization is the skill of time-telling, which is sometimes taught directly in the Grade 1 or 2 math curriculum. In the particular time-telling studies that were reported, however, the children were drawn from schools where it was not part of the primary curriculum.

relevant to a valued skill—and even had the opportunity to observe adults executing the skill with some regularity—but did not receive explicit instruction in how to execute the skill themselves.

In the study reported here, a skill was selected for which the subject population had received no prior formal training. They were then exposed to a period of carefully scripted instruction as part of the investigation. The skill that was selected for this purpose was musical sight-reading.

THE COGNITIVE BASIS OF MUSICAL SIGHT-READING

In recent years, musical sight reading has been shown to depend on cognitive capacities in much the same way as do other, more academic skills (Bamberger, 1973, 1978; Davies, 1978; Hildebrandt, 1987; Serafine, 1980, 1981, 1983; Wolf, 1976). The discovery of a cognitive basis for musical sight-reading has led researchers to other cognitive realms in search of clues as to the mechanisms underlying the sight-reading process. Naturally enough, particular attention has been devoted to the domain of text reading, because the reading of text also requires the interpretation of a set of visual symbols, and their conversion to a motor response with a strong auditory component. This line of study has proven to be quite fruitful, and many parallels between the two tasks have been demonstrated, both in structure and in process.

At a global level, research has examined the structure and logical organization of music as it relates to that of language, with a view to extracting the cognitive elements of music and explicating the interdependencies among them. From one such investigation, Sundberg and Lindblom (1976) concluded that melodies, like sentences, exhibit a hierarchical constituent structure that results from the application of a system of rules. This system determines which manipulations of musical elements are permissible and is directly analogous to that which is operative in the production of text. Sloboda (1978) has investigated this notion formally in a series of studies designed to examine the use of various musical-structural principles by expert versus novice sight-readers. In an early study (Sloboda, 1976a), he examined the occurrence of misreading errors in music for parallels with the well-documented phenomenon of proofreader's error in text reading. Musicians were required to play a number of musical selections to which several stylistically improbable alterations had been made. They were instructed to play the notes exactly as written. It was hypothesized that the knowledge of harmony and musical style possessed by skilled sight-readers would lead them to misread the notes they played in a fashion that was consistent with their knowledge of the larger whole. The results confirmed the hypothesis: Performance on unaltered notes was only 2% inaccurate, whereas performance on altered notes was 40% inaccurate. Furthermore, notes substituted by musicians for the altered ones tended to be those that had appeared in the original, unaltered manuscripts. Finally, the experts were not aware they had made any of these substitutions. It would seem, then, that proficient sight-readers automatically impose conventional structure on musical notation, regardless of the fact that they are specifically instructed not to do so.

Sloboda's (1976a) study also investigated the effects on performance of varying the position of alteration. From studies of text reading, it was known that readers identify words by first identifying the exterior letters, and then using the surrounding context, in conjunction with their knowledge of language structure, in order to "read" the most appropriate word. Musical sight-readers appear to utilize a similar strategy. They are more likely to correct altered notes appearing at the beginning or end of a phrase than those occurring in the middle. They are also more likely to alter notes in the treble clef (which usually establishes the pattern of a phrase) than in the bass. Sloboda proposed that music readers attend to those parts of the phrase that offer the most information, that is, those that establish the pattern of the phrase most conclusively. From his interviews with gifted sight-readers, Wolf (1976) concurred with Sloboda that musical sight-reading is essentially a pattern-recognition task.

In order to study the pattern-recognition process further, Sloboda (1974) adapted a technique originally devised by Levin as a method for examining the cognitive processes in text reading. The original method, termed the *eye-voice span* (EVS) is a measure of the number of words recalled beyond the point at which a text ceases to be displayed. EVS is known to be longer for more experienced readers or for structured material, and shorter for less experienced readers or unorganized material. Sloboda's (1974) adaptation of the technique, termed the *eye-hand span* (EHS), operates within the same paradigm as EVS but requires that readers play what they recall of the musical notation beyond the point at which the display is removed. Sloboda determined that EHS behaved analogously to EVS, and that a high positive correlation is evident between EHS and sight-reading ability. In addition, he found that EHS varied as a function of the degree of segmentation within the musically notated material.

In a subsequent study, Sloboda (1977) investigated the effects of phrase segmentation more closely, and suggested that phrase markers are of two types: physical and structural. In written music, such elements as rests and bar lines act as punctuation or physical markers, while rules for harmonic progression (such as scale or cadence) act as structural markers. Using the EHS technique, he tested the performance of accomplished readers on musical phrases that incorporated the various types of markers. The results indicated that the effects of physical and structural markers are independent, and that the latter always increase EHS, whereas the former do not necessarily. To account for these findings, he proposed that *harmonic* structural markers render the musical text more predictable, therefore reducing the processing load of the information, while *physical* markers allow the reader to determine where their analysis should start or stop, but do not decrease processing load. One might propose, then, that the acquisition of skill in musical sight-reading occurs through a gradual shift in emphasis from the perceptual to the semantic, that is, from utilizing the structure in the visual symbols to utilizing the structure of the music they represent.

Wolf (1976) suggested that music reading, like text reading, is merely a special instance of problem solving. On this basis, she proposed a cognitive model of sight-reading that has its origins in the tradition of information processing. Within the proposed system, information about musical notation, harmony, and musical style is stored in long-term memory (LTM) and is used to segment incoming information into meaningful units, which are then stored in short-term memory (STM). If there is a lack of knowledge of musical structure (from LTM), segmentation of incoming information will be less efficient, which in turn will lead to an overload on STM.

In summary, existing research on musical sight-reading illustrates the many parallels between this task and that of text reading, and indicates that it obeys the same general cognitive principles. If this is true, it follows that performance on the task of sight-reading should lend itself to a developmental analysis on the basis of cognitive-developmental theory. Moreover, because many children do not receive explicit training in sight-reading (which is, of course, not the case for text reading) it should be possible to select children at different ages who have not yet been exposed to such instruction, and to predict their response to a carefully developed instructional program, using cognitive developmental theory as a guide.

That was the purpose of the present study. The more particular goal was to see if the theory in chapter 2 could predict the response of children at different ages to a carefully scripted program of instruction.

A DEVELOPMENTAL ANALYSIS OF MUSICAL SIGHT-READING

The investigation was based on the premise that the same dimensional structure that had been found for 4- to 10-year-olds on tasks such as the Balance Beam or Time-Telling could be used for predicting children's performance in the task of musical sight-reading as well. In order for such predictions to be made, several "levels" of the task had to be constructed, which entailed the same dimensional progression as had been created in the earlier studies. Children in the dimensional stage (i.e., 4 to 10 years) then had to be given training in how to respond at each level.

At first glance, the selection of the "quantitative dimension" as the unit of analysis may seem to be a rather inappropriate one for music, especially in view of the previously cited literature on sight-reading, which demonstrates its similarity to the reading of verbal text. It must be remembered, however, that the study that was planned was a training one and that, just as novice readers must often rely on phonetic decoding to determine the correspondence between a printed word that they have not seen before and its aural referent, so novice musicians must often rely on the one-to-one numerical correspondence between the lines and spaces on the printed staff, and the strings, keys, or holes on their instruments.

While understanding and utilizing this one-to-one correspondence may not be *all* there is to learning how to sight-read music, it necessarily constitutes a major component—indeed, one that is basic to the acquisition of skill in this task domain. Moreover, given that this component is a central one, it follows that a musical "scale" must possess the same general dimensional properties as do dimensions such as distance on the balance beam, or time as displayed on a clock. There is a physical dimension, which can vary between two poles in a continuous fashion, and there is some culturally devised artifact (in this case, musical notation) for indicating the relative magnitude of any two values of the dimension along this continuum.

Once the task of sight-reading is understood in this fashion, it follows that 4- to 10-year-old children should progress through four substages in mastering it. There should be a preliminary substage, in which they can map global variation in tune (i.e., up and down) onto corresponding globally differentiated positions on the musical staff. Next should come a substage where they can map quantitative variation on to precisely specified position on a musical instrument (e.g., for the piano, the white keys). Next should come a substage where they can do this for two separate dimensions or scales (e.g., white keys and black keys). Finally, there should be a substage where they can make precise tradeoffs between these dimensions. The aim in designing the sight-reading task was to create a set of items that possessed this general structure, and that would maximally facilitate children's learning: by reducing information processing load to a minimum, by providing maximally salient perceptual cues, and by providing explicit verbal guidance in how to utilize these cues.

Items at Level 0 were designed to be appropriate for children at the predimensional stage, in which the child's processing strategy is one of global scanning along a single bipolar dimension. The dimension that was selected was musical contour—the rise and fall pattern of music—for which the required global judgment was "up high" versus "down low." Only two distinctively marked notes and their corresponding keys (middle C and F) were presented at this first level.

During the training period for Level 0, the children were shown the symbols indicated in Fig. 6.1. Middle C was marked in red and designated a spaceship, due to its perceptual similarity to a flying saucer. The F above it was marked with a happy face and designated the moon due to its similarity to pictures of "the man in the moon." The children were instructed that these markers on the piano corresponded to the *spaceship* and the *moon* on the musical manuscript. The children were also told that on seeing a spaceship they should play the spaceship key; and on seeing the moon, they should play the moon key.

Level 1 items were designed to be appropriate for children in the substage of unidimensional thought, in which a processing strategy for quantifying along a single dimension is available. It was speculated that at this level children would be able to understand a scale as a series of one-unit steps, and go back and forth between the music and a piano keyboard while maintaining their position in the scale in question. Accordingly, the second level of the sight-reading task introduced two more notes (D and E) that were conventionally notated, and situated between C and F. Because these new notes were not conspicuously marked, it was expected that children would be forced to coordinate contour with their previously consolidated counting structure, as a means for determining which of the two notes should be played. More explicitly, because each new note was one or two scale steps up or down from a distinctively marked note, the precise magnitude of this distance would have to be counted.

Training for Level 1 items involved explaining to the child that, when moving up toward the moon, the first new note (D) was one step away from the spaceship while the second new note (E) was two steps away from the spaceship. The child was also alerted to the fact that the notes would not always be presented in the same order. Level 2 was designed

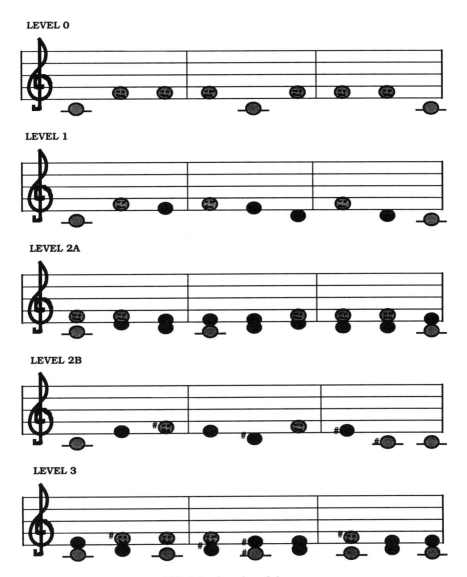

FIG. 6.1.   Sample task items.

to require bi-dimensional thought, that is, thought that requires one to quantify along two dimensions in a sequential fashion, but without integration. This third level of the task was divided into two parts, each introducing a different additional dimension. Level 2A introduced the child to simple harmonic intervals, that is, the playing of two notes simultaneously. Hence, the task was presumed to require the identification of two rather than one unit of a scale. In essence, two successive coordinations of the sort achieved at Level 1 were required. The child was told that when one note appeared above another the notes were to be played at the same time.

Level 2B exposed the child to sharps, which have the effect of raising a note by one semitone, thus constituting a half-step movement upward (to the right) on the keyboard. Again, the task was construed as requiring an evaluation of a dual sort: noting a position with regard to the white key (the natural note) and then the black key (its corresponding sharp) in sequence. The story that was told to facilitate this acquisition was as follows: "These signs (#) are called *turbo-boosts,* (in keeping with the video-game analogy). Turbo-boosts move the note away from the spaceship and bring it one little step closer to the moon." Attention was drawn to the fact that a sharp on the E functions differently from a sharp on the other notes, in that a turbo-boost E is a white key whereas a turbo-boost C, D, or F is a black key.

Level 3 items were designed to require elaborated bidimensional thought. This level of the task was structured such that simultaneous processing of two dimensions was necessary for successful performance. By presenting harmonic intervals that contained sharps, the task required that the child coordinate the interval and sharp dimensions previously encountered separately at Level 2. At this final level, children were told they would be using everything they had already learned, and would have to play two turbo-boost keys at the same time.

It should be noted in passing that the foregoing instructions were designed to reduce the cognitive load that would be involved in learning, and that they followed the general guidelines that have been suggested by developmental theories of instruction (see Case, 1978; Case, Sandieson, Dennis, 1986). It should also be noted that the particular simplifying techniques were consistent with the research on musical knowledge reviewed earlier. For example, it has been noted that proficient sight-readers possess knowledge of musical structure (harmony) that renders them capable of making inferences regarding subsequent musical phrases. By contrast novices are generally lacking in this ability (Sloboda, 1978). Since novices are not capable of making inferences on the basis of higher order structure, the task was constructed in such a way as to foster the establishment of lower order expectancies, through the use of the video game script and structure. The rationale for selecting a small set of notes (middle C, D, E, F) was similar, namely, to increase the redundancy of the musical description, thereby constraining the possible choices at each step and decreasing the load of processing the information (see Davies, 1978). Finally, because sight-reading has been shown to be a pattern-recognition task (Wolf, 1976), patterns inherent in the musically notated melodies were made more salient through the use of distinctive physical markers, such as bar lines, which segment the information into smaller chunks.

It was presumed that these features would serve to facilitate learning of the task, while drawing attention to relational information. This latter aspect has also received some attention in the music literature. It has been found that proficient sight-readers encode the relationships between notes rather than note names in deciphering written music (Sloboda, 1976b). The two notes, middle C and the first F above it, were selected for marking based on their conspicuous positions on both the piano and the staff. By structuring the task so that the novice would be required to attend to relational information rather than to specific information about each note, it was hoped to promote this more advanced type of processing strategy, and thus to provide as much assistance as possible in the acquisition of some elementary music-reading competence. In summary, then, the instruction was designed on the basis of findings from both the developmental literature and the literature on music reading, in order to be as effective as possible. The hope was to provide a strong test of the neo-Piagetian hypothesis that children tend to function at the same developmental level on novel tasks for which they receive direct training, as they do on familiar tasks, where no such training is provided but prior opportunities for informal learning are numerous.

AN EMPIRICAL INVESTIGATION OF CHILDREN'S RESPONSIVENESS TO INSTRUCTION

Method

Subjects

The majority of children were selected from the existing subject pool at the Center for Research in Human Development at the University of Toronto. The final sample consisted of 40 children, 10 in each of four age groups (4, 6, 8, and 10 years); there were 5 males and 5 females in each group. None of the children had any prior formal musical experience.

Procedure

Children participated in one session, which varied in length from approximately 15 minutes to 1 hour, depending on the particular child's rate of progress through the training sequence already described. Children were trained and tested at each level of the task, provided that they remained successful.

Levels 0, 1, and 2B each contained 8 musical sequences of 9 notes. Level 2A and Level 3 each included 8 musical sequences of 9 intervals. The entire task involved a total of 40 musical sequences. The 8 sequences for each level were placed, 4 per card, on 10 cards. However, only one melody was revealed to the child at any given time. At each level the melodies were arranged in order of difficulty and the cards were always presented in the same order. Training sequences were provided at each level. These training sequences were similar in form, but not identical, to those of the testing phases.

Training. Training involved the introduction and explanation of any new information presented at that particular level. During this time, the child was encouraged to ask questions. Errors were pointed out and corrected by the experimenter. Every effort was made to promote the child's understanding of the concepts being presented, and his or her general enjoyment of the task.

The video-game analogy, already described, was adopted as a bridging metaphor, with (spaceship and moon) markers placed on middle C and F on the piano, and these same symbols used to represent their respective notes on the manuscript. The remaining two notes were not marked or otherwise verbally labeled. The notation on the manuscript took the form of opaque red circles; red notes were used rather than black ones to increase their visual contrast with the staff.

Testing. Advancement to the testing phase was contingent upon correct playing of the training sequences. During testing, feedback was always in the form of encouragement, regardless of the child's actual performance. However, the child was allowed to correct self-detected errors. If at least 50% of the musical sequences for a particular level were correctly played, the child was advanced to the training phase for the subsequent level. The session was terminated when the child had either failed to achieve a score of at least 50% on the test of a given level, or had failed the training period at that level.

Predictions

It was hypothesized that each of the four age groups would exhibit a distinct pattern of performance on the sight-reading task similar to that reported in chapters 4 and 5. It was also hypothesized that the trend in mean scores would be linear, because the distance between substages is assumed to be equivalent in the context of neo-Piagetian theory. Finally, it was predicted that children's absolute level of performance would reflect an age-appropriate level of functioning, that is, that the majority of children in each age group would succeed up to the level predicted by the theory, but no further.

Results

Correspondence of Mean Scores to Predicted Trend

To investigate the first prediction, a series of one-way analyses of variance were executed, with the dependent variable being the highest level attained. Children were assigned a score of 0, 1, 2, or 3 as a function of their level of successful performance; for example, a child who was successful up to, but no higher than, Level 1 was assigned a score of 1.

Figure 6.2 illustrates the actual versus expected mean scores attained by each age group. In the first analysis, children who were successful at either Level 2A or 2B were assigned a score of 2. This analysis revealed that there was a significant difference in mean scores across age groups, $F(3, 36) = 42.32$, $p < 0.001$. The linear term was found to be highly significant, $F(1, 36) = 112.59$, $p < .001$. In addition, the data exhibited a significant quadratic component, $F(1, 36) = 9.00$, $p < .01$.

In order to isolate the source of the quadratic component, two further analyses of variance were conducted. The first of these excluded *Level 2B* from the analysis, so that it could be determined whether *Level 2A* was responsible for the quadratic trend. It was evident that there was again a significant difference in performance across age groups, $F(3, 36) = 30.32$, $p < .001$, and a highly significant linear component, $F(1, 36) = 78.98$, $p < .001$. However, the quadratic component also approached significance, $F(1, 36) = 6.93$, $p = .012$. In the subsequent analysis, *Level 2A* was excluded, to determine whether *Level 2B* was responsible for the original quadratic trend. The four age groups again differed significantly in performance, $F(3, 36) = 21.03$, $p < .001$, and the linear component was again significant, $F(3, 36) = 6279$, $p < .001$. This time, however, the quadratic component was non-existent, $F(1, 36) = 0$, $p = 1$. The deviation from the linear relationship was thus clearly attributable to the inclusion of the scores at *Level 2A*.

One last analysis of variance was executed which again included *Levels 2A* and *2B*. In this final analysis, *Level 2A* was rescored as 1.5 (rather than 2) when it represented the highest level successfully performed. *Level 2B* was scored as 2. The rationale for this rescoring was that *Level 2A* might represent a lower level of difficulty relative to *Level 2B*, but still be higher than *Level 1*. Again, the age groups showed a difference in performance, $F(3, 36) = 36.00$, $p < 0.001$. A highly significant linear relationship was evident, $F(1, 36) = 102.05$, $p < 0.001$. The quadratic component was not significant, $F(1, 36) = 3.30$, $p = 0.078$.

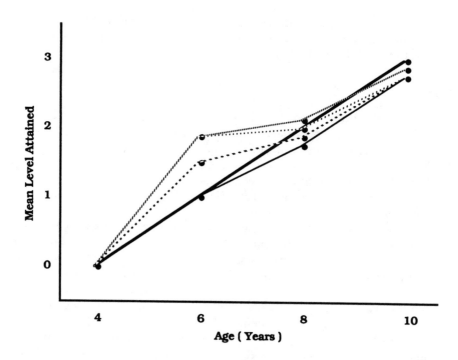

Legend

／   Expected

,,,,,,,,'''   Including 2A and 2B, scored as 2.0

,,,,,''''   Including 2A only

／   Including 2B only

....····'   Including 2A and 2B, scored as 1.5 and 2.0, respectively

FIG. 6.2.   Actual versus expected mean levels attained by age group.

Correspondence of "Ages of Ascession" to Predicted Trend

Two way analyses of variance were performed to investigate the effects of age and sex. These analyses revealed that sex was a non-significant factor in all three of the above analyses: $F(1, 32) = .07, p = .798; F(1, 32) = .05, p = .822; F(1, 32) = .59, p = .447; F(1, 32) = .06, p$

= .807; respectively. In addition, there were no significant interactions between age and sex: $F(3, 32) = .07, p = .977; F(3, 32) = .05, p = .984; F(3, 32) = .09, p = .960; F(3, 32) = .10, p = .959$; respectively. Groups were therefore pooled over sex for all subsequent analyses.

The second hypothesis was that children would perform successfully at each level of the musical sight-reading task up to and including, but not beyond, that which was designed to be appropriate for their particular age group. Table 6.1 lists the cumulative frequencies of children achieving a criterion of 75% (6 out of 8 correct) at each level of the task within each age group. Level 2A was excluded so that the linear relationship could be examined. The obtained frequencies were compared to the expected cumulative frequencies derived from a theoretical distribution consistent with the hypothesis. The distribution represented the hypothesis that 80% of the children would experience success at the predicted level of performance for their age groups, while the remaining 20% would be distributed equally one level above and below this predicted level. Examination of the expected and actual cumulative frequencies indicated a good correspondence between the expected and actual patterns of performance.

To examine the extent of this correspondence further, the theoretically expected distribution was superimposed on each of the four task levels separately, generating a total of 4 theoretical distributions representing the expected patterns of performance for each age group. Figure 6.3 plots the actual distributions of scores for each age group against the corresponding theoretical distributions.

The Kolmogorov-Smirnov one-sample analysis-of-fit test (S. Siegel, 1956) was subsequently applied to the cumulative frequencies. The actual distributions for each age group were compared to all theoretical distributions in order to isolate the theoretical distribution of best fit. (For example, the actual cumulative frequencies for the 6-year-old group were compared to the expected cumulative frequencies for the

TABLE 6.1
Actual (and Expected) Cumulative
Frequencies of Children
Attaining Criterion (6/8)

Level of Task	Age (years)			
	4	6	8	10
0	10 (9)	10 (10)	10 (10)	10 (10)
1	0 (1)	8 (9)	8 (10)	10 (10)
2B	— (0)	1 (1)	6 (9)	9 (10)
3	— (0)	1 (0)	3 (1)	8 (9)

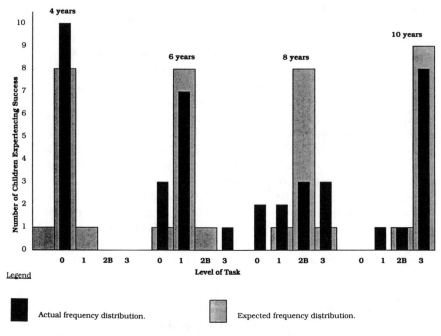

FIG. 6.3.   Actual versus expected frequency distribution by age group.

6-year-old group, as well as those of the 4-, 8-, and 10-year-old groups.)
These comparisons were performed in order to determine whether the
actual distribution for each age group best coincided with its respective
theoretical distributions (0, 1, 2, or 3) or with that of some other age
group. A total of 16 comparisons was executed. A summary of the
Kolmogorov-Smirnov analysis appears in Table 6.2. The results indicated that, for all age groups, the hypothesis that the actual frequency
distribution lies within the predicted theoretical distribution could not
be rejected, while all other hypotheses pertaining to other theoretical
distributions could be rejected with a high degree of confidence (see
Capodilupo, 1985).

Discussion

At the outset of this chapter, a case was made for the claim that musical
sight-reading is a cognitive task, the performance of which should be
subject to cognitive developmental constraints common to other tasks of
a similar nature. The results provided strong support for this conten-
tion, providing that the items from Level 2A were excluded. The question that naturally arises, therefore, is whether a theoretically defensible

TABLE 6.2
Summary of Kolmogorov-Smirnov
Analysis-of-Fit (One-Sample) Tests

Distribution	Level of Task	Age (Years)			
		4	6	8	10
80%	0	0.1	0.7*		
	1	0.9*	0.1	0.5*	
	2B		0.8*	0.3	0.7*
	3			0.6*	0.1

*$p = 0.01$ ($D > 0.490$)

reason for this exclusion can be found. In fact, there appears to be a rather straightforward rationable for the exclusion. Observation of children's performance while they were engaged in the task at this level revealed that, as predicted, their strategy involved the coordination of contour and counting for each note. However, by keeping one finger on the first note while determining the second, most children effectively eliminated the need for simultaneous storage of the products of these two actions. As a result, the task differed only minimally from that of Level 1, because it did not impose a further load on working memory capacity, or require the use of strategies that had not already been learned at the previous level.

Note that this interpretation fits well with the argument that was developed in the previous chapter, concerning the necessity of moving toward a representational theory of children's cognitive development (see also Case & Sandieson, 1987). If one sees the 6-year-olds' difficulty as involving the coordination of two distinct representations, each corresponding to a different dimension, one can readily see that Level 2A did not require them to exceed this capacity. Although it is true that two notes did have to be played, the children could understand both notes as occupying positions on the same scale: that is, the scale defined by the white keys. Because they understood the nature of the task conceptually, and were able to represent it mentally in a unidimensional fashion, they were able to find a way to circumvent the working memory load that is normally involved in making a second quantitative comparison while storing the product of a first. In effect, they were able to let their fingers do the storing for them. By contrast, at Level 2B, which appeared to involve a second scale (i.e., the notes were played predominantly on the "black" scale), children had no such general understanding of the notes' locations to guide them. Although the success of 6-year-old children on Level 2A was not predicted, then, it does appear to be understandable in retrospect, and to fit well with data from the previous two chapters. Together, what the three sets of data suggest is that there is the need to work toward a representational theory of development rather than a purely processing one.

The pattern of errors exhibited by various groups further supports this interpretation. For example, on Level 2A, the 6-year-olds would default to the global processing strategy of the previous level when their attempt to use a unidimensional strategy failed. Siegler (1978) has previously noted the occurrence of a similar default strategy in children's performance on the balance beam task. The pattern of errors for the 8-year-old group was also consistent with this interpretation, in that many of the errors involved a confusion about E-sharp (the *turbo-boost* E note)—the only sharp presented that corresponds to a white rather than a black key. It may therefore be speculated that these children were quantifying along two dimensions and that those two dimensions were the black versus white notes suggested by the keyboard, not the whole versus half notes intended by the task designer. The 8-year-old strategy thus reflected the sort of misconception or immature rule that is common when dimensional integration is not present. This confusion appeared to have been straightened out by the majority of 10-year-olds.

CONCLUSIONS

Three general conclusions may be drawn from the present investigation:

1. *Musical sight-reading as a dimensional task.* Musical sight-reading, like clock reading, money changing, or making predictions about a balance beam, may be regarded as a dimensional task, for which children acquire the appropriate underlying capabilities in the fashion suggested in previous chapters.

2. *Instruction is a developmental task.* Effective instruction—at least as a short term endeavor—should not be seen as introducing a performance bias that *overrides* children's cognitive developmental competencies. Rather, it should be seen as drawing on their developmental competencies, and utilizing these competencies in order to enable them to perform at their optimum developmental level (Fischer, 1980). This is not to imply that it is impossible for children to achieve a level of musical sight-reading competence beyond their optimum level, or that their "readiness" is completely fixed. Given appropriate scaffolding and practice of a developmental sort, one would predict that children should indeed be able to transcend these limitations to some degree, up to the limit of what Vygotsky (1962) called the

"zone of proximal development". The data do suggest, however, that a child's developmental level may be used to predict the sort of intervention that will be spontaneously comprehensible under the facilitating conditions provided by short-term instruction, and that many of these conditions are well specified by current developmental theories of instruction based on neo-Piagetian theory.

3. *Cognitive developmental competence is representational, not procedural, in nature.* Finally, children seem more able to circumvent their working memory limitations when the coordinating requirements are primarily procedural than when they are representational in nature. The present study thus joins those that have been summarized elsewhere (Case & Sandieson, 1987; Griffin, Case, & Sandieson, this volume) in suggesting that neo-Piagetian theories of development in general, and the theory described in chapter 2 in particular, need to be modified, if they are to do an adequate job of explicating what is common to children's development in several different content domains. The modification that appears necessary is to include an account of the development of children's general structures for representing information, as well as the more specific executive structures by which they process it.

Testing for the Presence of a Central Quantitative Structure: Use of the Transfer Paradigm

Robbie Case
Stanford University
Robert Sandieson
University of Western Ontario

As one examines the pattern of performance across the various tasks that have been reported in the foregoing chapters, and particularly as one begins to model the conceptual representations that underpin children's performance on them, it becomes increasingly difficult to believe that several different strands of development are involved. Rather, it seems more likely that there is one strand of development involved, which happens to be of relevance to four or five different domains of endeavor. Stated in more classic terms: It seems far more likely that children are assimilating each of the various tasks with which they are presented into one underlying central conceptual structure, than that they are representing each new problem, afresh, in a fashion that happens to be very similar.

To be sure, each of the different tasks that has been considered does require some unique form of understanding. What one needs to understand the operations of a balance beam is different from what one needs to know in order to decide who is happy at a birthday party. And this in turn is different from what one needs to know in order to tell the time on a clock, or to play a musical score. Moreover, if a child does not possess this specific knowledge, he or she will fail the particular task in question. Nevertheless, the fact remains that each of the tasks that has been considered entails a common core concept, and children move through the same developmental progression with regard to this concept, and do so at approximately the same rate. Thus, at a deeper level, it is difficult to resist the suggestion that what happens in the course of children's development is that they gradually move to higher and higher levels of understanding with regard to one conceptual structure, and that this movement governs the observed improvement in performance across a wide range of more specific tasks.

As soon as one interprets the data in this fashion, however, one is struck by the parallel between this sort of interpretation and the classic interpretation that was proposed by Piaget. Although the specific form of structure that is being proposed is somewhat different, the general claim is essentially the same. This poses a serious problem, for it was precisely the *deficiency* with Piaget's interpretation that led to the present research program in the first place! Before developing the notion of a central conceptual structure any further, therefore, it seems worthwhile to pause, and to review the criticisms that were leveled at the classic Piagetian position. In particular, it seems worthwhile to review the forms of data that were mentioned in the introductory chapters as being problematic for Piagetian theory.

PROBLEMS WITH THE CLASSIC STRUCTURALIST POSITION

Asynchronies in Cognitive Development

For the classic structural position, one of the major problems was that different tests of the same logical structure were often passed at very different points in children's development—with the décalages sometimes being as great as 12 years. Although one could imagine "performance" factors that would produce décalages of this magnitude, it was hard to reconcile their existence with the suggestion that structural changes were the major underlying impetus of cognitive development.

In the present context, the claim is similar to the classic one, namely, that with the acquisition of a new central conceptual structures comes the ability to solve a new class of developmental tasks. It is important to realize, however, that the data are different. Although there is clearly some variation from task to task in the age at which a particular structural understanding is reflected in children's performance, what the previous chapters suggest is that this variation is confined to the two-year period spanned by one substage. Accordingly, the phenomenon of décalage does not pose the same challenge to the present structural formulation as it did to the original one.

Individual Differences in Cognitive Development

A second set of data that were hard to explain within the classic structural framework were the low inter-task correlations among test items that were supposed to tap the same underlying logicomathematical structure. What these data suggested was that different individuals were developing along different paths, or passing logically equivalent problems for different reasons. Once again, this notion was difficult to reconcile with the classic view that one underlying logical structure was being acquired, and that the acquisition of this structure permitted a wide variety of more surface insights to be acquired.

Once again, the present claim remains similar to the classic one, but the data are different. When different tasks are grouped together because they all require the same form of dimensional thought, it turns out that the correlations among items within this group are actually quite high. In the study by Marini (chapter 4), for example, the correlations were in the low 80s and remained significant even when age was partialled out statistically.

Cross-Cultural Differences in Performance

For the classic structural position, a third problem was the fact that certain structural competencies (e.g., formal operations) that were supposed to be universal did not appear to emerge in certain cultures. Why this was so was not apparent. Although Piaget suggested that it was merely a problem with test content, no convincing proof was offered that a change in content yielded different performance.

For the present hypothesis, these data are not as problematic because the claim is somewhat different. All of the structural relations that have been specified (e.g., the relationship between the dollars and cents, or minutes and hours, or black notes and white notes) are semantic rather than logical ones, and are actually cultural inventions. That their acquisition should not be universal is thus not a problem for the theory.

Effects of Training on Performance

A final problem for the classic structural position stemmed from the results of training studies. Since the classic logico-mathematical structures were supposed to be acquired primarily by autoregulative mechanisms, it was hard to explain why short-term training of a verbal nature would have much effect. In those cases where it did have a strong effect, however, and where children passed a set of delayed posttests with clear insight, it was hard to explain why they did not transfer their insight to other tasks that were supposed to tap the same underlying structure.

In the present context, the first datum (the success of training) is not particularly problematic, because no assumption has been made that central conceptual structures are acquired exclusively by autoregulative means. It has been explicitly suggested that social factors play a vital role in the acquisition of local structures (Case, 1985; chapter 2). Thus, it would be inconsistent to suggest that social factors did not play a vital role in the acquisition of central conceptual structures as well. It would clearly be damaging for the theory, however, if no transfer of training was found. If children really do achieve Level 1 performance in money use, time-telling, the balance beam, and the sight-reading of musical notation because they acquire one central conceptual structure that applies to all of these tasks, and if they are taught this structure in a conceptually appropriate fashion, they should clearly transfer the structure to at least some of these other tasks for which it supposedly is the crucial central requirement.

Unfortunately, when one examines the literature on conceptual training, failure to transfer emerges as one of the major findings that almost all studies share in common. If this sort of failure were characteristic only of studies that attempt to train a general logical competence such as "concrete operations," one could perhaps dismiss them as irrelevant to the present argument. After all, there is a great difference between trying to teach something as general as "compensation," or "reversibility," and something as specific as a "mental number line." However, the literature on training more specific concepts reveals essentially the same pattern: Indeed, one of the most robust findings of this century is the failure to generalize such concepts in a convincing fashion (see Mc-Keough, this volume, for a review of the relevant literature).

In the past few years, isolated instances of transfer have begun to be reported (Bassok & Holyoak, 1989; Bereiter & Scardamalia, 1985; Brown, Collins, & Duguid, 1989; Field, 1982). So far, however, these studies have either focused on general metacognitive awareness with older children (for a review, see Perkins & Salomon, 1987) or else the teaching of a very specific principle. Thus, one could argue that no study has as yet focused on training precisely the sort of conceptual structure on which our developmental analyses have focused, and that this is the reason for the negative results. What we decided to do, therefore, was to conduct a set of training studies in which the sort of conceptual structure in which we were interested was trained, and to examine the pattern of transfer that resulted.

STUDY 1: TRAINING YOUNG CHILDREN TO "DIMENSIONALIZE" THEIR WORLD

The particular structure we attempted to teach was the one responsible for unidimensional comparison. For the purpose of instruction, we found it desirable to have a slightly more detailed conception of what this representation might entail. Accordingly, we developed the network representation indicated in Fig. 19.2 (see p. 332a). As the figure indicates, our assumption was that 6-year-olds' understanding of the number line includes the following six components:

1. Bidirectional knowledge of the number sequence: the ability to count up to or down from X, and to say for each number which other number will come "next" when counting in a particular direction.

2. Number-to-number correspondence: knowledge of how to map the number sequence onto a set of objects, such that each object is assigned one and only one numerical value.

3. Knowledge of cardinality: knowledge that, in mapping number names on to objects, each number represents the size of a different set.

4. Knowledge of the set generation principle: knowledge that the sets thus created form a continuum, and that one can generate the next one in either direction by either adding or subtracting one unit.

5. Knowledge of relative magnitude: knowledge of each number's magnitude, relative to that of each other (this knowledge implies an understanding of cardinality).

6. Knowledge of the dimensional utility of this information: knowledge that the overall number line thus generated can be used as a basis for determining the results of real-world quantity comparisons along such dimensions as length, time, size, tonal frequency, and so on.

The reader who is familiar with Gelman and Gallistel's (1978) influential work on number will recognize the first three of these components as the conceptual knowledge that is generally available for small numbers by the age of about 4. The other components appear to be ones that are normally acquired slightly later, at about the age of 5 to 6 years (Siegler & Robinson, 1982). For many children who do not come from social backgrounds where quantification plays a major role, however, both sets of these components may still be missing by the time the children enter school. This sort of population thus seemed best suited for conducting the sort of training study in which we were interested.

Method

Subjects

A group of subjects was selected from junior kindergarten in a school serving a population that had recently immigrated to Toronto from rural Portugal. A group of children in one classroom served as the treatment subjects (n = 12; mean age = 4.9 yr), while a group of children in a second classroom served as the control subjects (n = 12; mean age = 4.8 yr). At the outset of the program, several children in each group were not able to recite the number string from one to five, in either English or Portuguese. They were also not able to count small sets of objects without double counts, omissions, or other errors.

Training

The training exercises were designed to have an impact on each of the components of the structure illustrated in Fig. 19.2 (see chapt. 19, pg. 332a).

1. Recitation of the number sequence. The first set of activities involved oral recitation of the numbers from 1 to 10, both forward and backward. These activities were conducted in a game-like context, for example, a spaceship game, where the students counted down to "blastoff" for a space rocket.

2. Counting of objects. The second set of activities required children to count out sets of real objects. These activities were also presented in a game context. For example, the teacher pretended everyone was going on a picnic together, and the students were asked to count the appropriate numbers of knives, forks, spoons, plates, and so on. While one child did the counting for a particular set, the others were encouraged to check that no mistakes were made. A related exercise involved counting how many objects were left, as one object after another was taken away from a set.[1]

3. and 4. Adding and subtracting one unit from a set. In a third set of activities, children played a game where they counted a small set of cookies, and then a Cookie Monster came and ate one cookie from the set. The children had to predict how many they would end up with when they recounted the set. In a similar game, the "cookie fairy" came along and gave them one extra cookie. This provided a context in which they could be asked to guess (and verify) what number would result after an augmentation of a set by one unit. By the end of these two games, most children could count an array of objects, shut their eyes, and tell which of the two characters (the cookie monster or the cookie fairy) had come to visit by counting the new total. Thus, in effect, they could go in both directions: from knowledge of the nature of a one-unit transformation to knowledge of set magnitude, or from

---

[1] If children had trouble with "place keeping" while counting, they were shown the strategy of moving objects as they were counted, so that the objects that remained to be counted were distinct from those that had already been counted.

knowledge of set magnitude to knowledge about the transforming operation.

5. Deciding which of two numbers is "bigger". Children were engaged in a number of different activities such as the card game, War, in which two sets of objects are displayed, each on a different card, and the child has to determine which of the sets is "bigger."

6. Use of numbers for quantity evaluation. In a final set of activities, children were asked such questions as which of two necklaces would be longer when it was unfolded, one made of X beads, or one made of Y beads. In this exercise, they learned to make judgments on the basis of numerical values alone, and then check these judgments by placing the two sets side by side.

Within each of these training units, the instructional progression went from low numbers to high numbers, and from contexts that were "facilitating" to those that were "misleading," according to the general principles of instruction that have been spelled out elsewhere (e.g., Case, 1978).

Procedure

At the beginning of the training program, children were given a pretest to assess their knowledge of number, as well as a test with 4- and 6-year-old items from Marini's Balance Beam and Birthday Party Tasks (see chapter 4), and our own Time-Telling and Money Usage Tasks (chapter 5). The treatment group was then presented with 20 (10-minute) training sessions, spread out over a one-month period. The control group received a comparable period of instruction with the "Sticky Bears" computer program, a software package designed to teach children the names of the letters of the alphabet. At the end of the training, each group was given the original tests again, in order to see if any change had taken place.

Results

The majority of the treatment children showed at least some evidence of progress on the number knowledge test, with half showing a change of one level. They also showed some improvement on most of the transfer tasks. Because it is the transfer tasks that are the major focus of the present chapter, the pre- and posttest success rates are shown in Table 7.1. The table indicates the percentage of the total group that passed each item and those from the subgroup who passed, that is, those who

TABLE 7.1
Percentage of Children Passing Transfer Items: Study 1

Task	Treatment (n = 12)		Control (n = 15)	
	Pretest	Posttest	Pretest	Posttest
Near transfer				
More/less: Money	0	67 (100)*	0	7
Intermediate transfer				
Social: Birthday Party	16	75 (100)	0	0
Physical: Balance Beam	0	33 (57)	0	0
Remote transfer				
Misleading money comparison (5 vs. 1 + 1)	0	80 (92)	0	14
Time passage on clock	0	50 (86)	0	0
Blocks: 4 given, 3 more = ?	16	75 (86)	—	—

*Figures in parentheses indicate percentages for the subsample who mastered the training activities.

showed a clear indication of improvement on the test of number knowledge.

Children passed most of the items that were similar in content to those that were used in the training. However, they also passed items that had little in common with such items, and that presented either no cues that number comparison was the appropriate way to determine the answer or mixed (positive and negative) cues. Note that the only item for which children showed a low degree of transfer (i.e., less than 50%) was the Balance Beam. One reason may be that this was the test for which the children had the least specific knowledge. Another is that the washers that were used on the test were quite thin, and there was a strong illusion of visual equality between stacks that differed by only one unit.

Discussion

Compared to the results that are often found in the training literature, those in Table 7.1 are quite encouraging. Our interpretation is that in the past training has been oriented toward one of two general goals: training for relatively specific competencies, or training for extremely general heuristic skills. The former sort of training has, by and large, been successful, providing that children are clear on the nature of the task goal, and a reasonable variety of training materials are used (A. L.

Brown et al., 1983; Ferrara, A. L. Brown, & Campione, 1986). By contrast, the latter sort of training has yet to demonstrate any real success.

The sort of training that our exercises represent is based on an objective that is, in effect, intermediate between the other two. It is not intended to be "training for transfer," that is, training that gives the children a clear idea of how to reach a specific objective across a wide variety of different materials. On the other hand, it is not intended to train some sort of all-purpose heuristic, either. Rather, it is intended to be training for a central conceptual understanding, that is, an understanding that is applicable to a broad range of (but not all) tasks that children encounter in their everyday lives.

STUDY 2: CONTRASTING DIMENSIONAL TRAINING WITH TRAINING IN ENUMERATION

Although the amount of transfer in the first study was substantial, two issues were left unresolved by the data.

Locus of Instructional Effect

The first had to do with the locus of the instructional effect. In the first study, our basic theoretical suggestion was that the instruction permitted our 4½-year-old subjects to create a dimensional representation of certain fundamental quantitative problems, and that—armed with this conceptual representation—they were able to apply it to a variety of problems that, on the surface, were quite different from those used in the training. There is a simpler way of looking at the results, however. According to this second interpretation, the reason that the training was effective was that, in order to solve problems such as the Balance Beam using a 6-year-old strategy, children must be able count with considerable efficiency. In the normal course of events, 4-year-olds from this population are not able to count with sufficient efficiency. All instruction needs to accomplish to produce transfer is to increase the efficiency of children's counting to the point where it falls within the bounds of their working memory. Once this challenge is met, the task of solving problems via quantification no longer poses a problem because the counting routine has become more highly "automatized."

In order to help us choose between the "automatization" and "dimensionalization" interpretations we introduced a new control group. For this group, training focused on improving the efficiency of counting strategies and the range of materials to which they could be applied, without focusing on any sort of problem that might be construed as involving a new conceptualization of numbers. The details of the training have been provided elsewhere (Case & Sandieson, 1987). The general sequence was as follows: Children in the "automatization group" began with exercises that enabled them to become more efficient in counting small sets of objects in response to one of two forms of question: "How many objects (e.g., apples) are there here?" and "Can you count out this number (e.g., 3) of objects for me?" As they became more efficient in this process, they were gradually introduced to a number of more complicated counting situations, including (a) situations where a greater number of objects was present; (b) situations where the objects were arranged in a fashion that made them more difficult to count, because they were set out in a random array rather than a line; and (c) situations where the numerical part of the problem was presented in written/symbolic form, rather than orally. The reason that this latter condition was included was that it forms a central part of many math readiness programs, and is believed by many curriculum designers to help children develop an enriched representation for numbers.

Range of Generalization Produced by Training

Whereas the first unresolved issue had to do with the feature of our instructional intervention that produced broad transfer, the second had to do with the limits of such transfer, once produced. With one exception, the only transfer items that were included in the Study 1 were ones for which the conceptual representation that was taught was central. Thus, we had no firm sense of the limits beyond which transfer would not be present. The second objective of Study 2, then, was to probe these limits more carefully, by including a variety of additional transfer items that were more remote. Two new tasks were designed for this purpose.

Stick Copying Tasks. The first of these was a drawing task that required the children to copy a picture showing a series of sticks and fenceposts. The basic notion was that if students saw each line as potentially stretching from short to long, with a continuum of steps in between, they might conceivably count the number of posts (or sticks) before drawing, even though there was no explicit requirement for doing so.

Rhythm Copying Task. The second task was one in which the experimenter tapped out a number of beats for the child, and the child had to reproduce the same acoustic pattern. Students were required to reproduce a "secret knock" consisting of 2, 4, or 8 taps. Following Bamberger (1978), they were also asked if they could think of some way of writing down a picture of what they had heard, so that they could remember it later or tell someone else what to do. This second task was introduced because counting is a useful skill for success on it; however, there is no obvious way in which one can think of a series of 2 or 4 beats as lying along some "dimension."

Method

The foregoing paragraphs describe the activities that were conducted in the second study that were different from those conducted in the first, and that were designed to clarify the two issues left unanswered by it. In addition, we replicated those activities included in the first study. The most important of these was the execution of a lengthy training experiment, with one treatment and one control group, and a battery of pre- and posttest measures. The children who participated in the training were once again drawn from two junior kindergarten classes in a working-class neighborhood, which contained both native speakers of English and immigrant families from rural areas of Portugal. The children ranged in age from 4 to 5 years, with a mean age of 4 years, 6 months. They were given a pretest battery that consisted of the quantification, time, money, social-numeric, Balance Beam, and Stick and Rhythm Copying tasks. This was followed by 20 sessions of instruction with either the control or the experimental treatment, and a re-administration of the same items used in the pretest.

Results

The most important finding was that the pattern of results in the first study was replicated. The students found the training highly motivating. They also showed impressive gains in their conceptual understanding of number. Finally, they also transfered this understanding to a wide variety of novel contexts (see Table 7.2).

Locus of Instructional Effect. The first data of relevance to the locus question were those dealing with the pre- and posttest performance of the control group on the quantification scale. On this scale, the control group showed a significant overall improvement, $t = 6.22$, $p < .01$. Moreover, when an item analysis was conducted, the source of this improvement could be traced directly to those items that contained an explicit requirement for counting. When these items were treated as a separate scale, the control group showed a significant improvement, $t =$

TABLE 7.2
Percentage of Children Passing Transfer Tasks: Study 2

Task	Treatment (n = 14)		Control (n = 14)	
	Pretest	*Posttest*	*Pretest*	*Posttest*
Near transfer				
More/less: Money	0	79 (100)*	0	29
Intermediate transfer				
Social: Birthday Party	0	64 (86)	0	7
Physical: Balance Beam	0	36 (57)	0	7
Remote transfer				
Misleading money comparison (5 vs 1 + 1)	0	43 (71)	0	29
Time passage on clock	0	43 (71)	7	29
Sticks	0	58 (71)	0	14
Rhythm	0	0	0	0
Blocks: 4 given 3 more = ?	28	71 (86)	14	36

*Figures in parentheses indicate percentages for the subsample who mastered the training activities.

5.74, $p < .01$). and no significant difference in the magnitude of this improvement from that achieved by the experimental group, $p > .07$. By contrast, on the quantification items that required some form of dimensionalization, the control group showed no significant improvement, and did significantly worse than the experimental group. What these results indicate is that the two treatments had the contrasting effects that were intended: The experimental group learned to think in terms of quantitative dimensions, and thus to answer questions involving more and less or before and after. The control group merely learned to count more effectively, and to understand the meaning of written numerals.

The data on the transfer tasks, then, became of particular interest. Here the pattern of data was equally clear. On the few questions that could be solved simply by counting, without any requirement for dimensionalization, both groups made improvements, and there was no significant difference between the two groups in the magnitude of these improvements. On all the other items, the control group showed very little improvement, and did significantly worse than the experimental group. The results thus support the "dimensional" interpretation of the broad transfer that was obtained in the first study.

Range of Generalization. On the Stick Copying task, the treatment group significantly outperformed the control group on both items. Note that, if one were to take a restricted view of what the experimental training was producing, namely, the ability to answer questions about more or less, it would be difficult to explain this superiority. It would also be hard to explain why the control group, who spent all their time answering questions having to do with "How many?" did not improve, because that is all that success on these items requires. If one sees the difference between the two groups as a difference in the tendency to represent the world in terms of quantitative dimensions, however, the results become comprehensible. According to this interpretation, the experimental group no longer saw the stimulus materials simply as a long line of posts, which had to be copied. Instead, they saw the stimulus as a line with a length whose value was quantifiable, and of potential significance. By contrast, the control group saw the problem as one of copying a picture. They therefore had no particular reason to duplicate the exact number of items. This interpretation is congruent with another finding, which might otherwise seem anomalous: that there was no significant difference between the two groups (and a low incidence of overall success), on the Rhythm Copying task. On this task there was no obvious "dimension." Moreover, even if there had been—that is, even if the pattern of knocks had been treated as a temporal "line"— the task had to be solved in real time. Thus, there was no chance to return and actually check the number of knocks in the stimulus. That neither group showed any change on this measure is therefore to be expected.[2]

Discussion

The data that were reported for these studies involved a rather small number of subjects. In addition, because the training was invented in each case as it was being used, it was not recorded or analyzed in as much detail as we would ideally have liked. For both these reasons, it would seem worthwhile to replicate the study.[3] While some caution is in order, however, there is clearly cause for optimism. The sort of pattern we obtained in both studies was precisely the one that would be expected if children did indeed acquire, at age 5, a central conceptual structure

---

[2]Note a further implication: that if the Rhythm Copying task were changed so that a dimensional representation would help, the treatment group would then succeed.

[3]Such a replication has since been completed the results are congruent with those reported here and indicate that children also show strong transfer to the task of musical sight reading (Griffin, Case, & Capodilupo in press).

related to quantification, which permits them to make a transition to dimensional reasoning across a wide variety of content domains. When combined with the data mentioned at the beginning of the chapter (that is, the data on décalages, cross-cultural variability, and cross-task correlations), it would appear that the last of the classic arguments against the existence of such central structures collapses. Thus, we are faced with the exciting task of re-conceptualizing the nature of children's cognitive operational development in a fashion that revives—albeit in somewhat altered form—a Piagetian notion that was once thought to have been discredited: namely the notion of a general operational structure.

Conclusions

The general point with which we would like to conclude is that the notion of a *central conceptual structure* may provide a basis for forming a bridge between the general-system and domain-specific views of development that were described in the first chapter. In order to make this point as clearly as possible, we must first provide a slightly more formal definition of what we mean by a central conceptual structure.

Definition of a Central Conceptual Structure

By a "structure" we mean an internal mental entity that consists of a number of nodes and the relations among them. By "conceptual" we mean that the nodes and relations are semantic: that is, they consist of "meanings," "representations," or "concepts" that the child assigns to external entities in the world, rather than syntactic devices for parsing such meanings. Finally, by "central" we mean structures that (a) form the core of a wide range of more specific concepts, and (b) play a pivotal role in enabling the child to make the transition to a new stage of thought, where these concepts are of central importance. A *central conceptual structure* is, thus, an internal network of concepts and conceptual relations that plays a central role in permitting children to think about a wide range of situations at a new epistemic level and to develop a new set of control structures for dealing with them.

The Relevance of Central Conceptual Structures for Neo-Piagetian Theory

Within the context of neo-Piagetian theory, the notion of a central conceptual structure fills two potentially important roles. First, it allows one to show how children's conceptual understanding—not just their control structures—is limited by the general developmental changes that take place at approximately 4, 6, 8, and 10 years. Second, it allows one to specify how it is that children come to focus on the particular aspects of problems that they do at different ages, and to build appropriate task-specific problem representations. Viewed from this perspective, the notion of a central conceptual structure constitutes a natural addition to the theory that was outlined in chapter 2; what it adds is a more detailed account of the conceptual knowledge children must possess at any level of development, in order to construct control structures of the sort our earlier work suggested they possess.

The Relevance of Central Conceptual Structures for Modular ("Domain-Specific") Theories

From the perspective of modular theory, the notion of a central conceptual structure also has a number of features to recommend it. First, the notion seems reasonably close, if not identical, to the notion of a "domain-specific" theory (Carey, 1985; Spelke, 1988). The range of tasks to which such structures apply has the breadth that one would expect of such theories, and also the responsiveness to environmental input. Such structures are also rooted in a domain for which an innate "core" has been shown to exist (Starkey & Cooper, 1980). Finally, such structures appear to be subject to both kinds of transformation suggested by Carey (1985) as characteristic of modular theory change: strong re-structuring, which, in the present case, appears to take place between 4 and 6 years and corresponds to a major stage transition; and weak re-structuring, which appears to take place here between 6 and 10, and corresponds to substage transitions.

Although the notion of a central conceptual structure fits well with the modular notion of a domain-specific theory, and provides a possible basis for linking this notion with the more general or "systemic" notions that have been proposed by neo-Piagetian theorists, it would be too strong to claim that the empirical work we have reported so far demonstrates any real *need* for such a linkage, for our studies have as yet offered no proof that conceptual structures such as those hypothesized are subject to the sort of system-wide "upper-bounds" that neo-Piagetian theorists have hypothesized. To be sure, the studies have shown that central conceptual structures conform to the general forms implied by Fig. 19.1, and that they emerge at the appropriate ages. Their emergence has also been linked to a parallel growth in "number span" (Case, 1985). However, other investigators (Chi, 1977) have suggested that number span itself is a product of children's conceptual understanding. In order to demonstrate a need for linking modular with general-system theory, then, it is necessary to look at domains that do *not* require the understanding of number, and that evolve from a different biologically specified "kernel" (Klahr, 1989) or "core". If one could show that such structures also exist in other domains, and that they develop in the same fashion and at the same rate as children's central conceptual structures, then the case for linking the two sorts of theory would be greatly strengthened.

This general goal is the focus of the next section.

III

THE ROLE OF CENTRAL CONCEPTUAL STRUCTURES IN THE DEVELOPMENT OF CHILDREN'S SOCIAL AND EMOTIONAL THOUGHT

The notion of a central conceptual structure, developed in the previous section, appears to have the potential for bridging the gap between the modular and general-system positions regarding the process of intellectual growth. However, the data presented thus far do not present a very strong case that such a bridge is necessary. Although many of the features of the modularity position have been documented—structural coherence, strong restructuring, weak restructuring, and so on—the key feature relevant to general system theory has not. According to the general-system position, major structural change takes place across different domains of knowledge at approximately the same point in children's cognitive growth. Although the foregoing chapters presented many examples of restructuring occurring in synchrony, they presented no examples of such restructuring taking place in synchrony across completely different domains of knowledge. In fact, one way of restating the conclusion of the previous section is this: Tasks that *appear* to tap different domains of knowledge really do so only partially. In fact, they all include a component from the *same* domain of knowledge, namely, knowledge of number.

If the bridging potential of the notion of a central conceptual structure is to be demonstrated, it seems clear that an example must be found of such a structure in a domain that is completely non-numerical. It must then be shown that this second structure shows the same formal and developmental properties as the structure for number (e.g., a strong restructuring between the ages of 4 and 6, and a more continuous or weaker restructuring at 8 and 10).

Tackling this problem is the main function of the present section. The methodology includes four components: First, a non-numerical task is explored empirically, and a pattern that appears to meet the above mentioned criteria is induced. Second, a set of new tasks with different content is created, in order to show that the hypothesized structure is not content-specific. Third, the first two steps are repeated for several tasks that appear related to the first one conceptually, although they are drawn from domains that the developmental research literature treats as different. Finally, the elements of the hypothesized structure are trained, to see if the pattern of transfer is what one would expect if the underlying conceptual structure really is a central one.

Young Girls' Conception of Their Mother's Role: A Neo-Structural Analysis

Jill Goldberg-Reitman

With the exception of Kohlberg's work on moral development (Kohlberg, 1958), investigations of children's cognition in the 1950s and 1960s tended to follow Piaget's lead, and to focus primarily on children's understanding of logic, mathematics, and the physical world. Beginning with Flavell's (1968) study of children's role-taking, however, this one-sided emphasis began to change, and attention began to focus on children's understanding of their social world as well. During the late 1970s and early 1980s, there was a virtual explosion of work on this topic. Piagetian investigators probed such diverse topics as children's understanding of social institutions (Furth, 1980), social conventions (Turiel, 1978), friendships (Damon, 1977; Selman, 1980), and feelings (Chandler & Boyes, 1982), while other investigators explored such topics as children's understanding of other people's spatial perspectives (Flavell, 1977), emotional states (Borke, 1971), and referential communication (Glucksberg, Krauss, & Higgins, 1975). In the past few years, two further topics have been investigated in some detail: children's understanding of other people's minds (Astington, Olson, & Harris, 1989), and their understanding of their own self-processes (Higgins, 1991; Kopp & Brownell, 1991).

Despite this increasing interest in children's social cognition, relatively little attention has been paid to children's understanding of their mothers, and the many roles their mothers play in their lives. This lack of attention is somewhat surprising, because children's understanding of their mothers is of considerable potential importance. For example, it has even been suggested that social cognition in this area may develop earlier than social cognition in other areas (Clement, 1978), and that children's representations of their interactions with their mothers may provide the basic template for their interactions with a wide variety of significant others (Sroufe, 1979), thus contributing to their emotional well-being (or disorder) at later points in their development (Bowlby, 1969; Kernberg, 1976; Stern, 1985; Sroufe, 1979). Information regarding children's early representations of their mothers would thus appear to be of considerable practical as well as scientific importance.

In the study reported in the present chapter, an attempt was made to gather this sort of information, in a fashion that would lay the groundwork for an analysis of children's social representations in general. At the time the study was initiated (1982), several structural analyses of children's social cognition had already been conducted in the classic Piagetian tradition (Damon, 1979; Furth, 1980; Kohlberg, 1969; Selman, 1980; Turiel, 1978), but no "neo-structural" analysis—that is, no analysis which used the finer grained classification system neo-Piagetian theory provides—had been reported[1]. In addition to gathering new empirical data, then, it was my intention to lay the groundwork for such a neo-structural analysis, and thus to permit a more detailed comparison between children's social and non-social cognition.

Method

The first step in designing the study was to select several maternal roles for investigation, and to devise a set of materials that would permit children's understanding of each role to be assessed. The particular roles that were selected for this purpose were those involving protection, physical care, nurturance, and teaching. These categories were abstracted from the literature in sociology, social psychology, and family theory (e.g., Ainsworth, Blehar, Waters, & Wall, 1978; Bowlby, 1969; Lewis & Feiring, 1979; Lewis & Starr, 1978; Wilson, 1975), and were defined behaviorally as follows: *Protection* is any active attempt to keep a child from falling prey to a potential life threat; *physical care* is any act that fulfills a child's daily physical needs (such as eating), or that eliminates some source of physical discomfort (cold, dampness, etc.); *nurturance* is any attempt to comfort a child emotionally, when he or she is feeling badly; and *teaching* is any active attempt to impart knowledge, set limits, or instill some notion of right or wrong.

---

[1]As it turned out, Fischer and his colleagues were at work on a similar project at the time the present project was initiated (Fischer et al., 1984). The relation of Fischer's analysis to the present one is discussed in the concluding section.

Stimulus Materials

In order to assess children's understanding of these four functions, a set of pictures and stories was developed to mirror the sorts of real-life social interactions in which each function might be served. In keeping with the suggestions of Damon (1977) and Nelson and Gruendel (1981), the unit of analysis was interactive. Each story involved a mini-episode in which a mother and daughter interacted in one of the four ways delineated above. For each event in the interactive episode, a cartoon picture was created to depict the situation graphically, in the manner first suggested by Selman and Byrne (1974). Each individual cartoon picture was then explicated verbally as it was presented, so that the overall sequence formed an interactive episode or "script." The structure of each script was modeled on the story grammars of Schank and Abelson (1977). Each script was created so as to contain the following critical elements: (a) a setting or context, (b) an initiating event, (c) a reaction on the part of the protagonist (a little girl), and (d) an unspecified but predictable response to this reaction by the mother. An example is presented in Fig. 8.1; the verbal story-line is also indicated.

After presentation of the cartoon sequence, each child was asked the following questions:

- How do you think the little girl feels?
- What does the mommy do? Why?
- What is the mommy thinking? Why?
- How does the mommy feel? Why?
- What does the little girl do then? Why?
- What is the girl thinking then? Why?
- How does the little girl feel then? Why?

Each story had the same structure and length, and was followed by the same set of questions. A serious attempt was also made to equate syntactic and semantic complexity across the various stories. Eight stories

FIG. 8.1. Example of stimulus materials used to explore children's understanding of maternal roles and functions. (The function in this example is protection.)

were developed, two for each of the four functions. The verbal descriptions of the stories are presented in Table 8.1.[2]

Subjects

Subjects were 60 girls from middle to upper-middle income families attending neighborhood Roman Catholic schools in the metropolitan Toronto area. There were 10 subjects at each of five age levels: 4, 6, 10, 13, and 18 years. These particular ages were chosen because they represented the beginning and end of Stages 2, 3, and 4, as defined in Case's (1985) neo-Piagetian theory.

Selection of individual subjects was random, but within the following constraints: (a) the child could not have repeated a grade, (b) the child had to be nominated by her teacher as being of at least average intellectual capability, (c) the child had to be from an intact family, and (d) the child could not have been previously identified by the school system as suffering from an emotional disturbance of any sort. The reason for establishing these criteria was to obtain some idea of the *upper bound* of children's social understanding under optimal rearing conditions in a middle-class Western home.

In order to permit a comparison with the work reported in previous chapters, only the data for the 4- to 10-year-olds will be reported here. For these three groups, the mean ages were as follows: Group 1: 4 years, 6 months (SD = 2.79 mos.); *Group 2:* 6 years, 3 months (SD = 4.30 mos.); *Group 3:* 10 years, 5 months (SD = 4.49 mos.). Data for the other age groups are reported in Goldberg-Reitman (1984).

Procedure

Parental questionnaires were sent home to inform parents of the reason for the study, and to secure permission for their child to be included. Half the participants in each age group were then tested by the experimenter, and the other half by a paid research assistant. It was originally intended that all children be tested in one 45-minute session. However, due to the lengthy demands of the various tasks, this proved to be impossible for the 4-year-old group. Thus, for these children

---

[2]For one story in each of the four categories, a number of additional probes was presented, which inquired as to whether all mothers would react the way in which the child had indicated, and whether the child's own mother would react that way. In addition, several other cartoons were presented in which an interaction was depicted between the little girl and her older sister. Because the structure of these data was in general agreement with those for the first stories and questions, they are not reported further. The interested reader may find the relevant questions and data in Goldberg-Reitman (1984).

TABLE 8.1

Protection	Care
1. A little girl is up on the roof.	1. A little girl is outside.
2. She starts to slip down.	2. She gets all covered with snow.
3. The little girl calls "help!"	3. The little girls says, "I feel cold and wet."
1. A little girl is in bed.	1. A little girl is playing outside.
2. A fire starts in her room.	2. She gets all dirty playing outside.
3. The little girl coughs and cries out.	3. The little girl says "I feel yucky and gucky."

Nurturance	Teaching
1. A little girl is sleeping.	1. A little girl is doing a hard puzzle.
2. She has a bad dream and wakes up.	2. She gets stuck with a piece.
3. The little girl cries out.	3. The little girl says, "I'm stuck with this part."
1. A little girl plays with her favorite doll.	1. A little girl plays with her block house.
2. The doll's head falls off.	2. Her house falls down.
3. The little girl cries.	3. The little girl uses a naughty word.

testing was discontinued at a natural juncture, and each child received Part 2 on a subsequent day. No between-session interlude was longer than two days.

Once the child had been selected for study and rapport had been established, she was presented with the following introduction:

> I'm going to show you some stories and then ask you some questions about them. I'm going to be giving the same questions to children a bit younger than you and I want to see if you are better at answering them than the younger children are. Here is the first story . . .

After the story had been presented, the standard questions were asked in the order indicated. Each interview was transcribed before being analyzed.

Results

How Does Young Girls' Understanding of the Maternal Role Develop?

To answer this question, the responses given by all children were examined by age, across all four maternal role categories. Common characteristics of children's responses at each age were then abstracted. Based on these characteristics, prototypical response categories were created, which could extend across the boundaries of any particular situation, and which could potentially be exhibited by any child at any age. Each response protocol was then scored with respect to its conformity to the various prototypes for each cartoon sequence. A second rater, blind to all features of the study except the scoring procedure, rated each protocol in order to provide a measure of interrater reliability. The second rater was provided with the prototypical characteristics and a brief training period (see Goldberg-Reitman, 1984).

Age 4. Examples of typical 4-year-old responses for each cartoon sequence in each role category are presented in Table 8.2. As may be seen, 4-year-olds could make sensible simple predictions about the mother's reaction to each situation. An appropriate knowledge of the mother's reaction in each situation was demonstrated, and the reason for this reaction focused on the little girl's particular circumstances. Thus, even by this early age, it appeared that there already existed a clear "script" for mothers' and daughters' interaction for each general category of maternal role.

The critical features of children's answers at this stage were as follows: (a) The children described the mother's responses in terms of simple, one-step *actions,* that referred only to the story in question; (b) although the reasons behind the mother's behavior were realistic, most referred only to the little girl's situation, not her internal state; (c) The majority of children made no mention of the mother's or daughter's goals. These

TABLE 8.2
Prototypic 4-Year-Old Responses: Dyad Condition

Category	Situation	Mother's Action	Rationale for Mother's Behavior
Protection	Roof	Catches her.	Because she falls off.
	Fire	Sprays it out.	Because there was a fire in her room.
Care	Snow	Takes her inside.	Because she is covered with snow.
	Mud	Changes her dress.	Because she got mud on it.
Nurturance	Dream	Says, "It's okay."	Because she's having a bad dream.
	Doll	Fixes it.	Because the head fell off.
Teaching	Blocks	Spanks her.	Because she said a naughty word.
	Puzzle	Puts the piece in the puzzle.	Because she's stuck.

features appeared to characterize the majority of protocols. Thus, they were given operational definitions and established as criteria for raters to use in order to decide if any individual protocol was or was not prototypic. Interrater reliability was .87. The percentage of protocols falling within, above, and below the prototype bounds are presented in Table 8.3, together with the percentage of protocols displaying each of the individual features.

Age 6.   Examples from typical 6-year-old protocols for each situation are presented in Table 8.4. By this age, most little girls could explain a mother's interactions with her daughter in each situation using a future-oriented description. The mother's immediate plans or intentions for her daughter's physical, emotional, and educational well-being were mentioned in most of the protocols as rationales for the mother's actions. These plans usually referred to what the mother wanted and didn't want for her daughter or to the mother's likes and dislikes (or standards). Finally, at this age the rationale for the mother's behavior was taken one step beyond the specific story content, to the little girl's immediate future. Hence, the 6-year-olds typically (a) perceived the mother as displaying a complex set of behaviors in each familial situation, (b) recognized that the mother acted toward her daughter so as to effect certain desires or specific immediate plans, and (c) mentioned the future consequences toward which these plans or desires were oriented.

Interrater reliability for scoring the protocols of this age group was

TABLE 8.3
Percentage of Prototypic Responses Having Each of the Critical
Component Features for Level 1 (4 years)

	Role				
Critical Features for Level 1	Protection (n = 15)	Care (n = 19)	Nurturance (n = 19)	Teaching (n = 17)	Total (n = 70)
Mother performs only one action	87	69	89	88	83
Action or situation equals reason	93	89	95	88	91
Focus on immediate present as opposed to past or future	60	95	84	88	83
Overall conformity to prototype	70*	75	65	65	68
* % above	25	15	15	25	20
% below	5	10	20	10	12

TABLE 8.4
Prototypic 6-Year-Old Responses: Dyad Condition

Category	Situation	Mother's Action	Rationale for Mother's Behavior
Protection	Roof	Mother gets a ladder.	Because she has to get her down; she doesn't want her to hurt herself
	Fire	She has to phone the Fire Department.	Because she doesn't want her daughter to get hurt; that's bad.
Care	Snow	Take everything off and get some more clothes.	Because she doesn't want her daughter to get all wet and catch a cold. Because that's not good.
	Mud	Take her up and get her into a new dress.	Because you don't go out like that; you're not allowed.
Nurturance	Dream	Mummy will say, "Calm down."	Because she doesn't want her little girl upset.
	Doll	Mum will sew up the doll's head.	Because she doesn't want her little girl upset.
Teaching	Blocks	She'll say, "Don't say that again"	Because it is not nice to say a bad word.
	Puzzle	Mum will put it in.	Because she doesn't want the little girl to be stuck with the piece.

.85. The percentages of protocols falling at, above, and below the prototypic level for each feature are presented in Table 8.5, as are the percentages of protocols demonstrating each of the individual features.

Age 10. Typical 10-year-old responses are listed in Table 8.6. Children at this age characterized their mother's goals in a more general fashion, or at least postulated some more general disposition behind her specific intention. For example, if the rationale at age 6 for a mother's phoning the Fire Department was "because she didn't want her little girl to get hurt," then by age 10 this specific goal was explained by stating that the mother "cared" about her little girl. There was also a recognition of flexibility with respect to the mother's behavior. Social situations were no longer perceived as having definitive courses, because people were perceived as having complex repertoires and choosing multiple actions, any one of which could serve the same motive. Thus, although a 6-year-old asserted that the mother *would* phone the fire department, a 10-year-old's response typically conveyed flexibility through the use of terms such as "probably," "perhaps," or "maybe." If such flexibility was not

TABLE 8.5
Percentage of Prototypic Responses Having
Each of the Critical Component Features for Level 2 (6 years)

	Role				
Critical Features for Level 2	Protection (n = 15)	Care (n = 19)	Nurturance (n = 19)	Teaching (n = 17)	Total (n = 70)
More than one action, no flexibility	59	58	56	50	56
Mother's specific desires equals reason	77	63	67	75	71
Immediate future addressed	91	79	72	75	71
Overall conformity to prototype	75	75	70	65	71
* % above	10	15	10	15	10
% below	15	20	20	20	19

expressed in this fashion, then two or more discreet actions that the mother might perform were stated in an "either/or" format. For example: "The mother will call the Fire Department and get help for her little girl, or the mother will call the father." Although the 6-year-olds sometimes mentioned that the mother would perform more than one action, the two actions were normally components of the same plan, not alternative plans. Thus, the prototype for the 10-year-old child, against which all protocols were scored, included the following stipulations: (a) The action of the mother in the situation had to be described as emerging from a series of potential actions; (b) The mother's rationale for acting had to mention some enduring plan for the little girl's future, or had to emanate from a concept of mother one step further removed from (or more abstract than) her immediate desire or goal.

Interrater reliability for scoring the 10-year-old protocols was .75. The percentage of protocols falling at, below, and above the prototypic level is listed in Table 8.7, together with the percentage of protocols showing each of the prototypic features.

Are There Differences Across Function in Children's Level of Understanding?

What has been outlined thus far is how young girls' understanding of the maternal role develops, during the age range that is of interest in the present volume. To address the question of cross-role variability, children's level-scores for each maternal function were submitted to a four-way analysis of variance with repeated measures. Significant main effects were found for age, $F(4, 40) = 123.60$, $p < .00$, and for function, $F(3, 120) = 4.03$, $p < .009$). There was no significant interaction effect, and no significant effect due to any other variable.

TABLE 8.6
Prototypic 10-Year-Old Responses: Dyad Condition

Category	Situation	Mother's Action	Rationale for Mother's Behaviour
Protection	Roof	She'll probably say, "Oh don't panic or anything; just try to hold on," and she will go up and get her.	Because she cares about her and does not want her to get hurt.
	Fire	The mother probably puts out the fire and asks the daughter if she's O.K.	Because she wants to know. She loves her daughter and doesn't want her hurt.
Care	Snow	The mother will probably come out and take her in and get her clothes changed and make sure that she's dry.	Because she cares for her
	Mud	She probably brings her in and cleans her up and wonders how she got muddy.	Because she's all muddy and she's not that happy Because the mother cares.
Nurtur-ance	Dream	Mum probably talks to her and wants to know what was matter.	Because she wants her to feel better; she does it because she loves her
	Doll	She'll wonder how it fell off. Mum will probably try to get the head back on the doll and make her happy.	Because she wants her to play with the doll and not be unhappy Because she loves her.
Teaching	Blocks	She'll probably maybe hit her or something	Because she's trying to teach her not to say bad words . . . Because if she grew up like that she'd get into a lot of trouble . . . she may get a bad reputation.
	Puzzle	Mother puts the piece close by but not actually in.	Because she wants the little girl to learn about things and she doesn't want her frustrated.

The maternal function means for each age group are plotted in Figure 8.2. As may be seen, the variance due to differences in age appears to be much larger than that due to maternal function. Further analyses were conducted to assess the relative strength of these effects. Using the formulas for a repeated measures design outlined by Vaughan and Corbalis (1969, pp. 208–209), the estimated strength of

TABLE 8.7
Percentage of Prototypic Responses Having
Each of the Critical Component Features for Level 3 (10 Years)

		Role				
Critical Features for Level 3		Protection (n = 22)	Care (n = 23)	Nurturance (n = 22)	Teaching (n = 23)	Total (n = 90)
(i)	Flexibility of action	77*	70	77	83	77
(ii)	Possessive notion: overt recognition that the little girl "belongs" to mother	64*	52	50	52	54
(iii)	Mother's internal general state or abstract behaviour equals reason for action(s)	59*	61	64	52	59
(iv)	Focus on long term, future	32*	39	36	57	41
Overall conformity to prototype		75	70	75	65	71
* % above		20	20	20	15	19
% below		5	10	5	20	10

the age effect (ω^2) was 92.8%, while the estimated strength of the maternal function effect was less than 1%.

Discussion

As was mentioned in the introduction, the present study was intended to accomplish two objectives. The first was simply to gather some preliminary empirical data on how healthy middle-class girls understand their mothers' roles at different points in their development. The second was to lay the groundwork for a more general structural analysis of these conceptions, using neo-Piagetian theory. Had the children performed at widely different levels with regard to each of the four maternal functions, the second goal would have been difficult to accomplish. Because the majority of the variance in children's scores was determined by their age, however, the data seemed well suited for the second objective as well.

The general characterization of young girls' developing social conceptions that was proposed is as follows.

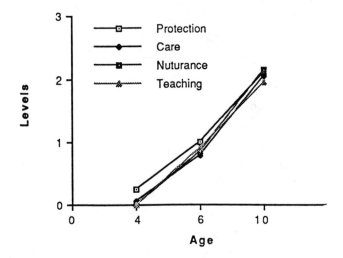

FIG. 8.2. Mean scores at different age groups, for the different maternal functions assessed.

Level 0: Maternal Roles as Scripted Actions

The characteristics that distinguished the answers of the 4-year-olds
were: (a) They could make appropriate predictions about a mother's
behavior toward her daughter; (b) they could explain their answers by
reference to the immediately preceding situation in which the daughter
found herself; and (c) both their predictions and explanations were
extremely simple, focusing only on one aspect of the predicted maternal
action, or one aspect of the situation that precipitated it. The appropri-
ateness of children's responses seemed supportive of Nelson and Gruendel's (1981) assertion that social "scripts" develop between 2 and 5 years,
and that children understand their mothers' role during this stage largely in terms of such scripts. This notion can be related to the neo-
Piagetian theory that was outlined in chapter 2 by noting the structure of
the cartoon sequences in which the children's capability for prediction
and explanation was demonstrated. Recall that all the cartoon sequences
contained one exemplar of each of Schank and Abelson's (1977) narrative categories: a setting, an initiating event, a response, and an outcome. It therefore seems reasonable to suggest that, by the age of 4,
children understand how these four categories are related to each other and can represent these relations in some intuitive fashion. The fact
that children could give an appropriate response for many specific situations that they never experienced personally (such as a fire, or falling off a roof) also indicates that their intuitive "category representa-

tions" must have taken on a reasonably general status by this time (Sugarman, 1982). In addition, their ability to move forward or backward through such a script suggests that their representations must have attained the sort of flexibility or "reversibility" that is characteristic of the end of the any developmental stage. Thus, one could suggest that children's mental representations of their recurring interactions with their mothers might have some general form such as this:

Script #1: Protection (4 yrs.)

(1) People and place: Baby near mother (e.g., in bed, backyard)
↑
next
↓
(2) Special event: Arrival of frightening person/object
↑
next
↓
(3) Response: Appeal to mother (call, gesture, cry)
↑
next
↓
(4) Outcome: Rescue (mother runs to baby and intervenes)

The notion of a maternal "role" which such a system of interrelations implies might be represented as follows:

Maternal Role #1: Protection (4 yrs.)

DANGER:

calls for help
→
Daughter   Mother
←
comes to save her

Finally, on the assumption that the child's ability to focus on and relate the items of the script in a reversible fashion leads to the consolidation of the script, the entire script might be represented in neo-Piagetian terms as a single unit, which could then be assigned a single symbol (A, B, etc.).

Level 1: Maternal Roles as Motivated Action Sequences

The first time the children saw their mothers as having the potential for acting in a fashion not rigidly scripted by their daughters' demands, but derived from their own independent wishes for their daughters' well-being, was at the age of 6. This datum fits well with Nelson's suggestion that children's understanding of recurrent action moves from scripts to "plans" during this age range (Nelson & Gruendel, 1981). The finding is also congruent with Kohlberg's conceptualization of children's moral reasoning at this age. For Kohlberg (1976), children begin to focus on satisfying other people's desires or wants at this age. This suggests that children's understanding of their mothers' role is part of a more general social understanding of the way in which motives or desires are related to scripted action. In turn, this suggests that a new understanding of maternal scripts may be emerging, which might be represented as follows:

Script #2: Protection (6 yrs.)

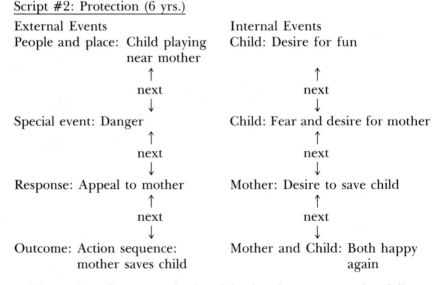

External Events	Internal Events
People and place: Child playing near mother	Child: Desire for fun
↑ next ↓	↑ next ↓
Special event: Danger	Child: Fear and desire for mother
↑ next ↓	↑ next ↓
Response: Appeal to mother	Mother: Desire to save child
↑ next ↓	↑ next ↓
Outcome: Action sequence: mother saves child	Mother and Child: Both happy again

The notion of a maternal role might then be represented as follows:

Maternal Role #2: Protection (6 yrs.)

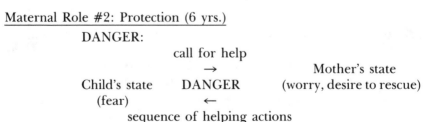

DANGER:

call for help
→   Mother's state
Child's state   DANGER   (worry, desire to rescue)
(fear)   ←
sequence of helping actions

The general insights implied by these representations might be thought of as entailing the coordination of two previously separate structures: a structure for analyzing event sequences or scripts, of the sort that was observed at the 4-year-old level (A), and a structure for analyzing a mother's intention or plan for a single event (B), which recent research suggests is available by the age of 4, as well (Astington et al., 1989; Bruchkowsky, this volume). In the context of neo-Piagetian theory, this sort of coordination (i.e., A-B) is characteristic of children at this age level (see Fig. 19.1, p. 436).

Level 2: Maternal Roles as Planned Action Sequences

In the present study, no attempt was made to select children from the middle substage of Case's dimensional period. If the foregoing analysis is correct, however, and children really do move to a new level of understanding of maternal scripts at the age of 6, it follows from Case's theory that, by the age of 8, they should be able to entertain two rather than one unit of the 6-year-old sort. This, in turn, suggests that one of the central features of the 10-year-old responses (their probabilistic or conditional nature) should also be present at the 8-year-old level. In effect, 8-year olds should already have begun to understand that mothers may have more than one desire, and that they may also select among more than one possible action sequence. Future research might investigate this possibility.

Level 3: Maternal Roles as Generalized Dispositions Toward Action

The critical features of the 10-year-old responses were: (a) that the children could envision multiple ways in which their mothers might respond; (b) that they could identify some more abstract maternal disposition, which was expressed by the particular behavior that was observed (e.g., "caring"); and (c) that they could also identify and make reference to some more remote or abstract set of goals that would guide the mother's selection of a particular action sequence. Once again, this is consistent with Nelson's (1981) suggestion that children's thinking progresses from scripts, to plans, to abstract goals. It is also consistent with Kohlberg's view that children begin to be concerned with exhibiting particular traits, such as "goodness" or "niceness," rather than simply particular behaviors that satisfy other people's particular desires at this age. Finally, the result is consistent with the general theory outlined in chapter 2, in the sense that the 10-year-old level is hypothesized to be the one where multiple units envisioned at the 8-year-old level are integrated in some fashion. In terms of this theory, the new knowledge might be symbolized as follows:

General Knowledge about Mother (10 yrs.)

A_1—Possible interaction———— B_1—Mother's thoughts and
       sequence #1   feelings (in situation)

                X—General dispositions/feelings about
                daughter that serve to integrate these
                interactions

A_2—Possible interaction———— B_2—Mother's thoughts and
       sequence #2   feelings (in situation)

Although this representation is rather global, it has the advantage of suggesting how the new behaviors that are observed might have their origins in earlier ones. It also suggests that children might be creating an integrated understanding of various other types of motivated maternal behavior as well. In particular, they might be integrating their understanding of the various behaviors that their mothers characteristically exhibit across each of the general categories of situation that were investigated, as well as within them. Either at this stage, then, or at the immediately following one, the maternal behaviors associated with protection, care, nurturance, and teaching should all be seen as stemming from the same source, namely, from the mother's care for her daughter's current and future well-being. This would mean that the child would, in effect, be constructing an abstract notion of a role similar to that found in the sociological literature, which might be represented thus:

Maternal Role #3: Protection (10 yrs.)

                Daughter $\rightarrow$
        has general needs (protection, care)
           $\uparrow \downarrow$ $\leftarrow$ Mother
       has general feelings and goals for

In fact, by the age of 12 or 13, children were talking quite explicitly in these abstract terms (Goldberg-Reitman, 1984).

Before concluding, one objection to the general procedure that was employed in this study must be considered. It could be argued that the strong cross-task consistency that was found in the present study was an artifact of the methodology. Because subjects' protocols were examined separately for each age group, in a direct attempt to induce a common structure across the various situations, it could be argued that there were also important differences across maternal functions in the subjects' protocols, which were missed, due to the desire to discover a set of cross-situational commonalities. Continuing with this line of argument, one could suggest that a different scoring system might have yielded cross-function differences rather then similarities.

This argument cannot be dismissed. It is quite possible that there *were* unique characteristics associated with each individual maternal function, and that this study did not detect them. One must remember, however, that the first aim of the study was to initiate a search for a *general* structural categorization in the social domain that might parallel the one proposed by Case and Sandieson for the quantitative domain (chapter 7). Second, the hypothesized prototypical features *were* empirically validated: both by the specification of objective scoring criteria and by the demonstration of a reasonable level of interrater reliability. Whatever aspects of the children's responses may have been different across different maternal functions, then, and may have gone undetected, the aspects of the children's responses that were common were objectively real, as was the fact that these aspects changed in a regular fashion with development.

The foregoing conclusion gains further support from a study that was conducted by Fischer and his colleagues at the same time as the present one (Fischer, Hand, et al, 1984). In their study, Fischer and his collaborators examined children's understanding of such roles as father and doctor, in a context where these roles could actually be "played out," after modeling by an experimenter. Under these conditions, 4-year-olds displayed a conception that they termed a "behavioral" role; 6-year-olds revealled a conception they termed a "true" role; and 10-year-olds evidenced a conception of multiple interacting roles (e.g., father and husband). Clearly, this empirical progression is directly parallel to the one reported here, with the behavioral role corresponding to a generalized action script (A), the "true" role corresponding to a more complex script that includes internal motivational components for each protagonist (A–B), and the conception of multiple interacting roles corresponding to multiple units integrated by some device such as a general disposition ($A_1 - B_1 \times A_2 - B_2$).

Given the close parallel between my results and Fischer et al.'s, as well as the parallel with the previous work by Nelson and Kohlberg, it seems reasonable to suggest that a central conceptual structure may underlie the different strands of social development that each investigator has examined at each age level, and that what varies from one task or context to the next may be the more specific that the child must analyze. In short, it seems reasonable to suggest that a sequence of central conceptual structures may exist for the domain of social cognition that is directly analogous to the one that was postulated in previous chapters for the domain of quantitative thought.

The Development of Empathic Cognition in Middle and Early Childhood

Marta Bruchkowsky
Credit Valley Hospital, Toronto

In the study reported in the previous chapter, Goldberg-Reitman presented children with a sequence of cartoon pictures depicting simple stories in which a little girl encounters some sort of problem, one that a parent might be expected to assist her with. She then asked her subjects how they thought the little girl in the story felt, how they thought the mother of the little girl would respond, why they thought she would respond that way and what they thought the mother was thinking and feeling. This paradigm is similar to the one that has been used extensively in the study of children's empathy. In this research, children are often presented with simple cartoon sequences that tell a story. After the story is over, they are asked how the main character in the story felt, why he or she felt that way, and how the story made them feel themselves (Hughes, Tingle, & Swain, 1981).

This literature is relevant to the topic of the present volume not just because the questions are similar to those that Goldberg-Reitman used and hence potentially useful in determining the generality of her findings, but also because they suggest a note of caution. In recent years, the standard empathy paradigm used for determining children's cognitive and affective capacities has been criticized on the grounds that cartoon pictures do not provide children with sufficiently realistic or comprehensive cues on which to base their analysis (B. K. Bryant, 1982; Rukavina, 1985), and that the paradigm relies too heavily on children's ability to report their thoughts and feelings verbally.

In an effort to mitigate these problems, recent investigators have presented children with videotaped vignettes, rather then cartoon sequences (Rukavina, 1985; Strayer, 1983, 1987). Even these new studies, however, are not without their problems. In Rukavina's study, for example, the actors that were used were adults, the affects they were asked to portray were subtle, and the dialogue was lengthy. In the study by Strayer, the vignettes were excerpts from commercial productions, such as *Poltergeist,* so the actual situations were more dramatic and vivid than those that children encounter in their daily lives. In addition, music was used quite extensively to intensify the affective experience. One could argue, therefore, that these methods do not provide a very realistic assessment of children's cognitive and affective capacities, either.

The first study described in this chapter was designed with two objectives in mind. The first was to correct some of the problems inherent in the standard empathy paradigm—both by preparing a more realistic set of videotaped vignettes for children to view and by including an analysis of children's nonverbal responses to these vignettes as well as their verbal ones. The second objective was to conduct a cognitive-developmental analysis of children's explanations for what they observed in the vignettes, and for what they themselves experienced. This analysis was designed within the same cognitive-developmental framework used by Goldberg-Reitman, which was reported in the previous chapter.

STUDY 1: THE DEVELOPMENT OF EMPATHY DURING THE DIMENSIONAL STAGE

Stimulus Materials

Three vignettes, one each depicting happy, sad, and angry situations, were written by the experimenter for the study and videotaped. All three vignettes were designed to have the same internal structure, consisting of two episodes, each with one salient event and one emotional reaction.

In the "happy" vignette, a little girl named Mary became frustrated because the friends she was phoning could not come over to play with her. This was Episode #1. Episode #2 began when Mary's friend Susan arrived with a surprise present, and ended with Mary opening the present and thanking Susan with great enthusiasm for buying her something she had always wanted.

In the "sad" vignette, Episode #1 consisted of an initial scene in which Mary and Susan were playing happily in the park with Mary's pet dog, Harry. Episode #2 began when a car hit Mary's dog (this event was indicated by the squeal of a car's tires off-screen) and ended with Mary crying on her mother's shoulder, saying that it was hard to believe her dog was dead, and that she would miss him so much.

In the "angry" vignette, Mary and her friend Susan were happily building a castle out of blocks in Episode #1. Episode #2 began when Alice walked in and said, "You think you're so smart, don't you!" Alice then broke the castle, at which point Mary jumped up and began yelling at her, asking how she could have done such a thing, and telling her how long and hard they had been working on the castle.

Two 13-year-old girls, one experienced in amateur acting and the other a professional actress, played the roles of Mary and her friend Susan. A graduate student portrayed Mary's mother in the "happy" and "sad" video. An 11-year-old girl with no prior acting experience played the role of Alice in the "angry" scenario. Judged only by appearance, the ages of the young girls could have been anywhere from 8 to 14.

The videotaping and editing were done with the aid of a professional technician. Once they had been filmed, the tapes were rated as to levels of "affective intensity" and "convincingness" by a group of adults. For all three videos, the raters evaluated the children's reactions as strong and appropriate to the events that were depicted. In no episode did any of the children provide a verbal label for what they were feeling.

Method

Subjects

Seventy-two children, 12 boys and 12 girls, from each of three age groups (4, 6, and 10 years), were selected for participation in the study. These ages were selected in order to represent the transitional substages and the upper limit of the Dimensional Stage, as in the study by Goldberg-Reitman (this volume, chapter 8). The subject pool was obtained from private homes, nursery schools, and public schools within the same general region. The socioeconomic composition of the subject sample was in the middle to upper middle-class range, and was relatively stable across age groups.

Children were selected for participation if they exhibited average to above-average functioning in language, as evaluated by their teachers; average to above-average levels of general intellectual ability, as assessed by the Ammons & Ammons Quick Test (R. B. Ammons & C. H. Ammons, 1962); no history of emotional problems or learning difficulties, as indexed by a referral to Special Services; and no traumatic family experiences such as death or divorce (within the previous six months) as determined by parental report. These selection criteria were used to obtain an estimate of children's "optimum level of performance" (see Fischer, 1980).

Procedure

Children were tested individually in a vacant room in their home or school. The experimental set-up of the room remained constant across the different testing locations, and is illustrated in Fig. 9.1. All children were seen for one session of approximately 40 minutes, during which the Quick Test was administered, followed by a set of warm-up questions designed to ensure that children possessed the relevant verbal labels for responding to the empathy questionnaire. The three videotapes and the empathy questions were then presented.

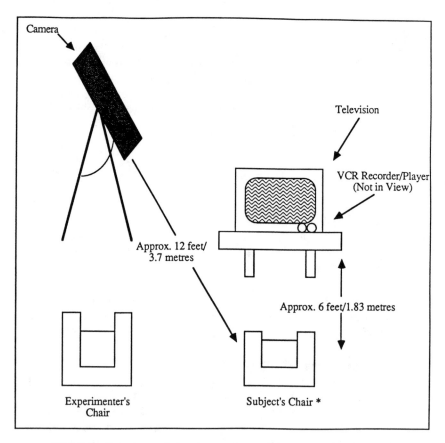

FIG. 9.1.   Experimental situation as observed from the subject's perspective.

Warm-up Questions.   Prior to viewing the first video, the children were asked the following questions.

Question A: "How do you feel?"
Question B: "Why do you feel '_____'?"
Question C: "What are some other ways people can feel?"

In most cases children responded with "fine" to Question A, and with "sad," "angry," or some other emotion to Question C. Children who did not mention "sad" and/or "angry" in response to Question C were told: "And people can feel sad (or angry) as well, right?" "What can make people feel sad (or angry)?" All children who were asked were able to answer the latter question. Thus, it was concluded that they had appropriate verbal labels for describing the feelings in the three videos.

Introducing the First Video.   The experimenter introduced the first video to the children as follows: "First, I am going to show you something on this television, and then I will ask you some questions about what you saw. Do you understand? Do you have any questions? Are you ready?" The video player and the camera were then turned on simultaneously. The examiner said to the child, "O.K., let's begin. Watch this." As soon as the video was over, the video player and the camera were turned off, and the Empathy Interview was administered.

Empathy Interview.   After the camera and television had been turned off, the child was asked five standard questions, following Hughes et al. (1981):

Question 1: "Tell me how you feel after watching that."	Answer 1: A1
Question 2: "Why do you think you felt '<u>A1</u>'?"	Answer 2: A2
Question 3: "How did Mary feel?"	Answer 3: A3
Question 4: "What made Mary feel '<u>A3</u>'?"	Answer 4: A4
Question 5: "Why did '<u>A4</u>' make Mary feel '<u>A3</u>'?"	Answer 5: A5

Introducing the Second and Third Videos.   The second and third videos were introduced in the same fashion as the first. After the third empathy interview was completed, the experimenter thanked the children for their help, and took them back to their classroom (or parents, if the session was being conducted in the home).

Record of Affective Response.   Throughout each video presentation, the camera was trained on children's faces in order to record their expressions. The camera was a standard videocamera recorder, which had a sound track as well as a video track. The record of the session that resulted thus contained a record of children's facial expressions, together with the soundtrack from the video the children were watching, which was synchronous with it. The sound track permitted the experimenter to match the children's facial expressions to the events that they were viewing.

Personality Measure.   Ten-year-olds were seen for a second session within three days of the first, in which the Children's Differential Diagnostic Test (CDDT; Weininger, 1986) was administered. Details of this projective test and its scoring are presented in Bruchkowsky (1989).

Experimental Design

The design was a randomized $3 \times 2 \times 3 \times 6$ factorial design, with blocks of size 2 and 3 replications. The design was chosen to permit a statistical analysis of main effects and interactions with respect to age (three groups), sex (two groups), affect (happy, sad, angry), and order of presentation (all six possible viewing orders of the three tapes).

Scoring Procedure

Feelings Attributed to Self and Others.   Children's responses to Questions 1 and 3 in the empathy interview were scored in the general fashion suggested by Feschbach and Roe (1968). According to their procedure, children are given credit for approximate responses along the pleasurable/unpleasurable dimension. For example, a response of "good" instead of "happy" is scored as correct. In the present study, this procedure was modified so that if children responded with "bad", they were asked whether they meant "bad-sad" or "bad-mad." Similarly, for equivocal responses such as "upset", children were asked to give a more specific label.

Explanation for Particular Feelings.   To determine the "cognitive level" of children's understanding of the emotion in question, a qualitative analysis of all responses to questions 2, 4, and 5 was conducted, using the categories identified by Goldberg-Reitman (Chapter 8) as a guide:

Level 0: Predimensional. Children were scored at this level if their reasoning focused exclusively on the salient external (observable) events depicted on the tape.
Level 1: Unidimensional. Children were scored at this level if their responses referred not just to the external aspects of the situation, but in addition, to some internal and/or motivational dimension.

Level 2: Bidimensional. Children were scored at this level if their thinking revealed an ability to focus on two internal features of the problem situation.

Level 3: Integrated Bidimensional. Children were scored at this level if they revealed an ability to focus on and coordinate two internal dimensions of a problem situation, in an elaborated manner.

The precise criteria that were given to the raters are described in Table 9.1. All three questions measuring empathic understanding were scored. A final score was then awarded on the basis of the highest cognitive level obtained across the three questions.

Facial Expression. A rating scale to evaluate children's facial responses was designed, based on the research of Ekman and Friesen (1975) and the System for Identifying Affect Expressions by Holistic Judgments (Affex) developed by Izard (1984). Ekman and Friesen (1975) conducted extensive cross-cultural research, and delineated three regions of the face capable of independent movement and relevant to facial affective expressions: (a) brow/forehead; (b) eyes/eyelids and root of the nose; and (c) lower face (cheeks, mouth, and most of the nose and chin). For each region of the face they provided verbal descriptions and photographs to describe the changes that occur for the six emotions of happiness, sadness, surprise, fear, anger, and disgust. Izard & Dougherty (1980) elaborated on the descriptions, added a videotape, described the two additional emotions of interest and contempt, and combined these into a system for rating affect expression.

The first item on the rating scale designed for this study entailed a global analysis of changes in terms of whether a brightening of the face

TABLE 9.1
Scoring Criteria for Developmental Levels of Children's
Empathic Explanations

Does the explanation refer to a salient event in the story involving the story protagonist?

No = Below Level 0   Yes
                                    ↓

Does the explanation refer to the story protagonist's internal state, in addition to a salient event in the story?

No = Level 0   Yes
                              ↓

Does the explanation refer to (a) more than one dimension of the story protagonist's internal state, or (b) the protagonist's internal state and an evaluation/judgment of that state?

No = Level 1   Yes = Level 3 [(a) or (b)]

occurred, indicating a change in the direction of a more positive/ pleasurable affective expression; a darkening of the face occurred, indicating a change in the direction of a more negative/unpleasurable affective expression; a brightening and a darkening of the face occurred sequentially; no change in affective expression was observed. This global analysis did not require that the rater provide a specific affect label or conduct a discriminative analysis of each of the three face regions, only a judgment as to whether one of these global changes occurred. When the three facial regions were attended to, interrater reliabilities ranged from .68 to .88.

Results

Facial Responses. The majority of children at all ages showed an appropriate brightening or darkening of their facial expression when the second episode of the vignette began, and the emotion-provoking event befell the main character. The nature of children's facial response was in accord with their self-reported feelings in the interview, and also with the feelings they attributed to the main character. All three age groups correctly labeled Mary's affect in the three videos as happy, sad, and angry, respectively.

Explanations of Affects. Where the three age groups clearly differed was in their ability to project themselves into the script, and to explain the reasons for the protagonist's feelings. Table 9.2 shows the percentage of children performing at each of the cognitive levels defined in Table 9.1. As may be seen, the majority of children performed at the level that would be expected to be characteristic of their age level, on the basis of Goldberg-Reitman's structural analysis. The typical sorts of responses that were generated were as follows:

Interviewer:	What made Mary feel sad?
4-year-old child:	Because Harry died.
Interviewer:	Why did that make Mary sad?
Child:	(silence)
Interviewer:	What made Mary feel sad?
6-year-old child:	Because her dog died, and she misses him.
Interviewer:	What made Mary feel sad?
10-year-old child:	Because her dog died, and she really loved him, and still really misses him 'cause he was her best friend.

TABLE 9.2
Distribution of Children Demonstrating Each Level of Empathic
Cognition on Happiness, Sadness, and Anger

| | | Stimulus Video | | | | | |
| | | Happiness | | Sadness | | Anger | |
Age	Level of Cognition	n	%	n	%	n	%
4	Below Level 0	4	16.7	5	12.5	2	8.3
	Level 0	13	54.2	11	45.8	14	58.3
	Level 1	6	25.0	10	41.7	8	33.3
	Level 3	1	4.2	0	0.0	0	0.0
6	Below Level 0	0	0.0	0	0.0	0	0.0
	Level 0	2	8.3	5	20.8	3	12.5
	Level 1	17	70.8	16	66.7	15	62.5
	Level 3	5	20.8	3	12.5	6	25.0
10	Below Level 0	0	0.0	0	0.0	0	0.0
	Level 0	0	0.0	0	0.0	0	0.0
	Level 1	3	12.5	7	29.2	4	16.7
	Level 3	21	87.5	17	70.8	20	83.3

Table 9.3 reports the mean scores of children at each age level. A score of 0 represents predimensional performance; scores of 1, 2, and 3 represent unidimensional, bidimensional and integrated bidimensional performance, respectively. A four-way multivariate analysis of variance was conducted to test the significance of the four main factors. The only significant effect was for age. There were no significant interactions.

The trend analysis revealed a strong linear relationship among the three age groups, $F(2, 72) = 207.86$, $p \leq .001$. The non-linear and quadratic effects were not significant. These data were then reanalyzed with alterations in the analysis of variance, to determine if the results would continue to be significant when the data were recoded to account for the gap between the 6- and 10-year-olds (created by the absence of 8-year-olds or Level 2 responses in this sample); and if the linear effect would continue to be significant when the data were recoded to account for the ceiling effect created by the impossibility of cognitive responses higher than Level 3. The results of the first analysis revealed that the age difference continued to be significant, $F(2, 72) = 87.92$, $p \leq .001$, when the data were readjusted to account for the gap between the 6- and 10-year-olds. The results of the second analysis revealed the maintenance of a strong linear trend, $F(2, 72) = 208.85$ $p \leq .001$) when the data were adjusted to account for the ceiling effect.

TABLE 9.3
Mean Cognitive Levels and Standard Deviations For
Age, Sex, and Type of Affective Video

| | | | Cognitive Level | |
Variable		n	M	SD
Age	4 Years	24	.25	0.68
	6 Years	24	1.25	0.91
	10 Years	24	2.61	0.80
Sex	Males	36	1.28	1.31
	Females	36	1.46	1.20
Type of Affective Video	Happy	24	1.43	1.32
	Sad	24	1.25	1.19
	Angry	24	1.43	1.26

Discussion

In the literature on empathy, three components of the total empathic response are normally distinguished: detecting the presence of an emotion in another person, taking that person's perspective or role in the situation that provoked this emotion, and responding with a vicarious emotional reaction of one's own. In the present study, there were no strong developmental differences in the first or the third of these components. The majority of children at all ages were able to detect and label correctly the affect displayed by the protagonist. They also showed a parallel affective response themselves, and correctly labeled this response when queried.[1] Because the situations the children were viewing were both familiar and powerful, these results are not surprising. Borke (1971) had already suggested that preschool children can diagnose other peoples feelings in simple situations and can react empathetically. Thus, this part of study merely served to confirm what was already known.

Given that there were no strong developmental differences in either of the other two components, however, the differences in the second component assumed a particular significance. For, even though the youngest children clearly *understood* the emotional predicament of the protagonist and responded to it, they did not appear to be capable of taking account of the protagonist's motivational or intentional stance in

---

[1]The one exception to this latter generalization occurred at the 10-year-old level, where a number of children with "chronically hostile" personalities, as assessed by the CDDT showed some brightening as well as darkening in response to the negative events, such as Harry's death, which appeared to represent a defensive reaction to the situation. For details of this analysis, see Bruchkowsky (1989).

explaining that state—at least not at the same time as they were keeping track of the external events that were taking place and the protagonist's emotional response to them. The capability for integrating motivational and behavioral script analyses was first seen in its unifocal form at the age of 6 years, and assumed a more fully elaborated and integrated form by age 10. In both of these latter respects, the results were very similar to those reported by Goldberg-Reitman in the previous chapter, and suggested the presence of a central structure that is applied to both tasks and formats.

STUDY 2: THE DEVELOPMENT OF EMPATHIC COGNITION DURING THE INTERRELATIONAL STAGE

In terms of the theory that was proposed in chapter 2, the results of Study 1 raise an intriguing possibility. The age of 6 years is hypothesized to be the beginning of a new stage of cognitive development, one whose structures are believed to emerge from the coordination of two well-consolidated structures from the previous stage. It could be the case, therefore, that 4-year-olds actually *possess* cognitive structures for analyzing other people's intentions and desires, but that they are incapable of *using* this knowledge in certain situations. Stated differently, their difficulty with Goldberg-Reitman's tasks and with the video tasks used in Study 1 here, may be in coordinating the sort of "motivational analysis" that an analysis of intentionality requires, with the sort of "script" analysis that these tasks also require, that is, encoding a novel sequence of external events and answering questions about what caused some particular event in the sequence or predicting what will occur next.

The possibility that children develop a rudimentary understanding of other people's motives and feelings during the interrelational stage gains some support from the existing literature on children's empathy (e.g., Hoffman, 1982) and from their success in labeling Mary's feelings in the videotapes. On certain tasks, such as those designed by Borke (1971), children are merely required to listen to a story about a familiar situation (e.g., a birthday party) and to say how the main character must be feeling. This ability to label feelings is typically seen by the age of 3 or 4, the age at which the "labeling" questions in Study 1 were successfully answered.

The possibility that children cannot use this understanding in more complex contexts until the dimensional stage gains support from studies such as those described by Chandler (1977), in which subjects are required to decenter from their own point of view, and take the point of view of someone else whose current situation is quite different. Typically these tasks yield results like those reported in the present chapter, namely, that the capacity under investigation is not seen until 6 to 8 years of age.

If children do develop the ability to comprehend and respond to other people's desires and feelings during the preschool years, but cannot use this ability when engaging in complex narrative analysis until the elementary school years, it should be possible to use the cognitive-developmental theory summarized in chapter 2 (Case, 1985) as an interpretive framework for charting the steps through which this development proceeds during the interrelational stage. To do so, however, one would first have to determine what the relevant unit of analysis should be for the interrelational stage. In Study 2 in this chapter, an hypothesis regarding the nature of these units was derived by examining the results of Marini's study of dimensional reasoning (this volume, chapter 3).

What Marini showed was that elementary children go through the following conceptual progression, in their understanding of how a peer might react to the receipt of a particular number of marbles as a birthday gift: At *Substage 1* (6 years), they understand that the degree of a child's happiness may be a function of the number of marbles he received; at *Substage 2* (8 years), they understand that the degree of the child's happiness may also be a function of how many marbles he had been hoping for; and finally, at *Substage 3* (10 years) they understand that the degree of a child's happiness may be a function of the *relationship* between these two variables, such that the greater the excess of what the child receives over what he or she was hoping for, the greater the degree of his or her delight.

In subsequent studies (e.g., Case & Sandieson, this volume, chapter 6), it was shown that children's success on Marini's task is a function of their ability to conceptualize *number,* not their ability to understand someone else's desires or feelings, per se. The conclusion that follows, then, is this: If the requirement for quantification is eliminated from Marini's task, children should be found to go through a similar progression during the interrelational stage on tasks where a qualitative rather than a quantitative judgment is necessary.

Study 2 (which was actually conducted before Study 1—See Bruchkowsky, 1984) was designed to test this possibility. It was hypothesized that, at substage 0 of the interrelational stage (1½ years), children should be able to respond to other people's feelings, based on the external appearance of their emotional display, including voice, body posture, facial features, and so on. At Substage 1 of the Interrelational

Stage (2 years), children should be able to understand that the quality of someone's feeling at a birthday party (happy vs. sad) can be a function of the quality of the gift they receive (nice vs. not nice). At Substage 2 (3 years), they should be able to understand that the quality of someone's feelings can also be a function of what they desire (e.g., a train vs. a doll). Finally, at Substage 3 (4 years) they should be able to understand that the quality of someone's feeling can depend on the relationship between what they desire and what they receive.

Method

Subjects

Forty preschoolers (19 boys and 21 girls) were selected for the study from an initial pool of 53 children. The criteria used to select children were: the ability to attend to and follow task instructions, the ability to complete two experimental tasks in succession, and a chronological age within the range specified for the interrelational stage.

From the initial sample, 10 children were assigned to Group 1 (mean age = 18 months, range = 15 to 21 months), 10 were assigned to Group 2 (mean age = 26 months, range = 25 to 27 months), 9 were assigned to Group 3 (mean age = 32 months, range = 33 to 40 months) and 11 were assigned to Group 4 (mean age = 49 months, range = 46 to 51 months). All subjects were attending day-care centers in three residential areas of metropolitan Toronto.

Stimulus Materials

Two hand-held female puppets, approximately 30 mm in length, were used for all levels of the task. Both their body postures and their facial expressions were manipulable. Two wooden stands were used to position the puppets. Additional materials included presents, as a doll, a toy car, and two identical toy bicycles (approximately 8–14 mm in length) one intact and one broken into several pieces.

Task Construction

Four levels of the task were constructed, one for each of the substages of the interrelational stage. At the preliminary level of the task (Level 0), the puppet's general feeling state was directly expressed by the experimenter, who was hiding behind her. At the next three levels, the children had to infer the puppets' emotional states on the basis of the information they were told about what the puppets wanted for their birthday, and what they received.

Warm-Up Period

Prior to the presentation of the tasks, each child was engaged in a brief discussion about various typical birthday events: "What do you like about birthdays? What do you do on your birthday? Do you get presents for your birthday? What is the best toy you ever got for your birthday? Have you ever been to a friend's birthday party?" The child was then told that he or she would be playing a birthday game with the experimenter.

As part of the birthday game, the puppets were given names, Jane and Sue. Then the child was told that both puppets were celebrating birthdays: "You know whose birthday it is today? It's Jane's birthday and it's Sue's birthday. Whose birthdays are today? Yes, you're right; Jane and Sue are *both* having a birthday today. And do you know what you and I are going to do? We are going to their birthday parties. Then we are going to find out how Jane and Sue feel about the presents they get for their birthdays." All explanations were repeated as often as necessary, until the child appeared to understand that the object of the game was to determine how the two puppets felt about the presents they received. The puppets were then placed on stands and turned around so that their backs faced the children. A birthday present was then placed behind each puppet, and in front of the child.

Level 0. At this level Jane was introduced first, and the child was given an opportunity to play with her. The experimenter then placed Jane on her hand, and told the child that they would now determine how she was feeling. The experimenter then put her head down behind Jane, and made Jane act like a very active and jovial girl who was laughing and singing. A smile was also put on Jane's face, and she was made to say things such as: "La, la, la, la, what a beautiful day; I have lots of toys and friends to play with, la, la, la, la." The child's reaction to these events was noted, and the first puppet was put away.

Next, the child was given an opportunity to play with Sue. The experimenter placed Sue on her hand and depicted her as a very sad and unhappy girl who was frowning, crying and leaning over with her head in her hands, saying: "Sniff, sniff, what a terrible day. I have no toys and nobody wants to play with me, sniff, sniff." Once again, the child's reaction to these events was noted.

The children were then asked, "Which puppet is crying? Which one is sad?" Immediately afterward they were asked, "Which puppet is laughing? Which one is happy?" Because these items were for the preliminary stage, the children were not actually required to answer the questions in order to "pass" the item. They merely had to demonstrate an affective response that was "in tune" with the puppets' feelings, either downcast or happy.

Level 1. At this level, Jane received a doll, but Sue did not receive anything. An alternate version of this level (1B) was also administered, where Sue received a "nice" bicycle for her birthday and Jane received a bicycle that was "not nice," because it was broken into several pieces. To pass this level, children had to understand the relationship between this external event (present no present, or nice vs. broken present) and each puppet's internal (feeling) state. Children were first asked, "How does Jane feel?" and "How does Sue feel?". Next they were asked, "If someone was crying, who would be crying?" "Is someone happy? Show me (point out) which puppet is happy." Finally they were asked, "Is someone sad? Show me (point out) which puppet is sad." In order to pass the items at this level, children did not have to supply a verbal label for the dolls' feelings. They simply had to point to the correct doll in response to each of the "show me" questions.

Level 2. At the second level, children had to consider what each puppet wanted for her birthday, in addition to what she received, in order to determine how she must be feeling. The experimenter asked each puppet what she wanted for her birthday and had the puppet "answer," by naming something (e.g., a train). This was repeated until the child was able to remember the present each puppet wanted, and to name it on request. The puppets were then turned around again, with their backs to the child. One puppet was given a toy car, while the other was given a train. The set of questions described in the previous paragraph was then repeated. In order to pass the item, children had to realize that the girl who received the bicycle was sad, and the girl who received a train was happy. (In an alternate version of the task at the same level, 2B, each puppet wanted something different (a bicycle, a car), but what the two puppets received was a bicycle and a doll.)

Level 3: At the third level, Jane and Sue each wanted something different for their birthday. Jane wanted a bike and Sue wanted a doll. However, neither puppet received the present she wanted for her birthday; instead, each one received what the other child wanted. Once again, the children were asked how each puppet felt.

Design and Procedure

All participants were administered the Empathy Task and Preschool Balance Beam Test (Liv, 1981; Marini & Case, 1989) by the experimenter. The children were seen for two sessions, approximately 15 minutes each in duration. These sessions occurred from one to two days apart.

The Empathy Task was administered at the first session and the Balance Beam Test during the second.[2]

The experimenter spent a minimum of three days at each of the three day-care centers, getting acquainted with all the children. She also dedicated two hours each day to playing on an individual basis with those children who were scheduled to be tested that day. Children were then taken out of the classroom and tested individually in a quiet area on the school premises. On several occasions a member of the school's support staff accompanied children during testing.

Results

Children as young as 1½ years were able to respond to the puppets' situation and display an affective response that was appropriate. For the "happy" episode, their faces showed clear "brightening" and for the "sad" episode their faces showed clear "darkening." Table 9.4 displays the mean scores and standard deviations for children's performance on the more cognitively oriented questions (1–3). The pattern of mean scores formed a clear linear progression. A trend analysis showed a highly significant linear relationship ($F(3, 36) = 35.51, p < .001$) and no significant quadratic or cubic trends, $F(3, 36) = -.520, p > .05$). A Scalogram Analysis was also conducted; the value for the coefficient of reproducibility was .99 and the value for the coefficient of scalability was .98, providing strong support for the notion that the items formed a natural Guttman Scale.

Table 9.5 displays the frequency and percentage of children across age groups who were successful in passing each level. As may be seen, the performance of children in the first two age groups satisfied the standard passing criterion of 50%. In the third age group, although all the children performed as predicted on the first two levels of the task, only 44% passed the task at the level specified for their age group. The same was true for children in the fourth age group: Although they performed as predicted on the first three levels of the task, only 45% succeeded at the higher predicted level.

Discussion

The reason many 4-year-olds failed the task where each puppet got the opposite present from the one she wanted may have been that the story was too complicated and confusing. Whatever the reason for their less than-optimal performance, however, it seems clear that the general trend of the results was in reasonable accordance with the theory: The

---

[2]Due to errors, this order of presentation was reversed for three children.

TABLE 9.4
Distribution of Mean Scores and
Standard Deviations for the Preschool
Empathy Test, by Age Group

Age	n	Mean age (months)	M	SD
1½	10	17.7	−0.30	.48
2	10	26.3	0.70	.68
3	9	37.0	1.67	.87
4	11	48.8	2.46	.52

vast majority of the 4-year olds could perform at least at Level 2, thus demonstrating an ability to take into account both what *happens* to someone and what he or she *wants* to happen, in evaluating their feeling state. At the time these data were first reported (Bruchkowsky, 1984), they might have been considered somewhat controversial. With the extensive work that has been done on children's theories of mind in the interim (Astington et al., 1989), however, they now appear far less so. Indeed, taken together with this literature, the findings suggests that the preschool period may be one in which a very general set of conceptual structures may be developing, which relate to children's models of other people's feelings and desires.

The results also suggest a potential resolution to a controversy in the field regarding the age at which such a general model emerges. The suggestion is that this argument is only resolvable if a clearer definition is provided of what one means by a "theory of mind." If what one means is some understanding that an external event can affect an expression of emotion, then this emerges at the age of 2. If what one means is that someone's desire or intention can be taken into account in predicting his or her internal reaction to something, then this emerges at about age 3.

TABLE 9.5
Frequency and Percentage of Children Passing Each Level of the
Preschool Empathy Tast

Age	Mean age (months)	Empathy Task Levels											
		0		1A		1B		2A		2B		3	
		n	%	n	%	n	%	n	%	n	%	n	%
1½	17.7	7	70	0	0	0	0	0	0	0	0	0	0
2	26.3	9	90	7	70	6	60	0	0	0	0	0	0
3	37.0	9	100	9	100	8	88	4	44	4	44	2	22
4	48.8	11	100	11	100	11	100	10	91	9	82	5	45

If what one means is that children have the ability to form a causal link between external events and internal events in predicting what someone will think or feel in a particular situation, and overcome potentially misleading cues, then this capability does not emerge until approximately the age of 4½, as the reversible structures of the interrelational stage are formed and consolidated. Finally, if what one means is that children have the ability to integrate a motivational analysis with a causal analysis of a novel event sequence, this does not emerge until the dimensional stage, at about 6 years.

General Conclusion

In the quantitative domain, children go through a series of substages during the preschool period in mastering the act of counting, at the same time as they are going through a similar set of substages in attaining a qualitative understanding of simple physical systems, such as a balance beam. Later, during the dimensional stage, they coordinate these two structures into the more general "dimensional structure," illustrated in Figure 19.2 (p. 356). Further progress results from children moving first to bidimensional, and then to integrated bidimensional thought.

What the present two studies reveal is a very similar progression. During the preschool period children go through a set of substages in learning about their own and others' internal desires, and the way in which these desires can influence their emotional reaction in a familiar context, such as a birthday party. At the same time, they develop an ability to follow simple stories—whether these are presented in verbal, cartoon, or video format—and to answer questions that require predicting what will happen next, as in Goldberg-Reitman's study, or explaining what has just happened by describing the event that immediately preceded it, as in the first study in the present chapter. What appears to happen as children move into the dimensional stage is that they coordinate these two sorts of structure into a more general structure that allows them to explain any event in a narrative in a conjoint fashion: that is, by reference both to the external event that preceded it, and to the protagonist's desires regarding future events. Finally, as they proceed through the dimensional stage, they become capable of taking two sorts of internal states into account, and then integrating these two states into a well-consolidated and coherent explanation.

If children's understanding of social events really does evolve in this manner, it follows that the underlying conceptual structure on which it is based must be a very general one, which—like the quantitative structure that was described in previous chapters—applies across a broad range of situations. As a minimum, the structure should apply, not just to situations where children are asked to *explain* a novel sequence of events, but to *imagine* and *describe* such a sequence. Children's performance on this latter sort of task (and its development), is the subjects of the next chapter.

170

A Neo-Structural Analysis of Children's Narrative and Its Development

Anne McKeough
University of Calgary

Contemporary interest in discourse analysis can be traced to the work of Bartlett (1932), who noted that structurally familiar stories were better remembered than structurally unfamiliar ones, and Propp (1968), who suggested that the entire corpus of Russian folk tales was based on a limited number of themes or "functions." In recent years, the ideas proposed by Bartlett and Propp have been elaborated and refined by cognitive scientists with an interest in discourse analysis. The models they have proposed may be divided into three broad categories: (a) those in which a knowledge of story syntax is hypothesized to guide and structure the narrative process (Mandler, 1982; Rumelhart, 1975; Stein & Glenn, 1979), (b) those in which a knowledge of the universal properties of human action is hypothesized to play this underlying function (Bower, Black, & Turner, 1979; Schank & Ableson, 1977; Wilensky, 1983), and (c) those more general models in which both syntactic and semantic elements have been integrated (de Beaugrande, 1982; Bereiter, 1983; van Dijk & Kintsch, 1983).

Notwithstanding their theoretical differences, the authors of these models have generally agreed on the following two propositions: that there is a gradual increase with age in the structural complexity of children's narratives, and that this increase may be attributed to some sort of age-related growth in information processing capacity. Investigators who have examined children's stories empirically have come to similar conclusions (Applebee, 1978; Biggs & Collis, 1982; Mandler, 1982; Peterson & McCabe, 1983; Rosenblatt, Gardner, & Winner, 1985). As yet, however, no attempt has been made to relate these two variables in a systematic fashion, or to suggest what specific values of processing capacity are necessary for generating which particular forms of narrative structure.

One possible way to accomplish this objective would be to use the theory that was outlined in chapter 2, and developed in succeeding chapters (e.g., Case & Sandieson, chapter 7). This theory hypothesizes that a general structural form is characteristic of children's thought at different ages, and that a particular value of processing capacity is necessary for constructing a structural form of each sort. According to the theory, 4-year-olds are supposed to be able to handle either of two relational structures in isolation. However, because their processing capacity for this sort of structure is hypothesized to be only one unit, they are not supposed to be able to coordinate two such structures, even under conditions that explicitly require them to do so. By contrast, 6-year-olds are supposed to have a processing capacity of two units and thus to be capable of assembling two such relational structures into a new unit of a higher epistemic sort. Finally, 8- and 10-year-olds are supposed to be able to integrate two units of the new kind into a more general structure, first in a tentative, and then in a systematic, fashion. This hypothesized progression could possibly be used as a guide in building a model of children's narrative in which both structural and process variables are formalized and related to each other in a more precise fashion.

In the present chapter, two studies are reported in which these were the general objectives. In the first, the method was inductive. A corpus of children's narratives was collected under conditions that were judged maximally conducive to the formulation of an integrated structural-process model. The two variables that were manipulated were the age of the participants (4, 6, 8, and 10 years), and the number of characters around which each narrative was supposed to center (1, 2, or 3). In the second study, the method that was used was deductive. Several hypotheses were formulated on the basis of the model that was formulated in the first study, and these were put to an empirical test in the second.

The reason it was necessary to begin with an inductive study is that the general theory spelled out in chapter 2 does not specify what type of relational units are available at the 4-year-old level for the domain of children's narrative, nor what sort of new unit might be created by their coordination. Thus, the object of the first study was to make such a determination empirically. Stated differently, the object of the first study was to examine children's narratives at the ages suggested by the theory, and to see if it might be possible to hypothesize an underlying structural progression that would fit the general characterization illustrated in Fig. 19.2 (p. 356). On the assumption that this sort of model could be generated, a second study was also planned in which several implications of the model were to be spelled out and tested.

STUDY 1: BUILDING A NEO-PIAGETIAN MODEL OF THE DEVELOPMENT OF CHILDREN'S NARRATIVE

Method

Subjects

Sixty middle-class children, aged 4, 6, 8, and 10 years, were selected according to a two-step procedure, in which teachers identified average to high average achievers, and then the Peabody Picture Vocabulary Test, Form L (Dunn & Dunn, 1988), was individually administered, to confirm that the children also had average to high-average verbal intelligence.

Procedure

Children were presented with two types of tasks: story telling and working memory. For the story telling part of the study, three stereotypic characters from children's literature were selected: a happy little girl, a kind old horse, and a cute little lamb. Four-year-olds were given two sets of instructions that directed them to include one or two characters in their stories, while 6-year-olds were given three sets of instructions specifying that one, two, or three characters be included. Eight- and 10-year-olds were given two sets of instructions requiring them to include two or three characters. The purpose of varying the number of characters was to determine if story structure would be affected by this variable. To control for the effect of the particular characters, a randomized block design was used. To control for order of presentation, a further randomization was employed within each block. Stories were recorded on an audio cassette and transcribed.

For the working memory portion of the study, two working memory measures were administered:

The Mr. Cucumber Test. Subjects were presented with a cartoon figure on which stickers had been affixed (Case, 1985, p. 350), and then presented with a blank figure and asked to point to the positions where the stickers had been present. The test increases in difficulty across five levels, as the number of stickers to be remembered increases from one to five. Three trials are presented at each level, and scores are obtained by averaging performance across levels.

The Opposites Test. Subjects were asked to listen as sets of familiar one-syllable words were recited, and to respond by furnishing the opposite of each word. This test also increases in difficulty as the number of words at each level increases from one to five. Five trials are presented at each level and again, scores are obtained by averaging across levels.

Results

The first step was to examine the 4- and 6-year-old stories to determine
if structural changes could be identified which reflected the hypothesized move from primitive interrelational units to a new "coordinated"
unit. The following stories were slightly above average in their coherence, but typical in their content.

Age 4

Jennifer
Once there was a lamb and a girl walking down to get home. So
they saw their mother's house and they went in and they saw their
mother. That's where they lived and they lived happily ever after.

Matthew
There was a little lamb that lived on grass and ate and got fat—fat.
Then—and people came to see him and then he got a gold medal.

Age 6

Ellen
There's a little girl. She was crying. So a boy came. No, a little—a
little, little girl came and said, "Do you want to play with me?" And
she stopped crying. And they played on the swings. And after they
played on the swings, they went on the slide. And then they went
on the teeter-totter. Then they walked along the beach. Then
they—they put their bathing suits on and they played in the water
and—ah—they—ah—and that's the end.

Jason
A horse was walking—walking along in a field and he saw a little
lamb in one of the places of the barn and it was a fence and it was a
little baby lamb and it—it was lonely. So the horse jumped in and
the lamb jumped onto the horse and then they got out. And then
they went to a place where there was nobody except them. And
they picked some blueberries and they ate them. And the horse
found some hay and he liked hay better than blueberries. And a
lamb found some grass and he liked the grass better than the
blueberries. And they went and lived together and they lived
happily ever after.

These stories could be analyzed in a number of ways. From the
present perspective, however, what is of interest that the 4-year-old
stories had the following properties: First, they were more like "happily

ever after" scripts than stories, in that the events were predictable and temporally and causally related in a single stereotypic event sequence. Second, the scripts had an episodic structure comprised of a setting, an initiating event, a response and an outcome, as noted in the work of Stein and Glenn (1979). *Settings* introduced characters, framed the story's time and place, and generally described the existing state of affairs at the outset: for example: "Once upon a time there was a lamb and a girl walking down to get home." Next, an *initiating event* begins the action sequence. Jennifer's characters see their mother's house as they are walking down the road. The initiating event then occasions a *response:* the lamb and the girl go into the house. Finally, the response yields an *outcome,* which brings closure to the episode: the lamb and girl finally meet up with their mother and live happily ever after. The second example, composed by Matthew, was similar. In the setting the listener is introduced to a lamb that lives on grass. The action is initiated when the lamb "eats" the grass and, in response, gets fat. In the outcome, Matthew reports that the fat lamb is displayed to an appreciative audience and wins a medal.

The episodes composed by the 4-year-olds varied considerably in the amount of material they contained. Some children produced elaborate versions of the prototypic story structure, such as those indicated here, whereas others managed only the "bare bones." Nevertheless, the stories clearly shared syntactic and semantic features. From a syntactic point of view, they followed a simple episodic format (i.e., setting, initiating event, response, and outcome). From a semantic point of view, they consisted of familiar well-scripted, social event sequences in which the motivation for action was never made explicit.

Six-year-old stories differed on two counts: First, they were composed of two coordinated episodes. Although the second episode retained the "happily-ever-after" orientation of the typical 4-year-old story, the first episode provided a context for the story and so gave it a different affective significance. The difference was based on the fact that a problem was presented in the first episode and solved in the second episode. The other distinguishing feature of 6-year-old stories was that the general form shifted from "script" to "plot." The action in scripts is based on a well-known set of events with an equally well-known temporal format, and so, is pre-determined. Plots, on the other hand, center around a problem and its resolution. In Ellen's story, a tearful child is comforted by a peer's offer to play; in Jason's story, a trapped and lonely lamb is rescued by a horse. In both cases, the course of events is determined, not by what *must* be, according to a predetermined script, but rather by what is needed to solve the problem, according to the character's perceptions. Thus, whereas 4-year-old stories were comprised of a single, primitive unit, a stereotypic social event, 6-year-olds' stories showed evidence of a higher order construction assembled by coordinating one event sequence, in which a problem is perceived, with a second event sequence, which seeks to resolve it. In other words, the locus of action control moved from the events themselves to the characters' response to and perception of events. In the process, children's first plots were born.

If the above analysis is valid, then it follows, according to Case's (1985) general theory, that 8-year-olds should be capable of considering two (and possibly multiple) plot units of the same sort, while 10-year-olds should be capable of integrating them in a more satisfactory manner. In fact, this appeared to be the case. Consider the following examples:

Age 8

Mary Jane
Once there was a little girl who was walking in the woods and she saw a helpless little lamb. And then she took it to her father.
But her father said "No," she can't keep it. So, then she built a little house in the woods for it and she kept it there and she brought food for her everyday.
And then her mother and father found out that she was keeping the lamb there. And so, they told her that they should send her to a place where lambs live.

William
Once upon a time there was a cute little lamb and a big, big horse, and every time the lamb got in trouble the horse would come to help him. And one day the horse was helping the farmer and the little sheep got in trouble. So—and the horse didn't come. And so the sheep was in trouble by a wolf. And so the sheep tried to outsmart the wolf and the sheep did because he hid behind a tree and the wolf couldn't find him.
And then he came back and he started to try to find the horse and he couldn't find him. And so, then he was looking around the barn and he saw the horse going off. So then he tried to follow the horse and he was following him around. And then he went to the lake to get a drink and the little sheep said to the horse, "Why weren't you here to help me when I was getting chased by the wolf?"
And the horse said, "Well, because I was helping the farmer". And the horse said, "Well—ah—next time I'll help ya." And that's it.

In each case one can see that the problem–resolution plot structure has been maintained, but also supplemented and considerably enriched. An intervening event or sequence of events has been generated, this time focusing on a complication that impedes resolution of the initial problem. In Mary Jane's story, the father adds to the problem by blocking the little girl's attempt to rescue the lamb. In William's story, immediate resolution of the lamb's problem is also stymied, because the horse fails to perform its usual rescue work. The stories are thus more complex from both a syntactic and a social/semantic point of view.

At 10 years, the stories became increasingly more elaborate. Not only did the number of complicating events increase, but, more important, the intervening complications were integrated more effectively with the original problem and its resolution.

The progression from scripts to plots, then to elaborated plots, and finally to integrated plots suggests that the structural sequence specified by the theory was maintained, albeit at a very general, "representational" level. The progression revealed by the data can be seen as a move from a consolidated primitive structure, A (scripted event sequence), to a new and qualitatively different coordinated unit, A—B (the plot composed of a problem [A] and a resolution [B]), to multiple units of the new sort,

$$A_1—B_1$$
$$|$$
$$A_2—B_2$$

(problem—failed attempt—problem resolution) to multiple units of the new sort that are integrated:

$$A_1—B_1$$
$$x$$
$$A_2—B_2$$

(initial problem (A_1) with solution-attempt (B_1) and subproblem (A_2) with solution attempt (B_2), yielding a plot + subplot structure.)

Of course, a great deal more is clearly going on in children's narrative development than this analysis indicates. Nevertheless, the analysis does capture one aspect of children's narrative development that appears to be general, and that includes knowledge about people's actions and motives as well as knowledge about how their actions and motives are typically rendered in story format.

If this analysis is valid, then according to the general theory in Chapter 2, the rate at which this structural progression takes place should be the same as the rate at which children's working memory grows, that is, from one to four units across the four age groups. As a preliminary test of this hypothesis, children's story productions were scored in terms of the *processing demands* of each type of story structure. Then, these "processing-demand" scores were compared to children's scores on the two working memory measures. Processing demands were analyzed as follows:

1. The simple four-event script structure (setting, initiating event, response, outcome) was treated as the basic story unit and, as such, was presumed to require an interrelational processing capacity of four units. These stories were assigned a score of 0 to indicate that their form was inter-relational, not dimensional.

2. The problem–resolution structure constructed with two basic units was presumed to require a dimensional working memory capacity of two units and was awarded a score of 1 to indicate it was the form constructed in the first substage of the dimensional stage.

3. The structure that includes a complicating event sequence was presumed to require three working memory spaces (one to store the initial problem, one for the complicating event, and one to complete the solution). This structure was awarded a score of 2, as it represented a form presumed typical of substage 2 of the dimensional stage.

4. Finally, any further elaboration that resulted in an integrated structure was presumed to require a processing capacity of one extra unit, for a total load of four. It was assigned a score of 3, to indicate its conformity to the form of the third dimensional substage.

After demonstrating the reliability of this scoring scheme by comparing its application by two independent raters ($r = .92$), repeated measure ANOVAs were conducted on the one- and two-character stories told by the 4- and 6-year-olds and on the two- and three-character stories told by all the children. These analyses revealed that there was a significant age effect, $F(1, 23) = 5.30$, $p < .01$ and $F(2, 48) = 7.70$, $p < .001$, but no significant task effect or Task × Age interaction. When processing capacities were assessed by the Mr. Cucumber Working Memory Measure and the Opposites Test, a positive correlation with structural complexity levels also emerged, $r = 0.39$, $p < .01$ and $r = 0.46$, $p < .01$.

Discussion

From an analytic point of view, the results of the first study were encouraging. It was clear that children's story structure was not affected by the number of characters, contrary to the intuitive belief that generating multi-character stories is more demanding. More important, the results suggested that the age-related growth in dimensional processing capacity from one to four units is paralleled by a change in the complexity of narrative composition that includes both a semantic and a syntactic component. Finally, by hypothesizing a processing demand for each different structure, a first step was made toward constructing a model of structural changes in children's narrative that could be mapped onto age-related increases in processing capacity on the one hand, and to neo-Piagetian theory on the other.

From an empirical point of view, the results were somewhat less impressive. When actively looking for a particular form of structural progression, there is a danger that one may simply "read in" a structure that fits the theory, but does not really provide a valid account of children's narrative development. The data on working memory do not rule out this possibility. Because the general working memory norms for these age groups were already known, the parallel between the structural progression and the growth of working memory—though certainly in accord with the theory—could also be an artifact of the inductive method that was employed. This being the case, it seemed desirable to provide a test of the theory's claims that would fit a more conventional "hypothetico-deductive" model. To this end, three implications of the neo-Piagetian model of narrative were articulated and tested.

A TEST OF THE NEO-PIAGETIAN MODEL

1. *Effect of Explicit Cuing.* According to the general theory, structural patterns in any domain are a function of general developmental limitations, and not an absence of the opportunity to learn what structural form is expected, or what form a finished product should assume. Thus, it was hypothesized that the structural patterns identified in the first experiment would be maintained across a range of story-telling tasks in which more explicit directions were presented concerning the desired form that a story was to take.

2. *Manipulation of Structural Complexity.* According to the general theory, the knowledge structures children can assemble are, to a considerable degree, determined by their working memory capacity. Thus, it was hypothesized that if the processing demand was lowered, and kept within the hypothesized parameters, younger age groups would be able to generate the content typical of more advanced age groups. This lowering of processing demand was accomplished by asking children to tell each half of a story, but not at the same time.

3. *Effects of Instruction.* According to the instructural theory that has grown up in conjunction with the developmental theory (Case, 1978; 1985, chapter 18), processing limitations can often be circumvented via instruction, providing: (a) that the advanced structure is reconceptualized in such a way that it fits with the children's existing mental representation; (b) that the complexity, and the working memory

demand, of the task are kept to an absolute minimum; and (c) that representational and working memory support are continued until the new story structure is consolidated. It was therefore hypothesized that, if these three conditions could be met, normally functioning 6-year-olds could be taught to produce stories that were structurally equivalent to those spontaneously produced by 8-year-olds.

STUDY 2: TESTING THE MODEL

Method

Subjects

Four groups of 20 children each, aged 4, 6, 8, and 10 years, were selected as follows: Teachers identified average to high-average achievers, and then the Vocabulary subtest of the Weschler Intelligence Scale for Children–Revised (Weschler, 1970) was used to verify the teachers' selections. Finally, the Mr. Cucumber Working Memory Test was used to ensure that subjects fell within the hypothesized working memory levels. Of the original 80 children, four 4-year-olds were excluded because they failed to produce stories and one 8-year-old was excluded because his production was not a narrative. No attempt was made to balance for gender. However, the number of boys and girls in each group was approximately equal.

General Procedure

All participants were seen individually in two sessions and asked to tell stories. A sub-group of 6-year-olds attended five additional periods of group instruction (for Session 3). All meetings were tape recorded and transcribed.

SESSION 1: EFFECTS OF EXPLICIT CUEING

To ensure that all age groups knew what was expected of them, the nature of the task was changed to include a specific request that they organize their story around a problem. The new instructions were: "Tell me a story about someone about your age who has a problem they want to solve—you know, make all better. It can be a real problem but it doesn't have to be—just about someone who has a problem they want to solve." In order to ensure that all age groups were also aware of the internal components of an age-typical plot structure, they were given additional cues that explicitly informed them about these components. For example, in a second task, the 6-year-olds were presented with a line drawing of a boy, and the structural components of a typical 8-year-old story and told: "Here's Joe. Joe wanted something really badly. But then something happened so that he couldn't get it. Tell me what he wanted, what got in the way, and what he finally did to get what he wanted."

If a child was unable to comply, the item at the preceding level was presented. If he or she succeeded, the next item higher in the developmental hierarchy was offered. This procedure ensured that every child was explicitly coached on the components of stories one level beyond his or her best spontaneous production and given a reasonable opportunity to exceed it.

Results

In spite of the change in procedure, the results remained much the same. In response to the problem–resolution directions, 4-year-olds typically generated several events depicting a problem, but failed to generate any subsequent events depicting a resolution. At 6 years, children were able to represent a problem and a resolution. Thus, the stories they generated appeared qualitatively different; in effect, they had a simple plot. Eight-year-olds went beyond the 6-year-old form of plot, producing a somewhat more elaborate set of failed attempts to resolve a problem before a resolution was presented. Finally, at 10 years, the children produced multi-faceted problems that necessitated well-planned, gracefully executed, resolutions. Sample stories are presented in Table 10.1.

To test the hypothesis that the majority of stories had maintained the pattern identified in the first study, stories were assigned scores based on the criteria outlined in Fig. 10.1. The reliability of the classification scheme was tested by having the stories scored by an independent rater (Cronbach's alpha = .95). The mean score for each group is presented in Fig. 10.2, along with the predicted levels of performance. A one-way ANOVA yielded a significant group effect, $F(3, 71) = 138.72, p < .001$. A priori non-orthogonal contrasts were computed on adjacent means ($p < .01$). Results demonstrated a monotonic relation, such that Age 4 < Age 6 < Age 8 < Age 10. A trend analysis revealed a significant linear component ($p < .001$) accounting for 85% of the variance; the nonlinear component accounted for 0%.

Finally the mean scores for each age group were plotted against a set of hypothetical values that were based on the assumption that each age group would achieve a mean score equal to that hypothesized by the

TABLE 10.1

Age 4:	Once I'm playing with my daddy with—with a ball and it go on the street.
Age 6:	There once was a girl that didn't know how to read. She went to school and she asked her teacher, "May I try to read?" And the teacher gave her a easy to read book. And then she started to try and read it and then she could read the whole book.
Age 8:	Once upon a time there was a boy named Sean and he didn't know how to get to school. So he asked somebody that went to this school and then watched how to get there. And he went to school and he did his math and then he came home for lunch and then he tried to remember how to get there and he got there. And then he did his work. And then the next morning they were doing work on the road and he couldn't go this way and so he had to go another way and he didn't know how to go. So he had to ask another person and he went that way and he did it and then he came home for lunch and went that way. And then he forgot how to go the other way so he had to go the same way that he usually went and he just went that way. And he went to school and he came back and he was going to his baby sitter's and he wasn't quite sure how to get there. So he had to go to his mom's house and then he came back the same way he usually does and he was late for school, and he asked his mom how to get to school.
Age 10:	This is a story called 'Why Me?'—Um—It's about a girl who's taking ballet. She's quite good at it and in a few weeks—um—she's gonna have to do a ballet exam to get into a company and she's working very hard. And then all of a sudden she gets stuck with diabetes and she's trying to fight it so she can go back to ballet and get into a—and get into a company. And she goes through a lot of things and like every morning she has to have a needle and she has to eat on time and she has to—um—she—ah—has to keep in shape and stuff like that and she has to eat a special amount of food and really watch for a thing called insulin reaction. And if she—what happens is she doesn't eat enough and there's too much—no—there's too much sugar in her body—no—there's not enough sugar in her body and she gets all dizzy and she—um—sometimes she faints and she has to eat sugar right away to regain her strength and stuff. She works hard trying to fight the diabetes and soon she gets out of the hospital and starts up back at ballet. And she's working really hard. And finally its the day of the exam and she walks in the room and she tries the best she can and she's—she—um—finishes the exam. And about two weeks later she gets a note and she's almost made the thing for the company but she didn't. She's an apprentice. And if she works really hard and gets better at her ballet and she will go into the company.

theory for that particular level (i.e., 0 for 4-year-olds, 1 for 6-year-olds, etc.). The deviation of each subject's score from that predicted for his or her age group was also computed. An ANOVA performed on the deviation scores failed to show any significant difference among the mean deviation scores of the four groups, $F(3, 71) = 0.57$, $p > .05$, nor was the grand mean effect significant, $F(1, 71) = 0.07$, $p > .05$. The

Does the story have a problem?
   NO = –1   YES
              |
      Is the problem resolved?
         NO = 0   YES
                   |
         Are there any failed attempts (or impediments) inserted be-
         fore the resolution?
            NO = 1   YES
                      |
            Is one impediment/attempt more significant than the oth-
            ers, with the ultimate resolution having a "well developed"
            or "carefully planned" feeling as a consequence?
               NO = 2   YES
                         |
               Is the "inner world" of the protagonist developed, in
               addition to his or her "outer world", such that a psy-
               chological orientation results?
               NO = 3   YES = 4

FIG.10.1.   Scoring criteria.

straight line obtained by empirical methods thus provided an excellent
fit to the one that was predicted theoretically, with no point lying further
from the line than any other.

In the analysis of the cued-component stories, the same scoring
criteria and statistical procedures were used. The mean scores for each

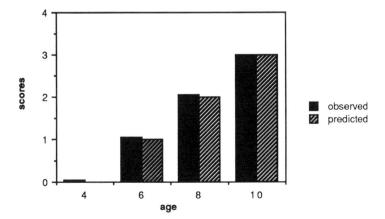

FIG. 10.2.   Predicted and observed mean scores for standard story telling task.

age group are presented in Table 10.2. A standard ANOVA yielded a significant group effect, $F(2, 57) = 63.90$, $p < .01$. An ANOVA performed on the deviation scores showed that there was no significant task effect, $F(1, 56) = 0.73$, $p > .05$, and no task by group interaction, $F(2, 56) = 0.21$, $p > .05$. Thus, explicitly telling children what sort of structure to produce—whether in general or specific terms—had no effect on the story structure they actually generated.

SESSION 2: MANIPULATION OF STRUCTURAL COMPLEXITY

According to the general theory, children who were cued to generate the components of the plot structure one level in advance of their highest spontaneous level were being asked to exceed their hypothesized working memory capacity, not to generate a type of content that was beyond their understanding. In order to validate this assumption, the more advanced structure was segmented into two parts: problem and resolution. According to the theory, this manipulation should reduce the working memory demand by one unit (i.e., one substage), and thus make it possible for children to do what they had failed to in the cued condition, namely, generate content typical of older children on request. To effect the manipulation, 6-year-olds were given an outline of a problem and a complication, accompanied by a line drawing of a girl and told: "Here's Peggy. She was lonely and then something happened that made her really cry a lot. Tell me why she was lonely and what happened *next* to make her cry a lot."

Following this they were asked to produce a solution to a dual-faceted problem: "Here's Janie. Today is her mom's birthday. Janie really wants to get her mom a birthday present but she has no money. Janie went into

TABLE 10.2
Means and Standard Deviations
for the Cued Story Telling
Tasks, 6-, 8-, and 10-year-olds*

	Cued Story	
Age Group	M	SD
6	1.05	0.61
8	1.95	0.52
10	2.85	0.37

*No task was developed for the 4-year-old group.

the family room to think. Then she saw the big mess she and her brother made when they had a pillow fight last night. Boy, would her mom be mad! What can Janie do about getting a present for her mom and about the messy family room?"

Other age groups were given parallel instructions, which broke the structure one level beyond their hypothesized level, into an initial and a final sequence.

Results

As before, scores were assigned to children's productions using the procedure indicated in Fig. 10.1. The results of two one-way ANOVAs revealed a significant age effect for the problem portion, $F(2, 57) = 82.08$, $p < .01$, and the resolution, $F(2, 57) = 25.53$, $p < .01$. ANOVAs performed on the deviation scores showed that, for the problem portion, all groups performed similarly, $F(2, 57) = 1.01$, $p > .05$, and that, when alpha was set at .01, the grand mean showed no significant vertical displacement, $F(1, 57) = 6.84$, $p > .01$. In effect, children described a problem that was one developmental level beyond their original one, thus demonstrating that this aspect of the test—by itself—was within their capabilities. For the resolution portion, the groups did not perform identically, however, $F(2, 57) = 9.61$, $p < .01$. An inspection of the marginal means revealed that 4-year-olds over-performed somewhat while 8-year-olds under-performed slightly. The ω^2 calculation indicated that the "X + 1" model accounted for 69% and 27% of the variance, respectively.

SESSION 3: EFFECTS OF INSTRUCTION

The final step was to attempt to teach children to produce a more advanced structure than they would produced spontaneously, using procedures that were designed to form a conceptual bridge between their current level and the next, and to keep the working memory demand of the learning sequence within their available capacity. The prediction was that children could be taught to tell narratives one level beyond their spontaneous level under these conditions.

Subjects

A subgroup of 6-year-olds who generated prototypic stories for their age group in Session 1 was selected for participation in the instructional phase of the study.

Procedure

In the first session, the component parts of children's original stories were highlighted and represented symbolically as 😲 (for the problem) and 😊 (for the resolution). Children were told that if they wanted to tell stories like those of older children they simply had to insert "something else they tried that didn't work." The experimenter modeled this by inserting a failed attempt in the original stories. The new story structure was represented as 😲 ☒ 😊 . In subsequent sessions, children generated content as the experimenter pointed to each symbol, first for only one component; then, after several sessions, for the entire story. Finally, each child was asked to compose a story without the aid of the cuing symbols (for a more detailed description, see Case & McKeough, 1990).

Results

Pre- and post-instruction stories were again analyzed using the scoring criteria outlined in Fig. 10.1. The results showed that the general structure of all stories increased by one substage after only 5 instructional sessions. That is, 6-year-olds replaced the simple "problem + resolution" plot structure with an expanded structure that included a problem, a failed attempt at resolution, and a successful resolution of the problem.

Discussion

The general notion that guided all 3 parts of the second study was that children's ability to construct a story with a particular type of content or structure would be limited by their level of development, and that both the "syntax," or "grammar," of their narratives and the "semantics," or "social structure," would reflect these limitations. The more specific structural constructs were the ones induced from Study 1: (a) Generating a familiar and temporally stable social episode was hypothesized to be within the capability of a child at the interrelational stage, but generating a second event sequence centering around the story character's intention or desires, which provides a context for a concluding episode, was hypothesized to exceed their capabilities; (b) such two-episode stories were hypothesized to emerge as children enter the dimensional stage, resulting in stories with a simple "plot"; (c) as children move through the dimensional stage, this plot is first elaborated by the insertion of additional "complicating events," so that it bears a closer resemblance to adult action tales in which the hero must first encounter a number of additional difficulties in his attempt to attain a goal, before he finally succeeds; (d) finally, by the age of 10, these intervening events can be planned out in advance, and integrated with the initial problem in such a fashion that a recognizable literary form begins to emerge, with a subplot that is related to the major plot in some fashion.

In order to test the robustness of these structural forms and the general mechanism presumed to underlie their development, a second study was conducted. This study showed that even when 4-year-old children were explicitly directed to produce stories with a simple problem–resolution plot, they failed to do so. In fact, no age group was able to produce plots that were characteristic of higher developmental stages, simply by being told what the elements of those plots were. When children were told the elements of either the first or second *half* of such plots, however, they were successful. These findings imply that it is the coordination of story elements, not an inability to produce a specific type of content, that is at the root of children's difficulty. This explanation is further supported by the results of the instructional study, which showed that children were successful in generating more advanced story structures when an instructional sequence was prescribed that: (a) formed a conceptual "bridge" between children's current level of functioning and the next level in the developmental hierarchy; (b) minimized the processing load of the production process; and (c) provided maximal external support for the coordination process until the new form of response was well consolidated.

It is quite possible that other theoretical frameworks could predict the effects of the instruction, or the difficulties that children had without the support that this instruction provided. For example, the notion that some form of social "scaffolding" is a desirable feature of instruction is a core postulate of Vygotsky's (1962) theory, and might well have led to a similar set of predictions. That other frameworks would also have been able to explain the particular structural forms that were characteristic of each age group at the outset, however, or the exact magnitude of the gain in both the segmented and instructional conditions, seems less likely. The results of the present study thus provide a substantial degree of support for the evolving neo-Piagetian theory that was described in chapters 2 and 7, and the more specific model proposed in the present chapter to operationalize this theory for the domain of children's narrative.

GENERAL DISCUSSION

Although the studies reported here were conceived exclusively as an investigation of children's capabilities for narrative composition, the particular narrative structures that were isolated appear to bear a substantial resemblance to those that were described in previous chapters, in the studies reported by Goldberg-Reitman (chapter 8) and Bruchkowsky (chapter 9). As the reader may recall, Goldberg-Reitman's study was designed to study children's knowledge of their mothers' roles, and Bruchkowsky's study was designed to study their empathic cognition. In both cases, children went from an initial focus that was exclusively on events at 4 years, to a focus that included some mention of the protagonists' internal state (e.g., a desire or goal at 6 years, to a focus that mentioned two or more such internal states in an integrated fashion at 10 years. If one makes the reasonable assumption that a "problem" constitutes an event that causes the story to center around the fulfillment of a simple desire or goal, then the present results may be seen to exhibit the same progression. It follows that children's narrative structures should not be thought of as demanding a unique set of understandings and processing capabilities, that is, ones that apply solely to the storytelling situation. Although the task of telling a story does indeed have specific requirements, it also has a more general requirement as well, one which would appear to implicate a more central conceptual structure. This structure is the one in which children begin to integrate their analyses of an action sequence with a motivational analysis, an achievement that Bruner (1986) refers to as tying together the "landscape of action" with the "landscape of consciousness."

When 6-year-old Jason says that a lamb is trapped and lonely, and that a horse comes along and rescues him, he is not tying together these two landscapes in a very sophisticated manner. Nevertheless, he does appear to be taking the first step in this sort of process, one that will becomes elaborated during subsequent years, according to the same general developmental timetable is revealed as in other content domains, or in other tasks in the domain of social cognition. Children's early narratives may therefore be seen as one of the primary stages on which they play out this emerging awareness of the landscape of consciousness, and come to understand its implications for the landscape of action more fully, using the social and literary forms that their society provides.

Young Children's Awareness of Their Inner World: A Neo-Structural Analysis of the Development of Intrapersonal Intelligence

Sharon Griffin
Clark University

By dividing reality into two parts, one can posit an external world of objects, actions, and events, and an internal world of feelings, desires, and judgmental attitudes toward these objects and events. Following an established tradition, these latter, inner, experiences can be referred to collectively as *intentional states*[1] (Brentano, 1960; Feigl, 1958; Olson, in press; Searle, 1983), and children's understanding of these inner states can be called *intrapersonal intelligence* (Gardner, 1983). A diverse set of findings suggests that children's understanding of intentional states changes dramatically between the ages of 4 and 6 years, and that a further change takes place between the ages of 6 and 8. Consider the following evidence.

Children as young as 3 readily acknowledge the experiences of being happy, sad, mad, and afraid, and describe these experiences in terms of observable physical characteristics, that is, by reference to actions and events. Older children, in contrast, describe these same feeling experiences in terms of psychological traits, that is, by reference to one or more intentional states (Harter, 1982). When one pursues children's understanding of feelings further, by asking where a feeling begins and where it resides, 3- to 4-year-olds locate happiness and fear in the action or object component of an event; 6-year-old's, in contrast, locate the same feelings in the self, which is clearly appreciated as distinct from both objects and actions (Fitzpatrick, 1985).

A parallel pattern appears to be present in children's understanding

---

[1]Intention is used here in the sense of reference, as opposed to the narrower sense of purpose or resolution.

of a class of judgmental attitudes collectively referred to as moral values. Summarizing a substantial body of evidence, Kohlberg (1976) suggested that moral value for the 4-year-old resides in external, quasi-physical happenings; in bad acts rather than in persons or standards. For the 6-year-old, moral value resides in performing good or right roles and in satisfying the expectancies of others (i.e., in the subjective world of intentional states). For the 8-year-old, moral value resides not only in conformity to shared standards but also in avoiding any violation of the will or rights of others.

A different set of findings gives us some idea of how intentional states are incorporated into children's understanding of their mothers' behavior. When Goldberg-Reitman (1984) asked children to describe what a mother would do in response to an event (e.g., a child falling off a roof) and to provide an explanation for their answer, she found no age differences in children's ability to predict an appropriate behavioral response (e.g., Mommy will catch her child) but significant age differences in the explanations provided. Four-year-olds justified a mother's action by exclusive reference to the antecedent event (e.g., because the child is falling); 6-year-olds justified a mother's action by reference to an intentional state (e.g., because the mother doesn't want her child to get hurt); and 10-year-olds justified the same actions by reference to two intentional states (e.g., because the mother loves her child and doesn't want her to get hurt).

Yet another perspective on children's intentional state understanding has been provided by Harter (1983), who asked 3- to 9-year-old children if they could experience two feeling states, happiness and sadness, at the same time. She found that 3- to 4-year-olds denied the possibility; 6-year-olds admitted the possibility, but claimed the feelings could be experienced only in a temporal sequence; and 8-year-olds acknowledged that the feeling states could occur simultaneously. In a similar vein, Gnepp (1985) found that 4-year-olds denied that one event (a small dog approaching) could have more than one emotional implication, but 6-year-olds readily acknowledged that this event could elicit happiness as well as fear.

Considered in conjunction, these findings suggest that children conceptualize both feelings and judgmental attitudes quite differently at these age levels. Two questions may therefore be raised: (a) How can these findings be explained and generalized?; and (b) How can they be related to developmental findings in other domains? To answer these questions, I will mention some additional findings, and advance a model of intrapersonal development that is congruent with the theory that was outlined in chapter 2, as supplemented by the modifications proposed in the second section of this volume. Finally, I will report a series of studies that were designed to test the model.

TOWARD A STRUCTURAL MODEL OF INTRAPERSONAL INTELLIGENCE

With intentional states defined as attitudes toward events, it can be suggested that any model of the development of intrapersonal intelligence must consider the forms of knowledge that are constructed for intentional attitudes and for events at each age level under consideration, and the way these two knowledge constituents are related in children's thought at the same age levels. When a 4-year-old's understanding is considered with respect to each of these structural components, and the available evidence is reviewed, the following picture emerges.

At 4 years of age, children's understanding of "events" extends well beyond a single event. They are able to connect four or five events in an "and–then" format and produce well-consolidated scripts depicting event sequences in their everyday lives (McKeough, this volume, chapter 10; Nelson, 1978; Nelson & Gruendel, 1981). The first-order temporal relations established between events appear also to be reciprocal in nature. Four-year-olds are thus able to predict a consequent event (e.g., a mother will catch her child) on the basis of an antecedent event (the child is falling) or explain the latter event by reference to the former (Goldberg-Reitman, this volume, chapter 8). Age level knowledge of event sequences can thus be modeled as a series of nodes (representing discrete events) and a series of two-way relations between them.

When one specific event is presented to a 4-year-old, independently of the sequence in which it is embedded, the child is able to relate this event to one or more discrete intentional states. As an earlier study in the present research program showed (Bruchkowsky, 1984; this volume, chapter 9), children of this age are able to assign the feelings of "happy" and "sad" to events that are instances of polar event categories (e.g., getting/not getting a present; see also Reiss & Cunningham, 1988). Similarly, they are able to assign the judgments of "good"/"bad," "want"/ "don't want," "like"/"don't like" to events that are instances of other polar event categories (Bretherton, Fritz, Zahn-Waxler, & Ridgeway, 1986). The reciprocal nature of these first-order, event–intention relationships is demonstrated by children's ability to produce an appropriate event as a definition for "happy," "sad," "good," and "bad" (Harter, 1982; Griffin, 1988) and to explain an event in a distributive justice task (e.g., giving self the biggest reward) by reference to an intentional state (e.g., "because I want it"; Damon, 1973; DeMersseman, 1976).

Two additional findings suggest that children's understanding of intentions at this age extends beyond a two-way event–intention relationship and encompasses a second intentional state as well. Bruchkowsky (1984; this volume, chapter 9) found that 4-year old children were able to attribute the feelings of "happy" and "sad" to events on the basis of whether the character got the present that she wanted (i.e., a bike) or got something else instead (i.e., a doll). Similarly, Gnepp (1985) found that 4-year-olds were able to assign happiness to an event in which "Mark got grass for dinner" when they were previously told that "Mark lives in Tree-land and eats grass whenever he can." Each of these studies suggest that 4-year-olds appreciate the relationship between a judgmental attitude (wanting, liking), an event (getting what I want or like), and a feeling state (happy). Age-level understanding of intentions can thus be modeled as a set of three nodes representing polar instances of these three categories, and two-way relationships between them. The resulting age-level intentional structure is depicted graphically in the top panel of Fig. 11.1, beside the corresponding event-structure.

When the organization of 4-year-old intrapersonal thought is considered, the question that naturally arises is whether 4-year-olds coordinate their understanding of event-sequences with their understanding of intentions. As has already been suggested, the available evidence suggests that they do not. Whereas 4-year-olds are perfectly capable of assigning intentions to isolated events, they do not use their knowledge of intentions to explain an event-sequence such as "a child is falling and mommy moves to catch her" (Goldberg-Reitman, 1984; this volume, chapter 8). When an event-sequence is presented to 4-year-olds, and an emotional attribution is requested for one event in the sequence, children at this age assign emotion on the basis of the single event, without reference to the intentional states associated with the consequent or antecedent event. In contrast to older children, preschoolers assign happiness to a character who "steals a ball" and "nobody sees him" (Barden, Zelko, Duncan, & Masters, 1980) and also to a character who "sees her friend on the playground" when that friend has stated in a previous event, "I don't like you anymore" (Gould, 1984).

At the 4-year-old level, children's understanding of feelings appears to be bound to the single event to such an extent that they claim the emotion resides within the event itself (Fitzpatrick, 1985). Whereas 4-year-olds appear to have constructed several discrete intentional structures (as well as several discrete event-sequence structures), they do not demonstrate an ability to coordinate two such structures in order to admit the possibility of feeling both happy and sad at one time (Harter, 1982), or to recognize that one event may have more than one emotional implication (Gnepp, 1985). On the basis of these findings, and consistent with the general theory outlined in the present volume, it was hypothesized that 4-year-olds would be able to entertain, at any one time, only one of the several knowledge structures that have been constructed, independently, during the interrelational stage. It was hypothesized

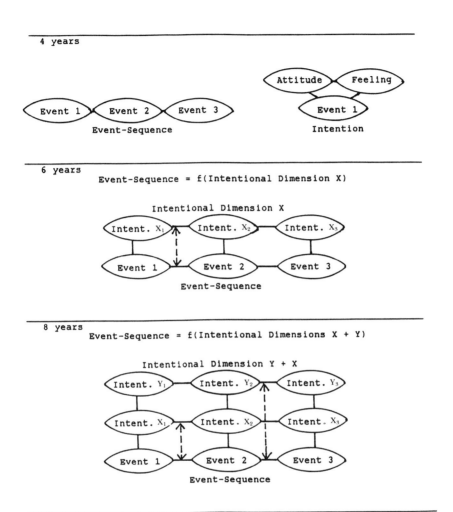

FIG. 11.1. Hypothesized knowledge structure underlying social understanding at different ages.

further that the ability to coordinate two such structures into a super-ordinate structure would appear in 6-year-old thought.

Using the same basic notion, 6-year-old intrapersonal thought was characterized as the coordination and hierarchic integration of two knowledge structures, the intentional structure and the event-sequence structure, which were present independently at the 4-year-old level. The higher-order structure constructed in the integration process can be modeled as: a set of nodes representing a sequence of events; a set of nodes representing the intentions associated with each event in the sequence; a set of second-order relations constructed between the intention nodes; and a set of second-order relations constructed between the event sequence itself and the sequence of intentions that parallels it. This structure is proposed as a model of 6-year-old intrapersonal understanding and is depicted graphically in the middle panel of Fig. 11.1

What are the implications of the proposed structural organization for 6-year-olds' understanding of their own internal states? First, this structure permits children to consider simultaneously, not only the relations between two distinct events (e.g., "I got a truck for my birthday and then my brother broke it"), but also the intentional states that are associated with each of these events (happy and then sad). One can expect, therefore, that 6-year-olds will admit the possibility of experiencing two emotions at one time, in a temporal sequence (as found by Harter, 1982) and will recognize that one event can have two emotional implications (as found by Gnepp, 1985).

Second, this structure permits children to recognize that intentional states vary along an event continuum, that intentional states are themselves related along an intentional continuum, and that happiness, for example, is related to sadness as a function of the relations between events. With this understanding, children should no longer conceptualize an intentional state, such as happiness, as a discrete feeling experience that is localized in a particular event. Happiness should now be conceptualized as a particular position along a continuum of intentions that spans two polar categories, happy and sad. Happiness should now be a function, not of an isolated event, but of the set of relations that obtain between events and their separate intentional implications.

When intentional understanding assumes a "dimensional" form, and is constituted by a set of relations between discrete intentional states and a set of relations between events, one can expect that any particular intentional state will be differentiated from the event in which it was formerly embedded. One can also expect that 6-year-olds will attribute intentional states to a higher order source. Given the beliefs of our own culture, it appears quite reasonable that one set of intentional states (i.e., feelings) will now be localized within the self, as found by Fitzpatrick (1985), and another set of intentional states (i.e., moral judgments) will now be localized in the internal world of others, or in the "expectancies" of others, as found by Kohlberg (1976).

This same structural organization should also permit children to use their intentional knowledge as a means to predict and explain the relations between events. It should permit them, in short, to engage in intentional thought. One can understand, therefore, why 6-year-old explanations for event-sequences should be couched in intentional terms

(Goldberg-Reitman, this volume, chapter 8) and why 6-year-olds, in contrast to 4-year-olds, should explain the action-sequences of walking, kicking, seeing, and hearing (Johnson & Wellman, 1982) and their own game-play behaviors (Griffin, 1985) by reference to mental states.

So far, the proposed 6-year-old structure has been discussed in very general terms, and the examples have suggested that children at this age level have constructed a higher order understanding of several intentional states (e.g., feeling states, judgment states). This structure can be further clarified by considering the age-level postulates of the general theory presented in chapter 2. In this theory, 6-year-old thought is labeled unidimensional, suggesting that only one domain-specific dimension can be considered at any one time. Eight-year-old thought, in contrast, is labeled bidimensional, suggesting that two domain-specific dimensions can be considered and coordinated simultaneously.

Using these theoretical characterizations, it may be hypothesized that 6-year-olds will consider only one intentional dimension at a time and the one considered will be the one that is most salient in the event-sequence situation. Because a 4-year-old is able to coordinate a single event with a feeling state and a judgmental attitude (e.g., want, like), it appears reasonable to propose that a 6-year-old will coordinate an entire event-sequence with a dimension of feeling *or* a dimension of judgment, but not both simultaneously. At the 8-year level, it may be hypothesized that two such intentional dimensions will be simultaneously considered and coordinated, as depicted in the bottom panel of Fig. 11.1.

There is some support for these age-level hypotheses in the findings that have already been mentioned. Recall that Goldberg-Reitman (chapter 8) found that 6-year-olds referred to one intentional dimension (e.g., a mother's judgmental attitudes) in the explanations they provided for a mother's behavior. Ten-year-olds (the next age group in the sample) referred to two intentional dimensions (i.e., a mother's judgmental attitudes and her feelings), in a coordinated fashion. Similarly, Kohlberg (1976) found that 6-year-olds explained moral-choice event-sequences by reference to "the expectancies of others" and 8-year-olds explained the same event-sequences by referring, additionally, to "avoidance of violation of the will or rights of others." In each of these findings, one distinct intentional standard appeared to be present in the responses of the 6-year-old group, and two coordinated intentional standards in the responses of the 8- to 10-year-old group.

In summary, the developmental model proposes three levels of intrapersonal understanding, for three substages of development. Each level is formally consistent with the age-level postulates of the general theory presented in chapter 2, and with the more specific conceptual structures proposed in chapters 4 through 10. The model also appears to account reasonably well for a diverse set of findings in the social domain and thus to offer an explanatory framework for unifying the results of several different research investigations. Several implications for intrapersonal understanding across this age range can also be derived from this model. Three that seemed most salient to me were formalized into a set of research predictions, which are presented in the next section.

Research Predictions

First, the model that has just been outlined proposes that children conceptualize intentional states quite differently at three different age levels. It is reasoned that, if the model has captured salient aspects of age-level intrapersonal thought, then the explanations children provide for four specific intentional states (happiness, sadness, goodness, and badness) should change systematically with age, in a manner consistent with the proposed structures. Specifically, it was predicted that 4-year-olds would explain these states by reference to an adjacent node in the proposed 4-year-old knowledge structure, and that happiness and sadness would be explained by reference to an event or a judgmental attitude and goodness and badness would be explained by reference to an event or a feeling state. Because the event node appears to be salient in 4-year-old intrapersonal thought, it was predicted that a majority of 4-year-olds would explain all four intentional states by exclusive reference to a behavioral event.

In the proposed 6-year-old structure, intentional states are interrelated along a higher order intentional dimension, which is itself functionally related to an event-sequence. It was predicted, therefore, that 6-year-olds would explain happiness, sadness, goodness, and badness by explicit reference to an intentional dimension and its functional relationship to an event-sequence. This reference was predicted to assume a full dimensional form (e.g., " 'happy' means my feelings turn from blue to happy because I got a doll I didn't have before") or a partially articulated dimensional form (e.g., " 'happy' means I feel really joyful when I get to play in tents"). Both forms depict an intentional state as an attitude toward an event. This awareness was thus expected to characterize 6-year-old responses and to be lacking in the explanations provided at the 4-year-old level.

In the proposed 8-year-old structure, intentional states are interrelated along two higher order intentional dimensions, which are themselves both functionally related to an event-sequence. It was predicted, therefore, that 8-year-olds would explain happiness, sadness, goodness, and badness by explicit reference to two intentional dimensions and their functional relationship to each other and to an event sequence. On the basis of previous findings, it was expected that the particular intentional dimensions used in 6- and 8-year-old explanations might vary across intentional states, with the feeling states of "happy" and "sad" being explained by reference to a feeling dimension and/or a judgment dimension (e.g., self's wants, likes) and the judgment states of "good" and "bad" being explained by reference to a judgment dimension (e.g., other's wants, likes) and/or a second focus on this dimension (e.g., avoidance of violation of the rights of others).

Second, the model proposes that 6- and 8-year-old children differentiate intentional states from the events in which they were formerly embedded and locate these states in a higher-order source. It was predicted, therefore, that 6- and 8-year-olds, in contrast to 4-year-olds, would locate not only happiness and sadness within the self (as found by Fitzpatrick, 1985, for 6-year-olds), but would also locate goodness and badness there.

Finally, the model proposes three levels of structural complexity and claims that these levels are formally consistent with the general forms and age-level norms postulated by neo-Piagetian theory. It was reasoned that, if the proposed levels really did fit the theory, then they should be formally consistent with levels of structural complexity in other domains for which a good theoretical fit had already been demonstrated. It was predicted, therefore, that the complexity of children's performance in the intrapersonal domain (scored by means of the proposed model) would be consistent, at each age level, with the complexity of their performance in the task of drawing (scored with Dennis's model, as outlined in chapter 13) and telling a story (scored with McKeough's model, as outlined in chapter 10).

Method

Sixty children from an urban, middle to upper-middle class population were individually administered a battery of tasks designed to assess the above predictions. The population included 20 four-year-olds (mean age = 4.0 yr), 20 six-year-olds (mean age = 6.0 yr), and 20 eight-year-olds (mean age = 8.1 yr), with each age group evenly divided by sex.

Children's explanations for four intentional states were elicited by providing some facilitating props (e.g., a Cabbage Patch doll who needs to know what the child knows) and by asking a set of three questions with respect to each intentional state: "What does it mean to be happy (sad, a good girl or boy, a bad girl or boy)? What else can it mean? What is happening when you are happy (sad, a good girl/boy, a bad girl/boy)?"

Children's responses to these questions (and all following tasks) were tape-recorded and transcribed verbatim. Intentional state understanding was operationally defined as the child's pooled responses to the three questions in the set and was scored in the following manner.

A score of 0 was assigned if the response production conformed to the predictions for 4-year-old intrapersonal thought. Thus, if a child referred exclusively to observable behavioral events or objects (e.g., " 'happy' means a birthday party, ice-cream, a cake; 'sad' means you cry—you go to bed and you sort of go under the covers and you sort of hide yourself; 'good' means you get treats, lots of treats"), he or she received a score of 0. Alternatively, if a child referred exclusively to an intentional state without mention of a related behavioral event (e.g., " 'bad' means you're angry, you're feeling sad") a score of 0 was also awarded.

A score of 1 was assigned if the response production conformed to the predictions for 6-year-old intrapersonal thought. Specifically, a score of 1 was assigned if the production referred jointly to a behavioral event and one of the following intentional dimensions: (a) feeling states (e.g., " 'happy' means *feelings.* I *feel* happy when I have a friend over to play with"), (b) personal judgments (e.g., " 'happy' means you're doing stuff *that you like* to do—when you go for holidays where you really like to be"), (c) other's judgments (e.g., "Being bad means you do everything *your mother doesn't want;* you throw a tantrum; you throw your clothes all over the room"), (d) social judgments (e.g., "'happy' means something *nice* happens; you have a birthday party; you get presents"; " 'being bad' means you just do something *wrong;* that's all: like being mean to your little sister").

A score of 2 was assigned if the response production conformed to the predictions for 8-year-old intrapersonal thought, that is, if the response referred jointly to a behavioral event and to two distinct intentional dimensions. One form such responses took was the coordination of an event with a feeling state and a judgmental attitude (e.g., " 'sad' means when you do something *wrong,* you *feel* so sad"), Another form such responses took was the coordination of an event with two judgmental attitudes that were categorically distinct (e.g., "being good means I'm doing *what I'm supposed to do,* like helping my Mom, and I'm not fighting or doing anything *I'm not supposed to do*"). A random sample of these response productions was scored by a second rater who was blind to the ages of the children, and interrater agreement was found on 58 of the 60 productions scored by both raters. (For a more detailed description of the scoring criteria for these tasks, see Griffin, 1988.)

The second prediction was assessed by asking children a fourth question that followed immediately after each of the question sets already described, namely: "When you are doing that activity [child's own example], where does the [happiness, sadness, goodness, badness] come from?" Responses were scored for provision of an *internal source* whenever the intentional state was located within the physical or psychological self (e.g., "it comes from my heart/my brain/my thoughts/my feelings"). Responses were scored for provision of an *external source* whenever the intentional state was located in an object, an action, or a bodily part that is available for external observation (e.g., "it comes from the sky, from my cake, from playing, from seeing myself in the mirror, from the tears"). The remaining responses fell into an "I don't know where it comes from" category.

The third prediction was assessed by administering Dennis's drawing task (this volume, chapter 13) and McKeough's story-telling task (this volume, chapter 10) to all children in the sample. Because this prediction addresses an issue that is the subject of a later chapter in this volume, the results of this component of the study are not reported in the present chapter, but are reported instead in chapter 15, where the issue of cross-domain synchrony in children's development is dealt with in a broader context.

The task-battery was presented to the subjects, individually, in one or two testing sessions, depending on the child's attention span. Older children typically completed the tasks in one testing session, whereas younger children often required two sessions; these were spaced less than a week apart. The order of task presentation was constant, with the happiness tasks given first, followed by the sadness tasks, the goodness tasks, the badness tasks, the drawing task, and the story-telling task.

Results

The "Meaning" Tasks

Table 11.1 presents the mean scores achieved by the three age groups on the set of intrapersonal tasks which requested a meaning for being happy, sad, good, and bad. It is apparent that each group performed close to age-level expectations on each task. Although the performance of the 4-year-old group is somewhat higher than the theoretical expectation of 0.0 and the performance of the 8-year-old group is somewhat lower than the theoretical expectation of 2.0, both of these deviations can be accounted for by the presence of floor and ceiling effects in the scoring categories provided for each task.

Before turning to a statistical analysis of these results, it may be useful to examine what they signify by describing them in operational terms. At a general level, they indicate that children's explanations for the four

TABLE 11.1
Mean scores of three age groups on the
meanings of four intrapersonal states
(standard deviations are in brackets).

Intrapersonal State	Age (years)		
	4	6	8
Happy	0.25 (.5)	1.10 (.5)	1.95 (.2)
Sad	0.25 (.4)	1.10 (.5)	1.80 (.4)
Good	0.35 (.5)	1.05 (.2)	1.90 (.3)
Bad	0.35 (.5)	1.05 (.4)	1.80 (.4)

intrapersonal states became systematically more complex with age. More specifically, they indicate that the 4-year-olds typically included only one of the domain-specific knowledge constituents that were jointly present, in a coordinated fashion, in 6-year-old productions. Six-year-olds, in contrast, typically included only two of the three knowledge constituents that were jointly present, in a coordinated fashion, in 8-year-old productions. The particular knowledge constituents included at each age level varied across tasks in specific content. However, in terms of general content, age-level responses conformed, in each case, to the content categories predicted by the model and operationalized in the scoring criteria.

The systematic increase in complexity with age is illustrated in the following summaries of typical age-level responses on each task.[2] (To highlight the knowledge constituents that were unique to each age level, and that differentiated one age-level from the next, the constituents that were common to all age-levels—by virtue of the retention of lower-order constituents in higher-order knowledge structures—have been omitted.)

• Being happy was defined as an external action *performed by the self* (e.g., playing) by 4-year-olds, as an internal feeling state (e.g., experiencing a positive feeling) by 6-year-olds, and as a coordinated feeling-judging state (e.g., liking something and experiencing a feeling in relation to this attitude) by 8-year-olds.
• Being sad was defined as an external action *performed by another* (e.g., mommy leaving) by 4-year-olds, as an internal feeling *or* judging state (e.g., experiencing a negative feeling *or* not liking something) by 6-year-olds, and as a coordinated feeling-judging state (e.g., not liking something and experiencing a feeling in relation to this attitude) by 8-year-olds.

---

[2]Although these responses typify those given by the majority of children, they do not exhaust the range of responses produced and scored at the same scoring level.

- Being good was defined as an external action that was *referred to the self* (e.g., doing my work, getting a treat) by 4-year-olds, as a value state or judgment (e.g., being nice) by 6-year-olds, and as two coordinated value states or judgments (e.g., being nice and never being bad) by 8-year-olds.
- Being bad was defined as an external action that was *referred to the self* (e.g., breaking something, getting a spanking) by 4-year-olds, as a value state or judgment (e.g., being mean) by 6-year-olds, and as two coordinated value states or judgments (e.g., being mean and not being obedient) by 8-year-olds.

As is apparent in each developmental progression described above, intrapersonal feelings and values were defined as physical behavioral activities by the majority of 4-year-olds, as unidimensional intentional states by the majority of 6-year-olds, and as bidimensional intentional states by the majority of 8-year-olds. Moreover, as indexed in the scoring levels achieved by the two older age groups, when one or more intentional dimensions were mentioned in the response production, they were typically accompanied by, and related to, events or event-sequences.

Figure 11.2 presents these results in graphic form, in relation to the

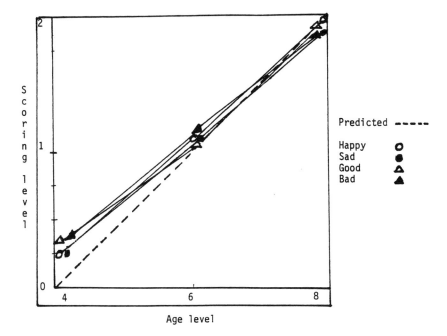

FIG. 11.2. Mean scores achieved by 3 age-groups on 4 tasks in relation to the predicted developmental progression.

predicted developmental progression. For each of the four sets of data displayed in this figure, a log-linear analysis indicated: (a) a significant Age × Level interaction ($p < .01$); (b) a significant Age by Level interaction, when this interaction was partitioned into the diagonal component ($p < .01$); and (c) a non-significant residual interaction. The results of the log-linear analyses indicate significant differences between the three age groups and non-significant deviations from the predicted diagonal form, on each task.

The results discussed so far indicate that the performance of three age groups was highly consistent in level of structural complexity across the four distinct intrapersonal tasks. The next question that was addressed was whether this consistency was present only in the group means, or whether it was maintained in individual subjects as well. Table 11.2 presents the pattern of performance of each individual child in the sample, at three age and complexity levels, for each task. This graphic display indicates that the majority of children responded at the predicted level on the majority of tasks and suggests that the cross-task synchrony found for age-level *groups* of children was also present in the performance of *individual* children within these groups. No child demonstrated a cross-task fluctuation that was greater than one scoring level and no sex differences were found.[3]

The "Source" Tasks

An analysis of age-level responses to the "source" questions indicated that an internal source was provided by a majority of 8-year-olds in the sample for each intentional state assessed (ranging from 85% to 100%), by a weaker majority of 6-year-olds in the sample (ranging from 60% to 75%), and by a minority of 4-year-olds (25% to 35%). The remaining 4-year-olds provided either an external source (35%) or an "unknown" source (35%). The results of a log-linear analysis indicated a significant interaction ($p < .01$) between Age and provision of an Internal Source for each intentional state assessed. When partitioned, this interaction was found to conform to a diagonal form, across three age levels for goodness and badness, and across two age levels (4 to 6 years) for happiness and sadness. These results support the prediction that 6- and 8-year-olds, in contrast to 4-year-olds, attribute happiness, sadness, goodness, and badness to an internal source.

When children's responses to the source task were compared to the meanings they provided for the four intentional states, it was found that 74% of the children who explained these states by exclusive reference to

---

[3]A more detailed analysis of these results is presented in chapter 15, where the issue of cross-task synchrony is discussed in greater depth.

TABLE 11.2
Pattern of performance of each individual child in the sample on 4 intrapersonal tasks

Level	Intrapersonal State	4 years	6 years	8 years
2	HAPPY		· · ·	· · · · · · · · · · · · · · · · · · ·
	SAD	·	· · · ·	· · · · · · · · · · · · · · · · · · ·
	GOOD		·	· · · · · · · · · · · · · · · · · ·
	BAD	·	·	· · · · · · · · · · · · · · · · · ·
1	HAPPY	· · ·	· · · · · · · · · · · · · ·	·
	SAD	· · · · ·	· · · · · · · · · · · · · ·	· · ·
	GOOD	· · · · ·	· · · · · · · · · · · · · ·	· · ·
	BAD	· · · · ·	· · · · · · · · · · · · · ·	· ·
0	HAPPY	· · · · · · · · · · · · · · ·	· ·	
	SAD	· · · · · · · · · · · · · · ·	· · ·	
	GOOD	· · · · · · · · · · · · ·	·	
	BAD	· · · · · · · · · · · · ·	·	
	Ss	ABCDEFGHIJKLMNOPQRST	ABCDEFGHIJKLMNOPQRST	ABCDEFGHIJKLMNOPQRST
	Sex	f f m m f m f f f m f m f m f m m f m	f m m f m f m m m f f f f f m m m m	f m m m f m m m m f f f m f f f

a behavioral event also attributed these states to an external source or an unknown source. In contrast, 77% of the children who explained these states by reference to an intentional dimension also attributed these states to an internal source. This degree of cross-task stability contributes to the confidence that can be placed in children's verbal "meaning" productions as an index of their awareness of their inner world.

Discussion

Children's responses to the tasks employed in the present study provided consistent support for the age-level predictions of the model. This support was manifested both in the content of children's productions, with intentional state information increasingly represented with age, and in their structure, with intentional state information integrated with behavioral event information at the 6-year-old level and becoming increasingly complex with age.

To avoid penalizing children for language immaturity, the scoring criteria permitted a child to obtain a score at any level with a "bare-bones" response (i.e., one which met the criteria for the postulated structure in a minimally articulated form). A number of children, however, produced more complete responses, which mapped directly on to the full structure postulated by the model. At the 6-year-old level, for example, several children defined happiness (or sadness, etc.) by reference to a *continuum* of internal states and its relationship to a *sequence* of events (e.g., "happiness means, well, like I'm all alone and then my feelings turn from sad to happy when I get to have a friend over"). Responses such as these lend support to a suggestion that is implicit in the model: that the postulated structures are actually inside children's heads, and are used by them to make sense of their internal and external worlds.

It is possible, however, that the findings reflect age-level language competence to a greater extent than they reflect age-level understanding. For example, the age-level increases in complexity could be attributed to older children producing lengthier verbal responses, and thus having greater opportunities for demonstrating increased complexity. To investigate this possibility, the median number of words produced by each age group on each set of tasks was computed. The results (see Table 11.3) revealed no significant differences between the 4- and the 6-year-old groups on any task. On two of the four tasks, the median number of words produced was actually less for the 6-year-olds. Substantial differences were found, however, between the 6- and 8-year-olds, with the older group producing almost twice as many words on the majority of tasks.

TABLE 11.3

Median number of words produced by three age
groups on intrapersonal tasks (Range is in brackets.)

Intrapersonal State	Age (years)		
	4	6	8
Happy	18 (5–73)	16 (6–30)	32 (13–72)
Sad	17 (4–50)	19 (4–56)	28 (12–52)
Good	13 (4–62)	17 (5–51)	34 (15–98)
Bad	23 (4–82)	18 (4–45)	34 (12–82)

To control for length of response, a post hoc analysis of the results was conducted. A subset of 5 response protocols (out of the 20 in each sample) was selected from each age group for each task, such that the responses of the subgroups would be identical in number of words produced; the number used for this selection was 18 words (i.e., the modal number of words produced by the total population). This subset of data was rated by a third rater who was blind to the ages of the children. The results of this analysis are presented in Table 11.4. With two minor exceptions, the mean scores obtained by this rater were identical to the scores obtained when the same protocols were coded by the first and second raters. These scores were also in close conformity to the age-level scores achieved by the total sample, as shown in Table 11.1. Although this analysis does not exhaust the number of language parameters that could conceivably influence age-level performance, it

TABLE 11.4

Mean scores by third rater of three age-level
subgroups (equated for length of response) on
four intrapersonal tasks. (Scores of second
rater are in brackets.)

Intrapersonal State	Age (years)		
	4	6	8
Happy	0.2 (0.4)	1.2 (1.2)	2.0 (2.0)
Sad	0.2 (0.2)	1.0 (1.0)	1.8 (2.0)
Good	0.4 (0.4)	1.0 (1.0)	1.8 (1.8)
Bad	0.2 (0.2)	1.2 (1.2)	1.6 (1.6)

Note. Each subgroup was comprised of 5 children whose response length was closest to 18 words (i.e., the modal number of words for the total population).

does indicate that the increased complexity of the older children's responses cannot be attributed to verbal fluency.

A second issue that is raised by the present findings is the consistency of children's performance across the four tasks. Although this consistency was predicted by the model, it contradicts subject-matter distinctions that are typical in the literature and requires an explanation. In the context of the present theory, an explanation of this finding is readily available. Consistent with the theory, the postulates of the model are couched at the level of deep structure and *general* domain content. Surface differences in content were largely ignored in the age-level scoring criteria: For example, intentional state information was scored in children's responses when reference was made to any one of several intentional dimensions. Had the focus of the model's predictions been more specific, in terms of surface content and/or structure, the results would undoubtedly have identified differences rather than consistencies in children's cross-task performance.

Given the strength of these findings, it appears that the level of generality struck in the present study was appropriate. For a limited set of intentional states, it appears to have captured a salient and general component of children's intrapersonal understanding. Although the study addressed only a limited set of the model's implications, its findings suggest that further investigation of the model would be a fruitful avenue for future research.

12

Testing for the Presence of a Central Social Structure: Use of the Transfer Paradigm

Anne McKeough
University of Calgary

In the previous chapters in this section, tasks have been described that have very different surface features. In spite of their different surface appearance, however, it has been suggested that they all require the same underlying structure for solution. This structure is one that encodes a sequence of social events, on the one hand, and the psychological "intentions" that motivate these events, on the other (i.e., judgments, feelings, desires)—and ties them into a single coherent entity. The problem with which the present chapter is concerned is whether this "intentional" structure plays a role in the development of children's social thought that is similar to the one played by the "dimensional" structure in the development of their quantitative thought. Recall that, in Section II, several different quantitative tasks were described that also varied widely in their surface features, yet shared a common underlying structure. As proof of this structure's developmental significance, it was shown that—when children are trained in the structure—they spontaneously begin to function at a higher level on all the quantitative tasks for which the structure is relevant. It follows that, if the intentional structure plays a similar role in children social-cognitive development, children trained in it should show a similar pattern of spontaneous improvement on all the tasks that have been described in the present section.

To train any structure thoroughly, it is useful first to describe the components of which it is comprised. Such a description is provided in Fig. 12.1. Following standard practice, the structure is defined in terms of its components and the relations among them. Concepts are depicted

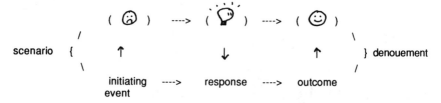

Fig. 12.1. Components of story structure typical of 6-year-olds.

at the structure's nodes, and the relations are represented by directional arrows. The gist of the diagram is as follows: By the age of 6, an initiating event is seen by children as causing internal disequilibrium of some sort, which sets a balance-restoring initiative or plan in motion. This plan is then translated into activity, which yields a resolution. As a result, affective equilibrium is restored. The intentional structure thus represents a set of causal relations between the external world of physical states and actions, on the one hand, and the internal world of feelings and mental states, on the other. Bruner (1986) has labeled these two strands the *landscape of action* and the *landscape of consciousness,* respectively, and this terminology would appear to capture the flavor of 6-year-old thought quite well. In the intentional structure, one could say that the landscape of consciousness is both differentiated from and coordinated with, the landscape of action.

If these two landscapes are present in a coordinated form in the thought of 6-year-olds, it follows from Case's (1985) theory that they should also be present in some more isolated and perhaps less differentiated form in the thought of 4-year-olds. That 4-year-olds are familiar with the landscape of action and represent it in scripted terms is clear from studies on their knowledge of narrative (McKeough, 1984; this volume, chapter 10; Nelson & Gruendel, 1981) and their knowledge of their mother's behavior (Goldberg-Reitman, this volume, chapter 8). That they are also aware of the landscape of consciousness is clear from studies on empathy (Bruchkowsky, this volume, chapter 9) and from current work on preschooler's theory of mind (Astington et al., 1989). Under certain experimental conditions, then, it is clear that 4-year-olds are capable of both sorts of thought, at least in rudimentary form.

Nevertheless, 4-year-olds fail to think "intentionally" on many tasks, as evidenced by the data reported in the previous four chapters. One explanation for their failure, and the one I favor, is that "naturalistic" applications of the intentional structure (as opposed to experimental elicitations) normally require the differentiation and coordination of its two parts, and this differentiation and coordination is hampered by systemic limitations in working memory. Although an unsophisticated or rudimentary form of intentionality is evident, it cannot be used as a tool in cognitive endeavors, because it cannot be taken as an "object," without some loss of the landscape of action.

The goal of the training program that is reported in the present chapter was to circumvent children's working memory limitations, while helping them differentiate and integrate the two landscapes; the reason for conducting the training was to determine whether 4½-year-old children would begin to perform at a higher level on a variety of intentional tasks, once they had a new structure of this sort in their repertoire. The general procedure for the study was as follows:

1. A set of tasks, possessing different surface features but thought to share the same underlying requirement (i.e., an intentional structure), was specified.

2. Children's level of performance on one of these tasks (narrative composition) was assessed.

3. An attempt was made to effect a developmental advance of one substage in children's performance on this task (which could thus be referred to as the "training task"), by teaching children the underlying intentional structure that it requires.

4. Children's level of performance on the other intentional tasks was assessed, to see if a difference of one substage became evident on these tasks as well, even though no training had been provided on their specific content.

Method

Tasks

The intentional tasks that were selected for study were as follows:

Understanding of a Mother's Role. The first task was taken from the study conducted by Goldberg-Reitman (this volume, chapter 8), in which young children's understanding of a mother's role was assessed. Goldberg-Reitman showed that 4-year-olds explained a mother's actions by exclusive reference to the landscape of action, whereas 6-year-olds made reference to the landscape of consciousness. Two of Goldberg-Reitman's cartoon sequences were used in the present study. In the first, a little girl wakes up coughing because a fire has started in her room, and calls out for help. In the second, a little girl who is sitting on a roof starts to slide off and calls out for help. According to Goldberg-Reitman, when asked what the mother will do, children in all age groups identify some appropriate behavior. However, when asked to explain why she will perform this action, 4-year-olds say that the mother will "put water on it because there's a fire in her room" or "will catch her because she's falling down," whereas 6-year-olds state that the mother will put out the fire or catch her because "she wants to save her little girl."

In the present study, each child was invited to "look at some comics." The experimenter then read the text for the cartoons in an animated fashion, while pointing to the appropriate pictures. A series of questions was then asked concerning the mental states of the little girl and the mother. Each participant's explanation of the state was also sought, as in the following typical exchange:

Experimenter: How did the little girl feel?
Subject: Scared!
Experimenter: Right, she felt scared. So what did the mommy do?
Subject: She getted water for the fire to be out.
Experimenter: Why did the mommy get water to put out the fire?
Subject: The fire's burning there (points to the first frame).
Experimenter: Right, there's the fire and the mommy got water to put it out. Why?
Subject: 'Cause—it's smoke, too.

The "why" probes were typically offered twice.

The criteria that were used for differentiating a pre-intentional from an intentional response were as follows:

Does the child reassert an event depicted in the comic strip (e.g., she's coughing, it's burning, she's falling)?

$$NO = Level -1 \quad YES$$
$$\downarrow$$

Does the child make additional reference to the mother's mental state (e.g., "she wanted," "she was afraid," "she didn't want") *or* to the mother's knowledge of the possible consequences of the incident (e.g., "she thinks the girl might hurt herself" or "she thinks to save her from falling")?

$$NO = Level \ 0 \qquad\qquad YES = Level \ 1$$

Empathic Cognition. The second task was taken from the study conducted by Bruchkowsky in chapter 9, in which subjects were shown videotapes of children in affectively laden situations and asked how the protagonist felt and why she felt that way. The particular videotape used in the present study was the one in which a young girl and her dog, Harry, are playing "fetch the ball." When the girl turns her attention from the game to her mother, telling her how much fun the two are having, Harry runs onto the road and is killed by a passing car.[1] An emotional scene ensues in which the little girl tearfully reveals that her dog is dead and that she will miss him greatly. Bruchkowsky determined that all age groups were able to identify the target character's feelings with considerable accuracy. However, they differed in the way they explained the reason for the feeling. Her results showed that 4-year-olds, once again, remained close to the landscape of action, whereas 6-year-olds moved to the landscape of consciousness; for example, 4-year-olds said that the little girl felt sad "cause her dog was killed." By contrast, 6-year-olds added that "he was her best friend" or that "she really loved him."

In the present study, the experimenter said, "Now I'm going to show you a video. Let's watch this." When the film was finished, each child was immediately asked "How did that make you feel?" and "How did the little girl feel?" Again, "why" probes were extended twice. For those young subjects who seemed upset by the vignette, the investigator helped them formulate a resolution by asking "What could happen to make the little girl happy again?"

The criteria that were used for differentiating a pre-intentional from an intentional response were as follows:

Does the child reassert an event depicted in the video (e.g., "the car hit him" or "the doggie got killed")?

$$NO = Level -1 \quad YES$$
$$\downarrow$$

Does the participant make additional reference to the little girl's feeling state (e.g., "she loved him" or "he was her best dog") *or* to the little girl's knowledge of the possible consequences of the incident (e.g., "she'll never be able to play with him again")?

$$NO = Level\ 0 \qquad\qquad YES = Level\ 1$$

Explaining the Meaning of Feeling Terms.   The third task was taken from Griffin's study in chapter 11, which inquired into children's understanding of affective labels. When Griffin asked children direct questions about feeling words, she noted that between the ages of 4 and 6 years,

---

[1]This event is not actually seen. What the viewer sees is a car driving down the nearby street. As the car starts to brake, the film cuts back to the girl, who hears the sound of its screeching brakes, turns, pauses, and then exclaims, "Oh no! Harry's been hit by a car!"

children move from thinking of an emotion as an event to thinking of it as a mental state arising from an event. Once again, then, they move from the landscape of action to the landscape of consciousness. In the present study, the particular feelings and judgments that the children were asked to explain were "happy," "sad," "good," and "bad." According to Griffin's data, "sad" is defined in terms of an event by 4-year-olds (e.g., "your mommy sends you to your room"). In contrast, sad is defined in terms of an intentional state by older children ("your feelings go down when your mommy sends you to your room").

The procedure used for administering the items in the present study was as follows: The experimenter said, "You know about feelings like happy and sad, don't you? Right. Tell me, what does 'happy' mean?" When the child answered, the experimenter queried: "Good. 'Happy' means 'X'. Can it mean anything else?" Then the child was asked "What's happening when you're happy?" And finally, "When 'X' is happening, where does the happiness come from?" The same series of questions was presented for each feeling word. The criteria that were used for differentiating a pre-intentional response were as follows:

Does the child refer to an action event (e.g., " 'happy' is when you get a toy" or " 'sad' is when your mom sends you to your room")?

$$NO = Level -1 \qquad YES \atop \downarrow$$

Does the child make additional references to a mental state (e.g., " 'happy' is when you feel happy") or to a social judgment (e.g., " 'good' is when you do what your mommy says")?

$$NO = Level\ 0 \qquad YES = Level\ 1$$

The foregoing three tasks were designated as the "transfer tasks." The final set of tasks were labeled the "training tasks."

Narrative.   The training tasks were taken from a series of studies I conducted (see chapter 10) in which children were asked to compose and recall stories. In the first study, I asked children to tell stories about various characters that appear frequently in children's literature. I determined that 4-year-old stories have the character of everyday scripts (i.e., stereotypic event sequences), whereas 6-year-old stories contain a simple plot (i.e., a problem–followed by a resolution). In a second study, I showed that this pattern remained, even when children were asked to tell a story about a peer "who has problems she wants to solve" or when they were explicitly cued as to what should be included in the story. At best, the 4-year-olds told stories in which a problematic event took place at the end of an action sequence. In short, they remained in the landscape of action. By contrast, 6-year-olds had little trouble organizing their stories around a problematic feeling state, experienced by the protagonist, that engendered the need for action.

Although 4-year-olds were unsuccessful in creating a landscape of consciousness when they were asked to compose stories, the rudimentary, undifferentiated representation of this landscape was evident in their story recall efforts. Because 4-year-olds can recognize the relation between an event and the mental state it typically engenders (Bruchkowsky, this volume, chapter 9), it was predicted that they would encode mental states as part of a gist item and so would accurately recall the gist of an intentional story. It was also expected, however, that mental states would be encoded and reported in much the same way as other events, that is, that the landscape of consciousness would be sacrificed due to limitations in working memory capacity, and the demand of reporting events in the landscape of action.

A second expectation was that working memory limitations would be seen in terms of the amount of detail which is recalled. A clausal analysis of the recall protocols of 4- and 6-year-olds had already shown that, although both groups recalled a story's gist satisfactorily, when it came to recall of details, the 6-year-olds performed significantly better than the younger children. A post hoc model had also been developed, which took into account the hierarchical nature of text structure (van Dijk & Kintsch, 1983) and predicted both groups' performance under the assumption of a single parameter difference, namely, the size of working memory (McKeough, 1986). In the present study, the mean expected scores generated on the basis of this model were compared to the observed scores on both the pre- and posttest.

The specific instructions that were given for the two story tasks were as follows:

(a) *Story Composition Task.* "I want you to tell me a story—a story about someone about your age who has a problem they want to solve, you know, make all better." If children failed to comply with the request or if they looked as though their attention had wandered from the task, the experimenter repeated the directions, adding, "It can be a true story, but it doesn't have to be—just about someone who has a problem they want to solve."

The criteria that were used for differentiating a pre-intentional from an intentional response were as follows:

Does the story have a coherent event sequence which culminates in a problem?

NO = Level −1   YES
                     Is the problem resolved?
                     ↓

                     NO = Level 0   YES = Level 1

(b) *Story Recall Task.* "Now I'm going to tell you some stories. Listen carefully, because when I finish I want you to tell the story back to me. Are you ready?" Three practice stories and one test story were read, with exaggerated expression. After each, the child was encouraged to recall as much of the story as he or she could. Although the experimenter engaged in "active listening," no leading prompts of any sort were given. The fourth (test) story was as follows:

> Once upon a time there was a boy named Tim who lived on a farm. He was very lonely because his friends lived a long way away. So, he decided he'd like a pet to play with. He asked his dad if he could get a dog, but his dad said "No! We have enough animals to look after around here!" But the boy kept asking and asking. Finally his dad said, "Okay. But you have to take care of it." So the boy got a puppy and he did take very good care of it. But one day, when the boy was doing his work, a car came along the road and killed the puppy. The boy was very sad because he loved the puppy a lot. But his dad had seen that he had taken good care of the puppy and so he got him a pony! Now the boy is happy with his new pet.

Scoring Criteria

1. Parse each recall protocol into clauses. The statement "There was a boy named Tim that lived on a farm," for example, is parsed into three clauses: "there was a boy," "named Tim," and "that lived on a farm."

2. Identify each case as a gist or detail item. The test story was originally analyzed by a panel of experts who identified certain clauses as gist items. In the present study, each child's recall protocol was analyzed according to this template: Clauses that match the gist identified by the experts were recorded as gist items; all other clauses were considered detail items.

3. Quantify the number of gist and detail items contained in each protocol.

In a previous study, this type of clausal analysis revealed that, whereas both 4- and 6-year-olds could both recall the story's gist, there was a

significant difference in the number of detail items recalled, means of
6.3 (*SD* = 4.07) and 10.65 (*SD* = 4.28), for the 4- and 6-year-olds,
respectively. In the present study, these means were used for comparative purposes, to examine the difference in children's performance
before and after instruction.

Subjects

Twenty-nine 4-year-olds (mean age = 4.10 yr) were selected for
inclusion in the study from the classrooms of middle class urban schools.
There were two treatment groups, 15 subjects in the experimental
group and 14 subjects in the control group. A two-step selection procedure was used. First, teachers identified average learners, and their
designation was verified using the Vocabulary subtest of the Wechsler
Preschool and Primary Scale of Intelligence (WPPSI; Wechsler, 1967).
Those having scaled scores in the average range (i.e., between 9 and 15
scaled score points) proceeded to the second selection task, which involved telling a story. The purpose of this second screening task was to
ensure that the selected population was functioning at or below the level
specified for 4-year-olds on the training tasks before narrative instruction commenced. All the selection tasks were administered individually,
and responses were tape-recorded.

Procedure

After the children's performance on the story composition task had
been assessed, the sample was divided into experimental and control
groups, which were matched for sex, ability, and socio-economic background. Next, the Story Recall task was administered. Finally, the children in each group were given approximately 15 instructional sessions
of 30 to 40 minutes each. Following the current practice in kindergarten,
this instruction was offered in small groups of 4 to 8 children each.

Experimental Group. The experimental group received instruction designed to help them tell stories that were one developmental level higher
than those they told spontaneously. The general procedure employed
was the one proposed by Case, Sandieson, and Dennis (1986): (a) Make
the children aware of their current representation of the task domain in
question; (b) build a conceptual bridge from the children's current level
of functioning to the next level in the developmental hierarchy, by
framing the new knowledge structure in a conceptually meaningful
fashion, and keeping the working memory demands of the new procedure to a minimum; and (c) provide working memory support and
practice while children are consolidating the new structure. The im-
plementation of this procedure was effected as follows:

(a) *Current Representation.* In an effort to make the children aware of their current representation, the notion of a story as a sequence of discrete but related events in "the landscape of action" was focused on. The stories the children told were depicted as "cartoon stories" (i.e., sequences of comic strip frames) that reported the flow of action. Figure 12.2 presents an illustration.

The specific steps were as follows:

1. Introduce the concept of picture stories in comic strip form.
2. Draw a series of four empty comic strip frames across a page, leaving space for additions.
3. Invite one child to tell a story about familiar characters (e.g., a little girl and a kind old horse).
4. As the recitation proceeds, depict the salient features of each event in a line drawing.
5. Invite a second child to "re-read" the story. Point to the appropriate frames one at a time, to guide the child in this process.
6. Encourage peer critique and review; that is, stimulate discussion of the story, personal reflections, and so on.

This attempt to externalize what was believed to be children's internal representation of narrative appeared to be meaningful and helpful. Children repeatedly requested that the instructor "draw the boxes" before the story telling began, and seemed to understand the visual representation almost immediately. The instructor moved to the next step when all children had generated a sequence of integrated events at least six times.

(b) *Conceptual Bridging.* The second step involved building a "conceptual bridge" to the next level in the developmental hierarchy, that is, to a simple plot structure. Recall that this structure was an intentional

Once when I was in Disneyland, I saw Mickey Mouse. And then we were going into a balloon till .. um.. go up in the sky and then .. um.. we saw lots of things in the sky and then the balloon came down and we got out and we went to see a show.

Fig. 12.2.   Illustration of "landscape of action" story told by 4-year-old.

one, one which included a representation of consciousness in addition to action. The steps in effecting the conceptual bridge were as follows:

1. Add an "intentional aspect" to the first part of the children's landscape of action stories. The teacher said, "You all told me such good stories and you made them up all by yourselves! Now I want to see if you can finish off a story that I make up. Do you think you can? Yes? Well, let's see!" As the teacher related the problem portion of the story, she sketched the events as a comic strip. "Once upon a time there was a little boy who was riding his bike. He hit a big hole and he fell off. His knee was bleeding and so he felt very, very unhappy. Now, who can finish the story?" One child was picked from those who volunteered. The instructor "read" the picture story and then the child related his or her answer (e.g., "the boy is crying and he calls his mom and she gets a band-aid and puts it on his knee"). The instructor completed the "picture story" on the blackboard as the child reported the events.

2. Differentiate the landscape of consciousness from the landscape of action. The dialogue continued as follows: "You were able to finish it! No problem! That's a great story! Look here. First the boy is riding along on his bike and he falls off because he hits a big hole. Ohhhh! Look at the blood on his knee. He feels very unhappy. Look, he's crying." At this point, the instructor depicted the protagonist's mental state, with a "sad face," above the appropriate frame. The instructor continued: "Then the boy thinks of what to do. He gets an idea, doesn't he?" (At this point the teacher represented this mental state as a light bulb above the appropriate frame.) "What is his idea?" One child volunteered: "He calls his mommy and she puts on a bandage." The instructor commented, "That's right; and he feels better. He feels happy again." The depiction of the final mental state (a "happy face") was then drawn above the last frame.

As the preceding instructional protocol demonstrates, the type of depiction shown in Figure 12.2 was altered so that, in addition to the action sequence, it represents the protagonist's mental state (i.e., "sad" or "happy"), and his or her plan (i.e., the protagonist's idea for solving the problem). The result was a cartoon sequence of the sort drawn in Fig. 12.3.

3. Encourage peer critique and review.
4. Recycle through steps 1. and 2. for each child in the group.
5. Have children generate a further round of stories. One child was

Instructor: "Once upon a time there was a little boy who was riding his bike. He hit a big hole and he fell off. His knee was bleeding and so he felt very, very unhappy.."

Student: "The boy is crying and he calls his mom and she gets a bandaid and puts it on his knee."

Fig. 12.3. Instructed intentional story.

asked to "tell the problem part of the story" and a second child to "think of an idea to make it happy again." This time the clausal relations were highlighted by drawing in the directional arrows. The purpose of this activity was to help the children construct an integrated or coordinated representation of the new structure.

6. To further integrate the structure, with icons in view across the page, ask one child to compose an entire story. Again, sketch the story. A sample story composed under these conditions is presented in Fig. 12.4. As can be seen, the procedure for effecting the bridge to the landscape of consciousness involved (a) pairing the action scripts with a symbol for the protagonist's mental representation and (b) focusing on a planned manipulation of the mental representation.

(c) *Working Memory Support.* The procedures already described were also expected to minimize the load on children's working memory.

1. The pre-intentional representation of narrative as a sequence of discrete but interrelated events was depicted as a "picture story," and so the internal representation was externalized, thereby providing the child with a guiding referent.

2. Stories having an intentional structure were represented in two strands—one depicting the physical world, the other the mental world. Again, the externalizing of the internal representation provided a "holding place" for past and yet-to-be-composed events.

3. Finally, toward the end of the instructional sequence, first the action sequence and then the mental state depictions were faded out, and children were asked to tell a story without the cuing support. This is a standard procedure in the behaviorist tradition, but is rarely used by developmentalists because of their preoccupation with conceptual meaning. As was indicated in chapter 2, however, the present theory presumes that there is an interaction between children's ability to "make meaning," and the automaticity of the operations they possess

Once upon a time there was a little girl and boy and they went to a park but they asked their mom if they went and they said, "No." But they got an idea. They went to the store and they got some wood and they builded the park. And they got some equipment for swings and slides and they built wood with .. for the.. They builded a little bench for them to eat supper on and they built a bed so they could sleep there.. with a house on top.

Fig. 12.4. Post-instruction 4-year-old intentional story.

for doing so. Operations that are not as automatic as children's maturational level permits consume too much working memory; conversely, as operations become automatic, more working memory becomes available and thus control can gradually be internalized.

Control Group. The instruction used with this treatment group was based on a "process approach," following the work of Donald Graves (1983). Three overarching principles guide this approach:

1. *Children learn to compose by being exposed to good models.* Graves and his colleagues have advocated that teachers surround children with good literature by reading to them and by engaging in story telling, choral speaking, and drama. Moreover, to be effective teachers of writing, teachers are encouraged to write themselves, because, according to Graves, teachers must understand "the craft of writing" as well as "the craft of teaching." To this end, he suggests that teachers model the steps of the composing process using their own work.

2. *The purpose of composition is to share with an audience.* For Graves, the main reason for mastering forms and conventions of discourse is so that the work can be understood by others. Consequently, children are encouraged to select topics about which they have something to say (typically, experiences in their personal lives or from story books) and are then given feedback from oral presentations of their stories. Ultimately, after revision, the production is put "between covers," and the published version is made available to parents and peers.

3. *Children learn to compose by composing.* This approach stipulates that it is critical for children to write every day in a predictably structured environment. While the approach is open-ended and interactive, Graves suggests additional activities teachers may use, which are similar across the grades but must be adapted to the needs of each group.

A typical application of these three principles to kindergarten instruction is as follows:

(a) Introduce each session with a "mini-lesson" directed to the whole group, focusing on a single topic of activity for the group (e.g., topics for stories).

(b) Set a general activity for the group (e.g., present a picture related to one of the possible story topics and discuss it). Then, compose a group story about it.

1. Elicit from the children a description of what is happening in the picture.
2. Invite the children to compose a story about the picture, modeling how stories should begin.
3. Invite individuals to generate content and record the utterances in print on the blackboard.
4. Read the story back to the group and invite revisions (e.g., "Is there anything else we want to put in our story?" "Is there anything we want to change in our story?").
5. Make additions and deletions, as indicated.
6. Answer questions concerning conventions of print (e.g., capitals, periods, letter formation) and spelling (especially initial consonants).

(c) Set an independent activity for the children, based on the group activity (e.g., invite the children to draw a picture pertaining to their own stories).

1. While the children work independently, confer, as needed, with individuals or a small group, focusing on topic selection.
2. While the children work independently, suggest to those students who are having difficulty getting started that they might look around to see what others are doing in order to get some ideas.
3. While the children work independently or in pairs, confer, as needed, with individuals or small groups concerning issues determined by an ongoing analysis of the children's work.
4. Encourage children to make "editorial" changes, as a result of the conference (e.g., "so, is there anything else that you want to put in your picture?").

(d) Invite all the children to print a story about the picture. While a few 4-year-olds attempt to do their own printing, the majority may require a scribe at this point.

(e) Confer with individual children concerning changes to the printed text, focusing on choice of language, sequencing of events, and story frames.

(f) Invite the children to share their productions with the large group and to take comments and questions from their classmates.

(g) Publish the productions in a class volume, which might be distributed to parents, kept in the classroom, or placed in the school library.

As can be seen from the above outline of classroom activities, no effort is made to move beyond the form of story organization and expressive language that children use spontaneously. Instead, the approach focuses on the children's experiences in daily activities and with literature, and develops their mode of expressing these experiences through activities such as conferring, revising, and publishing.

Posttest

Children in both the experimental and control groups were reassessed on two story tasks: composition, and recall. The three transfer tasks that were described earlier were also presented. Because these tasks were thought to entail the same conceptual underpinnings as the training task, it was assumed that, if the training had successfully advanced pre-intentional children to the intentional level on story telling tasks, the change should yield comparable progress on the transfer tasks. Conversely, if no increase was made as a result of the story training in children's underlying central conceptual structures, then children should remain at a pre-intentional level on the transfer tasks.

Results

Story Composition

Although the experimental and control groups performed similarly on the story composition task before the instruction commenced, their postinstruction scores were significantly different, $t(27) = 6.47$, $p <$ .0001. As Table 12.1 shows, the mean for the experimental group was .93, indicating that the intentional level had been attained, whereas the mean for the control group was only .15.

Story Recall

Recall that in a previous study, (McKeough, this volume, chapter 10; Study #2), 4-year-olds were found to report significantly fewer detail clauses than 6-year-olds when retelling an intentional story. In the present study, a comparison of the pre- and postinstruction recall protocols showed that, whereas the preinstruction scores of both groups

TABLE 12.1
Pre- and Posttest Scores for Training and Transfer Tasks, M (SD)

| | Training Tasks | | | | Transfer Tasks | | | | | |
| | Composition | | Recall | | Mother's Role | | Empathy | | Feeling Labels | |
Group	M	SD	M	SD	M	SD	M	SD	M	SD
Control										
Pretest	0.00	0.00	5.14	2.91	—	—	—	—	—	—
Posttest	0.15	0.38	4.23	1.31	0.20	0.37	0.14	0.36	0.21	0.47
Experimental										
Pretest	−0.07	0.26	6.23	3.35	—	—	—	—	—	—
Posttest	0.93	0.26	8.27	2.63	0.57	0.46	0.64	0.50	0.98	0.47
Normative data from earlier studies:										
4-year-olds	—	—	6.30	4.07	—	—	—	—	—	—
6-year-olds	—	—	10.65	4.28	—	—	—	—	—	—

were similar to those obtained in the original study, the postinstruction scores of the experimental group showed an increase in the number of detail clauses, approaching but not reaching that of the original 6-year-old group (see Table 12.1). The postinstruction scores of the control group showed no such increase, $t(26) = 4.14$, $p = .0002$.

Transfer

The developmentally trained children used intentional reasoning to solve the more distantly related transfer tasks more frequently than did the control group. The percentage of subjects performing at the intentional level on each type of task is displayed in Table 12.2, along with the percentages obtained in the original studies. As can be seen, the performance of the 4-year-old experimental group approached that of the original 6-year-olds, whereas the performance of the control group was similar to that of the original 4-year-olds. The means and standard deviations of the various groups are shown in Table 12.1. One-tailed t-tests showed a significant difference between the experimental and control groups for all three transfer tasks: for understanding mother's motivation, $t(28) = 2.42$, $p = .011$; for empathic cognition, $t(26) = 3.04$, $p = .003$; and for definition of feelings, $t(27) = 4.41$, $p = .0001$.

In summary, the results showed that children in the experimental group not only met criterion-related standards on the most direct training test, but demonstrated transfer to story recall tasks and to other intentional tasks, as well.

TABLE 12.2
Percentage of Children Scoring at the Intentional Level on
the Transfer Tasks

	Transfer Tasks		
Groups	Mother's role	Empathy	Feeling Labels
Present 4-year-olds			
Control	27	14	33
Experimental	67	67	93
Normative data from earlier studies:			
4-year-olds	20	26	22
6-year-olds	81	57	88

Discussion

The finding that the developmental approach was successful, not just in teaching specific content, but in producing general transfer, is significant from both a theoretical and a practical point of view. From the viewpoint of the present volume, the primary significance of the results is theoretical. What the data suggest is (a) that the conceptual underpinnings of the various tasks are actually represented in the mind of the child by a common conceptual structure, and (b) that training in this structure can play a role in bringing about the developmental transition from 4- to 6-year-old thought. In terms of its formal properties, this intentional structure shares many properties with the dimensional structure that was described in the previous section. It seems reasonable to suggest, then, that the two structures are subject to common constraints, and develop according to the same general timetable. The nature of the successful instruction gives further weight to this conclusion, because the instruction was designed according to the same general principles as the instruction that was successful in teaching the dimensional structure, and it had the same sort of broad impact (Case & Sandieson, this volume, chapter 7).

Another relevant theoretical issue, which has not been considered at any length in the present volume, is how to teach new concepts so that children can use them in a wide range of contexts. Although many studies have attempted to produce knowledge transfer, the majority have been successful in yielding local change only (Perkins & Salomon, 1987). Historically, the move from classical learning theory (Skinner, 1950) to the information-processing paradigm brought about a shift in the focus of educational research from attempts to shape specific skills through successive approximation to training very general "metacognitive" skills (A. L. Brown, 1975; Pressley, 1982). However, transfer proved resistant even under these altered conditions. Although metacognitive skills clearly could be trained, their application appeared to be limited largely to tests of "near" transfer. In other words, transfer of knowledge was effective only when the surface features of the two tasks were highly similar.

Children's failure to engage spontaneously in "far" transfer has led researchers to turn their attention from teaching general metacognitive skills to teaching strategies or procedures designed to facilitate "knowledge accessing." In this latter approach, investigators either cue children's retrieval so that they will apply or transfer knowledge gained during training to novel tasks (Bereiter & Scardamalia, 1985; Ferrara et al., 1986), or vary training along a continuum, ranging from "specific and highly representative" to "general and less representative" (Glick & Holyoak, 1987). In this latter case, the learner is offered an opportunity to construct rules by which to classify tasks according to their conceptual and strategic requirements and to develop a more general sense of the range of tasks to which any given structure is applicable.

In an attempt to explain the mechanisms underlying knowledge transfer, Cormier (1987) has hypothesized the operation of an abstract process in the expert that first extracts "critical dimensions," which are common or invariant across a range of tasks, and then decontextualizes them. When it comes to categorizing tasks along such a continuum, experts, with their elaborate classification structure, have a clear advantage over novices. Whereas novices classify according to surface features, experts call on elaborate knowledge networks consisting of both declarative knowledge and knowledge of task goals (Chi & Rees, 1983), discerning similar goals through the morass of dissimilar surface features.

Although the present study was not conceived within this framework, the framework does offer an alternative way to look at the success of its results. It could be said that the children were provided with a more expert-like knowledge structure, which enabled them to see beneath the surface features of the transfer tasks and discern their conceptual similarity to the training task. It should be stressed, however, that the knowledge network on which the training was focused was not one that was taken from true "experts," but rather from children who were one developmental stage more advanced than those being trained. Moreover, rather than having to extract and decontextualize critical dimensions from the tasks, children in the present approach were helped to construct a developmentally more advanced structure through a procedure that provided an external representation of their initial conceptual structure and then utilized this external representation to help the children expand it. If we are to achieve the level of success that we want in classrooms, this may turn out to be a crucial variable.

Turning to the practical implications of the study, it seems important to mention that, traditionally, the 4- to 6-year-old shift has been a point where researchers have found it necessary to focus on "readiness" activities and to delay direct instruction until this readiness is present. Our successful attempt to help children cross this barrier in the domain of social cognition was, in effect, a new form of readiness training. Rather than being aimed exclusively at the promotion of task-related skills, though, the training was aimed at teaching central conceptual structures, that is, structures with wide yet delimited application to scholastic tasks.

It is conceivable that, in the future, this form of training might be extended to other areas, and serve to provide a basis for a new generation of readiness curricula. Moreover, for certain populations, it may turn out that the provision of such curricula will be necessary before full participation in the regular school curriculum will be possible.

IV

THE ROLE OF CENTRAL CONCEPTUAL STRUCTURES IN THE DEVELOPMENT OF CHILDREN'S SPATIAL THOUGHT

The question that is addressed in the present section is whether there are central conceptual structures in the spatial domain that are parallel to those in the numerical and social domains. As compared to the previous two sections, the data that are presented are somewhat incomplete. In the first chapter, a study is reported in which a spatial structure with the appropriate conceptual properties is induced from a set of empirical data. A new set of tasks is then generated to determine whether the hypothetized structure can be used to predict children's performance in novel situations. This procedure is then repeated in the next chapter for a second set of spatial tasks. It is then shown that the conceptual structures underlying the two developmental sequences are formally similar in a number of important respects, and are closely linked in the development of individual children. The one study that has not yet been conducted is the sort that was reported in chapters 7 and 12: namely, a training study in which the hypothesized structure is taught directly and the pattern of transfer is observed.

Notwithstanding the importance of the missing study, the data in this section still present an intriguing and suggestive picture of children's spatial development and its relationship to development in other domains. Moreover, this picture has a special significance for the issue of cross-domain specificity in cognitive development, because spatial cognition, unlike social cognition, is unquestionably distinct from numerical cognition in its neurological substrate as well as in the information and the operations it entails. To the extent, then, that central conceptual structures play the role in spatial cognition that the authors of the next two chapters suggest, and develop in the fashion that they hypothesize, one must explain the overall pattern in terms that span biological as well as conceptual boundaries.

Stage and Structure in the Development of Children's Spatial Representations

Sonja Dennis
Winthrop College

Distinctive qualities mark the artwork of children at different periods in their development. This phenomenon attracted attention over a century ago, and has continued to be of interest in modern times (Lowenfeld & Brittain, 1970). Although early writers were content to describe the sequence of changes in children's drawings in general terms (Clark, 1897; Cooke, 1885; Eng, 1931; Goodenough, 1926; Harris, 1963; Kellogg, 1967; Luquet, 1927), more recent scholars have reacted against this practice and pointed out its shortcomings (Freeman, 1972; Gardner, 1980).

As Beilin (1971a) has noted, the description of a stage can perform two functions. First, it can provide an empirical generalization of a particular type of developmental phenomenon. Second, it can locate such a description within a formal developmental theory, which attempts to explain developmental phenomena as well as describe them (p. 172). The early literature on children's art was largely restricted to the first function. Luquet's (1913, 1927) work provides a good illustration. Children were said to begin their drawing development when they entered the *Scribbling Stage*. Next, during the stage of *Fortuitous Realism*, they were said to produce a combination of scribbles and distinguishable forms, which they labeled in a post hoc manner. Next, during the stage of *Failed Realism*, they were said to represent objects by graphic symbols that resembled their referents, but only globally. More precise pictures of objects were said to be produced during the stage of *Intellectual Realism*, when children draw the particular parts of objects that they know define them, without regard to visual appearance. Finally, in the stage of *Visual Realism,* children were said to depict objects as they might appear visually, by means of graphic rules and procedures that render the various objects in spatial perspective.

As both Freeman (1972) and Gardner (1980) have pointed out, such a characterization of drawing is adequate to permit empirical generalization. It can also serve to highlight dimensions of change that may be of developmental significance: For instance, the particular progression described by Luquet suggests an underlying movement from intellectual to visual knowledge. What is missing, however, is "an account of drawing as part of some more general developmental process" (Gardner, 1980, p. 12).

The research reported in the present chapter is an attempt to move in this direction, that is, to characterize the stages in children's drawing in such a fashion that they can be linked to the more general stages of their cognitive growth and to suggest the process by which they move from one of these stages to the next. As was indicated in chapter 1, several new formulations of stage theory emerged during the early 1980s, as a result of efforts to strengthen the explanatory power of Piaget's theory (Case, 1985; Fischer, 1980; Halford, 1982; Mounoud, 1982). The work reported in the present chapter was initiated during this period, and was conducted in the hope that the new generation of theories might offer a more powerful framework within which to describe the changes that take place in the domain of drawing.

The theory chosen for this purpose was the one described in chapter 2. In order to locate children's drawing within the context of this theory, I first collected a sample of children's drawing under facilitating conditions, and proposed a model that would relate the structure of children's knowledge about visual representation to the more general structural forms described in the theory. The next step was to test this model, in a hypothetico-deductive fashion.

STUDY 1: BUILDING A STRUCTURAL MODEL OF CHILDREN'S VISUAL REPRESENTATIONS

The objective of the first study was to examine the changes that take place in children's drawing during the period from 4 to 10 years of age, within the broader context that has been outlined in previous chapters. Because the theory specifies a set of four structural levels, as well as four working memory levels, which are hypothesized to be related, the study examined children's drawing behavior and their working memory performance at each age specified by the theory: 4, 6, 8, and 10 years. The specific goals were (a) to determine whether children's drawings would show qualitatively different patterns at these ages, and (b) to determine whether there was any correlation, at either the group or individual level, between performance on measures of working memory and any drawing stages that might be proposed based on the theory.

Method

Subjects

Subjects were 75 kindergarten and elementary school boys and girls, all of whom attended an upper-middle-class school in Toronto. They were divided, by age, into four groups: There were 16 four-year-olds (mean age: 4 years, 5 months), 22 six-year-olds (mean age: 6 years, 3 months), 19 eight-year-olds (mean age: 8 years, 4 months), and 18 ten-year-olds (mean age: 10 years, 4 months). The subjects were screened, using the PPVT (Dunn & Dunn, 1988), to ensure that they were of average to above-average intelligence and thus suitable for providing a good picture of optimum development, under conditions where the ability of interest, drawing, does not form an explicit part of the school curriculum. All of the children scored within the range of 100 to 120 IQ points.

Tasks and Materials

Three tasks were administered, two measuring working memory and one measuring drawing performance.

Mr. Cucumber Test. This test contains pictures of an imaginary Mr. Cucumber who has a number of colored dots on various parts of his body (e.g., left eye, right hand, left foot). The picture was presented for 5 seconds, and the child was instructed to remember the spatial locations of the dots for later recall. Although the children often attempted to place their fingers on the colored dots, this was not permitted because this seemed to facilitate encoding and/or provide an external mnemonic. Immediately after removal of this stimulus, a grid was shown for about 1 second. This was followed by the presentation of a second picture of Mr. Cucumber, without the colored dots. The child was asked to point to the positions where the colored dots had appeared in the previous picture. The test was divided into six levels of difficulty, corresponding to the number of dots appearing on Mr. Cucumber's body. At the first level, there was only one dot. The number of dots was then increased by one dot for each successive level; at each level three different problems were presented. The test began with a brief training session, and ended when a subject incorrectly identified the spatial location of dots for three consecutive problems at a given level. A final score was calculated by assigning ⅓ of a point for each problem for which recall was perfect.

The Opposites Test.   In the training phase, children initially listened to a list of paired adjectives read by the experimenter and were required to respond with the opposite of each adjective when the experimenter called out one of the adjectives in the pair. This was designed to ensure that the polar adjectives were familiar. During this phase the experimenter might have said, for example, " 'Big' is the opposite of 'small'. What is the opposite of 'small'?" The subject then responded "big." This procedure continued until the nine sets of adjectives in the test were practiced: big–small, up–down, good–bad, right–left[1], wet–dry, tall–short, hot–cold, love–hate, and fat–thin. The adjectives chosen were all simple, one-syllable words. The test was structured in a similar way to the preceding one. There were five levels of difficulty corresponding to the number of adjectives presented. At the lowest level, only one adjective was presented. The number of adjectives was then increased by one unit for each successive level. The child was required to recall the opposite of each adjective that the experimenter called out. For example, if the experimenter said "up, tall", the child was required to respond with "down, short." Each level contained five problems. The test ended when the child failed all problems at a given level. The final score was calculated by assigning ⅕ of a point for each correctly paired adjective.

Drawing Task.   The experimenter gave the following instructions: "Draw me a picture that shows a little girl (boy) your age, doing something that makes her (him) happy." For this task, a standard-sized sheet of white paper (8 ½ in. × 11 in.) and colored crayons were supplied.

Procedure

Subjects were tested individually in a quiet area. The Mr. Cucumber Test was administered first, followed by the Opposites Test, and then the drawing task. The specific items at each level of the Mr. Cucumber Test are presented in Dennis (1987).

Results

The similarities and differences among the pictures drawn by each age group were noted, and the prototypical characteristics of pictures at each age were described as follows:

---

[1]"Wrong" could be substituted for "left."

4 years: A human figure and an object are drawn. The human figure, which is globally represented, includes: head, trunk, arms, and legs. Legs appear more often than arms. Hair is included in roughly half the pictures. The sex of the figure is ambiguous.

6 years: A human figure and an object (or another person) are placed in a graphically defined setting. The sky is represented as a narrow line of blue color at the top of the page. The ground is a narrow line of brown or green at the bottom of the page. People and objects are located on the baseline (ground). There is an empty space between the sky and ground. In general, more features are included in the drawings of the human figure.

8 Years: People and objects are drawn in a scene that now includes a front (near) and a back (far). The scene features both sky and ground. The ground is a strip of color at the bottom of the page, as before. The sky is filled in, in the space that used to be empty, so that it meets the ground. The effect this produces is that of a "background." People are drawn in more detail, and there is evidence of more interaction between people and objects. Depth is recognizable for the first time, both in the representation of the human figure and in the relationship between the principal human figure and other objects.

10 Years: The structure of the picture is less rigid than those described above. Different kinds of settings are represented. For instance, a sporting field or arena might be depicted, rather than just a general outdoor scene (i.e., sky and grass) for context. Scenes are often represented from a point of view that differs from a frontal view, the typical presentational format of scenes found earlier. Perspective is captured in some pictures. Depth is often portrayed as continuous space, rather than as polar space where front and back are juxtaposed. Both human figures and scene elements are well differentiated.

An example of each type of picture is presented in Fig. 13.1.

The foregoing age-related characterizations were used to generate performance scores. Drawings that contained more features of the 4-year-old prototype than any others were assigned to Level 1; those that came closest to the 6-, 8-, and 10-year-old prototypes were assigned to Levels 2, 3, and 4 respectively. In addition to the experimenter's ratings, an independent judge blindly rated a sub-sample of the drawings made by each age group. Overall agreement was 94%. The mean scores for the 4-, 6-, 8-, and 10-year-olds were .91, 2.0, 2.9, and 3.5, respectively.

FIG. 13.1.   Sample pictures drawn by children at 4 years (top left), 6 years (top right), 8 years (bottom left), and 10 years (bottom right).

Working Memory

Each subject's average score was computed from the two working memory tests. The mean working memory scores for the 4-, 6-, 8-, and 10-year-olds were 1.4, 1.9, 3.1, and 3.3, respectively.

Correlational Analysis

A Pearson correlation coefficient was computed for the drawing and working memory scores. The positive correlation between drawing and working memory performance was significant ($r = .76$, $p < .01$). With age partialed out, the magnitude of the correlation between the two measures was reduced, but remained significant ($r = .25$, $p < .01$).[2] Figure 13.2 depicts the mean scores for the working memory and drawing measures as a function of age. There is a clear linear trend, as the theory predicts, if children's prototypic performance conforms to the general structural forms it describes.

Analysis of Spatial Structure

Given the general pattern that the foregoing analysis revealed, the next step in examining the results was to search for parallels between the structure of children's art, as reflected in the defining descriptions, and the more general structural forms that are hypothesized by Case to characterize different developmental levels during this age range (see Figure 19.2, p. 356). The following model was suggested on the basis of this analysis.

Preliminary Substage: Operational Consolidation (4 years).   At the preliminary substage, three or four types of elements (dots, lines, circles, etc.) are coordinated and consolidated into a recognizable symbolic unit, whose parts on the page have a spatial relationship to each other that is isomorphic to their relationship in the world (e.g., "eyes" farther away from near edge of paper than "mouth" = eyes above mouth). The categorization of each graphic element as a distinct object "part," and the spatial arrangement of these "parts" into a recognizable "whole" is hypothesized to require a relational working memory of four units, which is the same as a "dimensional" working memory of one unit (see McKeough, this volume, chapter 10).

Substage 1: Operational Coordination (6 years).   The structures at the next level are qualitatively different, and involve a focus on a higher set of relationships, those involving the organization of the whole set of objects

---

[2]For a higher estimate, of this correlation, based on the relationship between working memory and the planning component of drawing, see Morra, Moizo, & Scopesi (1988).

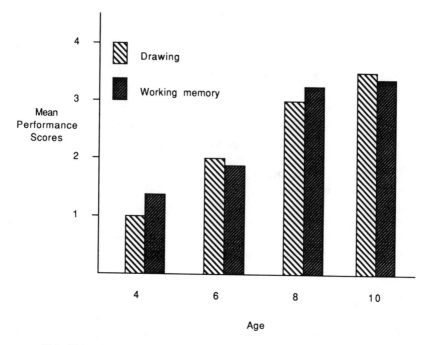

FIG. 13.2.   The relationship between drawing and working memory
performance scores as a function of age.

created at the end of the previous stage into a setting or scene. This
scene constitutes the higher order spatial unit that is characteristic of the
dimensional stage in this domain. It is hypothesized that the construction of such a scene requires, as a minimum, the successive pair-wise
spatial mapping of distinct objects, each of which in itself requires one
unit of working memory. The working memory required for transition
into this stage is two units.

Substage 2: Bifocal Coordination (8 years).   The change at this level is a
minor one. The additional element is of the same general sort found at
the previous level, but now a "scene" is included in the background. This
permits the child for the first time to represent depth, albeit in a
somewhat primitive fashion. In order to do so, it is hypothesized that the
child must store a "pointer" to one scene (the foreground scene) while
actually focusing on the second (the background). The introduction of
depth in this fashion is hypothesized to require an additional unit of
working memory.

Substage 3: Elaborated Coordination (10 years).   The new element at this level is a device that elaborates on the acquisition of the previous level, such that the two units already depicted may be connected in a more integrated fashion. This means that spatial depth is depicted such that fore-, middle-, and background are all present. In effect, the middle ground "links" the foreground and background, producing an integrated scene in which depth appears to be continuous. The construction of such a continuum is hypothesized to require an additional working memory unit, yielding a total of four.

Discussion

The foregoing structural analysis suggests that, during the period known as the dimensional stage, a major qualitative shift in children's drawings appears between 4 and 6 years, followed by two more minor shifts or elaborations at 8 and 10. This pattern implies that, for the ages examined, there is a parallel between children's performance in drawing a picture and in other problem-solving tasks. Prior to stage transition, a new element (or process) is unitized. As the child moves into the new stage, two units are coordinated into a higher order unit. As the child progresses through the stage, two higher order units are combined, but not yet integrated. Finally, at the end of the stage two higher order units are well integrated. The results thus indicate a positive relationship between drawing performance and a more general developmental trend, possibly mediated by the growth of working memory.

These findings led to the proposal of a linking model, but they were not considered a critical test of it. In order to conduct such a test it was necessary (a) to change the instructions, so that the children were made aware of the elements of more complex drawing, and thus had a better chance to perform at a higher level, (b) to standardize the instructions, so as to control the content of the pictures more closely, and thus be sure that content and structure were not being confounded, and (c) to make sure the children had remembered the instructions, so that any deficiencies in performance at lower ages could not be attributed to simple memory deficits. In the second study, an attempt was made to meet each one of these conditions.

STUDY 2

Study 2 was designed to test the structural model that was proposed in Study 1. Five drawing tasks were constructed. Each succeeding task required that more objects be depicted than the previous task. Each succeeding task also provided explicit instructions regarding how the children were to relate the objects that were rendered. In effect, two types of information were presented: content information and relational information. The tasks were developed so that the first task would provide an explicit account of the pictorial structure that 4-year-olds typically generate, and each succeeding task would present explicit descriptions of the pictorial structures that 6-, 8-, and 10-year-olds typically produce. The last task was designed to require a level of performance that went beyond what was predicted at a 10-year-old level of performance, thus preventing a ceiling effect. The five tasks were:

1. *Human Figure Task.* "Draw a picture of a man."
2. *Girl–Tree Task:* "Draw a picture of a girl standing in a park next to a tree."
3. *Boys–Fence Task:* "Draw a picture of two boys shaking hands in a park with a fence just behind them."[3]
4. *Couple–Baby–Tree Task:* "Draw a picture of a man and a woman holding hands in a park. Their baby is in front of them and a tree is very far away behind them."
5. *Mother–Window Task:* "Draw a picture of a mother looking out the window of her house to see where her son is playing, in the park across from where they live. She only sees her son's face, because he is peeking out from behind a tree."

These tasks meet the following criteria: (a) They present the instructions in sufficient detail that failure at any level cannot be blamed on a lack of understanding of what is expected; (b) they require that each age group (and each child) generate the same content, thus eliminating any confusion of structural phenomena with age-related changes in the type of content that children typically choose to depict; (c) they are arranged in gradations of difficulty, thereby presenting the opportunity for children to perform at their highest possible level, by applying what they learn on lower level tasks to tasks at higher levels; and (d) they control for the possibility of a long-term memory confound, because the instructions are explained and repeated until children at all ages can say them back "by heart."

Predictions

On the assumption that the structure of children's drawings would be unaffected by the manipulations described, two predictions were advanced.

---

[3]Note that this task cannot be solved by rendering the figures and fence in side view and using a single ground line, as it would if figures only were required, or if the two boys were facing the same direction.

1. The pattern of success and failure, would be as follows:
   Age 4: Pass Task 1; fail Tasks 2 through 5.
   Age 6: Pass Tasks 1 and 2; fail Tasks 3 through 5.
   Age 8: Pass Tasks 1 through 3; fail Tasks 4 and 5.
   Age 10: Pass Tasks 1 through 4; fail Task 5.
2. Working memory performance should still be positively correlated with drawing scores when structural rather than descriptive criteria are used for scoring.

Method

Subjects

Of the 120 subjects tested, 116 completed all the tasks. Subject distribution in the four age groups was as follows: 26 four-year-olds, 30 six-year-olds, 30 eight-year-olds and 30 ten-year-olds. The mean age and standard deviations, by group, were: 4 years, 6 months (SD = 2.5 months); 6 years, 6 months (SD = 3.5 months); 8 years, 5 months (SD = 3.7 months); and 10 years, 5 months (SD = 4 months). For the most part children came from middle- and working-class backgrounds. Principals and teachers assisted in selecting the subjects according to age (no 5-, 7-, 9-, or 11-year-olds participated) and intellectual status (each participant was judged by his or her teacher to be within the normal range).

Tasks and Materials

Seven tasks were administered: the two working memory tasks described previously and the five drawing tasks. Standard-sized (8 1/2 in. × 11 in.) sheets of white paper, pencils, and colored pencils were supplied.

Procedure

Subjects were administered the tests in the order described. The two working memory tasks were presented in the first session. In general, one drawing task was administered per day and subjects were tested individually. Two exceptions were made to this rule: (a) The human figure task was administered in groups varying from 4 to 25, depending on the availability of children at a particular time; and (b) many subjects were allowed to complete the human figure task and the girl–tree task on the same day, with several hours intervening. This was permitted because the only redundancy effect possible was one that was not going to be analyzed: a person being depicted in both tasks. Also, there were no specific second-order relations (e.g., next to, behind) in the human figure task that could carry over to the girl–tree task.

Drawing time was unrestricted. The drawing tasks were usually completed in 3 to 30 minutes, depending on the age of the subject and the level of the task. Younger children required less time than older children to complete their drawings. Tasks lower on the complexity scale were completed in less time than those higher on the scale. Instructions for a task were read twice at the beginning, and once again when the subject appeared to be halfway through the picture. After the subject announced that he or she had completed the drawing, the instructions were repeated once more and the subject was asked to check the picture to ensure that it had been completed to his or her satisfaction. The instructions were also read again at any time during the drawing session, if the subject so requested.

The foregoing procedures were varied slightly for the 4-year-olds. Questions accompanied the instructions at the beginning of drawing Tasks 2 through 5, which they had to answer correctly before proceeding. A test was also administered at the beginning of Task 3 to check the child's understanding of the concepts "in front" and "behind." In this test, children were asked to "Put the frog behind the alligator," (the alligator was already on the table, in front of the child) and to "Put the teddy bear in front of the frog," (Here the alligator was removed and a teddy bear was handed to the child).

Scoring

Each drawing was assigned a picture structure score according to its structural level. For the purpose of this chapter, the score number matched the substage level (i.e., 0 for the preliminary substage, 1 for the first substage, and so on). Intermediate (one-half) scores were assigned in any case where the drawing seemed above a given level, but clearly did not reach the next level. A score of −1 was given for scribbling.

The general criteria for levels were as follows:

Preliminary Level (score = 0). The objects had to be recognizable, but they could not be organized into a foreground "scene."

Level 1 (score = 1). The spatial organization of a foreground scene arrangement had to be present, but a background scene could not be depicted.

Level 2 (score = 2). In addition to the foreground, background objects had to be differentiated, but the two scenes could not be clearly interconnected (The background object often appears to be floating in this case.)

Level 3 (score = 3). The fore-, middle-, and background had to be differentiated in the scene and had to be interconnected to produce an appearance of continuous depth.

Level 4 (score = 4). Children could only demonstrate this level of structural organization on the most difficult task. In this task, children were asked to depict two scenes (a "mother in a house" scene and a "son in a park" scene) such that the mother (in the first scene) could see the face of her son (depicted in the second scene) but not his body, because the body was hidden behind a tree.[4]

A more detailed account of the scoring procedure is presented in Dennis (1987), and is available on request.[5]

Results

One hundred sixty of the 580 drawings in the sample were scored by an independent rater. The percentage of agreement was 75%. When converted into a reliability coefficient, the resulting gamma statistic was .96.

The assumption that the five drawing tasks would form a hierarchical scale was supported by a Guttman scale analysis. Only 6 of 116 subjects deviated from a Guttman scale pattern. The coefficient of reproducibility was .99 and the coefficient of scalability was .94.

The mean working memory capacity scores for ages 4, 6, 8, and 10 years were .98, 1.99, 2.79, and 3.22, respectively. A significant developmental trend in working memory performance was found when a one-way analysis of variance for age was conducted, $F(3, 112 = 104.14, p < .01$. The mean score for each age group differed significantly from each other group. When the observed scores were compared to the expected working memory values of 1, 2, 3, and 4 for ages 4, 6, 8, and 10 years, only the 10-year-olds' scores were found to be discrepant, being much lower than expected. This deviation of the observed pattern from the predicted one was examined further, as follows: The deviation of each subject's score from the expected value for that age was computed and a one-way ANOVA was performed to test whether the displacement was a significant one. This analysis indicated significant differences among the mean deviation scores of the four groups, $F(3, 112) = 14.92, p < .01$, and a significant grand mean effect, $F(1, 112) = 28.71, p < .01$. Hence, the linear displacement of the observed values from those predicted by the theory was significant.

Table 13.1 shows the percentage of subjects passing the drawing tasks by age group. For any given age group, a predetermined minimum of 50% of the individuals passing constituted a pass. Such a lenient crite-

---

[4](Ed.) Note that "point of view" considerations must determine the relative position and orientation of persons and objects in each scene. In effect, two three-dimensional representations must be coordinated to form a higher order representation in which the criteria regarding line of sight from one scene to the next are met.

[5]In the original scoring system scores were 1 unit higher than the values noted here, to permit easier comparison with the working memory scores.

TABLE 13.1
Percent of Subjects Passing the
Drawing Tasks, by Age Group

Age (years)	Task				
	1	2	3	4	5
4	92	23	8	0	0
6	100	70	40	0	0
8	100	97	87	33	7
10	100	100	100	43	20

rion was used because these tasks were exploratory. The bold-face section of Table 13.1 indicates the hypothesized passing region. With respect to the first hypothesis, the pass-fail predictions for ages 4, 6, and 8 years were all verified: 4-year-olds only passed Task 1, 6-year-olds passed Tasks 1 and 2, and 8-year-olds passed Tasks 1, 2, and 3. Contrary to expectation, however, the 10-year-olds showed a ceiling level of performance at Task 3, like the 8-year-olds. Therefore, only 19 of 20 predictions were confirmed.

Table 13.2 presents the mean picture structure scores by age and task level. The coefficients of reliability for the structural scale were good. The overall reliability coefficient for the intercorrelations of the set of items in the scale was .86, and the reliability coefficient increased to .92 when Task 1, which introduced an artificial floor on the performance level of 6-, 8-, and 10-year-olds, was removed. (In Table 13.2 the mean picture structure score is summed across Tasks 2 to 5 only.)

To test the hypothesis about the role of working memory, the correlation between working memory and picture structure scores was examined. The positive correlations between all pairs of variables were high and significant: age and working memory, $r = .86$, $p < .001$; age and total structure score, $r = .82$, $p < .001$; and working memory and total structure score, $r = .80$, $p < .001$. The age-partialed correlation

TABLE 13.2
M (SD) of Picture Structure Scores on Drawing Tasks 1 to 5, by Age

Age	Task					Grand Mean, over Tasks
	1	2	3	4	5	
4	0.0(.37)	0.3(.62)	0.4(.95)	0.4(.42)	0.0(.75)	0.3(.58)
6	0.3(.46)	1.1(.65)	1.6(.76)	1.5(.18)	1.3(.81)	1.4(.61)
8	0.1(.31)	1.8(.81)	2.3(.62)	2.2(.86)	2.4(.99)	2.2(.67)
10	0.3(.65)	1.8(.79)	2.7(.33)	2.5(.66)	3.0(.93)	2.5(.50)

coefficient between working memory and total structural score was also positive and significant $r = .34$, $p < .001$. This can be interpreted to mean that roughly 11.6% of the variance in drawing is explained uniquely by working memory, when any one level of chronological age is considered. Hence, there seems to be a direct relationship between working memory and drawing, which is separate from the obvious common relation that both variables share with chronological age. Any direct comparison of absolute scores on the working memory and drawing tasks is problematic, however, for the following reasons: Although no time limits were placed on the child during the drawing phase, the working memory tests required the child's instantaneous response. Second, whereas the child was free to correct errors in the drawing by starting over, the working memory tests were administered under stringent time constraints and provided little room for error. Third, the drawing tasks provided a way of optimizing all children's performance by allowing them to draw all five pictures, whereas the working memory task was terminated when the child reached a level of persistant failure. Finally, although points were credited for success at levels beyond a child's ceiling in both tasks, it is difficult to assess the comparability of the two scoring methods.

As an initial attempt to correct for these differences, each individual's best performance on each task was examined. The best drawing performance score was assessed as the highest level achieved by an individual on any of the five tasks. Similarly, the best working memory performance score was the highest level at which any success was indicated, irrespective of whether all the items at that level were passed. One unit was then added to each drawing score, to make the absolute value correspond to working memory demand rather than to substage number.

Based on the new scoring procedure for scoring the 4-, 6-, 8-, and 10-year-olds' performance their mean working memory scores, were 1.5, 2.6, 3.5, and 4.1, respectively and their mean drawing scores were 1.7, 2.5, 3.6, and 4.0, respectively. The relationship between these two performance measures is shown in Fig. 13.3. A two-way ANOVA indicated a significant age effect, $F(3, 112) = 113.99$, $p < .001$) and no significant Task effect or Age by Task interaction. The absence of a task effect suggests that each group's best performance on these two tasks may be comparable in absolute terms, and not simply correlated. Based on this post hoc examination, it is plausible to suggest that there may be some sort of one-to-one relationship between the maximum number of elements that children can hold in their working memory, and the maximum number of elements they can integrate into a coherent spatial "whole" while drawing. Recent work by Morra, Moizo, and Scopesi (1988) gives further weight to this suggestion.

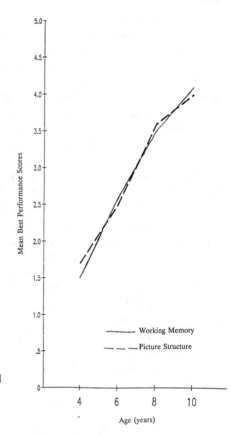

FIG. 13.3. The relationship between working memory and picture structure scores measured according to best performance.

GENERAL DISCUSSION

In earlier work, Case (1985) described how children first come to use a pencil as a scribbling tool during the sensorimotor stage, and how, as they enter the interrelational stage, they gradually differentiate and coordinate different types of line drawings into coherent spatial patterns. He also suggested that this progression conformed to the general sort of structural change that is seen in other domains during the sensorimotor and interrelational periods. In the present investigation, this same type of analysis was continued into the dimensional stage. Two predictions were generated as a consequence: (a) that a qualitative change in drawing performance would occur between 4 and 6 years of age, with a progressive elaboration between 6 and 10, and (b) that measures of working memory capacity and drawing performance would be correlated. The prediction regarding the structural changes in children's drawing was partially supported by the data, as indicated by the pass/fail patterns of the four age groups across the five drawing tasks. Contrary to expectation, the 10-year-olds performed similarly to the 8-year-olds. The absence of a developmental difference between the 8- and 10-year-olds, however, was paralleled by a similar absence of difference in their mental processing limitations, as measured by working memory. On this measure, children aged 4, 6, and 8 demonstrated working memory capacities equal or very close to the theoretical expectation, while the 10-year-olds' mean working memory score (of 3.22) fell short of the expected value (4) by a relatively large margin. It was presumed that a working memory score of 4 was necessary in order to pass Task 4. Thus, the difficulty that Task 4 posed for this age group might be attributed to their relatively low working memory capacity. Despite the 10-year-old group's deviation from the predicted pass/fail performance pattern, then, the data for this age group can still be viewed as supporting the general theoretical model.

This interpretation is also supported by the correlational analysis. The correlation between working memory and drawing was significant. When age was partialed out, although there was a decrease in the strength of the positive association, the correlation coefficient remained significant. Therefore, working memory accounts for some of the variance in drawing within an age group. Stated differently, for children of the same age, individual differences in working memory are still related to individual differences in the structure of the pictures that are drawn, with children performing up to the level that the size of their working memory suggests is their upper bound.

The findings reported in the present chapter help clarify the link between the structure of children's art at various ages (which has been studied and classified into stages for many years) and the more general structure of their developing cognitive system. The findings also provide support for the notion that changes in the size of working memory play a role in potentiating these general systemic changes.

Horizontal and Vertical Structure: Stages and Substages in Children's Motor Development

Denise T. Reid
University of Toronto

Early studies of children's motor development were aimed at describing the movement patterns of children at different ages, as they gradually acquire the motor competencies that are characteristic of the human adult. Some of the best known studies concentrated on infant competencies such as locomotion and grasping (Ames, 1937; Halverson, 1931; McGraw, 1940, 1941; Shirley, 1931), and preschool achievements such as throwing, skipping, and jumping (Bayley, 1935; Gesell et al., 1940; McCaskill & Wellman, 1938).

Since the "cognitive revolution," there has been a considerable shift in emphasis. Researchers have now begun to investigate the information processes that enable humans of any age to learn *new* motor responses, using their existing neuromuscular capabilities (Fitts, 1954; Keele & Posner, 1968). Closed- and open-loop theories of motor control have provided the principal framework for addressing the issues that have emerged from this line of inquiry (Adams, 1971; Bernstein, 1967; Keele, 1968; Schmidt, 1975). Although information processing theories have been useful in explicating the process of short-term motor learning, they have not as yet cast much light on the longer term changes that take place in the course of human development. Todor (1979) has initiated a program of research that addresses this latter question. Drawing on the developmental theory formulated by Pascual-Leone (1970), he and his colleagues have analyzed children's speed of performance on a set of classic motor-learning tasks, and shown that many of the developmental changes that take place can be explained by postulating an age-related growth in the size of children's *M-space*, or working memory (Mitchell, 1977; Sifft, 1978; Thomas & Bender, 1977; Todor, 1975, 1979).

Inasmuch as the theory outlined in chapter 2 builds on Pascual-Leone's theory, while adding a stronger structural component to it, it seemed that it could also be used to extend our understanding of children's motor development, and to expand the range of tasks and ages for which motor-learning predictions could be made. By applying the theory to the domain of motor development, I thought a reciprocal contribution might also be made to the theory itself, particularly regarding the issue of what is general and what is specific in cognitive development. The study of motor development would appear to offer a particular advantage for examining the issue of task specificity, because children's motor development can be assessed without resorting to verbal protocol analysis. One can therefore build up a picture of what sorts of developments are common to this domain and other domains not clouded by reliance on common methods of assessment.

FINE MOTOR DEVELOPMENT IN PRESCHOOL CHILDREN

The first study was inductive. A small group of preschoolers was observed as they performed a variety of familiar motor tasks that involved the use of eating utensils. Eating tasks were chosen for two reasons: First, children have a great deal of experience with these tasks, and understand their general purpose from an early age; second, such tasks are often the focus of rehabilitation therapy for the neurologically handicapped (e.g., adult stroke victims, children with cerebral palsy). Any study that contributes to a better understanding of these tasks thus has the potential to make a practical contribution as well as a theoretical one.

In order to get a preliminary sense of children's ability to use eating utensils, several groups of preschoolers of different ages were observed while they were engaged in a variety of mealtime activities. These informal observations were then followed by an attempt to formalize the developmental changes that appeared to be taking place in terms of the general theory that was outlined in chapter 2. Finally, on the basis of these preliminary formulations, a set of new tasks was developed and administered to different groups of children in the same age ranges. The following is a brief summary of the general structural levels that were hypothesized and the new tasks that were developed as exemplars of them.

STRUCTURAL LEVELS IN THE USE
OF EATING UTENSILS

Substage 0: 1 to 1½ years. At this substage, Case's theory suggests that children are supposed to be capable of executing responses that involve the representation and control of a single relationship: most frequently, a relationship between one object and another (Case, 1985; Case & Khanna, 1981). In the domain of eating tasks, the sorts of relationships that children appeared to be mastering were the spatial relationships between different sorts of food, and the utensils most frequently used for eating them. It was therefore hypothesized that 1½-year-olds, but not 1-year-olds, would be able to perform a variety of tasks in which a simple, differentiated motor movement was applied to a particular eating utensil, in order to bring it into sustained relationship (normally involving physical contact) with some sort of food or food-substitute. The principal task on which the pilot subjects were observed was retrieving pablum with a spoon. The new tasks that the second group of subjects were given were:

1. scooping yogurt with a spoon;
2. using a spoon to stir a cup filled with water;
3. sticking the tines of a fork into a banana;
4. sticking a knife into a ball of Play-Doh;
5. moving the tynes of a fork along a table in a straight line;
6. inserting the point of a knife into a hole.

Note that these tasks all require that some familiar eating utensil be brought into some specific sort of spatial relationship with a second object. What varies is the nature of the eating utensil, the nature of the second object, the nature of the relationship that is required, and the nature of the motor response that must be applied in order to produce the relationship. Some variability in children's familiarity with the required responses is no doubt present as well.

Substage 1: 20 to 28 months. At approximately 2 years, according to Case's theory, children should become capable of solving problems that require two relational features to be mastered and coordinated with each other, such that a new "inter-relationship" emerges. Very often the first relationship is presumed to become "background" as this process takes place, while the second relationship becomes the object of focal attention (Case, 1985). In observing children's performance on a variety of eating tasks, it seemed that by this age they were capable of more than simply bringing an eating utensil into contact with their food: They appeared to be capable of maintaining or controlling this contact, while some sort of spatial displacement was executed. For example, in Task 1., children could now bring the back of a fork into contact with a piece of soft food (e.g., a banana or a cooked carrot) and maintain this contact, while pressing the fork downward into it, thus executing a sort of controlled "mashing."

Children were asked to imitate several actions demonstrated by the experimenter, in order to test the generality of this capability. These were:

1. bringing a fork down onto the top of a banana, and then mashing it;
2. placing a spoon on a penny, and then using the spoon to push the penny along a line;
3. bringing the edge of a spoon up against a pea at the bottom of a deep bowl, and then pushing the edge of the spoon against the side of the pea so that the pea rolled into it;
4. bringing the tine of a fork against the surface of a pea, and then slowly piercing it;
5. inserting a knife into a hole in a paper plate, and then pushing the knife downward until it jabbed into an object immediately below the hole; and
6. laying the cutting edge of a dull knife against a piece of flat Play-Doh, and then using the edge to score the dough.

As the reader may verify, each of these actions requires that one object be carefully oriented in relation to another object, and that this orientation then be maintained while the first object is displaced along some particular spatial axis.

Substage 2: 28 months to 3½ years.   According to the general theory, children at this substage are supposed to become capable of thinking in terms of two distinct interrelationships, rather than just one. The changes in children's mealtime activity at this level appeared to involve the displacement of an eating utensil along two axes. For example, in Task 1., children could now score a ball of Play-doh with a knife, rather than just a flat sheet. On this task the child must focus on maintaining contact between the knife and the Play-doh while displacing the knife along the two spatial axes that are necessary to describe the ball's circumference. To test the hypothesis that this capability was a general one, the following additional tasks were designed:

2. using a spoon to pry open a pop-up lid: This task requires placing the edge of the spoon under the lid's edge, and then maintaining

this contact while pushing the spoon handle downward in a curvilinear fashion;

3. using a fork to lift a noodle off a plate: This task requires placing the edge of the fork at the side of the noodle, then pushing the fork under the noodle and up (again in a curvilinear fashion); and

4. using the edge of a spoon to make a scallop-shaped slice through a banana: This task also requires the subject to make sustained contact between a spoon and a second object and then to make a curvilinear motion with the spoon.

5. putting a spoon through the hole in the lid of a container, and pulling up to remove the lid

6. flipping a carrot by putting a spoon on the edge, and moving it down and to the side (the action involved was the same as in making the scallop-shaped banana slice).

Substage 3: 3½ to 5 years. At this final substage, children are supposed to be able to elaborate on their earlier bifocal responses. They are also supposed to be able to integrate the elements of these responses in an on-line (as opposed to sequential) fashion (Case, 1985). It was therefore hypothesized that they would be able to control the action of a tool in a more precise, circular fashion. For example, in Task 1., they were expected to be able to twirl a cooked spaghetti noodle onto a fork, a task which requires maintaining control of a fork in an upright position, while rotating it through 360 degrees; this requires sustained, on-line control of the fork's movement about two axes simultaneously.

The additional tasks that were designed at this level were:

2. using a knife to score a circle on a flat piece of Play-Doh: Like the twirling noodle task, this task requires on-line control of biaxial movement, through a full 360 degrees;

3. removing an unwanted piece of "sticky food" (actually a block of Play-doh) from a fork, using only the friction between the plate and the food as an aid. This task requires extracting the fork from the block with a curvilinear movement of the sort children can demonstrate at the previous level; however, it requires more careful control of this movement: The fork must push the food down against the plate (because otherwise the food simply accompanies the fork along its curvilinear trajectory) while it "exits" from the food along a curvilinear trajectory;

4. scooping a pea onto a spoon from a plate, without an edge to roll it up against. Once again, this task requires a careful biaxial movement of the utensil in the hand, coupled with a sideways "finishing motion" in which the edge of the spoon is tilted up as the pea is lifted;

5. getting a small block of "food" (Play-doh) to fall over and into a

spoon, by quickly pulling the spoon backwards while it rests on top of the block, and then scooping the spoon underneath it; and

6. cutting through a bagel, while the experimenter stabilizes it, a task that requires *resisting* the tendency of the curved surface of the bagel to displace the knife in a curvilinear fashion.

Substage 1: 5 to 6 years (Unidimensional Stage).   At this new stage, children are hypothesized to become capable of coordinating two entire relational systems, and focusing on a new, higher order relationship as a consequence (Case, 1985). When they are at the dinner table, children at this level appear to be capable of coordinating two different utensils, each of which is responsible for a different function: for example, stabilizing a piece of soft meat or bread with a fork, while slicing through it with a knife. Note that this requires that one tool perform a biaxial motion while the other stabilizes the food along two axes simultaneously. The other tasks that were devised to test the generality of this capability included:

1. cutting through an apple with a knife and a fork; and
2. lifting a pea between a spoon (held in one hand) and a fork (held in the other).

Procedure

Because the purpose of this first study was primarily inductive, a small number of children was selected on a rather arbitrary basis from a local day care center, and presented with the items that have just been described.

Results

Details of each task's presentation are available on request. The number of children passing each task at each age level is presented in Table 14.1. As may be seen, for each task the results confirmed the predictions.

Discussion

The pattern of results in the data was encouraging and was taken as an indication that the hypothesized model should be formalized and put to a more rigorous test.

GROSS MOTOR PERFORMANCE FROM BIRTH TO ADOLESCENCE

Generalization of the Theoretical Model

Prior to conducting the second study, a generalized model was formulated, which could apply to the full range of children's motor performance from birth to adolescence. The assumptions underlying this gener-

TABLE 14.1
Percentage of Children Passing Each Item at Each Level

Items	8–15 mo (n = 1)	16–20 mo (n = 2)	21–26 mo (n = 3)	27–41 mo (n = 5)	42–54 mo (n = 6)
	(12 mo)	(x̄ = 19 mo)	(x̄ = 24 mo)	(x̄ = 33 mo)	(x̄ = 48 mo)
Level 0					
Scoop yogurt	0	100	100	100	100
Stir liquid	100	100	100	100	100
Fork in banana	0	100	100	100	100
Knife into Play-Doh	0	100	100	100	100
Fork along table	0	100	100	100	100
Poke knife through hole	100	100	100	100	100
Level 1					
Mash banana	0	0	66	100	100
Push penny	—	—	—	—	—
Scoop pea	0	0	100	100	100
Jab pea	0	0	100	100	100
Poke knife through and into	0	0	100	100	100
Knife track	0	0	66	100	100
Level 2					
Play-Doh slice	—	—	—	—	—
Pop-up lid	—	—	—	100*	100*
Noodle lift	0	0	0	100	100
Slice banana	—	—	—	—	—
Pull-up lid	—	—	—	100*	100*
Carrot flip	—	—	—	100	100
Level 3					
Twirl noodle	0	0	0	0	83
Cut-out-circle	0	0	0	0	100
Release block	0	0	0	0	100
Scoop pea on plate	0	0	0	0	83
Block flip	0	0	0	0	66
Bagel slice	0	0	0	0	83

— = task not presented

*n = 2

alized model were as follows: First, the progression from uniaxial to biaxial to integrated biaxial control is not confined to fine motor development; it is present in gross motor tasks as well, since it depends more on the understanding of spatial relations than on the particular form of neuromuscular control that is required to produce these relations. Second, the progression from uniaxial to biaxial to integrated biaxial control is not confined to the interrelational stage. It is present at the sensorimotor and dimensional stages as well. Third, the sort of movement over which axial control is possible does vary from stage to stage: At each successive stage, the units children control and operate on are of a higher order than those at the stage before. Fourth, the nature of the appropriate unit for analysis at the sensorimotor stage can be determined by "backing down" from the Level 1 capability of the interrelational stage, with the aid of a "halfing" rule. Finally, the nature of the appropriate unit for motor analysis at the Dimensional Stage can be determined by moving upward from the Level 3 interrelational capability, with the aid of a "doubling" rule. Illustrations of both of these rules follow.

Analyzing Motor Development During the Sensorimotor Stage

As has already been mentioned, the element on which interrelational tool use was hypothesized to depend was the ability to move one object through space, and bring it into contact with another, in some particular fashion. The question that was asked, therefore, was how this act could be reconstrued as involving some form of "integrated biaxial control" over two more primitive units. Stated differently, the question was how this unit could be reconstrued as involving two separate and integrated "halves." The answer suggested was that the axes of the tool's displacement with respect to the *body*, rather than with respect to some other *object*, should be thought of as the earlier focus of the child's attention. The following predictions were therefore advanced: At Substage 1 of the sensorimotor period (4 to 8 months), children should be able to control the use of a graspable object along a single axis, where this axis is defined with respect to their own bodies; at Substage 2 (8 to 12 months), children should be able to control the use of a graspable object along two self-referenced axes; and at Substage 3 (1 to 1½ years), children should be able to control the use of a graspable object along two self-referenced axes simultaneously (or three axes in a sequential fashion).

Analyzing Motor Development During the Dimensional Stage

In the domain of utensil-use, the "doubling" that was introduced in the first study was the use of two tools simultaneously (as in the case of the fork and knife). In order to conceptualize this capability in a more general fashion, the question was how the act of carving with a knife could be thought of as involving a higher order control system with a unitary mental focus. The answer proposed was that, by treating the stabilizing tool as "background" and the slicing tool as "foreground," children might, in effect, be visualizing the knife as sawing back and forth through an imaginary plane or *mental corridor.* Thus, the predictions were: Children at the first substage of the dimensional period (5 to 6 years) should be able to control the use of a tool along a single mental corridor; children at the second substage of the dimensional period (7 to 8 years) should be able to control the use of a tool along two such corridors; and children at the final substage of the dimensional period (9 to 10 years) should be able to control the use of a tool along two such corridors in an integrated fashion (or three corridors in a sequential fashion).

In effect, then, the assertion was that children moved through three general stages, in their understanding of the spatial relations on which controlled motor movement is dependent. In the first, they constructed an understanding of spatial axes as defined with regard to their own body. In the second, they constructed an understanding of the spatial relations of external objects in a flat plane. In the third, they constructed an understanding of spatial relations in "free space."

TASKS USED TO ASSESS THE VALIDITY OF THE GENERALIZED MODEL

Sensorimotor Level 1

In order to assess the sensorimotor capability that was presumed to be characteristic of Substage 1, children of 4 to 8 months were encouraged to imitate the experimenter, who modeled the act of moving pegs along a straight track in a small box (see Fig. 14.1a), in order to ring a bell. The prediction was that 5- to 8-month-old children (but not 3 or 4-month-olds) would be able to monitor the action and reaction produced by the tester, and then generate a similar action and reaction themselves. Note that this action required the baby to displace the peg along a single self-referenced axis, namely the sagittal one.

Sensorimotor Level 2

At the next substage, the prediction was that infants would be able to execute a task that involved control along two such self-referenced axes, rather than just one. The apparatus used to test this hypothesis was similar to the one used at the previous substage, but in this case the infants needed to move the peg through two tracks set at right angles to each other (Fig. 14.1b). This response was considered a biaxial control structure, because it required control of an object's movement along both the frontal and sagittal planes.

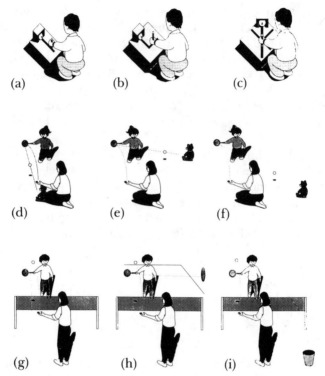

FIG. 14.1.   Parallels in motor performance across stages.
Top Row: Sensorimotor Stage: Left to Right (Substages 1, 2, 3)
Middle Row: Interrelational Stage: Left to Right (Substages 1, 2, 3)
Bottom Row: Dimensional Stage: Left to Right (Substages 1, 2, 3)

Sensorimotor Level 3

At this substage it was predicted that infants would be able to execute a task that required on-line integration of the previous structures. As shown in Fig. 14.1c, children were presented with a third box, which required them to move a peg through a diagonal track. While children might well be able to slide the peg along the track in a direction that was generally forward or sideways, it was hypothesized that, when they arrived at the point of intersection of the two tracks, they would have to exert an active and very precise control of the peg's movement about the sagittal and frontal axes simultaneously, or else the peg would slip into one of the two incorrect tracks.

Although the diagonal peg task was the principal one that was designed to assess the presence of integrated-biaxial control at this stage, two other measures were also administered in order to assess the roots of developments that were anticipated at the next stage. In the first of these tasks, children were asked to use a racket to push a stationary ball toward a target that was positioned directly in front of them (Fig. 14.1d). In order to succeed, children had to move the racket in the same diagonal fashion as in the peg task: a little bit forward and a little bit laterally, while monitoring the progress of the ball.[1]

In the second additional task, children were asked to catch a moving ball that was rolled toward them across a table. To succeed at this task, it was presumed that they would have to monitor the ball as its position varied in a forward–backward fashion (i.e., along a sagittal axis), and to coordinate this monitoring with the action of moving their own hands along the frontal axis (apart–together). Note that this coordination would also have to be done on-line, in order to time the closing of the hands with the ball's arrival.

Interrelational Level 1

At the first substage of the interrelational period, the hypothesis was that 2-year-old children would be able to coordinate the two competencies just described: that is, bringing a dowel into contact with a ball in order to control its forward movement and making contact with a rolling ball as it arrived at a proximal point. As a result, for the first time, they should be able to execute a task which requires them to monitor a ball as it rolls towards them, and to strike it with an object such as a bat, thus rolling it back along the same (sagittal) axis. While this new coordination is complex from the point of sensorimotor development, from the perspective of interrelational development it can be said to involve a new sort of simple, uniaxial control: In effect, the child must monitor the ball's arrival and departure along the single axis that runs along the floor from the experimenter to the end of the child's racket.

Interrelational Level 2

At the second substage, the hypothesis was that 3-year-old children would be able to control a ball's movement along two externally referenced axes in succession, first tracking its displacement along the sagittal axis (Fig. 14.1d), then directing the ball toward a target that was stationed along the frontal axis at a right angle to their non-dominant side (Fig. 14.1e).

Interrelational Level 3

At the third substage, the hypothesis was children aged (3½ to 5 years) would be able to execute a task that was similar, except that the target was positioned along a diagonal rather than a right-angled path

---

[1]For further theoretical and empirical support of this notion, see Olson (1970).

to the child's non-dominant side (Fig. 14.1f). Again I hypothesized that children would have to coordinate their monitoring of the displacement of the ball along the frontal and sagittal axes simultaneously, as they made contact with it. In effect, they would have to aim the ball a little bit forward and a little bit sideways simultaneously, just as they had had to move the stick at the corresponding substage of the sensorimotor period.

Once again two additional tasks were designed to assess the precursors of higher order motor control. The first task involved making global contact between a racket and a ball that was moving through free space. The second task involved throwing a ball in free space to a target. The first task was presumed to require an on-line coordination of two interrelational structures: one for moving a tool through free space to make contact with a moving object, and one for tracking a moving object whose position varied along two axes simultaneously (forward–backward, upward–downward). The second task was also presumed to require an on-line coordination of two interrelational structures: one for controlling the biaxial or "pendular" movement of the arm, in order to propel the ball forward in a straight line, and the other for coordinating the release of the ball from the hand, in order to attain the right degree of loft, to propel the ball from the child to the experimenter.

Dimensional Development: Level 1

Children in the first substage (6-year-olds) were presumed to be capable of a new level of uniaxial control, in which they could coordinate the two structures whose presence was assessed by the two tasks just described. The new capability was that of using a racket to strike a freely moving ball in such a fashion that it would travel back along the same trajectory as it had just traversed (Fig. 14.1g). This latter requirement was introduced by throwing a ball to the children from behind a net, and demanding that the child hit the ball back over the same net with his or her racket. The new psychological entity or mental unit that children were presumed to have constructed was a spatial corridor or *free space axis* along which a ball could travel and return.

Dimensional Development: Level 2

At the second substage, 8-year-old children were expected to be capable of biaxial tool use in the same context. This capability was assessed by pitching them a ball, and asking them to hit it toward a target that was set at eye level, at right angles to their non-dominant side

(Fig.14.1h). The new task was presumed to require focusing on the first free-space corridor along which the ball moved toward them (sagittal), and then "decentering" and focusing on a second (frontal) corridor.

Dimensional Development: Level 3

Ten-year-olds were presumed to be capable of integrated biaxial control. This was assessed by pitching a ball to them in free space, and asking them to strike it back over a net and toward a target that had been placed along a diagonal path (Fig. 14.1i). As at the previous two stages, control of the ball along the diagonal was presumed to result from activating two structures simultaneously, one for directing it along the frontal axis and one for directing it along the sagittal axis.[2]

In summary, the foregoing motor tasks were designed to conform to the general model of motor control and its development that had been constructed on the basis of the more specific analysis of preschoolers' use of eating utensils. Two of the major assumptions tested were: the notion that there is a substantial degree of horizontal structure in development, structures that are observed on fine motor tasks with one sort of tool should thus be observed on gross motor tasks where a different sort of tool is required; and that there is also a substantial degree of vertical structure. Recurring cycles of development should thus be identifiable from one stage of development to the next.

Procedure

The full details of the administration of each task are described in Reid (1987). The tasks were administered to 10 children at each of the age levels hypothesized as critical by the general theory. Each task was administered individually, in the school gym, for the preschool and school-age children. For the infants and toddlers, a quiet room was used.

Results

The mean ages and standard deviations of each age group are presented in Table 14.2. At each stage, the mean performance scores were examined to see if they fell on the predicted straight line, formed by presuming that the mean score of subjects who were at the preliminary

---

[2]For related dimensional analyses of diagonality and its construction, see Olson (1970), Simon (1972), and Halford (1974).

TABLE 14.2
Mean Scores of Different Age Groups on Different Batteries of
Motor Tasks

(a)   *Infants on Sensorimotor Sequence (N = 40)*

| | Developmental Classification of Age Group | | | |
	Substage 0	Substage 1	Substage 2	Substage 3
Mean Age	4.3 mos	8 mos.	12.3 mos.	19 mos.
Mean Score	0.0	1.1	1.88	3.13
Standard Deviation	0	.32	.29	.21

(b)   *Preschool Children on Interrelational Tasks (N = 30)*

| | Developmental Classification of Age Group | | |
	Substage 1	Substage 2	Substage 3
Mean Age	2.2 yr	3.2 yr	4.7 yr
Mean Score	0.99	1.97	2.91
Standard Deviation	.27	.29	.37

(c)   *Schoolchildren on Dimensional Tasks (N = 30)*

| | Developmental Classification of Age Group | | |
	Substage 1	Substage 2	Substage 3
Mean Age	6.8 yr	8.8 yr	10.7 yr
Mean Score	1.23	1.80	2.58
Standard Deviation	.42	.26	.51

substage would be 0, while the mean scores at the next three substages
would be 1, 2, and 3, respectively. The resultant analyses indicated no
significant deviation from expectation for any age group.

Discussion

A number of conclusions can be drawn from the results reported in
Table 14.2. The first is that children at each of the first three stages of
cognitive development are capable of solving qualitatively different
types of spatial problems. For children in the sensorimotor stage, the
problems entail making simple graspable objects do their bidding, that
is, move in desired directions. For children in the interrelational

stage, this first problem assumes a background status, and the new problem involves using an object in one's hand as a tool in order to make a second object do one's bidding. For preschool children, objects can only be "driven" along a precise axis if their movement is constrained to a flat plane. For elementary school children, objects can be directed along corridors in free space.

A second conclusion relates to the form of mental representation that children employ for encoding and solving these three problem types. At least as a heuristic, it seems reasonable to assume that the three forms of representation differ. Ultimately, each form of representation may have to be modeled in some sort of analog format. For the present, though, it seems useful to think of children at the first stage as thinking in terms of the frame of reference provided by their own body and the directed actions it is capable of applying to an object (e.g., push, swipe, and push and swipe simultaneously). At the second stage children can think in terms of an external reference plane and the mental "tracks" or "lines" that objects can be made to trace with a bat or some other tool, as they move along such a plane (straight ahead, sideways, ahead but a bit to the side, etc.). Finally, one may view children at the third stage as thinking in terms of three-dimensional Euclidian space and the mental corridors that an object can trace as it passes through such a space after impact with a tool such as a bat or a racket (up and out to center court, up and out to the side, up and out to left-center court, etc.).

Because progress within each stage was so regular, a third conclusion is that the construction of each new frame of reference is accomplished only gradually. The representations children can construct at the first substage appear to require that the object's movement be specified along a single spatial axis. Those at the second substage appear to require specification along two spatial axes, at least in sequence. Finally, those at the third substage appear to require specifications along two spatial axes simultaneously, or along a third axis.

One final noteworthy aspect of the data, concerns the linkage between the tasks that a child can perform at the last substage of any major period and those he or she can execute at the first substage of the next. The integrated biaxial representations that are formed at the end of any stage—when fully coordinated—appear to serve as the basis for transition to the next stage. Thus, for example, when the biaxial control of the grasped object's movement can be coordinated with the biaxial specification of another object's movement path, one has, in effect, "constructed" a two-dimensional plane over which one can guide another object. Similarly, when the triaxial control of a grasped object's movement can be coordinated with the triaxial specification of another object's movement, one has, in effect, constructed a three-dimensional framework, within which one can guide an object with the tool in one's grasp. A further transition may be possible at the 10-year-old level, making for the possibility of dual-frame coordination within free space. This would, for example, enable one to impart a spin to an object with a tool, in order to make it describe different forms of curving arc en route to its intended destination.

These four conclusions are all quite speculative, and place a rather heavy emphasis on spatial representation, as opposed to neuromuscular control. The utility of such an emphasis was explored in a third study.

HORIZONTAL STRUCTURE IN CHILDREN'S CONSTRUCTION OF THIRD-ORDER SPATIAL RELATIONS

Before describing the third study, it is worthwhile to compare the results that have been reported so far with those that were reported by Dennis in chapter 13. The focus of Dennis's study was considerably different from the present one, in that it concerned children's mastery of a culturally based system of artistic representation. It was also similar, however, in that it required the use of a tool, coupled with higher and higher forms of spatial representation. As Case (1985, chapter 8) has pointed out, children first master the use of a pencil as a graspable object during the Sensorimotor Stage, grasping the shaft of a pencil, while monitoring the pencil as it comes into contact with a flat plane. This can be thought of as directly analogous to the competence of bringing an eating utensil, such as a spoon, into contact with food in that both require the child to focus on and control a spatial relationship between two objects.

During the Interrelational Stage, the close parallel with utensil use continues. During the first substage, children first master the use of the pencil to create marks on a flat plane. However, the only marks they can imitate with any accuracy are restricted to those that move along a single axis, that is, straight lines. Children then extend this competence during the second substage to include the production of two straight lines along intersecting axes or single curvilinear lines (at 2½ to 3½ years). Finally their competencies are elaborated during the final substage, with the result that crosses, circles, and so on, can be made. It is at this point that the resultant products can be recognized and labeled as people or objects.

Transition to the third stage of representation in drawing bears a somewhat more remote resemblance to development in the motor domain. Nevertheless, a clear analogy is still present. The "scenes" that children create in their drawings as they move from the relational to the dimensional stage are ones where all the individual objects on the paper are aligned in a single spatial corridor. A second such corridor then appears in the background at the age of 8 years, followed by some sort of attempt at integration at the age of about 10.

Given the foregoing formal parallel between children's development in the two domains and the 10-year period over which this parallel is maintained, the possibility that a central conceptual structure for space exists must, clearly, be considered.[3] If such a structure does exist it follows, of course, that the development of individual children should proceed at about the same rate on these two different tasks. Although certain children might be far more skilled on one task than the other, the general conceptual understanding of space on which their skills depend, and the general sort of motor control that they exhibit when operating within this understanding, should develop at approximately the same rate.

The third study was designed as a preliminary test of this hypothesis. The same 40 children who had been given the "free space" sports tasks were also presented with two other measures. The first was a modified version of the initial drawing task presented by Dennis in chapter 13. In the present study, the instructions were "Draw me a picture of a girl (or boy) about your age, doing something they like to do outside." Scoring of children's drawings was conducted using the system devised by Dennis.

The second additional task was the Visual-Spatial Span Test. This task was designed by Crammond (this volume, chapter 16) to measure memory span for non-verbal information in children, and is a modified version of the Mr. Cucumber spatial task that was described in chapter 13. This task was used for two reasons: First, the task requires children to localize the position of an object along two axes in a flat plane; it should therefore be mastered at about the same time as other biaxial capabilities of this sort, that is, at about 4 years of age. Second, the task's difficulty can be increased incrementally, thus testing the prediction of neo-Piagetian theory that quantitative and qualitative changes in any domain should be closely linked.

The details of the task and its administration are described in the chapter 16. Basically, children are required to remember the location of one or more shaded cells in a 4 × 4 matrix. Three trials are then presented at each of several levels, with the number of shaded cells to be remembered increasing by one unit from each level to the next. After

---

[3]Note that this idea, or one much like it, was originally postulated by Piaget and Inhelder (1956) and has been further developed by Olson (1970) and Olson and Bialystok (1983).

three successive failures at any level, testing is discontinued. The final score is the total number of items on which the subject is correct, divided by the number of items per level (in this case, 3).

Results

The first step in the analysis was to compare the group scores for the two additional tests with those for the Stage 3 motor tasks. As is indicated in Fig. 14.2, the three sets of data are virtually indistinguishable. All three fell along the predicted straight line, and there were no significant differences among the means.

The next step was to determine whether, if the tests were treated as independent estimates of the same underlying parameter, the results would form a single Guttman scale. This analysis was approached using a technique originally developed by Bereiter and Khanna (Khanna,

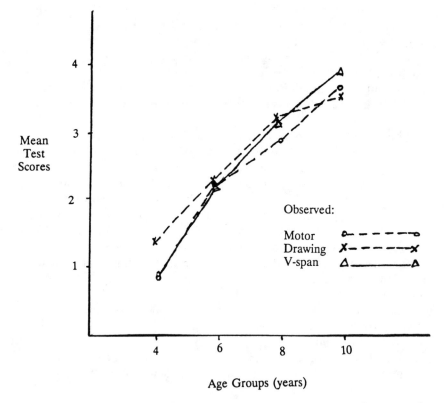

FIG. 14.2.   Observed mean scores on the motor, art and visual-spatial span tests.

1985, p. 59), wherein all possible sets of items are formed (e.g., Set No. 1: Level 1 from the art task, Level 2 from the motor task, Level 3 from the span task, Level 4 from the motor task. Set No. 2: Level 1 from the motor task, Level 2 from the art task . . . etc.). The percentage of these sets that form perfect Guttman scales is then determined. The results from this test were very strong, and indicated that children's performance on the heterogeneous task sets yielded a perfect Guttman scale 100% of the time: no child failed Level X on one scale while passing Level X + 1 on the same scale or any other.

In the same vein, when the data on individual subjects were examined, it was found that the majority of children performed at the same level across the three tasks. Thus, for the majority of children, there was a clear modal level of functioning, with only a minor deviation of one substage in a few cases (see Table 14.3).

Discussion

The first and most obvious finding is that development in the motor domain bears a strong formal similarity to development in other domains in its general structure. Second, at least at higher age levels, development in the motor domain appears to depend on the presence of spatial structures that are quite general or "central" in nature.

CONCLUSION

I would like to conclude by making two general points. The first concerns the relationship of the present work to the more classic studies that have been conducted in the field of motor development: those exploring the information-processing mechanisms that underlie motor learning

TABLE 14.3
Percentage of Subjects Showing Varying
Degrees of Asynchrony at Different
Age Levels

Age (years)	Perfect Synchrony	Split of one Substage
4	90	10
6	100	0
8	90	10
10	80	20

Note. $n = 10$ in each group.

(Adams, 1971; Keele & Summers, 1976; Schmidt, 1975) and those examining the neuromuscular and biomechanical capabilities on which these mechanisms depend (Diamond, 1989; Scott, 1983). It is important to realize that the present study was not designed to challenge the assumptions that underlie these information processing or neurophysiological studies, but rather to supplement them, by suggesting that the learning of any specific motor task, even one whose biological substrate is known, may be seen in a developmental context as being dependent on a broader structural progression, one which requires an increasingly sophisticated understanding of space.

A similar point may be made with regard to the neo-Piagetian research that was cited in the introduction. This research focused on the general information-processing constraints to which children's motor performance appears to be subject, during the 6- to 10-year-old period (Mitchell, 1977; Sifft, 1978; Thomas & Bender, 1977; Todor, 1975, 1979). The present results present no challenge to these studies either. Indeed, if anything, they confirm them by demonstrating a close parallel between quantitative and qualitative change. What the present results suggest in addition, however, is that these earlier results should also be seen in a somewhat broader perspective, wherein the developments that occur between 6 and 10 years of age are seen as entailing a recapitulation, at a higher epistemic level, of developments that occurred earlier at lower levels.

Exactly what the neurological basis of such a recapitulation might be is not clear. However, given the strong implication of a neurological substrate subserving factors in most motor functioning, this is clearly a possible area for future research. A similar conclusion applies to the relationship between the spatial developments that have been described in this chapter and the previous one, and the developments that were described in the two previous sections. To the extent that these developments are controlled by different neurological systems, the structural parallels that have been found across systems must either be located within these separate systems (e.g., in their internal structure and pattern of developments) or in some common central system, which establishes constraints to which all the more specific systems are subject.

V

CROSS-DOMAIN SYNCHRONY AND ASYNCHRONY IN THE ACQUISITION OF DIFFERENT CONCEPTUAL STRUCTURES

The results reported in the previous three sections indicate that children's central conceptual structures in three different domains undergo major and minor restructurings of the same general nature, during the same general time periods. In and of themselves, however, such data do not resolve the question of whether these changes are controlled by a common underlying mechanism. As an illustration, consider the following example: Suppose that a group of 8-year-olds achieved a mean score of 2.0 on two test batteries, each of which was designed to assess their level of functioning in a different conceptual domain (e.g., numerical and social understanding). If one examined only the group data, one might easily conclude that development in the two domains was controlled by a common underlying mechanism, because the average level of functioning of the population would be identical in each. Suppose further, however, that only half the individual children actually showed an even profile across the two domains, while one quarter of the children showed profiles in which performance on the numerical battery was three full substages ahead of performance on the social battery, and the remaining quarter showed profiles that were exactly the reverse. Clearly, the existence of so many children with extreme discrepancies in their level of functioning would call into question the conclusion of a common underlying mechanism. It would seem more likely that development in the two domains was controlled by a *different* mechanism that just happened to produce similar results for half the subjects.

The foregoing example is, of course, an extreme one. In view of the

267

even developmental profiles *within* developmental domains, which were reported in earlier sections, one could even argue that such a scenario would be unlikely. Nevertheless, the example illustrates an important point. The issue of developmental generality cannot be resolved simply by examining the performance of an entire age cohort, on two tasks from different domains. In addition, one must examine the performance of individual children *within* each age cohort, and determine whether their cross-domain profiles are symmetrical.

In the present section, a start is made in this direction. The particular conceptual domains that are examined are those discussed in previous sections, namely, numerical, social, and spatial reasoning. For the most part, the measures that are used are the same as well. Instead of focusing primarily on group data within each domain, however, these final chapters focus on data from individual children across domains. In addition, an attempt is made to consider a broader *range* of individuals than in previous chapters, including those who would be most likely to show developmental profiles that are uneven.

Some of these studies yield data that are closely in line with what one would expect, on the basis of the existing literature. There are some surprises as well, however, and these are of considerable theoretical import.

Parallels in the Development of Children's Social, Numerical, and Spatial Thought

Robbie Case
Stanford University
Sharon Griffin
Clark University
Anne McKeough
University of Calgary
Yukari Okamoto
University of California, Santa Barbara

In the context of cognitive developmental theory, the question of whether the mind should be thought of as a general or modular device is normally translated into the question of whether children's development in different conceptual domains does or does not take place at the same rate. It is with this question that the present chapter is concerned. In three of the studies that were reported in earlier chapters supplementary measures were presented, in order to address this question in a preliminary fashion. The present chapter begins with a review of these studies, and a presentation of the additional data that they generated. A fourth study is then described, which was designed to test the conclusions from the first three studies in a more rigorous and systematic fashion.

A DEVELOPMENTAL COMPARISON OF CHILDREN'S STORIES AND LINE DRAWINGS

In a study that was reported by McKeough (chapter 10), children's stories were classified as falling into one of four developmental levels. At the lowest level were stories in which a problem was mentioned, but no solution was offered. These stories were classified as pre-intentional and were assigned a score of 0. At the next level a problem was mentioned, followed immediately by a successful attempt to resolve it; these stories were classified as uni-intentional (and scored 1). At the next level, a problem was mentioned and was then followed by a complicating event before it was resolved. These stories were classified as bi-intentional, and assigned a score of 2. Finally, at the highest level, stories contained a

269

problem and a sub-problem, which were presented in a well integrated fashion, and both were satisfactorily resolved; these stories were classified as having an integrated bi-intentional plot and were assigned a score of 3.

The same children who performed the story-telling task in this study were also presented with the drawing task designed by Dennis (this volume, Study 1, chapter 13). Pictures in which the figures hovered in space and were randomly distributed about the page were classified as pre-axial (score = 0). Pictures in which the figures were aligned in a horizontal row on a ground line were classified as uniaxial (score = 1). If a second horizontal row was introduced as background the pictures were classified as biaxial; other pictures that gave clear evidence of foreground-background differentiation using techniques such as occlusion were classified at this level as well (score = 2). Finally, pictures that included some middle ground between the foreground and background were classified as having an integrated biaxial composition (score = 3).

With the data from these two tests in hand, the question that was addressed was whether individual children's progress through these two separate developmental sequences took place at the same rate—as one might expect if some sort of general, systemic factor were operative—or whether development more frequently took place at considerably different rates, as one would expect if development were more modular or domain-specific.

Method

Subjects

Subjects were the same 60 children described in Study 1 in chapter 10. There were 9, 16, 19, and 16 subjects respectively, in the 4-, 6-, 8-, and 10-year-old groups.

Procedures

The procedures were also the same as those described in previous chapters. Both tests were administered on an individual basis, with the drawing task always being given in a separate session, several days after the story tasks had been completed.

Results

Analysis of Group Data

The mean scores of each age group on each task are illustrated in Fig. 15.1. As may be seen, the performance of each age group was remarkably consistent across the story and the picture drawing tasks.

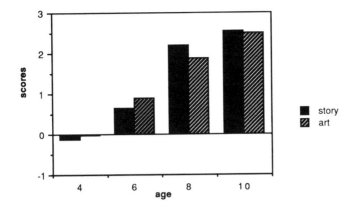

FIG. 15.1.   Mean scores on narrative and drawing tasks at 4 age levels
(Study #1).

An analysis of variance revealed a highly significant effect due to age, and a nonsignificant effect due to task.

Analysis of Individual Data

The individual data are presented in Table 15.1. These results also indicate a parallel in the rate at which children mastered each successive task level. At most ages, the majority of children scored at the same level on both the story and the drawing tasks. The percentage of subjects who performed at the same level on both tasks was somewhat lower in the two older groups than in the two younger groups, however, and at the 10-year-old level, there were even a few subjects (2/16 or 12.5%) who showed a discrepancy in performance of two substages.

TABLE 15.1
Percentage of Subjects Showing
Various Degrees of Developmental
Asynchrony at Different Age Levels
(Study 1)

Age (years)	Amount of Asynchrony		
	None	One Substage	Two Substages
4	75	25	0
6	73	27	0
8	58	42	0
10	46	41	13

Discussion

As in the study reported by Marini (this volume, chapter 4), the degree of concordance for individual subjects was not as great as that for the entire group. However, the degree of concordance was still higher than would be expected if one assumed that completely different mental modules or forms of intelligence were involved, each with its own unique developmental trajectory. It was also of some interest to note that, even in the two subjects who showed a discrepancy of two substages, performance was not at an adult level on one task, and a child-like level on the other. Rather, performance was one substage ahead of age-level expectations in one domain, and one substage behind these expectations on the other. The hypothesis of an age-typical upper bound or "optimum level" is thus not precluded by these data, providing one does not view this level as completely immutable.

A DEVELOPMENTAL COMPARISON OF CHILDREN'S STORIES WITH THEIR BALANCE BEAM SOLUTIONS

In a second study that was conducted by McKeough (Chapter 10) children were presented with a more focused set of story telling tasks that could be classified according to the same general scoring scheme. This time, the children were presented with the balance beam task in a subsequent session, using the procedure developed by Marini (this volume, chapter 4). Responses to this task were classified as predimensional (no evidence of numerical quantification: score = 0), unidimensional (numerical quantification of weight only: score = 1), bidimensional (numerical quantification of distance from the fulcrum, when weights on the two sides are equal: score = 2), or integrated bidimensional (quantification of the difference on each dimension in cases of weight–distance conflict: score = 3).

Subjects

Subjects were the same 75 children that were described in the second study in chapter 10. There were 16 four-year-olds, 20 six-year-olds, 19 eight-year-olds, and 20 ten-year-olds.

Procedures

The procedures were also the same as those described in previous chapters. Both tests were administered on an individual basis, with the balance beam task always being given in a separate session, several days after the story tasks had been completed.

Results

Analysis of Group Data

The first step was to determine whether performance on the balance beam followed the same pattern in these subjects as had been found in previous studies. In fact, it did. A one-way ANOVA revealed a significant group effect, $F(3,71) = 112.01$, $p < .01$, with follow-up *a priori* tests revealing (a) a significant difference between all adjacent age groups, (b) a significant linear component to the trend ($p < .01$), and (c) no significant quadratic component. When the mean scores were compared to the predicted values and the deviation scores analyzed, a further ANOVA indicated that the three age groups did not differ significantly from each other in their deviation scores and that the grand mean showed no significant vertical displacement. In short, the overall fit of the data to the predictions was excellent, with no one group showing a deviation from the predicted linear trend that was greater than any other, and the predicted linear model accounting for 78% of the explained variance.

To compare the performance of the subjects on the balance beam with their performance on the narrative task, another ANOVA was conducted on the deviation scores, using the data from both tasks. The mean scores for each group on each task are illustrated in Fig. 15.2. As may be seen, the 2 sets of means were almost identical. As a consequence, when an ANOVA was conducted on the combined mean deviation scores, it showed no significant differences as a function of age, $F(3,71) = 2.18$, $p > .05$, and the grand mean did not show any significant vertical displacement from the expected one, $F(1,71) = .38$, $p > .05$.

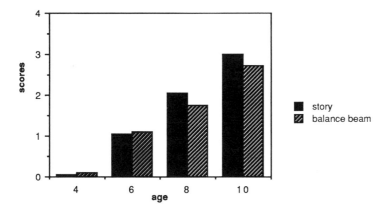

FIG. 15.2.   Mean scores on narrative and balance beam tasks at the 4 age levels (study #2).

Crucial to the issue of cross-domain parallels, there was also no significant Task effect, $F(1,71) = 2.79$, $p > .05$, and no significant Task $\times$ Age-group interaction $F(3,71) = 1.52$, $p > .05$.

Analysis of Individual Data

When the performance of individual subjects was examined, a number of individual children were found who performed at different levels. The data for this comparison are presented in Table 15.2. As may be seen, those children who showed an asynchronous pattern of performance were always in the minority. Furthermore, of these, only 2 children showed a split in functioning of more than one substage. Finally, of these two children, none performed more than one substage beyond their age-predicted optimum level. Nonetheless, the amount of asynchrony was far from trivial.

Discussion

In neither of these first two studies was the degree of concordance within individual subjects as great as it was within the age cohort as a whole. In both studies, however, the degree of cross-task concordance was sizable and was greater than would be expected if children's performance in each domain followed a unique developmental trajectory. It could possibly be argued that such concordance is not sufficient, in and of itself, to undermine the assumption of domain-independent cognitive growth. Even for two domains in which growth is independent, the appearance of cross-domain uniformity can be produced if common factors are introduced that impose common performance constraints on what otherwise would be revealed as quite different levels of competence. In the present case, however, the two tasks differed dramatical-

TABLE 15.2
Percentage of Subjects Showing
Various Degrees of Developmental
Asynchrony at Different Age Levels
(Study 2)

Age (years)	Amount of Asynchrony		
	None	One Substage	Two Substages
4	56	44	0
6	80	20	0
8	84	11	0
10	50	40	10

ly in the type of operation required, as well as in the response format, stimulus array, and question format. Unless one were to argue that most children happen to acquire the specific experience relevant to each task at virtually the same rate, then, it is hard to escape the conclusion that the developmental constraints to which both sets of tasks are subject have at least some common component, whose nature must be sought in the functioning of their general cognitive system.

A DEVELOPMENTAL COMPARISON OF CHILDREN'S AWARENESS OF THEIR INNER WORLD WITH THEIR STORIES AND THEIR LINE DRAWINGS

The same children who performed the intrapersonal tasks in the study reported in chapter 11 were also presented with the story-telling task and the drawing task in a subsequent session. The methods used to present the story and drawing tasks were identical to those described in Study 1. The method of task presentation for the intrapersonal tasks was the one developed by Griffin (this volume, chapter 11). Children's responses to requests to provide meanings for "happy," "sad," "good," and "bad" were classified as pre-intentional (internal states defined as behavioral events: score = 0), uni-intentional (internal states defined as attitudes toward events, with one intentional dimension mentioned: score = 1), or bi-intentional (internal states defined as attitudes toward events, with two intentional dimensions mentioned: score = 2).

Subjects

Subjects were the same 60 children described in chapter 11. There were 20 subjects each at 4, 6, and 8 years.

Procedures

The procedures were also the same as in chapter 11. All tests were administered on an individual basis, with the intrapersonal tasks always being presented first, the drawing task second, and the story task last. Depending on a child's attention span, the tasks were administered in a single session or in two sessions spaced less than one week apart.

Results

Analysis of Group Data

The mean scores on six tasks (i.e., four intrapersonal tasks, one drawing task, and one story task) are illustrated in Figure 15.3. As may be seen, the developmental progressions formed by the group means

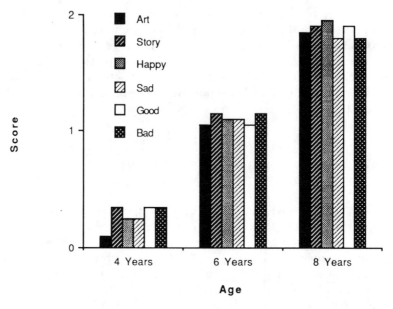

FIG. 15.3.   Mean scores of 3 age groups on 6 tasks (study #3).

were consistently linear, parallel, and of equal magnitude, suggesting that development across all tasks takes place at the same rate, at least at the group level.

Analysis of Individual Data

Table 15.3 presents the pattern of performance of each individual child in the sample across the six tasks. This graphic display indicates that a majority of children performed at the predicted level on the majority of tasks, and shows quite clearly that the cross-task synchrony found for age-cohorts was also present in the performance of individual children within each cohort. Deviation from the modal level of performance typically took the form of a one-substage deviation across one or more task pairs, and was insufficient to mask the dominant developmental pattern. Only 3 children of 60 (or 5%) showed an asynchrony in performance of more than one substage across any of the six tasks.

A more rigorous assessment of cross-domain consistency was obtained by computing the percentage of children at each age-level who performed at an identical level across selected groups of tasks. Cross-domain concordance for all three age-groups is shown in Table 15.4. Because the 6-year-old group was the only one whose performance was free to fluctuate in two directions, it was considered to provide the most

TABLE 15.3

Pattern of performance of individual children on six tasks drawn from three content domains (Study 3)

		YEARS		
SCORE	TASKS	4	6	8
2	ART			
	STORY			
	HAPPY			
	SAD			
	GOOD			
	BAD			
1	ART			
	STORY			
	HAPPY			
	SAD			
	GOOD			
	BAD			
	ART			
	STORY			
	HAPPY			
	SAD			
	GOOD			
	BAD			
	Subject	ABCDEFGHIJKLMNOPQRST	ABCDEFGHIJKLMNOPQRST	ABCDEFGHIJKLMNOPQRST
	Sex	ffmmfmmffmfmmmfm	fmmfmmmfffffmmm	fmmmfmmmmffmmffff

TABLE 15.4
Percentage of children at three age levels
with consistent performance across various
task combinations (Study 3)

| | Age Group (years) | | |
TASKS	4	6	8
Cross-Domain			
Art-Story-Happy	70	70	75
Art-Story-Good	60	75	65
Art-Story-Modal Intrapersonal	70	80	70
Art-Modal Social*	80	90	90
Within Domain			
Happy-Sad	90	70	75
Good-Bad	90	80	80
Happy-Sad-Good-Bad	70	50	70
Across all 6 tasks	55	50	55

*Note: When consistency was not found, the typical
pattern was a one-level split across tasks. Only 3 children showed a two-level split.

reliable estimate of cross-task concordance. A substantial majority of the
6-year-olds (70 to 98%) performed consistently in all cross-domain comparisons considered. Consistency was also high (70 to 80% at the 6-year-
old level) across pairs of tasks drawn from the intrapersonal domain,
although it fell to 50% at the 6-year-old level) when all four intrapersonal tasks were considered.

Discussion

Whether one considers the average scores of the entire group of children, or the individual scores of particular children within this group,
the degree of concordance in the third study was of the same general
magnitude as in the first two studies. Moreover, there was at least some
indication that this concordance was greater across broadly defined
structural domains than it was across individual tasks within a domain.
When the intrapersonal tasks were averaged and compared with performance on the spatial task, the concordance of absolute scores was
very high, with no subject showing an asynchrony as high as 2 levels. The
same was true when modal (rather than average) performance on the
intrapersonal tasks was compared with performance on the spatial task,
or when modal performance across all social tasks (including the story
task) was compared with spatial performance.

By contrast, children's performance within the set of intrapersonal
tasks was more varied, with the greatest difference occurring between

the tasks that required meanings to be given for "sad" and "good." There are a number of specific factors that might differentially affect children's performance on these two items. For example, differential anxiety might be produced by self-attributions of sadness vs. goodness; differential environmental support might also be available for acting in a manner that could be described as good vs. sad. Either of these factors might produce the sort of asynchronies that were providing a better meaning for good than sad.

Notwithstanding the difference in these two items, it is important to note (1) that 50% of the 6-year-olds still functioned at the same level across these two tasks and (2) that 80% of the children functioned at the same level when average intrapersonal performance was compared with performance on the spatial task. That the average performance on a battery should be more stable than performance on any particular item is not surprising. As long as individual items really are measuring some common underlying structure, one would expect this on statistical grounds alone. That average scores on the social battery should yield the same absolute values as performance on the spatial task for each age group, however, is by no means guaranteed by this statistical manipulation. Indeed, if development were truly modular, one would expect the reverse: Since average scores more accurately reflect the sophistication of underlying structures, and since structures from different modules develop at different rates (according to the modular hypothesis), children's average social scores should be more likely to diverge from their spatial scores. Since they do not, what the data in Table 15.4 suggest is that—regardless of their neurological or experiential substrates—the central conceptual structures children construct in different domains are subject to a common general-developmental constraint, which is system-wide in its nature.

A DEVELOPMENTAL COMPARISON OF CHILDREN'S DIMENSIONAL AND INTENTIONAL THOUGHT

The performance pattern reported in the previous sections of this volume is consistent with the notion that at certain key points in development, children acquire central conceptual structures that influence, but do not completely determine, their performance across a wide array of specific tasks. The performance pattern across the three studies reported in this chapter is consistent with this notion, and suggests further that different central conceptual structures appear to develop at approximately the same rate. However, as Rushton, Brainerd, and Pressley (1973) pointed out, the most rigorous way to investigate any hypothesis about the relationship between two underlying conceptual structures is not to give one task from one domain, and one or more tasks from a second. Rather, it is to present multiple measures from two different domains, so that task variance and structural variance can be disentangled. In our final study, this was the strategy we adopted.

Tasks

The tasks we administered were designed to chart the rate of development of the two central conceptual structures that were described in Sections II and III, namely those relating to dimensional and intentional thought. The first three dimensional tasks were the Balance Beam, the Birthday Party, and Distributive Justice tasks, which were described by Marini in chapter 4. The next two dimensional tasks were the Money Knowledge and Time-Telling tasks, which were described by Griffin, Case, and Sandieson in chapter 6. The final dimensional task was a modified version of the Number Knowledge test that was described by Case and Sandieson in chapter 7 (for the details of these modifications, see Case, Griffin, & Capodilupo, in press).

The tasks we used to assess children's intentional thought were the Mothers' Motives task, (Goldberg-Reitman, chapter 8), the Empathic Cognition task, (Bruchkowsky, chapter 9), the Story-Telling task (see McKeough, Study 2 chapter 10) and the Definition of Feelings task (Griffin, chapter 10). Two new tasks were also developed, in order to assess children's understanding of Psychological Verbs (Astington, 1985), and their understanding of Affective Change. A description of these last two tasks, and of the procedures that were used in administering the entire group of tasks, may be found in Case, Okamoto, Henderson, and McKeough (in press). A more detailed account is available in Case, McKeough, Okatomoto et al. (1990).

Subjects

There were 148 children from a wide range of social and economic backgrounds who were tested. The mean age of the children in the sample was 6½ years. The sample was drawn from kindergarten and first-grade classrooms in six different schools. Three of the schools were private, three public. Two of the public schools and one of the private schools served middle to upper-middle socioeconomic status (SES) families, who came predominantly from Anglo-American backgrounds. The remaining public school and the other two private schools drew from a relatively low SES population and served children from African-American and Hispanic as well as Anglo-American backgrounds. All but a few children spoke English as their first language.

RESULTS

Analysis of Group Data

Once again, the first step was to examine the group data to see whether performance on each task was at the level that would be expected for the age of the population in question. The mean scores and standard deviations for each task are presented in Table 15.5. The scores in Table 15.5 correspond to developmental levels, that is, a score of 0 indicates a typical 4-year-old performance, a score of 1 a typical 6-year-old performance, and a score of 2 a typical 8-year-old performance. What the data show is that the absolute level of children's performance was very close across all the tasks. In fact, the average level scores on the two batteries showed no significant difference, [$t(1, 147) = 1.52, p > .10$].

TABLE 15.5
Mean Performance on Each Task

Tasks	Mean	SD
Dimensional Tasks:		
Balance Beam	1.05	.75
Birthday Party	0.99	.75
Distributive Justice	0.83	.51
Money Knowledge	1.01	.61
Time Telling	1.07	.58
Number Knowledge	1.21	.45
Average Quantitative(a)	1.03	.44
Intentional Tasks:		
Story Telling	1.01	.89
Psychological Verbs	0.92	.60
Mothers' Motives	1.14	.73
Affective Change	0.89	.57
Definition of Feelings	1.20	.63
Empathic Cognition	1.37	.71
Average Social(b)	1.08	.44

Notes.

(a) The Average Quantitative score for one child with a missing level score on the Distributive Justice task was computed based on his responses to the other five tasks.

(b) The Average Social score for each of the seven children with a missing level score on one of the social tasks was computed based on their responses to the other five tasks.

Analysis of Individual Data

The assumption on which the analysis of the individual data was predicated was that the first six tasks could all be treated as tests of one underlying structure, and the second six tasks could all be treated as tests of another. In order to verify this assumption, a factor analysis was conducted. For this purpose, the data from the two new tasks (Psychological Verbs and Affective Change) were combined, due to problems of low reliability.

With the data thus re-coded, children's individual scores on the entire battery were submitted to the variant of alpha factor analysis that extracts orthogonal factors and submits them to varimax rotation, using Kaiser's criterion for determining the total number of factors (i.e., eigenvalues greater than 1; Kaiser & Caffrey, 1965). A further oblique rotation was then conducted, using the Oblimin procedure that is available on SPSS (Nie, 1986). The factor loadings from the two procedures were very similar and are given in Table 15.6. As may be seen, both solutions were in close conformity with the analyses in previous chapters. The six dimensional tasks all showed their strongest loadings on the first factor, and the six intentional tasks all showed their strongest loadings on the second. This being the case, it seemed acceptable to generate an average

TABLE 15.6
Factor Loadings: Oblique
(and Orthogonal) Rotations

	Factor	
Tasks	I Quantitative	II Social
Quantitative Tasks:		
Time Telling	.78 (.77)	−.09 (.30)
Number Knowledge	.77 (.72)	.05 (.30)
Money Knowledge	.74 (.74)	−.10 (.16)
Balance Beam	.67 (.62)	.11 (.29)
Birthday Party	.61 (.62)	−.13 (.08)
Distributive Justice	.30 (.30)	−.03 (.11)
Social Tasks:		
Story Telling	.09 (.25)	−.64 (.64)
Definition of Feelings	−.08 (.09)	−.62 (.58)
Mothers' Movites	−.06 (.10)	−.58 (.55)
Empathic Cognition	.16 (.31)	−.56 (.58)
Pictures*	.09 (.19)	−.37 (.38)

*Note This variable was created by combining the Affective Change and Psychological Verbs tasks.

(or more, accurately, a weighted average) of the scores on each set of tasks, in order to obtain an estimate of children's level on the underlying structure that each set of tasks had been designed to assess.

The pattern of cross-structural synchrony that resulted is presented in Table 15.7. Once again, the general pattern was one of synchronous rather than asynchronous performance: Only two children showed a mean discrepancy of a full substage between their average quantitative and social scores; approximately 70% of the children were within one-half a level on the two scales.

CONCLUSION

In this chapter, the results from four different studies have been presented. In the first, children were presented with one measure from the social domain (Story-Telling) and one measure from the spatial domain (Drawing). In the second, they were presented with one measure from the social domain (Story-Telling) and one from the numerical domain (Balance Beam). In the third, they were presented with several measures from the social domain (Definition of Feelings [Happy–Sad], Explanation of Judgements, [Good–Bad] and Story-Telling) and one from the spatial domain (Drawing). Finally, in the fourth, they were presented with six measures from each of the numerical and the social domains. The pattern across these four studies was extremely coherent. In neither study where only two measures were administered did any child ever show a discrepancy in his or her level of conceptual reasoning that exceeded two substages, and the great majority of differences were confined to one substage in their magnitude. In the study where multiple measures were administered in one domain, the percentage of individual children showing an asymmetry in performance of one substage across domains was reduced, and no two substage discrepancies were reported. Finally in the study where several measures were administered in each of two domains, the percentage of subjects showing a

TABLE 15.7
Percent of Children with
Cross-Structural Synchrony
and Asynchrony

Difference	Percent
Within 1/2 substage	69.60
1/2 to 1 substage	29.05
1 substage to 1 1/2 substage	1.35

split as great as one substage fell to less than 2%. Moreover, these splits, when they did occur, tended to involve underperformance, not over-performance, in a particular domain. If taken at their face value, then, these data suggest that wide differences in children's performance are more likely to be the result of different specific items of task knowledge than different levels of development across entire conceptual system. That is not to say, of course, that the small differences that were found are insignificant, or that all conceptual development can be reduced to a single factor. To the contrary, the results from the factor analysis indicate that two factors can be extracted from the group of conceptual tasks, with one factor corresponding to each central conceptual structure.[1] What the results do suggest, however, is that—even though each central conceptual structure is a distinct and coherent entity—different central conceptual structures progress along the same general lines. The results also suggest that—whatever their separate origins—such structures nonetheless are subject to the same set of general developmental constraints. In short, the results suggest that there is an element to development that is modular or domain-specific, and an even stronger element that is task specific but an element that is general as well.

We return to the implications of this suggestion in the final chapter. First, however, it is necessary to consider the extent to which the findings reported in the present chapter may be generalized to other populations: particularly those whose individual modes of functioning, and/or experience may vary more widely across conceptual structures than was the case for the children who participated in the present set of experiments.

---

[1]Note that two of the numerical tasks (Birthday Party and Distributive Justice) contained social content, while two of the social tasks (Intentional Verbs and Affective Change) contained numerical content; thus, a "surface" interpretation of the common task variance is not viable. It is only their underlying conceptual content of the tasks that was similer.

16

Analyzing the Basic Cognitive-Developmental Processes of Children with Specific Types of Learning Disability

Joanna Crammond
McGill University

When viewed from the perspective of the theory that has been developed in the present volume, cognitive development appears to be remarkably synchronous, at least in middle childhood. At each of the four modal ages of the dimensional stage, most children demonstrate parallel performance across a broad array of tasks, including those that tap the same underlying conceptual structures, and those that tap different ones. Although asynchronies in functioning across such tasks are not uncommon, they appear to be limited to one substage in the great majority of cases (Case, Marini, et al., 1986; Case, Griffin, McKeough & Okamoto , this volume, chapter 15).

The present chapter addresses the question of whether cross-domain synchronies of this sort are found only in average children, or whether they also appear in children who have been identified as exceptional in some way. This question is of considerable theoretical interest, because the even developmental profiles that have been reported could conceivably be an artifact of the selection procedure used. In most of the tests that have been reported so far, teachers have been asked to select children of average to above-average intelligence. It could be that a synchronous pattern of development is characteristic only of such average children. Worse still, it could be that such children are not even average, but merely perceived to be such by their teachers, because they happen to display an unusually even pattern of development to begin with.

The particular atypical children that I studied in the present project were those of who have difficulty in learning a particular type of subject matter in school, in spite of having an IQ in the average to above-average range. Three subtypes of such children were considered: Those who were classified as *reading-disabled, math-disabled* or disabled in both subject areas. In the educational literature these children are often referred to collectively as *learning-disabled.*

PREVIOUS RESEARCH ON CHILDREN WITH LEARNING DISABILITIES

To be classified as learning-disabled, children must attain IQ scores within or above the average range, but have achievement scores significantly below their chronological peers. It is normally stipulated, as well, that their achievement difficulties cannot be attributed to socioemotional or neurological factors. In recent years, deficits within the short-term memory system have consistently been cited as characteristic of such learners (Bauer, 1977, 1979, 1982; Bauer & Emhert, 1984; Cohen, 1982; Cohen & Netley, 1981; Mann, Liberman, & Shankweiler, 1980; L. S. Siegel & Linder, 1984; Torgesen, 1977, 1978; Torgesen & Houck, 1980). In view of the demonstrated importance of short-term memory for reading (Daneman & Carpenter, 1980; Doctor & Coltheart, 1980; Jorm, 1983; Perfetti & Lesgold, 1977; Stanovich, 1986; Torgeson, 1985), this finding makes good sense. What remains unclear, however, is whether these deficits are general or specific, and whether they play a role in producing disabilities in other school subjects.

Several neuropsychological studies (Salame & Baddeley, 1982; Shallice & Warrington, 1970; Warrington & Shallice, 1972) have reported selective memory impairment (verbal or visual) in subjects with localized brain damage. Such findings point to the existence of separate memory systems for verbal and visual information, and give some a priori support to the notion that memory deficits in reading may be specific to the verbal domain (Monsell, 1982; Shankweiler & Crain, 1986). Early investigations of this question did not reveal a modality-specific deficit, but these studies were confounded by the use of nonverbal tasks employing stimuli that could be verbally encoded (see Jorm, 1983; Torgesen, 1985). When more abstract spatial materials were used to assess visual spatial memory, the deficits for reading-disabled children tended to disappear (Ellis, 1981; Ellis & Miles, 1978). Moreover, in studies that manipulated the ease with which visual stimuli could be encoded verbally, further support was obtained for the hypothesis that reading deficits are specific to the verbal mode (Swanson, 1978, 1983, 1984).

Given the possible specificity of reading disabilities, recent reviewers and researchers have pointed out the danger of treating disabled learners as a homogeneous population (Fletcher, 1985; L. S. Siegel & Heaven, 1986; Stanovich, 1986); empirical research has confirmed this. For example, (Rourke and Strang 1978a; 1978b, Strang & Rourke, 1983) have suggested that learning-disabled children be classified into subtypes according to their pattern of performance on the Reading, Spelling, and Arithmetic subtests on the Wide Range Achievement Tests (WRAT; K. F. Jastak & S. R. Jastak, 1978). Results of a more recent study (Fletcher, 1985) have provided further validation for this hypothesis: Using a selective reminding procedure to assess the storage and retrieval functions of memory for both verbal and nonverbal materials, Fletcher reported that (a) children whose primary disability is in arithmetic show age-appropriate verbal skills but poor visuospatial skills, (b) children whose primary disability is in reading tend to demonstrate the opposite pattern (although the difference between verbal and visual spatial memory is not statistically significant), and (c) children with both reading and arithmetic difficulties have deficits in both verbal and nonverbal memory. L. S. Siegel and Linder (1984) reported similar data.

Given that an asymmetrical pattern of cognitive functioning exists, a further issue that arises is whether these deficits are exclusively in so-called *strategic* processes, as has been suggested by a number of investigators (Bauer, 1977; 1979; Bauer & Emhert, 1984; Cohen & Netley, 1981; Torgesen, 1977), or whether they also have some cause that is more basic, such as the speed or span of verbal processing. A number of investigators have suggested that these latter factors are critical (Denckla & Rudel, 1976; Lorsbach & Gray, 1986; Spring, 1976; Spring & Capps, 1974; Spring & Perry, 1983), although, as Stanovich (1986) has pointed out, the two categories of difficulty are by no means mutually exclusive.

The goal of the present study was two-fold: to determine whether reading- and math-disabled children show asymmetrical developmental profiles when viewed from the perspective of Case's (1985) theory, and to determine whether the difficulties they reveal include problems in basic processing speed. In the present study, *working memory* measures were used rather than traditional short-term memory tasks in order to examine the first question. As the name implies, working memory involves a system that is responsible for both processing and storing information, and it is this system that appears to be most closely related to school tasks, such as arithmetic and reading (Baddeley, 1986; Daneman & Carpenter, 1980). An additional advantage of such measures in the present context is that they have been shown to play an important role in potentiating the development of higher conceptual structures and strategies (Case, this volume, chapter 2), and can be scored using the same system as measures involving problem solving. Working memory measures have also been shown to be dependent on speed or efficiency of functioning (Case, 1985, p. 361). Thus, they seem a likely candidate for examining the question of more basic processes as well.

The tasks that were used in the present study were variants of those designed by Case and his colleagues to measure working memory in middle childhood. To assess working memory for verbal information, the Counting Span task developed by Case and Kurland (1978) was used. Although this test requires children to generate numbers, it has been shown to load with verbal rather than spatial factors in previous studies. To assess nonverbal working memory, a spatial span test was designed that was analogous to Case and Kurland's Mr. Cucumber task, but which precluded the possibility of verbal encoding by the use of more abstract visual-spatial materials.

STUDY 1: ASSESSING THE NORMATIVE PATTERN OF CHILDREN'S DEVELOPMENT ON VERBAL AND SPATIAL WORKING MEMORY MEASURES

Because both of the spatial measures were new, the first study that was conducted was normative. Subjects participating in the study were children from the same four age levels as in the previous studies reported in this volume: 4, 6, 8, and 10 years. It was predicted that there would be a systematic increase in working memory across this age range for both the verbal and nonverbal tasks, as well as a systematic increase in the speed of processing.

Method

Subjects

Forty-four subjects participated in the study. The children were drawn from a school located in a middle-class residential area of a suburban city. There were 9 four-year-olds; 13 six-year-olds; 13 eight-year-olds, and 9 ten-year-olds.

Tests

The Counting Span Test materials and procedures have been outlined elsewhere (Case, 1985; McKeough, this volume, chapter 12). Briefly, children are required to count sets of small green dots. There are a total of 18 sets, containing 1 to 6 cards each, on which a number of randomly arrayed yellow and green dots have been placed. For each set, the total numbers of green dots for each card must be stored and recalled in order when the last card is removed.

The materials for the Visual Spatial Span Test consisted of a series of 4 × 4 matrices (2 cm × 2 cm cells) drawn on white cards (21.5 cm × 14 cm). Each set of three cards had a different number of black cells (1 to 5), for a total of 15 stimulus items. The number of black cells in the matrices increased by 1 at each level. The response card contained an empty matrix. A blank card was presented between the stimulus and recall matrices. The purpose of the blank card was to minimize the possibility of performance enhancement due to iconic storage. To control the use of mnemonic strategies, matrices having some sort of symmetry or familiar pattern were eliminated from the set of potential test items. The actual test items are shown in Fig. 16.1.

For each span task, a measure of operational efficiency was also obtained. Operational efficiency on the Counting Span test was assessed using the Counting Speed measure developed by Case, Kurland, and

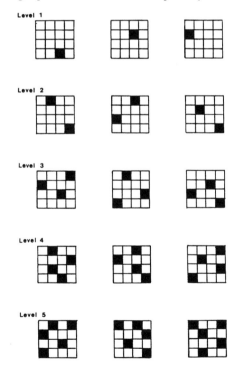

FIG. 16.1. Visual spatial span test.

Goldberg (1982). The materials are similar to those of the Counting Span test: a set of eight cards with randomly arrayed yellow and green dots. Children are asked to count the items as fast as they can without error, and their score is the average number of milliseconds it takes to count each dot.

The Spatial Localization Speed test served as a measure of operational efficiency for spatial span. The test materials used to assess the efficiency of this operation were similar to those used on the Spatial Span test, and consisted of two sets of matrices (10 matrices per set), with each matrix containing one randomly placed blank cell. Once again the response matrix used is an empty one. Subjects were asked to point to the cell in the blank matrix that corresponded to the cell that was "filled in" on the stimulus matrix, and their average time to do so in milliseconds was recorded.

Procedures

Children were tested individually by the experimenter in a small room provided by the school for this purpose. The testing session lasted approximately 30 minutes. The order of task administration was Counting Speed (1st half), Counting Span, Counting Speed (2nd half); Spatial Localization Speed (1st half), Spatial Span, Spatial Localization Speed (2nd half).

Measures

Counting Speed Test.   For the Counting Speed test the examiner demonstrated on a practice card how the subject was to count only the green dots and ignore the yellow distractors. The importance of counting aloud while touching each dot with a "pointing finger" was emphasized. The child was required to practice counting the green dots quickly and accurately while being timed by the examiner. Once mastery of the correct procedure was demonstrated, the set of eight test cards was placed face down in front of the child. The cards were presented sequentially to the child, who was required to count the green dots as instructed on the practice trial. The time from the card being turned over until the subject had counted the last green dot on the card was recorded, along with any miscountings. This was repeated for each card.

Counting Span Test.   For administration of the Counting Span test, the child was then told he or she would have to count the green dots as before, but would have to remember the number of green dots counted on the card and would not be timed. A practice card was presented and the child counted the green dots as previously instructed. A blank card was then placed over the card and the child was asked to recall the number of green dots counted. Once the child answered correctly, testing commenced. If a child recalled any of the three 1-card sets correctly, a practice run of a two-card set was administered in order to ensure that the child understood the importance of recalling both totals in the order presented. Then the three 2-card sets were administered; if any of the three sets at the second level was correctly recalled, all three sets at the next level were administered, and so on, until a child failed all three trials at one level.

Spatial Speed Test. The procedure for the Spatial Localization Speed test was formally identical to the Counting Speed test, and was explained to the child using a practice item. The practice stimulus card was turned over and placed on the table above a response card containing an empty matrix, which was directly in front of the child. The child was instructed to point to the cell in the empty matrix that should be filled in so that it would exactly match the stimulus card. The child was then told that more cards would be shown, and each time he or she would have to touch the cell in the empty matrix that should be black. The importance of responding quickly and accurately was stressed. Children were requested to place their pointing finger on a colored spot below the response card between test items. Once the procedure was understood, 10 trials from the first set were presented. Response latencies represented the interval from the time the stimulus card was turned over until the child touched a cell on the response matrix.

Spatial Span Test. For the Visual Spatial Span test, the children were instructed to remember the squares in the matrices that were black. A practice stimulus matrix (containing one black cell) was presented for 2 seconds, and the child was instructed to look at the matrix, and remember which cell was black. The stimulus card was turned over and replaced with a blank card for 2 seconds. Finally, a card with an empty matrix was presented and the child was required to demonstrate recall by touching the cell that should be black. Once the child understood the task, the test items were presented following a similar procedure. If a child's recall was correct on at least one of the items presented at any level, all three items at the next level were administered.

Scoring

For both the Counting and Visual Spatial Span score, subjects were assigned a point for each level at which they were able to recall correctly at least two of the three items presented. If a subject recalled a single set correctly at any one level, an additional one-third of a point was given. To determine a child's Counting Speed, the times recorded to count dots on cards for the two sets of trials were summed, and the total was divided by the actual number of dots counted (78 plus or minus any dots counted twice or missed). Hence, Counting Speed reflected the average time to count a dot. To determine Spatial Localization Speed, the response latencies for the two sets of trials were summed, discounting latencies on which subjects responded incorrectly. The two fastest and two slowest latencies were also eliminated, as is common in reaction time research. The total was then divided by 16 minus the number of incorrect responses. Hence, Spatial Localization Speed reflected the average time to locate the position of a cell in the matrix and point to it on trials that were correct.

Results

Working Memory

The group means and standard deviations for the span measures are presented in Table 16.1. Results of separate ANOVAs indicated a significant age-group effect on Counting Span and Visual Spatial Span (p's $< .001$). A trend analysis revealed a significant linear component for age groups on Counting Span and Visual Spatial Span (p's $< .001$), and a small but significant quadratic component for Counting Span ($p < .05$); this was because the difference between the 10- and 8-year-olds' scores was not quite as great as that between other adjacent age groups.

The Counting Span and Visual Spatial Span mean scores were not significantly different. This indicates that, at the group level, there is a high degree of synchrony in development across the two domains. To examine the issue of individual development the percentage of children within each age group showing different degrees of developmental asynchrony was tabulated. These data are presented in Table 16.2.

TABLE 16.1
Span Scores, *M (SD)*, by Age Group

		Span Measure	
Age (years)	n	*Counting*	*Visual Spatial*
4	9	1.07 (0.15)	0.96 (0.39)
6	13	2.08 (0.64)	1.95 (0.62)
8	13	3.13 (0.44)	2.88 (0.79)
10	9	3.41 (0.47)	3.59 (1.08)

TABLE 16.2
Percentage of children in each group
showing varying degrees of
developmental asynchrony

Age (years)	Developmental Asynchrony		
	< 1	1–1.66	1.67–2
4	100	—	—
6	69	23	8
8	61	31	8
10	67	22	11

As may be seen, the majority of subjects at each level showed discrepancies of less than one level. This is essentially the same pattern revealed on the more content-oriented tests described in previous chapters.

Operational Efficiency

Reciprocal transformations of the speed scores for each individual were conducted in order to homogenize group variances. The reciprocal score represented the rate at which an individual performed a task, measured in operations per second. The group means and standard deviations are reported in Table 16.3. ANOVAs conducted on each rate measure indicated a significant age effect. The trend analysis indicated a developmental change that was similar to the one reported for the Span measures. The change in Spatial Localization Rate with age was positive and linear. The function best describing the relationship between Counting Rate and age included a linear and a quadratic component.

Relationship Between Span and Processing Rate

The mean span scores were plotted against their corresponding processing rate scores. For each task, the relationship between processing rate and span was monotonic and approximately linear. As operation-

TABLE 16.3
Processing Rate Scores, *M (SD)*, by Age Group

Age (years)	Rate Measure	
	Counting	*Spatial Localization*
4	1.613 (0.337)	0.510 (0.121)
6	2.642 (0.360)	0.837 (0.128)
8	2.174 (0.369)	1.001 (0.102)
10	3.010 (0.284)	1.191 (0.162)

al efficiency increased, so did memory span. Regression analyses conducted to further examine the relationship between span and processing
rate indicated that for each task, processing rate accounted for a significant proportion of the variance in span ($p < .001$). As expected, the
correlation between Counting Rate and Counting Span was significant (r
$= .76$) and remained so after age had been partialed out ($r = .35, p <$
$.05$). The correlation between Visual Spatial Span and Spatial Localization Speed was significant ($r = .77$) and approached significance after
the influence of age was partialed out ($r = .27, p < .08$).

The intercorrelations among the span and speed measures are presented in Table 16.4; all were significant at the $p < .001$ level. As may be
seen, correlations of similar magnitudes were observed among all span
and rate measures, which suggests that one factor accounted for performance on all four measures.

TABLE 16.4
Correlations Among Measures: Study 1

	Visual Spatial Span	Counting Rate	Spatial Localization Rate
Counting Span	.65	.76	.85
Visual Spatial Span		.52	.77
Counting Rate			.77

Discussion

The above findings are consistent with those reported by Case et al.
(1982) and Case (1985) on their tests of verbal and spatial span and
speed. What they suggest may be summarized as follows: First, one
factor is responsible for producing a large proportion of the variance on
both speed and span measures, for both verbal and spatial content.
Second, modality-specific differences in development are not large for
normal populations, being on the average confined to one substage.
Finally, the relationship between speed and span is reciprocal and linear.

There was one finding that was discrepant from those of earlier studies:
namely, that the Spatial Span scores showed no deceleration in rate of
growth between the 8- and 10-year-old levels, and thus did not give rise to a
significant quadratic component in the trend analysis. A possible explanation for this anomaly is that older subjects may have received slightly
enhanced Spatial Span scores by perceiving higher order patterns or
"chunks" in the stimuli.[1] In spite of this one anomaly, however, the results

---

[1]If so, this trend should disappear if the spots were presented in a serial rather than a
simultaneous fashion (see Capodilupo, 1990).

on the new measures were deemed close enough to those of previous studies to permit the two major questions regarding learning-disabled children to be addressed. This was done in a second study.

STUDY 2: VERBAL AND SPATIAL SPAN AND SPEED FOR READING- AND MATH-DISABLED STUDENTS

The object of the second study was to compare the performance of three groups of learning-disabled students, relative to a control sample, on the four measures for which normative data were obtained in the first study. The specific predictions were (a) that children with a reading disability would perform poorly on the verbal memory and speed tasks when compared to controls, but no differently on the nonverbal tasks; (b) that children with an arithmetic disability would perform poorly on the spatial memory and speed tasks when compared to the controls, but no differently on the verbal memory tasks; and (c) that children with disabilities in both reading and arithmetic would demonstrate poor performance on all four tasks, relative to controls. These predictions were based on previous studies cited in the introduction, as well as unpublished studies by L. S. Siegel (personal communication, 1987).

Method

Tests

The following standardized tests were administered to all subjects: IQ tests: the Vocabulary and Block Design subtests of the WISC-R; achievement tests: the Reading and Arithmetic subtests of the WRAT-Revised, and the Word Attack test of the Woodcock Reading Mastery Tests-Form A (Woodcock, 1973); and the experimental span and speed measures from Study 1 and the Digit Span test from the WISC-R.

Procedures

Testing was conducted by the experimenter. Subjects were seen individually in a small testing room. The WISC-R subtests were administered first, followed by the experimental span and speed measures, using the same procedure outlined in Study 1. The WRAT-R Reading and Arithmetic subtests were presented next, followed by the Woodcock Word Attack test.

Subjects

Fifty-four children ranging in age from 7 years, 5 months to 10 years, 11 months participated in the study. All control children, and a majority of the learning-disabled children, were drawn from schools in the same suburban city as in the normative study. The remaining learning-disabled children were obtained from a psychoeducational clinic in Toronto. Subjects represented a wide range of social classes.

In order to qualify for the study, all groups of subjects had to meet the following criteria: an estimated IQ score on the WISC-R of at least 90^2, a chronological age between 84 and 132 months, and no evidence of emotional difficulties or neurological problems, as indicated by school records. In addition, subjects qualifying for the control group had to obtain WRAT-R Reading and Arithmetic scores above the 34th percentile, and subjects qualifying for one of the learning disability groups had to meet the following criteria: The reading-disabled (RD) group had to have WRAT-R Reading scores below the 26th percentile and Arithmetic scores above the 34th percentile; the arithmetic-disabled (AD) group had to have WRAT-R Arithmetic scores below the 26th percentile and Reading scores above the 34th percentile; and the reading- and arithmetic-disabled (RAD) group had to have Reading and Arithmetic scores below the 26th percentile. These criteria are ones that have been used in other studies by L. S. Siegel, and thus are appropriate for testing the hypothesis regarding the domain specificity of the two disabilities.

Results

Performance on Selection Measures

Separate ANOVAs revealed that the four groups were not significantly different on either age or Full Scale IQ. Thus, all learning disabled groups met the basic criteria for being classified as having a specific disability, rather than a general deficiency.

On the Word Attack test, the scores from the two groups with reading disabilities (RD and RAD) were essentially equal and significantly below the other two groups; there were negligible differences emerging between AD and control groups. This indicates that the reading-disabled samples had the specific pattern of abilities that was required by the operational definitions in order to conduct a valid test of the questions that were of interest. Relative to the control and AD groups, the RD and RAD children were at a disadvantage in reading isolated nonsense words.

The same pattern was present on the WRAT-R Arithmetic test, in reverse. On this test the AD and RAD groups scored significantly lower

[2]Full Scale IQ scores were estimated using the Vocabulary and Block Design Short Form of the WISC-R, and the full scale estimation procedure suggested by Sattler (1982).

than the RD and control groups, while the within-pair differences failed to reach significance (AD vs. RAD and RD vs. control). Once again, this indicates that the AD and RAD groups demonstrated the profile that was required by the operational definition.

On the WRAT-R Reading test one anomaly was present. Although the AD group scored higher than the RD and RAD groups, which was as planned, it scored significantly worse than the control group, which was not. Thus, while the AD sample was clearly arithmetic-disabled, there was some evidence that it may have been slightly reading-disabled as well, though not as disabled as the RD or RAD groups. The implication of this will be considered in the discussion. The mean scores for all selection measures are presented in Tables 16.5 and 16.6.

Symmetry of Developmental Profiles

The mean Counting and Visual Spatial Span scores for all experimental groups are given in Table 16.7. As may be seen, the pattern of performance demonstrated by the control and RAD groups was the predicted one: an even pattern of performance across the two measures, with the disabled group achieving scores that were lower by almost three years than the original normative sample.

The general pattern of the AD group, however, was not as predicted. Although a small modality-specific deficit did appear to be present in the spatial mode, the post hoc comparison for this trend did not reach significance ($p < .12$).

The pattern of the RD subjects was not even close to the one predicted. Like the doubly-disabled subjects, the mean scores showed an

TABLE 16.5
Characteristics of Learning Disabled Subgroups and Controls, *M (SD)*, on Achievement Tests

Group	n (Male/Female)	Age (years)	WRAT-R (percentile)		Woodcock grade percentile
			Arithmetic	Reading	Word Attack
RAD	20	9.18	11.08	5.72	13.55
	(12/8)	(0.55)	(6.75)	(6.25)	(12.99)
RD	8	8.92	56.88	10.88	16.50
	(6/2)	(1.09)	(14.71)	(7.83)	(10.93)
AD	8	9.33	13.13	45.00	63.63
	(3/5)	(0.89)	(8.39)	(9.35)	(20.70)
Control	18	9.28	63.00	65.61	65.94
	(11/7)	(0.87)	(18.63)	(19.22)	(18.98)

TABLE 16.6
Characteristics of Learning Disabled Subgroups
and Controls, M (SD), for Estimated IQ and
WISC-R Subtests

Group	WISC-R Estimate	Subtest	
		Vocabulary	Block Design
RAD	103.20	10.30	10.80
	(9.44)	(2.32)	(3.22)
RD	105.38	11.13	10.75
	(14.65)	(2.90)	(4.17)
AD	105.13	10.50	11.38
	(8.49)	(2.27)	(1.30)
Control	110.39	11.28	12.28
	(7.93)	(2.11)	(2.16)

even rather than an asymmetrical profile, with both types of span measure being significantly lower than that of the controls.

In Table 16.8, the percentages of individuals showing varying degrees of asynchrony in the development of verbal and spatial span are presented. As with the normative sample, the majority of individuals in both reading-disabled groups showed absolute levels of development that were within one substage of each other. Moreover, among those who showed a one-substage discrepancy, verbal span was ahead of spatial span as often as the reverse. Thus, there was no strong evidence in the individual data either for the predicted asymmetry in developmental profile.

In keeping with the pattern of mean scores, a slightly higher percentage of AD than control subjects showed a split of more than one substage. Moreover, all children with performance discrepancies of more than one level showed higher spatial than verbal span. Thus, there was some evidence of a trend in the predicted direction in this group. In line with the results of other chapters, however, discrepancies of more than one substage were rare.

TABLE 16.7
Span Scores, M (SD), for Learning Disabled
Subgroups and Controls

Group	Counting Span	Visual Spatial Span
RAD	2.55 (0.58)	2.58 (0.85)
RD	2.75 (0.56)	2.75 (0.73)
AD	3.13 (0.47)	2.38 (0.95)
Control	3.30 (0.47)	3.15 (0.87)

TABLE 16.8
Percentage of Individuals in Each
Group Showing Various Degrees of
Developmental Asynchrony

	Developmental Asynchrony		
Group	< 1	1–1.66	1.66–2
RAD	65	30	5
RD	75	25	0
AD	50	37.5	12.5
Control	72	22	6

Implication of More Basic Processes

The correlation coefficients between span and speed scores were $r = .38$, $p < .01$ for Counting Span and Counting Rate, and $r = .44$, $p < .01$ for Visual Spatial Span and Spatial Localization Rate. When the effects of age were partialed out, the resulting coefficients remained significant ($r = .30$, $p < .05$ and $r = .41$, $p < .005$, respectively). A regression analysis conducted for each task indicated that processing rate was a significant predictor variable for span. The mean scores for processing rate are shown in Table 16.9. As indicated in Figure 16.2, the general form of the relationship between speed and span was the same as for the normative sample.

Discussion

Two questions were addressed in the second study: First, do learning-disabled children show a more asymmetrical pattern of development than normal children, of the sort that would be expected from the learning disabilities literature, and second, are more basic processes (rather than just strategies) implicated in such differences.

TABLE 16.9
Processing Rate Scores, M (SD), for Learning
Disabled Subgroups and Controls

	Processing Rate Measures (operations/second)	
	Counting	Spatial Localization
RAD	2.704 (0.437)	1.061 (0.179)
RD	2.654 (0.484)	0.971 (0.162)
AD	2.749 (0.521)	1.046 (0.119)
Control	2.923 (0.340)	1.085 (0.166)

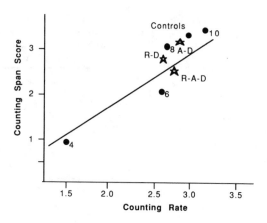

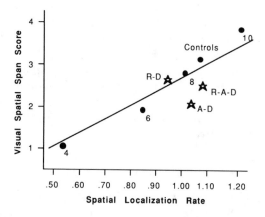

FIG. 16.2. Relationship between span and processing rate
at different age levels (4, 6, 8,
and 10 years) from Study 1,
and in three groups of learning
disabled children; reading-
arithmetic disabled (RAD),
reading disabled (RD), and
arithmetic disabled (AD). Top
panel gives figures for Counting Span; and bottom panel for
Visual Spatial Span.

From the point of view of the literature on learning disabilities, the
answer to the first question was somewhat surprising. The RD and RAD
groups met the defining criteria that have been proposed in the literature. Moreover, their performance on the verbal span and speed measures was the same as has been reported in previous studies (e.g., Mann,
1986): that is, there was a large and statistically significant deficit in
performance on both the verbal measures. What was lacking, however,
was any evidence that this disability was specific to the verbal mode.
While one might possibly dismiss this result as being due to vagaries of
sampling, or to the high within-group variance on the criterion measures, there have been an increasing number of other studies in recent
years in which the modality-specific hypothesis has encountered similar
difficulties. Either the trend showing poorer performance on one sort of
test has not reached significance (Fletcher, 1985), or it has not emerged

at all (Capodilupo, 1990). An alternative way to interpret the findings on the RD and RAD groups, then, is to take them at their face value, and to ask why previous research appeared to give such strong support to the modality-specific hypothesis.

In this connection, it is important to recall that the very first studies on reading-disabled children did not show any evidence of a modality-specific deficit in verbal working memory. What they showed was a general deficit, that is, a deficit that appeared on both verbal and spatial measures (Jorm, 1983; Torgesen, 1985). It was only once the apparent flaw in these early studies was corrected (namely, altering the nonverbal measures so that they did not permit verbal labeling) that reading disabled children appeared to be equivalent to normal controls on spatial measures (Ellis, 1981; Ellis & Miles, 1978; Katz, Shankweiler, & Liberman, 1981; Liberman, Mann, Shankweiler, & Werfelman, 1982). As other investigators have also noted, however (e.g., Fletcher, 1985), these new tasks were not without their problems, either. In creating tasks where verbal labeling would not be a problem, investigators changed the task format as well as the nature of the stimulus materials. In certain cases, the requirement for serial production was eliminated, while in others the requirement for recall was eliminated (and replaced by a recognition method). In the present study, however, the possibility of verbal labeling (which might be a factor in the Mr. Cucumber test) was eliminated, without introducing these other confounds. It is quite possible, then, that reading-disabled children suffer from a deficit in any measure that involves active, ordered retrieval of the products of earlier processing. In short, it is quite possible that they suffer from a general working memory deficit. If so, this would help explain the results reported by Segalowitz (in press), who found that reading disability did not correlate with EEG patterns in the verbal and visual processing areas, but did correlate with EEG patterns in the frontal areas, which are assumed to play a major role in controlling working memory (Diamond, 1989; Goldman-Rakic, 1989).

Returning to the question with which this volume is primarily concerned, then, we see that the results of this study confirm, rather than challenge, the results of previous studies reported here. The studies in the present chapter show a strong degree of cross-domain synchrony in the group and individual data, in the central processes (span and speed) on which children's cognitive development is presumed to be dependent. Even for the one group that did show a trend in the direction of a modality-specific deficit, namely the "pure" AD subjects, this trend was not manifest in a greater percentage of asymmetrical profiles. Rather, it was simply manifest in a skewed distribution of these profiles, such that most subjects who showed a one-level split in functioning did so in the predicted direction. The present findings thus join those reported in other studies investigating the presence of horizontal structure in normal children (Case, Marini, et al., 1986; Griffin & McKeough, this volume, chapter 15), and suggest that these findings cannot be dismissed as simply being due to artifacts of sampling.

With regard to the second question, it would appear that speed of processing bears the same relationship to span in learning-disabled populations as it does in normal populations; thus, such differences as obtain between groups should not be attributed exclusively to strategic factors.

SUMMARY AND CONCLUSION

The two goals of the present study were to examine the developmental profiles of learning-disabled children on working memory measures, to see if reading- and mathematics-disabled children showed a predictable pattern of modality-specific deficits; and to determine whether basic processes, such as speed, are implicated in whatever differences the groups do show.

The answer to the second question was clearly affirmative. Wherever span deficits were present, speed differences of the expected magnitude were apparent as well. The answer to the first question was more equivocal: Although there were clear working-memory deficits in reading-disabled and math-disabled children—often as much as three years in magnitude—the differences for the former group were not specific to the verbal mode, and the differences for the latter group showed only a weak tendency to be specific to the spatial mode. Overall, then, what the results suggest is that the specificity of processes leading to particular scholastic deficits must be sought for elsewhere. With regard to the core capacities of speed and span that are the focus of neo-Piagetian theory, reading- and math-disabled children, while clearly slower in their overall level of development, do not show any greater cross-domain asymmetry in their development than do other children.

17

Stage and Structure in the Development of Children with Various Types of "Giftedness"

Marion Porath
University of British Columbia

In a number of tests of neo-structural theory, a synchronous pattern of development has been found: The majority of children have been shown to function at the same cognitive-developmental substage, or to evidence asynchronies in functioning of only one substage, on tests that measure two or more central conceptual structures, or two or more basic capacities on whose presence these structures depend (Case, Marini, et al., 1986; Case, Griffin, McKeough, & Okamoto, chapter 15; Crammond, this volume, chapter 16). As Crammond (chapter 16) has pointed out, however, this pattern of results could be an artifact of the selection process. In most of the studies that have been conducted, teachers have been asked to provide the experimenter with children of average to above-average intelligence. It could be that a synchronous pattern of development is not typical of the population in general, but only of children who are judged to be of typical or average intelligence by classroom teachers.

In Crammond's study, the children who were tested were deliberately selected to show an atypical pattern of abilities, yet the proportion of asymmetrical developmental profiles remained approximately the same. It is important to realize, however, that the children who were tested in her study were exceptional only in terms of their school achievement. In terms of their IQ they were still within the normal range. This feature of the study is important, because it has been suggested that asymmetrical developmental profiles are most common at the extreme ends of any IQ distribution (Jackson & Butterfield, 1986; Sternberg & Davidson, 1985).

In the present study, I decided to examine the performance of children who were at the upper end of the IQ spectrum. This end of the spectrum was judged to be of greater theoretical significance than the lower end because it is the performance of high-IQ children that constitutes the strongest potential threat to the neo-Piagetian claim. The existence of specific disabilities in development can be explained by postulating the absence of some task-specific knowledge, talent, or neurological prerequisite (e.g., adequate eyesight). The existence of a specific developmental "gift," however, is much harder to account for. For if there really is an age-typical upper bound to children's level of thinking—as all neo-Piagetian theories maintain—and a given child performs exactly at this level in most domains, there is no construct in neo-Piagetian theory that would explain how he or she could exceed this limit by several substages in one particular domain on genuinely novel tasks.

Whether or not gifted children are developmentally advanced in any cognitive domain has been an issue that has received considerable attention in the research literature. However, the pattern of results has been equivocal. Some studies have suggested that gifted children are not developmentally advanced, at least on the sorts of tasks that were developed by Piaget (Brekke, Johnson, Williams, & Morrison, 1976; A. L. Brown, 1973; Lovell & Shields, 1967; Webb, 1974). Other studies have yielded findings that suggest the opposite (Carter, 1985; Goodnow & Bethon, 1966; Jacobson & Robinson, 1987; Keating, 1975; Jacobson & Robinson, 1977; Shayer, Kuchemann & Wylam, 1976). This lack of agreement could possibly be ascribed to the different selection criteria that have been used. As Pascual-Leone (1969) pointed out, Piagetian measures tend to have a high "disembedding" requirement. Moreover, this same requirement is present on many nonverbal IQ tests such as the Raven's Progressive Matrices or the WISC Block Design (Case & Globerson, 1974). If the gifted population were selected with a verbally loaded test such as the Stanford-Binet, Terman & Merrill, 1973, then one would be unlikely to find that they performed a full stage-level beyond their chronological peers on a Piagetian test battery. By contrast, if they were selected with a test such as the Raven's Progressive Matrices (J. C. Raven, Court, & J. Raven, 1983) or WISC Block Design, they might very well perform in a superior fashion on Piagetian tasks.

In the present study, in order to guard against this possible confound, three groups of gifted children were studied: those with extremely high scores on both the verbal and nonverbal subscales of a standard intelligence test; those with an extremely high score on only the verbal subscale; and those with an extremely high score on only the nonverbal subscale. By comparing the performance of these three groups to that of a normal population, I hoped to maximize the chances of finding children with asymmetrical developmental profiles, and to evaluate the magnitude and frequency of these asymmetries. I also hoped to cast further light on the controversy as to whether gifted children are developmentally advanced—that is, whether their gift lies in the rate of their cognitive development—or in some other aspect of their functioning.

Method

Subjects

Subjects were drawn from western and central Canada. The western sample was drawn from a parochial school system; the central sample was drawn from a variety of public, private, and parochial schools. Both samples were predominantly Caucasian and of high socioeconomic status. Thirty-six 6-year-old children with different patterns of giftedness participated in the research: 18 generally gifted children, 12 verbally gifted children, and 6 spatially gifted children. Forty-two children of average ability formed a pool of subjects from which chronological- and mental-age control groups were selected. Children were included in the study on the basis of teacher and/or parent nomination, and the following additional criteria: To qualify as *generally gifted,* subjects had to have a Full Scale IQ of at least 130, with superior scores on both the verbal and performance scales of either the WPPSI or the WISC-R. To qualify as *verbally gifted,* subjects had to have Verbal IQs of at least 125 and Performance IQs in the average range (100–120) on the same tests. To qualify as *spatially gifted,* subjects had to have Performance IQs of at least 125 and Verbal IQs in the average range on the same measures. To qualify as control subjects, children had to have IQ scores in the normal range on both the Verbal and Performance subscales.

Procedures

Three other groups of tests were administered: tests of children's existing conceptual structures; tests of children's working memory span or speed; and tests of children's ability to create new knowledge structures, using their existing working memory and experimenter feedback.

Tests of Children's Existing Conceptual Structures. The tests of children's existing conceptual structures have been described in previous chapters. Marini's version of the Balance Beam task (chapter 4) was used to assess children's structures for logico-mathematical thought, and was administered using the procedures reported by Case, Griffin, McKeough and Okamoto (chapter 15). Because two trials were presented at each level, subjects' final scores were computed by dividing the total number of problems passed by 2. The coefficient of interrater agreement for this scoring procedure was .98.

McKeough's story-telling task was administered to assess children's social-narrative structures, using the procedures described in chapter 10. In a few cases, children told stories whose structure was clearly above one of the levels described by McKeough, but which did not meet her criteria for the next level. In these instances, an intermediate score (e.g., 2.5) was assigned. Interrater agreement was .80 using this procedure. The stories were also scored for complexity using a story grammar approach developed previously (McKeough, 1982). It had already been demonstrated that the degree of complexity in children's stories develops in relation to their narrative structures (Case, Marini, et al., 1986; McKeough, 1982, 1986). Whether this would be true for a gifted population, however, was not certain.

Finally, Dennis's drawing task (chapter 13) was used to assess the spatial structures implicit in children's art. The instructions that were used were: "I need to find out the *best* sort of drawing children your age can do. I'd like you to help me by drawing a picture which shows a little girl (boy) your age doing something that makes her/him happy. Remember, do your *very best*."

Tests of Working Memory.   In order to permit a comparison with the studies reported by Crammond (chapter 16) and Rich (1979, 1982), two working-memory measures were administered: the Counting Span and Visual-Spatial Span tests. The Counting Speed and Visual-Spatial Speed tests were administered as well, using the same procedures and scoring methods described in Crammond's study.

Tests of the Structural Assembly Processes.   Two measures were used to assess children's ability to assemble new structures within their existing capacity limits.

The first of these was a test of "dynamic assessment" developed by Campione, A. L. Brown, Ferrara, and Bryant (1984), to operationalize Vygotsky's (1962) concept of the zone of proximal development. In this task, children are presented with a letter completion task that is known to be difficult for their age group, and then given a series of hints until they reach a correct solution. The letter series used was DXEXFXGX——. The scoring criterion was the number of hints the child required to get the correct answer.

The second test in this category was the Guided Restructuring test devised by Rich (1982). In this task, subjects are asked to count a series of dots and ×s using a variety of novel counting procedures. The number of errors they make (i.e., perseverative intrusions from the standard counting sequence, or from earlier trials) is assumed to be a measure of the ease with which children can modify their existing procedures using their available working memory capacity and adult guidance.

Results

The Visual-Spatial Speed test exhibited severe reliability problems and was therefore dropped from the battery prior to any analysis. The remaining analyses are presented and discussed in three parts.

Comparison of Generally Gifted Children with Controls

The first question that was examined was how the generally gifted children performed relative to control children of the same chronological or mental age. The descriptive statistics of relevance to this question are presented in Table 17.1. As may be seen, the mean scores of the gifted children generally fell between those of their chronological age (CA) and mental age (MA) peers, with performance on some tests lying closer to one group, and on other tests lying closer to the other group.

The data from the three groups were submitted to two general classes of analysis. First, an analysis of mean scores was conducted, using multivariate analyses of variance. A significant group effect in the multivariate vector (Pillai's Trace = .69, $p < .01$) was obtained. Tukey's Honestly Significant Difference (HSD) test was used to explore the locus of this effect more precisely, with alpha set at .05. This test showed that the gifted children achieved a level of performance that was significantly higher than their CA peers on only two tasks: the Balance Beam and Letter Completion tasks. For both of these tasks there was no significant

TABLE 17.1
Descriptive Statistics For Each Task: Study 1

	M (SD) by group[a]		
Task	*CA Peers*	*Generally Gifted*	*MA Peers*
Balance beam	1.94 (0.57)	2.50 (0.57)	2.69 (0.43)
Story telling	2.28 (0.65)	2.19 (0.52)	2.47 (0.61)
Story complexity	8.00 (7.45)	10.22 (9.74)	18.44 (14.89)
Art	2.08 (0.52)	2.36 (0.61)	2.69 (0.71)
Counting span	2.44 (0.57)	2.83 (0.69)	2.96 (0.67)
Counting speed[b]	531.28 (80.10)	484.06 (61.37)	416.06 (74.26)
Visual-spatial span	1.70 (0.84)	2.05 (0.96)	2.93 (0.82)
Letter series[b]	6.22 (3.28)	2.83 (3.38)	2.61 (3.18)
Restructuring[b]	9.17 (6.27)	6.56 (6.28)	3.11 (3.16)

[a]n = 18 in each group.
[b]Lower scores are indicative of better performance.

difference between the gifted children's mean and that of their MA controls. On the other seven tasks, performance by the gifted children was significantly lower than that of their MA peer group and was not significantly different from that of the CA group.

To provide convergent evidence on the nature of these differences, the correlation matrix in Table 17.2 was also analyzed using a principal components analysis. Because the Story Complexity score correlated strongly with the Story Telling score (having been derived from the same task), the possibility that it might unduly influence the factor loadings because of method variance was avoided by dropping it from the analysis. Prior to rotation, two factors were identified with eigenvalues greater than 1. All measures showed a substantial loading on the first factor. However, because there were two clear clusters in the data, a rotated solution was deemed preferable, and thus an oblimax rotation was performed. Table 17.3 presents the factor pattern and structure from this analysis. As may be seen, the first factor, which accounted for 39% of the variance, was defined by the Span and Speed tasks, the Drawing task, and the Cognitive Restructuring task. The second factor, which accounted for 14% of the variance, was defined by the Balance Beam and Dynamic Assessment tests. Only one task, the Story Telling task, showed significant loadings on both factors. As a result, the two factors themselves were only modestly correlated ($r = .20$).

As is no doubt apparent, the analysis of children's mean scores on the eight tasks and the analysis of the correlations among the eight tasks were consistent in the general pattern they revealed. The gifted children performed at a different level from their CA peers on only two tasks, the Balance Beam and Dynamic Assessment Task. These two tasks not only showed higher mean scores than the other tasks; they also loaded on a separate factor.

TABLE 17.2
Correlation Matrix: Study 1

	BB	St	A	CSpa	CSpe	VS	LS	CR
BB	1.00							
St	.05	1.00						
A	.06	.16	1.00					
CSpa	.13	.16	.17	1.00				
CSpe	−.29	−.22	−.38	−.45	1.00			
VS	.26	.32	.26	−.36	−.48	1.00		
LS	−.38	−.04	−.31	−.33	.38	−.30	1.00	
CR	−.30	−.22	−.19	−.27	.58	−.47	.36	1.00

Key to terms: BB = Balance Beam; ST = Story Telling; A = Art; CSpa = Counting Span; CSpe = Counting Speed; VS = Visual-Spatial Span; LS = Letter Series Completion; CR = Cognitive Restructuring.

TABLE 17.3
Pattern and Structure Matrices: Study 1

Task	Pattern		Structure	
	Factor I	Factor II	Factor I	Factor II
Balance beam	.17	−.69	.31	−.72
Story telling	.67	.58	.56	.45
Art	.52	.03	.52	−.07
Counting span	.57	−.10	.59	−.21
Counting speed[a]	.75	−.18	.79	−.33
Visual-spatial span	.76	.00	.75	−.14
Letter series[a]	.37	−.62	.49	−.70
Restructuring[a]	.66	−.27	.70	−.35

[a]Values were inflected on these variables because of the inverse nature of the scores.

Discussion

Two questions are raised by the foregoing data. First, what do the Balance Beam and Dynamic Assessment tasks have in common? Second, why did these tasks show a pattern that is different from all the others? One possible answer to these questions is that on both the Balance Beam and Dynamic Assessment tasks, children are presented with feedback from the experimenter on their performance, and can utilize this feedback to improve their performance. By contrast, on most of the other tasks, such feedback is not provided. These two tasks might thus be said to index the amount of *learning* children are capable of at their developmental level whereas the other tasks might be said to index their *developmental capacity* and/or optimum level (Fischer, 1980).

The one task that was intended to assess children's learning, but which did not appear to do so, was Rich's Guided Restructuring task. Two reasons may be suggested. First, the task requires that a number of "double-counting" routines be executed, and may thus be more appropriate for children at the bi-dimensional than the uni-dimensional stage (Case & Threadgill-Sowder, 1990). Stated differently, the task may be too heavily capacity-loaded for children who are only 6. Second, gifted children appear to find this task rather boring, and spend more time trying to make it interesting than trying to avoid the errors that they make when double-counting is required. For this reason, the test may also have had very little loading on learning.

As was mentioned earlier, the literature on the gifted has not resolved the question of whether such children are developmentally ahead of their chronological peers, or different from them along some orthogonal dimension. If the interpretation of the data just presented is correct, the latter conclusion is more likely to be correct. Thus, one may ask why the literature has not been uniform in demonstrating this sort of pattern. If gifted children do not have more developmental capacity than their CA peers, or function at a more advanced structural level, why have certain studies shown their performance to be at a higher level, on batteries of Piagetian tasks?

The explanation that was proposed at the outset of the study had to do with the sorts of selection measures that have been employed and the degree to which they pose a spatial-disembedding component. Given the controls in the present study, however, it seems clear that this interpretation is not tenable. A more likely explanation is that certain studies may, unintentionally, have implicated a learning factor, while others have not. In fact, in most of the studies where MA equivalence has been reported (e.g., Goodnow & Bethon, 1966), the tests have been administered in a fashion where children start with simple tasks, and move on to more complex ones. Thus, these studies have implicitly incorporated some opportunity for learning. By contrast, in studies where this sort of procedure has not been used, CA-equivalent performance, not MA-equivalent performance, has been the norm.

While this explanation is admittedly post hoc, it is in accord with two neo-Piagetian studies that have been reported since the present investigation was initiated. In the first of these (Fischer & Canfield, 1986), gifted children performed at the same developmental level as their CA peers, when these levels were defined in terms of Fischer's theory. The gifted children revealed their superiority in greater "elaboration" within a level, which in Fischer's theory is ascribed to learning. In the second study (Globerson, 1985), gifted children demonstrated CA-equivalent performance on a set of tests that were deemed measures of "pure developmental capacity," or "M-space" (Pascual-Leone, 1970). By contrast, they demonstrated MA-equivalent performance on tests where assessment of M-space was deemed to be confounded with learning and field factors.

The pattern emerging in the neo-Piagetian literature thus appears to be more differentiated than the one that emerged in the classic Piagetian literature, and more consistent as well. It also seems in accord with work being done within other theoretical frameworks (e.g. Sternberg & Davidson, 1983). As long as there is some basis for distinguishing between learning and development, gifted children appear to show their superiority on the former function and not the latter.

Comparison of "Asymmetrically Gifted" Children with Other Groups

The second question was how groups of asymmetrically gifted children would perform relative to other groups. In view of the small number of subjects that were involved, any answers to this question must

TABLE 17.4
Descriptive Statistics for Each Task: Study 2

Task	M (SD) by group[a]					
	CA Peers		Verbally Gifted		MA Peers	
Balance beam	1.96	(0.45)	2.21	(0.40)	2.50	(0.43)
Story telling	2.17	(0.69)	2.71	(0.45)	2.54	(0.66)
Story complexity	7.67	(8.51)	25.67	(29.19)	24.33	(24.31)
Art	2.13	(0.53)	2.38	(0.68)	2.58	(0.70)
Counting span	2.47	(0.61)	2.58	(0.59)	2.69	(0.64)
Counting speed[b]	521.50	(85.27)	501.92	(88.80)	443.92	(110.64)
Visual-spatial span	1.42	(0.78)	2.00	(0.84)	2.78	(0.87)
Letter speed[b]	6.33	(3.00)	4.75	(3.60)	4.58	(3.45)
Restructuring[b]	9.58	(7.17)	11.58	(4.17)	5.00	(4.67)

[a]$n = 12$ in each group.

[b]Lower scores are indicative of better performance.

be considered tentative. The mean scores for these groups are presented in Tables 17.4 and 17.5. As may be seen, the general pattern of performance was the same as for the symmetrically gifted children. Children performed at an intermediate level between CA and MA controls on most measures, with performance more frequently falling closer to the CA controls than to the MA controls. There was one notable exception to this rule, however. The verbally gifted children outperformed their MA peers on the Story measure, notwithstanding the fact that their performance on the Verbal Span measure was inferior. Similarly, the spatially gifted children outperformed both control groups on the Drawing measure, despite the fact that their performance on the Spatial Span test was inferior.

TABLE 17.5
Descriptive Statistics for Each Task: Study 3

Task	M (SD) by Group[a]					
	CA Peers		Verbally Gifted		MA Peers	
Balance beam	2.00	(0.55)	2.25	(0.27)	2.58	(0.38)
Story telling	2.33	(0.82)	2.25	(0.42)	2.83	(0.41)
Story complexity	11.50	(11.88)	12.33	(7.92)	24.67	(21.03)
Art	2.25	(0.42)	2.92	(0.58)	2.83	(0.98)
Counting span	2.39	(0.65)	2.61	(0.57)	2.94	(0.83)
Counting speed[b]	476.17	(42.96)	479.50	(85.99)	400.50	(99.41)
Visual-spatial span	2.00	(0.60)	2.05	(0.65)	3.17	(0.59)
Letter series[b]	7.50	(3.08)	3.83	(2.79)	2.33	(3.67)
Restructuring[b]	6.33	(3.33)	6.67	(5.13)	2.83	(3.37)

[a]$n = 6$ in each group.

[b]Lower scores are indicative of better performance.

In view of the fact that the asymmetrically gifted children outperformed children who were matched with them in terms of IQ on structural tests in their area of giftedness (but not in the more basic capacity tests), it may be speculated that some special achievement motivation may be involved, as well as talent. Asymmetrically gifted children may come to recognize their own gifts, and to devote a disproportionate amount of time and energy to their cultivation. If this is true, it would mean that they would come to tasks such as picture-drawing or story-telling with an experiential advantage over their more generally gifted peers, and also have a higher motivation to achieve on them.

Given that the asymmetrically gifted groups were performing at a higher level than other children on the two structural tasks related to their particular talent, it seemed particularly worthwhile to examine the frequency and magnitude of the asynchronies they revealed when their functioning was classified in terms of the theory that has been outlined in the present volume. As is shown in Table 17.6, the pattern was not unlike that in the study reported by Crammond (this volume, chapter 16) for her AD subjects. The asymmetrically gifted groups did not show a particularly high number of substage "splits," nor did they show splits of particularly large magnitude. What they did show was an uneven distribution of splits. That is to say, when a split of the normal magnitude did occur, it was almost always in the direction of their special talent.

Subsidiary Analyses Contrasting Specialized and General Development

Although the pattern of synchronous development shown by asymmetrically gifted children is consistent with the theory that is being developed in the present volume, it is not what one would expect on the

TABLE 17.6
Percentage of Gifted Children Subjects Showing
Various Degrees of Developmental Asynchrony
on the Story and Art Tasks

Group	None	One Substage	Two Substages
Generally gifted	55	17[a]	0
		28[b]	
Verbally gifted	50	33.3[a]	8.3[a]
		8.3[a]	
Spatially gifted	50	0[a]	0
		50[b]	

[a]Verbal ability ahead of spatial ability.
[b]Spatial ability ahead of verbal ability.

basis of the literature on gifted children. Nor is it what one would expect on the basis of the literature on child prodigies or mental modularity (Feldman, 1986; Gardner, 1983). In all these cases, different strands of development are spoken of as though they were completely, or almost completely, independent. It is also presumed that a child may function at an adult level in his or her domain of special competence, while still exhibiting performance that is childlike in all others. How, then, is this discrepancy to be explained?

One possible explanation is that accounts of prodigies' abilities are often based on anecdotal data, and thus, considerably exaggerated. However, I do not accept that explanation. The impression I got from talking with the verbally gifted children was the same as that reported in the literature on mental modularity, namely, that in certain ways these children's verbal performance was truly precocious, and much more like that of adults. I therefore decided to re-analyze the entire corpus of stories that these children had generated, looking for more specific attributes of language in which they might be more advanced. The variables that I chose to examine were *tokens*, the number of words produced (Loban, 1963); *types*, the number of different words produced (Loban, 1963); the number of "mature" words produced (where a mature word was defined as one that did not appear on Finn's list of frequently used childhood words; see Hammill & Larsen, 1983); and the thematic maturity of the story. For thematic maturity, the criteria were those suggested by Hammill and Larsen (1983): (a) giving a personal name to main characters, (b) giving proper names to animals, robots, and so on, (c) using direct dialogue, (d) using dialogue suitable to the characters, and (e) attempting humor. Finally, a score was assigned for the use of mature grammatical constructions for sentence or clause combination.

Descriptive statistics for each of these scoring categories are presented in Tables 17.7 to 17.11. Note that, on virtually every measure, the

TABLE 17.7
Descriptive Statistics for Tokens per Story, by Group

	Tokens		
Group	Range	M	SD
CA Peers	19–325	83.61	71.66
Gifted	24–298	98.28	78.27
Spatially gifted	47–206	113.67	72.17
MA Peers	35–437	149.94	100.36
Verbally gifted	37–712	188.75	180.93
Grade 9—high language proficiency (Loban, 1966)		291.88	

TABLE 17.8
Descriptive Statistics for Types per Story,
by Group

Group	Types		
	Range	M	SD
CA Peers	10–81	40.94	18.22
Gifted	17–136	51.44	33.07
Spatially gifted	33–88	56.33	24.97
MA Peers	26–165	69.50	33.23
Verbally gifted	27–259	87.67	62.41

verbally gifted children were substantially superior both to their CA and MA peers. This suggests that one must distinguish between the general level of structural organization a child can achieve in a verbal production, which is subject to some form of central developmental limitation, and the form of language that is used, which appears less centrally constrained.

Discussion

The attempt to resolve the controversy between modular and general-system theorists leads one to conclude that both are right in their own way. In those aspects of children's development having to do with the creation of central conceptual structures, the modularity of development, while it is clearly present, is relatively unpronounced. The great majority of children tend to have a modal level of development at which they function across different conceptual domains, with deviations from these levels generally being no more than one substage. By contrast, in other, less "conceptual" domains, development is far less constrained by

TABLE 17.9
Descriptive Statistics for Mature Words per
Story, by Group

Group	Mature Words		
	Range	M	SD
CA Peers	5–30	13.61	6.57
Gifted	5–60	20.78	15.57
Spatially gifted	9–43	22.83	14.11
MA Peers	10–78	27.56	16.86
Verbally gifted	10–122	36.08	32.19

TABLE 17.10
Descriptive Statistics for Thematic
Maturity, by Group

Group	Thematic Maturity		
	Range	M	SD
CA Peers	0–2	0.67	0.68
Gifted	0–2	0.72	0.83
Spatially gifted	0–2	0.83	0.75
MA Peers	0–3	0.94	0.94
Verbally gifted	0–5	1.25	1.36

central factors such as working memory, and modularity of the mind is more apparent.

If this is the case, one might expect that even child prodigies, those extremely rare children who appear to display adult levels of performance by early or middle childhood (Feldman, 1986), might still show relatively normal levels of general development across a variety of conceptual domains, including the domain in which they exhibit their unusual performance. A systematic investigation of this hypothesis must await further investigation. Nevertheless, the data that are already available appear to support it. For example, using the method just described to score the detailed data on a 5-year-old writing prodigy provided by Feldman (1986), the pattern shown in Table 17.12 emerged. In language development, the subject's performance was indeed prodigious. Although he was only 5, most of the indices revealed him to be functioning at an adult level. In the general conceptual level of his narrative, however, he was functioning only one substage ahead of age-typical values, that is, at the level attained by typical 7-year-olds.

An analysis of the childhood drawings of Paul Klee that have been preserved in the Berne museum (Porath, 1988) yielded a similar pattern. Using the criteria from the Goodenough Draw-a-Man test (Harris, 1963), I found Klee's 6-year-old performance to be equivalent to that of an adult, as required by Feldman's definition of a prodigy. And indeed,

TABLE 17.11
Percentages of Subjects Who Used Immature (score-1) and
Mature (score-2) Grammatical Strategies, by Group

Score	CA Peers	Gifted	Spatially gifted	MA Peers	Verbally gifted
1	89	61	100	83	58
2	11	39	0	17	42

TABLE 17.12
Comparison of Analysis of a Story by Randy, A Writing Prodigy, with
Data Found for Other Groups

Measure	Randy	CA Peers	MA Peers	Verbally Gifted Peers	Grade 9 High Language Proficiency (Loban, 1966)
Tokens	521	83.61	149.94	188.75	291.88
Types	239	40.94	69.50	87.67	
Mature words	110	13.61	27.56	36.08	
Thematic maturity	5	0.67	0.94	1.25	
Combinatorial strategies	2	1.11	1.17	1.42	

the intuitive feeling one gets in inspecting his drawings is one of prodigious talent. Nevertheless, the fact remains that, in his general organization of space, as reflected, for example, by the degree of foreground–
background differentiation, he was only functioning about one substage
in advance of his chronological age.

GENERAL DISCUSSION

What appears remarkable about children with very high IQs is not how
different their general level of cognitive development is from that of
children with normal IQs, but rather how similar it is. In the present
sample there was no evidence of any developmental advance in the
mean speed, span, or structural complexity scores of the generally gifted
group, except on the two measures where adult feedback was provided,
and students received credit for taking advantage of these hints and
modifying their responses. From the viewpoint of the literature on
giftedness, what this pattern of results suggests is that gifted children
might better be thought of as exceptionally rapid learners rather than as
exceptionally rapid developers, at least in regard to their central conceptual structures. From the viewpoint of neo-Piagetian theory, this
finding suggests that the hypotheses that have been proposed by neo-
Piagetian theorists, which have been shown to hold for "average" (Case,
Griffin, McKeough, & Okamoto, chapter 16), retarded (Rich, 1979,
1982), and learning-disabled (Crammond, this volume chapter 16) samples, may now be extended to generally gifted samples as well. Such
children show a characteristic or "modal" pattern of development, with
deviations from this mode being relatively modest in magnitude, and the
overall level being strongly influenced by a factor on which working
memory measures show a strong loading.

The situation for the asymmetrically gifted children does not appear to be very different, although the number of cases that are available is, by definition, quite low. Here what one finds is that, as long as the analysis is restricted to measures with a strong conceptual, or capacity component, the pattern of development is also remarkably even, and at the level one would expect for their chronological age group. One does not find many instances where children are more than one substage advanced, even in the area of their special gift.

Finally, the same general conclusion appears to be true for child prodigies. While their level of conceptual development in the area of their special talent is advanced, it is unlikely to be advanced by more than about one substage. What they are more likely to show is an unusually high level of functioning on tests that do *not* have a strong conceptual or capacity or loading, but which tap their special talent in a more direct and specific fashion.

From the viewpoint of the present volume, then, two general conclusions would appear to be warranted. The first is that there does, indeed, appear to be some sort of general structural line of development, for which a relatively inelastic upper limit on children's functioning exists. This limit is seen on any task where children must conceptualize things afresh, without much adult assistance. The second conclusion is that there are also aspects of development that are relatively "encapsulated," and immune from this general structural limitation.

Finally, from the viewpoint of the literature on the gifted, the general conclusion is that gifted children should not be viewed as being different from other children in their rapid rate of intellectual growth. Rather, they should be seen as having a special gift. For some children this may be a gift for rapid learning of any sort of academic material, particularly with adult guidance. For other children it may be a gift for learning a type of content that lies within some cognitively encapsulated domain, and that they experience as having some particular personal significance. In either case, the development of their central conceptual structures proceeds in a fashion that is much like that of their more typical peers; however, their acquisition of data and skills in their area of giftedness is likely to be very rapid, and should be encouraged.

18

Cross-Cultural Variation in the Structure of Children's Thought

Thomas A. Fiati*

The data that have been reported thus far in the present volume, like those that have been reported in other neo-Piagetian research programs (Fischer, 1980; Mounoud, 1986), reveal a substantial degree of synchrony in children's general conceptual development. In the studies in Sections II, III, and IV, this synchrony appeared across tasks with different content that shared the same underlying conceptual structure. In the studies by Case, Griffin, McKeough and Okamoto (chapter 15) this synchrony appeared across tasks with different content *and* conceptual structure. Finally, in the studies by Crammond (chapter 16) and Porath (chapter 17), the pattern appeared across a wide range of ability patterns.

This relatively uniform pace of development is consistent with the classical Piagetian position, according to which the mind's underlying conceptual structures are presumed to be both general and universal. It is important to realize, however, that virtually no neo-Piagetian theorist would interpret the data in this fashion today. The sort of universalism that is proposed in neo-Piagetian theory is not seen to reside in the mind's conceptual structures, per se, but rather in the upper bound to which the structuring process is subject. Stated differently, what is seen as universal is the mind's *potential* for constructing central conceptual structures, once a particular developmental capacity has been attained.

The difference between the classic and neo-structural perspectives is nowhere more apparent than in their interpretation of cross-cultural data. According to the classic structural position, the apparent diversity

---

*Thomas Fiati was killed in an automobile accident a few days after submitting the final draft of his doctoral thesis. The present chapter has been excerpted from that thesis; short connective passages have also been added, where necessary, to provide continuity with the rest of the volume.—*Ed.*

in the development of children from different cultures is just that: a surface phenomenon, which belies an important commonality both in the underlying structural sequence and in the final level in that sequence that is achieved. The apparent differences that are recorded are presumed to be a function of the fact that measurement devices are often unsuited for use with non-Western cultures due to the fact that they utilize content with which such cultures have little experience (Piaget, 1972).

According to the neo-Piagetian position, however, the apparent diversity across different cultures is real. Different cultures have followed different paths in their own historical evolution. Thus, they have exploited their universal human potential in different ways, and assembled different conceptual structures as a consequence. Similarly, they now induct their children along different structural paths and provide them with different forms of experience. Even when two structural paths appear to be identical across different cultures, there are likely to be subtle differences among them, either in the absolute level to which children progress, or in the details of the steps along the way.

In an important sense, then, the data on cross-domain synchrony that have been presented thus far must be regarded as unrepresentative. More precisely, they must be seen as representative of the situation that exists when several different conceptual domains receive approximately equal emphasis within a culture, and a substantial proportion of the developmental variance is thus attributable to universal factors of an endogenous nature.

In the present chapter, a study is reported in which this qualifying condition is not met. While the sorts of central conceptual structures that we examine remain the same as in earlier studies (i.e., numerical, social, and spatial), the sorts of children whose development we examine are quite different. Three groups of children are described, who, by virtue of their cultural and educational histories, may be presumed to have differential access to the experience that is relevant to the three conceptual structures we have discussed. We then report a study in which the level of attainment by these children on these structures is compared.

DESCRIPTION OF THE SAMPLING AREA

The geographic area in which the research was conducted was the Ho District of the Volta Region of West Africa. As Fig. 18.1 indicates, the Ho district is bordered on the west by the Volta River, and on the east by the Republic of Togo. The people of the region are Ewe, and were once ruled by the British under the territorial government of Togoland. In 1956, when their neighbors to the west were in the process of attaining

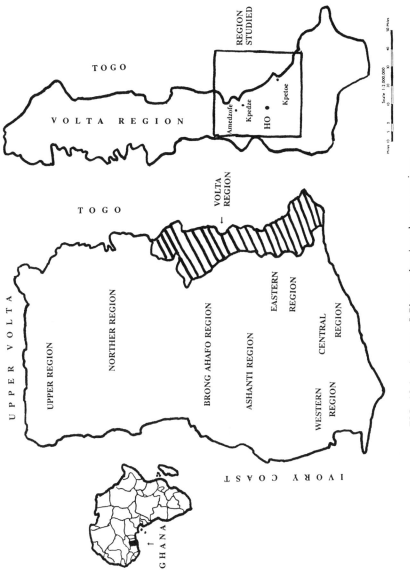

FIG. 18.1. A map of Ghana, showing the ten regions.

321

independence from Britain, the inhabitants of the Volta decided by plebiscite to join them and become part of the new African state of Ghana. In spite of their incorporation into this larger political unit, they have retained their unique cultural and linguistic identity.

From the perspective of the present volume, there were several advantages of the Volta region as the location for a cross-cultural study. The first was the wide range of physical and cultural environments that co-exist within this region, in close spatial proximity. The second was the varied role that quantitative dimensions play in these environments. In the most traditional settings—where indigenous patterns of socialization have been maintained over the centuries—counting and dimensionalization play very little role in daily life. By contrast, in the urban centers, Western ways have overshadowed those of the local culture, and dimensionalization plays a very important role indeed. Finally, the author was born and raised in a small village in this region. Thus, he was able to conduct the study in a fashion that otherwise would have been impossible.

The City Sample

Of the various settings from which samples of children were drawn, the largest and most Westernized was the city of Ho itself. The city of Ho has a population of about 40,000, and is situated on well-drained, level land bordering the long Ewe range. At Ho, the mountains undulate into a saddle, making it possible for roads to connect the towns and villages on the northern and southern sides of the divide. Five such routes converge at Ho, making it a natural transportation center. In addition, the main east—west road in the region passes through the town, linking central Ghana on one side with the former French colony of Togo on the other. Ho's central location has led to its selection as the administrative capital of the district. At present, the city contains such facilities as the regional hospital, post office, and telecommunications center. It also contains the regional administrative offices of the central government, a military base, and the offices of the local District Council. Finally, the city contains the educational headquarters of the various churches, which provide much of the schooling in the region under guidelines laid down by the Ministry of Education.

Although Ho is privileged with regard to the centrality of its location, it does not have a completely adequate supply of water. There are no large rivers nearby, so pumping stations must depend on underground reserves. Because these become seriously depleted during the dry season, people are often forced to rely on their own private stores of rain water. Another drawback of life in Ho is the absence of cheap electrical power. Until 1984, Ho's only source of power was a diesel generator. Since that time, a power line has been put in from the Asombo Dam on the Volta. However, there is still no industrial base in the city. Thus, the majority of the inhabitants are either in the government or service sector of the economy.

With its large population, Ho has many schools of varying quality. For children at the primary level there are 19 schools, most of which are financed by the Ministry of Education but run by one of the local churches. These schools admit children at the age of 6 years, and offer six years of basic education. The curriculum is fairly standard by Western standards, although it is supplemented by courses in Ghanian language and religious knowledge. At the middle level there are 13 middle (or senior public) schools, which admit children from the primary schools and offer two to four years of further instruction. These schools, too, are usually financed by the Ministry but run by one of the local churches.

For most students, middle school is the terminal point of their education, from which they either enter the labor force directly or take vocational training. A limited number of select students, however, sit for the Common Entrance Examination. If successful, they are then admitted to a 5-year academic program in one of the two secondary grammar schools in the city. These schools provide an advanced Western curriculum, which is aimed at preparing for the Cambridge Ordinary Level ("O-level") or Advanced Level ("A-level") examinations.

In addition to these public facilities, there are 4 "preparatory schools" in Ho, which serve as private alternatives to the public primary and middle schools. These "prep schools" train children of the military and civilian elite. They admit students in first grade and prepare them for secondary school directly. The program in these schools is more intensively academic than in the public schools, and takes place in English rather than Ewe. Graduates of the prep schools normally sit for the Common Entrance Examinations without attending middle school, and then go on to secondary school to complete their education.

For the purpose of the present study, children from each of the major types of public school were tested: one primary school, one middle school, and one secondary school. In addition, children from one private preparatory school were examined. In each case, the headmaster of the school was contacted via a mutual friend, and the purpose of the study was explained to him. After the headmaster had met with the senior investigator and granted his approval, an appointment was made to meet the students. On the appointed date, the class register was requested for students in Grades 1, 3, and 6, and children were selected at random according to the dates of their birth. Proximity to the modal ages of 6, 9, and 12 years was the criterion for selection.

Testing of students was done on an individual basis, either in the headmaster's office, or under a nearby shade tree. Both Ewe and English were used as media for communication, with the testing done in whichever language each individual child appeared to find most convenient.

The Town Sample

Children in the town sample were obtained from two different locations: Dzolo Kpuita and Amedzofe.

Dzolo Kpuita. Dzolo Kpuita is a small town of less than 2,000 inhabitants, which is located about 18 miles from Ho, at a crossroads near the Togo border. At one time the town was quite a busy spot, with its own market and a growing immigrant population from nearby Togo. In recent years, however, its population has dwindled as people have migrated to the more prosperous border town of Kpedze, about 8 miles away. Dzolo Kpuita remains the administrative center of the local subdistrict, and thus still boasts a post office, a court, and the local council offices. It also has a medical clinic, a public school, and a middle school. The majority of its inhabitants, however, are subsistence farmers, who sell their produce in nearby Kpedze.

The schools in Dzolo Kpuita are run by the Evangelical Presbyterian Church, which also runs the public schools from which children were selected in Ho. As might be expected, the schools in Dzolo Kpuita lack many of the facilities and equipment that are present in Ho. In fact, they often do not have enough texts or paper to go around. Although the curriculum is ostensibly the same as in Ho, there are considerable differences in the training that is actually provided, with everyday instruction in Dzola Kpuita containing a great deal more singing and rote memorization of Bible passages than in Ho. Although some of the graduates of middle school go on to attend secondary school at Kpedze or at Ho, the majority enter a trade or start to farm the land as soon as they complete their elementary education.

The children who participated in the study in Dzolo Kpuita were drawn from both the primary and the middle school. The headmaster of each school was approached in the same manner as at Ho. The selection of the sample and the testing of the children was also done in the same fashion.

Amedzofe. As one ascends the mountains to the north of Dzola Kpuita, one experiences a sharp transition in climate. The brown savannah grass of the valley gives way to the lusher vegetation of the hills, and the air becomes markedly cooler. The second town in which testing was conducted was Amedzofe, which is situated at an altitude of about 2,000 feet, near a narrow road that passes through the mountains. The cool air and seasonal waterfall of the village were probably the factors that made it the choice of the first German missionaries who came to the Volta region, as a location for their seminary. The building they constructed in the 1890s is still standing, and now functions as a teacher training college for the Evangelical Presbyterian Church.

In spite of the presence of the teacher training college, the town of Amedzofe remains almost exclusively rural in character. There are no industries, and the only other large buildings are the post office and a medical clinic. As at Dzolo Kpuita, the majority of the population are subsistence farmers. Not only are the crops at Amedzofe different, but transportation to and from the town is much more difficult, especially during the rainy season. By and large the townspeople must depend on human transport to cart their produce to the neighboring valley markets to be sold.

Unlike Dzolo Kpuita, there is no pipe-borne water in Amedzofe, although nature does provide a copious supply of springs that flow throughout the year. Electricity is another amenity that is lacking, and thus the residents must rely on kerosene lamps for nighttime illumination. The situation at the college is somewhat different, because the organization has its own electric generator and a truck. Even here, however, life still has a strong rural flavor. For example, when their truck breaks down, it may take weeks to repair, leaving the college teachers and students isolated from the outside world.

In spite of its isolation, Amedzofe has a strong educational ethic. Perhaps due to the presence of the Bremen seminary, its inhabitants were quick to recognize education as an avenue for social mobility during colonial times. Thus, unlike most rural locations, Amedzofe can boast many families that have been literate for three and four generations. Although many members of these families have long since relocated to urban centers, they often return to visit their relatives on holidays and retain a strong attachment to their village. Some also return to spend their old age there, supported by their government pensions. There is thus a sizable community of older inhabitants who have no formal connection to the college, but who nonetheless wait with eagerness for the newspapers and letters that arrive on the college truck. The church is also well attended on Sunday, with the entire congregation reading from their Bibles and hymn books with ease.

Like Dzola Kpuita, Amedzofe boasts one primary school and one middle school, each run by the same (Evangelical Presbyterian) church. The facilities in these schools are much the same as in Dzola Kpuita, and subject selection and testing were conducted in the same manner.

The Village Sample

Traveling south-eastward from Ho is a first-class road that runs almost parallel to the Togo border. Sixteen miles along this road one reaches a large town called Kpetoe, which is about a mile from the Togo border and has a population of about 4,000. The position of Kpetoe makes it a natural spot for the exchange of goods, both legal and illegal, between Ghana and Togo. Apart from its commercial importance, Kpetoe is also of considerable importance for the marketing of agricultural produce. It is situated on a wide stretch of fertile savannah, where grains, legumes, and vegetables can be cultivated. Because it is quite close not just to Togo but to Ho, there is always a ready market for these commodities.

Although there are a few wealthy farmers in the vicinity of Kpetoe, the majority of farmers in the area are relatively poor, and depend on traditional methods of agriculture. The small hinterland villages in which these farmers live were the third source of children for the present study. A total of five such villages were visited: Agbesia, Adokpa-Korfe, Asafotse-Korfe, Blido-Korfe, and Amuzu-Deveh. Each of these villages contains from 15 to 30 households, and the average population ranges from 100 to 200. With the exception of Agbesia, which can be reached by motorable road, all the other communities have to be reached by walking through the bush, on trails that average 3 miles in length and contain numerous natural hazards, such as poisonous snakes and insects.

As might be expected, these isolated villages present a sharp contrast with the settlements from which the rest of the sample was obtained. In all the other locations, for example, there are a substantial number of dwellings in the western style. By contrast, in the villages virtually all the buildings are traditional huts made of mud bricks and grass roofs. A household normally consists of at least two such buildings. The large one, made up of two or three rooms, is the bedroom block. The smaller one, which is basically an open shed, is the kitchen. The fuel used in the kitchen is wood, and cooking is done on an open clay hearth. To the rear of the kitchen one normally finds a small structure that houses the chicken coops and the pens for the goats and sheep.

One very important facility that the villages lack is clean water. During the rainy season, the villagers can depend on nearby ponds and brooks for their drinking water. However, in the dry season, these sources disappear. The villagers are thus forced to walk 3 or 4 miles through the bush to the nearest well, and to collect water in pots that they must then carry back to their village on their heads. Unfortunately, this water is often of poor quality. Thus, there are many water-borne diseases in the locality, with guinea worms, hook worms, and round-worms the most frequent.

For those who must travel the bush paths, there is also the potential danger of a bite from a poisonous snake or insect. Treatment in the case of such attacks is left to traditional healers or to the older men in the village. Serious emergency cases can be carried to Kpetoe in a cloth hammock. However, because this entails a journey of several hours, some do not make it this far and are buried in the local graveyard at the outskirts of their village. Whenever there is a death of any sort, the whole village is involved in the funeral, and the mourning ceremonies last from 2 to 3 days.

Despite the occupational and environmental hazards that the farmers confront, they have a strong attachment to their villages and to their traditional way of life. Each village is an independent entity, with its own chief whose ancestry dates back to the founding of the village. The role of the chief includes acting as arbiter in family disputes, receiving visitors, and presiding over all meetings that deal with the welfare of the people. As might be expected, there is a strong sense of community among the members of each village, which is no doubt heightened by the fact that most of them are blood relations.

Village life proceeds in much the same fashion each day. Work begins at dawn, with the women cleaning the compounds and heating up breakfast while the men sharpen their cutlasses and hoes before heading out to the surrounding farms. The men work continuously until mid-morning, after which they take a rest from the sun and eat the breakfast that the women have prepared. After breakfast, the women often visit their vegetable plots, while the men inspect the traps they have set in the surrounding bush to catch the rodents that form the main source of meat in their diet. At mid-afternoon, when the worst heat from the sun has subsided, everyone resumes serious work until evening. The men then help the women gather wood for cooking, and everyone returns home. Once the women have served supper, the evening is spent shelling peanuts by the fire, and enjoying story-telling sessions or listening to the village elders. These more senior citizens can often be counted on to narrate personal experiences of historical events, which the younger members of the village listen to with considerable enjoyment. After story-telling, a great silence descends, and everyone goes to sleep.

Schooling is not a priority in the hinterland villages. During the late

1960s, the Nkrumah government made an effort to build a school in every village, even the most remote. Since Nkrumah's time, however, the village schools have all been closed, and no further emphasis has been placed on either schooling or literacy. In fact, at present there is considerable resistance to the very idea of schooling. Children are needed to help in the everyday work of the village. Although this work is arduous, it assures a reasonably comfortable subsistence. Moreover, even if children were not needed, the bush trails are sufficiently hazardous that parents would not want their children to travel through them on a daily basis. Finally, there is no obvious benefit to be obtained from attendance at a regional school, because reading and writing play no important role in village life. The few individuals who did succeed in becoming literate during the Nkrumah days did not manage to obtain government jobs, and thus had to continue their subsistence farming in the traditional fashion.

Because a major focus of the present study was on dimensional thought, it is important to describe the traditional village approach to matters of physical causality and measurement. With regard to physical causality, the villagers do not favor Western "scientific" forms of explanation. For example, they are still far from recognizing a causal link between the impurity of their drinking water and the occurrence of guinea worms, even though the worms cause intense inflammation of the tissue and permanent crippling of the joints, and could be eliminated with appropriate sanitary measures. Nor do the villagers understand the importance of the anopheles mosquito in the causation of malaria. Like rainlessness, both plagues are presumed to be caused directly by God, and whatever other explanations others may offer are deemed irrelevant.

Although the villagers have become nominally Christian in the last 15 years, and are visited on Sundays by itinerant ministers, they have largely assimilated the new teachings to their more traditional ways of thought, and regard the major advantage of the Christian God as His patient nature and His relaxed attitude toward animal sacrifice. In former days these sacrifices used to consume virtually all the villagers' yearly profits, and thus constituted a considerable hardship. To please the Christian God, the villagers work hard during the week, take their rest on Sundays, and count their blessings during years that bring copious rains and bumper harvests.

There is a similar lack of emphasis in village life on Western forms of measurement. Such measurement as does take place is informal, and does not draw on standard units. For example, the unit of length for twine is a double stretch of the arms, with 12 arm-lengths being called a rope. The distance between objects is measured in units that can vary from the segment of the index finger to the distance between two well-known towns. In cooking, the women talk about the number of calabashes of cooking oil or palm wine when they need to describe a particular volume. However, a calabash is defined as the volume a thirsty person can drink without having to stop to take a breath. Thus, even here, the notion of standardization is lacking, and there is no reason to talk about quantities involving double digits.

In the area of weight, which is of most direct relevance to the present study because the balance beam test was used, there is no common unit whatever. Trading in the local markets is not done by weight, but by the quality and approximate quantity of goods. Money is also not a factor, because goods are exchanged without this intermediate medium. Finally, measurement of time via clocks or watches is absent, as is contact with the outside world via radio, telephone, or television. Although it would be a mistake to assume that the villagers live in a totally "undimensionalized" world, it is safe to assert that the intense focus on quantitative dimensions that is present in Western culture is absent from village life.

Given the nature of life in the hinterland villages, it was necessary to obtain the sample of children in a different fashion. The principal investigator started at Agbesia, where he was the guest of a relative. He was taken by this individual to the chief's house, and introduced in the traditional manner. The chief and the elders then asked questions, to make sure that there was no hidden agenda, such as forcing the village to pay taxes or pressuring their children to go to school. Permission was then granted to proceed with the study. Subjects for the study were recruited the following Sunday by going from house to house and asking for volunteers. Although many of the younger children were eager to participate, a good number of the teenagers were hesitant to volunteer for fear of betraying their illiteracy. Many of them provided ingenious excuses for not participating, and had to be assured that they would not be forced to go to school as a result of the testing, regardless of their performance. The actual testing was conducted in a room provided by the chief. When this became too hot, a neighboring shade tree was used for the same purpose.

Before testing began, subjects were encouraged to talk about their experiences in farming and hunting, and the things they would like to acquire when next they went with their parents to the market at Kpetoe. Once testing began, the subjects seemed to be very attentive. Frequent breaks for conversation were taken nonetheless, in order to maintain a relaxed atmosphere and to prevent fatigue.

The procedure that was followed in the other villages was similar, except that the chief normally appointed someone else to escort the investigator from house to house in order to obtain the consent of the parents and children.

Comparison of the Areas Sampled

Obviously, the first way in which sampling areas varied was in their degree of Westernization. Along this dimension, the hinterland villages of Kpetoe were the least Westernized, Ho was the most Westernized, and the two town samples lay somewhere in between. The second way in which the sampling areas varied was in the quality of schooling they provided. The hinterland villages again occupied one extreme, with the private schools in Ho occupying the other, and the public schools in Ho and the town schools lying somewhere in between. Given that a major focus of the study was on dimensionalization, the difference between the two town samples was also of some interest. In terms of the number of western amenities that were present, and the proximity to Western-style markets, the valley town of Dzola Kpuita had the edge over its more isolated rural counterpart, the mountain town of Amedzofe. On the other hand, Amedzofe was the more Western from the viewpoint of its emphasis on literacy. Thus, were literacy the critical factor in dimensional thought, one would expect the advantage to favor the children in Amedzofe.

Method

Measures

Dimensional Tasks. The primary measure used to assess children's dimensional reasoning was the Balance Beam task, which was given under the standard conditions used by Marini (this volume chapter 4). The only difference was that, after the initial familiarization period, the series of testing trials that followed were ones in which predictions and explanations were requested, but no feedback on their adequacy was given. The second measure that was given was the Counting Span test. Again, this was given under the standard conditions, which include a period of familiarization and practice followed by a period of testing with no feedback.

Social Tasks. Had the central social structure that was described in Section III of the present volume been identified at the time the study was initiated, almost any of the measures that were described in that section could have been adapted for use in the local culture. Because the present study was conducted prior to the isolation of this structure, however, the only social measure about which the author felt confident was one developed by Marini (1984). This measure is intended to assess teenagers' ability to diagnose some abstract "quality" that characterizes a person's behavior in an initial story, and then use this quality to make predictions about their subsequent behavior in other story situations. At Vectorial Level 1, one such quality is implicit and of relevance to the outcome of the second story; at Vectorial Level 2, two such qualities are implicit and relevant to the second story's outcome; finally, at Vectorial Level 3, two such qualities are relevant, and must be integrated in some fashion. Because every adult Ewe—from villager to Ho sophisticate—is prepared to characterize other individuals in terms of such traits, it was felt that this measure would not be inappropriate for use in any of the sampling populations.

Of course, Marini's stories were designed for an urban Canadian sample, and thus their content was not appropriate for use in the present study. For this reason, they were rewritten by the author so that they would be more representative of the sorts of situations that are encountered in traditional Ewe culture. Table 18.1 presents illustrations of Marini's original Canadian stories, and of the Ewe counterparts that were designed for the present study. The full details are available elsewhere. (Fiati, 1987).

Spatial Tasks. Had the spatial structure that was described in Section IV been isolated at the time the present study was conceived, any of the measures used by Dennis (chapter 13) or Reid (chapter 14) could have been adapted for use in the present context. Once again, however, the present study was actually completed before those two studies were undertaken. Thus, in the absence of such measures, we used two of the classic spatial tests in the literature: the Raven's Progressive Matrices (Raven, 1962) and the Embedded Figures Test (Karp & Konstadt, 1963). The version of the former task that was used was the Standard Colored Matrices, without any modification to take account of the local culture. The version of the latter task that was used was one designed for African culture by Van de Koppel and Van Helfteren (1982). The general requirements of this test are the same as for the standard Children's Embedded Figures Test (Witkin, Dyk, Faterson, Goodenough, & Karp, 1962). However, both the nature of the figure that is "hidden," and the design in which it is hidden, are modified to resemble classic African objects and patterns. Scoring for both tests followed the standard procedure laid down in the test materials: no attempt was made to convert the subjects' raw scores to neo-Piagetian levels.

TABLE 18.1
Sample Stories Used For Social Task at a Vectorial Level Together
With Model Stories on which they were based

Level 0   Canadian Story[1]

Jack needed a new book for school, so he went into the store and joined the line to pick one up. There was only one book left for each person in the line. While he was counting his money someone grabbed the last book that should have gone to him. As the other person went to pay for the book Jack left the store.

What type of person is Jack?

Ewe Story

Kwaku needed a new hoe so he went and placed an order at the local blacksmith. A week later the local blacksmith sent for Kwaku to come and pick up the hoe, which was ready. When Kwaku went to pay for the hoe, someone else came and offered a higher price and bought it. Kwaku left the blacksmith's workshop without saying anything either to the blacksmith or to the other person.

What type of person is Kwaku? Why?

Level 1   Canadian Story

One evening as Jane was waiting to buy tickets for the theater, another person tried to get ahead of her. Jane told the person that she did not like people getting in the line ahead of her and asked the person to move. The next day, when Jane arrived at school, she went to her history class. There she found an older student had taken her books and was using them.

What do you think Jane did?

Ewe Story

The mobile cinema van arrived in the village and pitched a large screen in the grounds for a public film show. Malam was waiting quite early in front of the screen. But as the show was about to start, his senior brother sat in front of him, blocking his full view. Malam told his brother that he did not like people blocking his view, and that he sat there first. He asked his senior brother to move. The next day when Malam was about to go to farm to cut trees, he was told that his senior brother had earlier come to borrow his only cutlass, and was just going through the other gate.

What do you think Malam did? Why?

Level 2   Canadian Story

When Robert was visiting the computer fair, he became very interested in one of the latest models. While waiting to get information on the display model, Robert noticed that several people had been served before him. He told the salesman he had been waiting for some time and would like to be served. Later that afternoon, as Robert was entering the school, he saw a student carrying a large cardboard box having problems opening the door. Robert offered his assistance by opening the door so that the student could get in. He then went to his class and found that an older student was sitting in his seat.

What do you think Robert did?

Ewe Story

It was the planting season and Kofi went to acquire a plot from the clan land. He cleared a small path around the plot to outline the boundaries of his intended farm. When he arrived the following day, someone was busy clearing the same plot. He told the person that he was the first to acquire the plot and asked the person to move. While he was working on the farm, someone approached him to ask for directions to a neighbor's farm. Kofi stopped his work and offered to take the person where he wanted to go. Later that day he went to his farm and saw that a relative of his was using his stored palm leaves to cover her new yam mounds to shield them from the hot sun, without his prior consent.

What do you think Kofi did? Why?

Level 3   Canadian Story

Cathy was waiting in line to get her skates sharpened and just as her turn came up they announced that the shop was closing. Cathy told the people at the shop that she had been waiting a long time, and she wanted her skates sharpened before they closed the shop. After skating she went over to see her friends. Late in the afternoon she remembered that she had to be home because relatives were coming, so she excused herself and started to leave when her friend asked her for help in finishing an assignment. Cathy helped her friend with the homework and then left for home. On her way home she slipped and ruined her favorite pants. When she got off the bus a person approached her asking for direction.

What do you think Cathy did?

Ewe Story

Yao went to the local store to inquire about the price of some new cutlasses. At the store, the store-keeper was serving other people, even those who came after him. Yao told the store-keeper he wanted to be served since he was there earlier. On his way to the farm that afternoon he remembered that he had to bring his gourd of water to the farm, so he went back home for it. When he arrived at home his brother asked for help in fixing his fence. Yao helped him fix the fence and left for his farm. Since he was rushing to get to the farm, he tripped and broke his gourd that he had had for a long time. When he arrived on the farm he found that someone who did not have a hoe was using his without permission.

What do you think Yao did? Why?

---

[1]All Canadian stories are from Marini (1984); all Ewe stories are from Fiati (1987).

Subjects

The sampling and testing procedures have already been described. The number and estimated ages of each sample are described in Table 18.2.[1]

---

[1]Age is another variable that is not quantified in the rural villages, so it was estimated from children's height, in the manner described in Fiati (1987).

TABLE 18.2
Primary Level Factorial Research Design Showing Cell Sizes

| Age (years) | Educational Environment | | | |
	Urban Public	Urban Private	Rural Public	Rural Non-Schooled
6	6	8	6	6
9	6	7	6	9
12	6	6	10	8
n	18	21	22	23

Predictions

On the assumption that Western schooling would be the most power-ful variable of relevance to dimensional reasoning, we predicted that there would be a large and significant difference in the developmental level achieved on the dimensional tasks, with the city sample (especially the privately schooled) performing at the highest level, the hinterland village sample performing at the lowest level, and the two town samples performing at an intermediate level.

On the assumption that the acquisition of social narrative structures would be unaffected by the degree of Western schooling, as long as the tests contained content that was equally familiar to all, we predicted that there would be no differences across the various sampling areas on these tasks.

Finally, for the Western spatial test, the Raven's matrices, we pre-dicted large and significant differences, with the nature of these differ-ences varying as a function of the degree of Westernization of the sample. No formal prediction was made as to whether these differences would be eliminated by the presence of African content on the African Embedded Figure Test (AEFT). Given the fact that the disembedding operation itself has been shown to be subject to cultural variation (Berry, 1976), however, some differences were anticipated on this measure as well.

Results

Dimensional Tasks (Balance Scale and Counting Span)

The mean scores relevant to dimensional thought are presented in Table 18.3. As may be seen, for each task there was a linear increase in scores with development, and a regular but non-linear increase in scores with the quality of schooling. Univariate tests revealed no significant

TABLE 18.3
Adjusted Balance Scale Test (BST) Scores Compared to Counting
Span Test (CST) Scores, M (SD), by Age Group

		Non-Schooled	Rural Public Schooled	Urban Public Schooled	Urban Private Schooled
6	CST	0.33 (.30)	0.62 (.25)	0.58 (.17)	.92 (.39)
M (SD)	BST	0.00 (.00)	1.00 (.00)	1.00 (.00)	1.13 (.35)
9	CST	0.48 (.38)	0.89 (.34)	1.33 (.21)	1.57 (.25)
M (SD)	BST	0.78 (.44)	1.00 (.00)	1.33 (.52)	1.29 (.49)
12	CST	0.62 (.45)	1.30 (.31)	1.50 (.35)	1.89 (.58)
M (SD)	BST	1.13 (.35)	1.67 (.71)	1.50 (.55)	2.00 (.00)
Total	CST	0.49 (.39)	0.98 (.42)	1.21 (.45)	1.41 (.58)
M (SD)	BST	0.70 (.56)	1.29 (.56)	1.31 (.48)	1.43 (.51)

Note Grand Means for Counting Span and Balance Scale tests are 2.02 and 2.18 respectively.

difference as a function of degree of Westernization, per se. Performance of the children in the sample from Ho and in the two town samples was virtually identical. As predicted, however, there was a significant difference as a function of schooling, with the unschooled group performing considerably less well than the publicly schooled group, and the publicly schooled groups in all three locations (Ho, Amedzofe, and Dzolo Kpuita) performing slightly less well than the privately schooled group for each measure. There was no schooling by development interaction. As a glance at the righthand column of Table 18.3 will reveal, there was also no large task effect: Mean scores on the Counting Span and Balance Beam tests were quite consistent within age groups; the small differences that were present were not significant.

Although the close correspondence in absolute levels between the Balance Scale and Counting Span tests had not been formally predicted, it was of considerable theoretical interest, and in line with the general theoretical position outlined in chapter 2. What it signifies is that, for any given level of Counting Span, children achieved the same absolute level of reasoning on the Balance Beam as would be predicted from an analysis of the working memory demand of the task (see Case, 1985, chapter 5). Stated differently, schooling had an effect on both variables that was not just in the same direction, but of the same absolute magnitude as well.

Spatial Tasks

The data on the spatial measures are presented in Fig. 18.2. As may be seen, on the Raven's, Matrices, there was a significant Age × Environment interaction, $F(6,68) = 6.54$, $p > .001$. In the youngest subjects, the

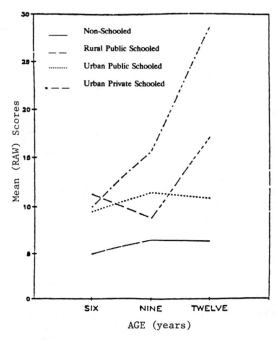

FIG. 18.2. A graph of Ravens colored matrices primary level mean scores by age by environment.

only difference of any substance was between the schooled and un-schooled subjects. With age, however, a significant difference emerged among the groups of schooled subjects as well. By and large, these differences were as expected, with the exception of that between the urban public schools in Ho and the two rural public schools in Amedzofe and Dzolo Kpuita. This latter comparison favored the rural group, due either to the transfer of the more talented urban students to other schools in the urban system or to some other factor.

Turning to the AEFT (Fig. 18.3), we see that the pattern was similar at the 6-year level: The only significant difference was between the schooled and the unschooled subjects, $F(1,68) = 25.17$, $p < .001$. What is noteworthy, however, is that no further difference emerged with schooling or development. Although it is sensitive to the presence or absence of schooling, then, the AEFT does not appear sensitive to the exact *nature* of children's schooling, or to more subtle differences in the degree of Westernization. The age by environment interaction and the other group comparisons failed to reveal any significant differences.

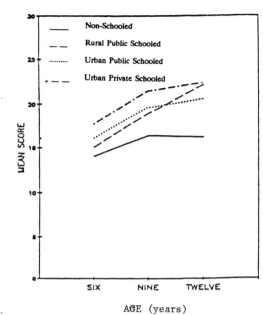

FIG. 18.3. Mean scores on
African Embedded figure test.

Social Tasks

The data on the social measures are presented in Table 18.4. The performance of the oldest (middle and secondary school) subjects was as predicted, in that no environmental differences of any consequence emerged. There was a very slight tendency for the middle school subjects in Ho to do worse than their counterparts in the towns, $F(1,46) = 4.46, p < .01$. However, that effect was probably due to the fact that the more talented urban students are encouraged to go on to the junior secondary or grammar schools.

Before concluding, it is worthwhile to mention the results of two supplementary studies that were conducted in order to clarify the pattern of performance that was observed on the Counting Span test. This test is often considered a test of "capacity." However, in the present context it was considered to be a reflection of operational efficiency, that is, differences on the test were presumed to result from differences in counting efficiency, which, in turn, were presumed to result from differences in the value the local subcultures place on this skill, and the amount of practice children receive in it. Two supplementary studies were done to check this hypothesis and both were supportive of it (Fiati, 1987).

Discussion

That children's performance should vary with their schooling is not surprising. Nor is it surprising that performance should vary with de-

TABLE 18.4
Secondary Level Results for Tasks from 3 Structural Domains,
M (SD), by Group

Group	n	Balance Beam M (SD)	Social Task M (SD)	African Embedded Figures M (SD)
Non-schooled	10	1.10 (0.31)	3.80 (0.42)	17.80 (3.19)
Urban Middle Schooled	8	1.38 (0.52)	3.50 (0.53)	24.13 (1.96)
Rural Middle Schooled	10	2.00 (0.00)	4.00 (0.00)	23.20 (1.48)
Junior Secondary	11	2.09 (0.54)	4.09 (0.54)	23.36 (2.20)
Secondary Grammar	14	2.36 (0.74)	4.21 (0.70)	25.07 (1.73)
Total	53	1.85 (0.69)	3.96 (0.55)	22.85 (3.30)

gree of Westernization. These two results have been among the most consistently replicated in the cross-cultural literature (see Berry, 1976; Cole & Scribner, 1974; Dasen, 1972, for reviews). The precise manner in which children's performance varied with these two variables, however, was much more interesting, and is of direct relevance to the question of how to interpret the pattern of individual and developmental differences in earlier chapters. The relevant data will be discussed under two general headings, as a function of whether they suggest the presence of cross-cultural universality in cognitive development, or cross-cultural variability.

Cross-Cultural Universals in Cognitive Development

There were three results that were identical to those which have been obtained with Western samples, and which fit very well with the theory that was outlined in chapter 2, and elaborated in subsequent chapters.

Relationship Between Operational Efficiency and Short-Term Storage Space. The first was that African children's mean scores on the Counting Speed and Counting Span measures could be fit to the data produced by children raised in a Western culture (Kurland, 1981). Coupled with the systematic difference in span as a function of schooling, this finding suggests the following: First, children in the various groups had no difference in their biological capacity for storing numerical quantities. Rather they differed primarily in terms of the automaticity of their quantitative operations. Second, while the efficiency of such operations may vary from group to group, the *relationship* between efficiency and short-term storage does not. This relationship therefore becomes a likely candidate for a developmental universal, an attribute of the human cognitive system that has some universal biological basis.

Relationship Between the Availability of Short-Term Storage Space and the Possibility of Constructing Sophisticated Cognitive Structures. The second finding in this category was that the absolute score each group attained on the Counting Span test was very close in magnitude to its score on the Balance Beam task. This result is not demanded by neo-Piagetian theory. The Balance Beam task is a complex one, which requires that children observe, reflect on, and form hypotheses concerning the operation of a physical system that many of them have never seen before. One might therefore expect that quite a range of factors (including previous specific experience with such systems, previous experiences in scientific experimentation, talent for quantitative/causal analysis, and cognitive style) might have a strong influence on the score received. Indeed, at the individual level, this is known to be the case (see Case, 1985; Siegler, 1978).

That the mean scores for each group were so close in the present study, however, has two interesting implications. The first is that—at least for this culture—one does not need to postulate some additional factor such as differences in exposure to the scientific method or cognitive style to explain the poor performance of the older children. Although the 16-year-olds in the unschooled environment did no better than the 6-year-olds in schooled Western populations, this is also true of schooled Western adults, when their working memory is artificially reduced to the same level (Case, 1985, chapter 17). In accord with the interpretation that was advanced in Section II of the present volume, then, it would appear that what holds many children back on the Balance Beam is the availability of the relevant *numerical* structures. As a corollary, it would appear that an important goal of scientific training should be to develop these numerical structures.

The second implication is that, just as a particular value of operational efficiency may be a universal requirement for attaining a particular value of working memory, so a particular value of working memory may be a universal requirement for constructing a complex conceptual structure in which this working memory is implicated.

Minimal Terminal Level of Structural Development. The third result that fits well with neo-Piagetian theory was a concealed one, but important nonetheless. This was that no adult group—whether schooled or unschooled, strongly or minimally Westernized—failed to develop to the 6-year-old level on any of the structurally oriented measures. There is no a priori reason why this should be the case. Consider the Balance Beam, for example, where the familiarization phase indicates that quantification is important. In order to perform at the 6-year-old level, subjects need to realize that the quantity of weights on each side is relevant. They also need to have some sort of mental representation analogous to that of a "number line." Given the minimal emphasis on quantification in the life of the village hinterlands, it is of considerable interest that all the subjects in this group found the general set of questions meaningful. It is also of interest that they all appeared to have constructed a representation of numbers by the age of 16, and to interpret the Balance Beam results in these terms.

Of course, it would be a mistake to draw too strong an inference from the study of subcultural variation in one particular non-Western society. Nevertheless, when coupled with the studies by Saxe, Guberman, and Gearhart (1987) and the work of the neo-nativist theorists that was summarized in chapter 1, it would appear reasonable to suggest the following hypothesis: Certain domains of development, such as number, are ones to which all human beings are innately sensitive. In this domain, a certain minimal level of development is achieved in all cultures, along the same lines as in the West, for a combination of biological and universal-experiential reasons.

Cross-Cultural Variability in Cognitive Development

In view of the apparent universality of the basic cognitive system and the parameters that constrain its development, the non-universality of the operations and structures that are acquired at higher developmental levels takes on added significance.

Automaticity. The first factor that varies from one ecological, educational, or cultural environment to the next is the automaticity of the basic operations in the domain that any test assesses. As has already been noted, the relationship between span and speed appears to be culturally universal. What is clearly not universal, however, is the absolute values of speed and span to which a particular form of cultural experience gives rise. In the quantitative domain, this variable appears highly susceptible to schooling, as one would expect given that quantification does not play a great role in children's lives outside of the school, but does play an important role in school itself (Stigler & Perry, 1988). In environments where such quantification plays a highly significant role in daily commerce, one might well expect that such effects would be greatly attenuated, if they were present at all (Carraher, 1985; Saxe et al., 1987).

Working Memory. In the present theoretical system working memory and the efficiency of basic operations are presumed to be intimately linked. Thus, the same conclusions and predictions may be drawn with regard to this variable as were drawn for automaticity. One can expect measured working memory to vary from culture to culture, notwithstanding the fact that there is a basic working memory system whose underlying capacity is universal.

Terminal Level of Structural Development. A third variable which varied, both across tasks and across environments, was the highest level of cognitive development that was reached in each domain that was assessed. In line with the predictions, the level that was reached in the quantitative domain turned out to be as strongly related to the presence and quantity of schooling as did the level that was reached in the spatial domain. It was also of some interest to note that, in the hinterland villages where Western-style science is not practiced, the highest level of development was only bidimensional.

For both the social scale and the AEFT, however, the highest level of development appeared unaffected by the nature or quantity of schooling. The presence or absence of schooling did appear to affect the level of development in the case of the lower ages, however, in the age at which children began to realize their potential on the AEFT. This effect was unpredicted, and an intriguing, one. Why 16-year-olds in the hinterlands should offer solutions that are indistinguishable from those of their more highly educated town and urban peers, while their younger siblings lag considerably behind, is not clear, and is worthy of further investigation. One possibility is that life in schools might encourage a particular analytic stance toward intentionality, which oral story-telling does not (see Olson, 1980), and that this was obscured at the highest level either by a scoring effect or by a ceiling effect. Another possibility is that an unschooled environment delays, but does not arrest, development along this line, so that what was recorded was a developmental lag. Because genuine developmental lags—that is, lags that do not result in different ultimate levels—are extremely rare (notwithstanding the frequency of the label in Western school systems), this possibility is also worthy of further investigation.

Line of Cognitive Development at Higher Structural Levels

A final variable that could be subject to strong cultural variation was not examined directly in the present study, but was suggested by the variables that were studied. This is the line of structural development at higher cognitive levels. Given that a certain minimum level of structural development appears to be achieved by all cultures, but that development beyond that—at least in the direction observed in the West—does not appear to be universal, it may be that developmental lines can diverge at this point in different cultures.

There was at least some indication of this possibility in the analysis of children's social narrative structure. In addition to the structures that were expected and assessed, children had other high-level ways of interpreting social behavior that were not tapped by the present scoring scheme. Note that, in classic structural theory, this sort of difference would have to be assumed to be non-structural in nature. In contrast to classic structural theory, however, neo-structural theory allows for the existence of unique structures in different cultures, which have widely varying forms and which are not universal in nature. This is perhaps most easily seen in regard to drawing, where one can imagine different high-level systems for representing space on a two-dimensional surface (e.g., realistic vs. non-realistic), or music, in which one may see different forms of composition that are highly abstract but not Western in their nature. It seems quite possible that similar differences exist with regard to systems for interpreting social and physical behavior as well.

Summary

In contrast to the earlier chapters in the present section, the present chapter reported a study in which children's level of conceptual development was not uniform across the three general conceptual domains studied in the present volume. For those subsamples of children who lived in a completely non-schooled and non-Western environment, the level of numerical representation lagged far behind the level of spatial and social representation, with the degree of the lag being explicable in terms of the degree of automization of basic numerical operations, which in turn, was linked to the degree of Western-type schooling. In spite of the lag in conceptual development in these areas, however, it was clear that there was no general conceptual deficit (because attainment was high in certain spatial and social areas). The same underlying relationship was also obtained between the automaticity of basic functions, such as speed and span, and the construction of higher order structures.

VI

CONCLUSION

In this final section, the question that motivated the present program of research is restated, and the data that were gathered to address it are summarized. An attempt is also made to indicate the way in which our thinking about the question evolved in the course of our investigation, and to review the reasons that we felt obliged to postulate the existance of a new construct: namely, the central conceptual structure. Finally, the notion of a central conceptual structure is formally defined, and used as a basis for integrating several different bodies of theory that are currently regarded as either incompatible or incommensurate. As might be expected, the answer to the original question which this synthesis implies is one that is intermediate between the two classically polarized positions.

19

The Mind and Its Modules: Toward a Multi-Level View of the Development of Human Intelligence

Robbie Case
Stanford University

The present monograph is multiply authored, but reports the results from a single research program. Thus, before concluding, it seems worthwhile to review the general nature of the issue that this program of research was designed to explore, and the way in which our thinking about the issue evolved in the course of our investigation.

GENERALITY AND SPECIFICITY IN COGNITIVE DEVELOPMENT

An issue that has played a central and controversial role in the field of intellectual development, virtually since its inception, is the question of whether the human mind should be seen as developing in a general or a specific fashion. Those favoring the former position have tended to characterize children's development as proceeding through a sequence of general stages, often ones that are presumed to be universal in their character, whereas those favoring the latter position have preferred to characterize children's development as proceeding along many fronts at once, at different rates, in a continuous and contextually sensitive manner.

Over the past 50 years, there has been a dialectical progression in the debate between proponents of these two positions. The first theories that were proposed reflected a system-wide perspective, according to which development was seen as monolithic, universal, and endogenously regulated (Baldwin, 1894/1968; Piaget, 1950, 1970). The next generation of theories reflected a more local perspective, according to which development was seen as situation-specific, non-universal, and exogenously regulated (Gelman, 1969; Klahr & Wallace, 1976). More recently, a new generation of theories has emerged, in which a balance has been struck between these two perspectives. The precise nature of this balance still differs from theory to theory, however, and remains tilted, at least slightly, in one of the two classic directions. On the one hand, there is a class of theories in which the changes in children's concepts and skills are acknowledged to have a strong specific character, but their rate of change is seen as being regulated by a system-wide change in processing capacity (Case, 1985; Fischer, 1980; Halford, 1982; Pascual-Leone, 1970, 1988). These theories are often referred to as "neo-Piagetian," because they retain many of Piaget's core epistemological assumptions. On the other hand, there are two alternative classes of theory in which children's development is acknowledged to have a component that transcends isolated tasks or situations—but where this general component is presumed to be restricted to certain neurologically defined "mental modules" (Carey, 1985; Gardner, 1983; Spelke, 1988), or to certain culturally defined "domains of knowledge" (Chi, 1988; Rumelhart & McClelland, 1987).

In the second chapter, a theory was described that falls into the neo-Piagetian camp. According to this theory, much of children's development stems from a change in their intellectual control structures. These control structures are specific entities containing three components: a representation of the essential features of some particular class of problem, a representation of the goals that this problem class most frequently occasions, and a representation of a sequence of operations that will bridge the gap between the problem's initial and terminal states. Because children's control structures are specific to particular classes of problem, and because these problems become increasingly "culture-bound" as children grow older, this theory implies that children should show different patterns of development as a function of a variety of specific factors such as the culture or subculture in which they are raised, the particular problems they encounter within that culture most frequently, and the models the culture provides for successful problem solution. The theory also implies that children's development should vary as a function of a variety of specific motivational or socio-emotional factors, which have their effect by influencing the goals children pursue most frequently, and the methods they find most attractive for achieving those goals.

Although all the foregoing factors are specific, their action is hypothesized to be constrained and potentiated by a set of changes that are system-wide and that have a strong biological component. These

changes influence the highest level of intellectual operation that children can execute successfully under optimal environmental conditions,
as well as their working memory for the products of such operations. As
these upper limits shift, children's control structures are believed to
progress through a universal sequence of four recursive cycles in each
problem domain to which the children have any long-term exposure,
and in which they maintain a long-term interest.

These four cycles are illustrated in Figure 19.1. As discussed earlier,
within each of the four cycles, a universal sequence of changes is postulated: At the first substage, children assemble a new class of operations,
by coordinating two well-established executive structures that are
already in their repertoire. As their working memory grows, and as they
practice these new operations, they enter a second substage in which
they become capable of executing two such operations in sequence.
Finally, with further growth in working memory, and with further
practice, they enter a third substage in which they become capable of
executing two or more operations of the new sort in parallel, and
integrating the products of these operations into a coherent system.
Once consolidated, these integrated systems then function as the basic
units from which the structures of the next stage are assembled.

In the third chapter, the foregoing theory was examined to determine
what sort of solution it implies to the dilemmas posed by classical developmental theories of either the system-wide or domain-specific sort.
It was suggested that most of these dilemmas can be resolved in a
satisfactory manner, one that suggests a testable explanation for data
that appear anomalous from either of the two classical perspectives. It
was also suggested that the theory contains new elements of its own, ones
suggesting the existence of developmental phenomena that can be investigated in their own right. Many such investigations have already
been launched, and have shown promising results (e.g., Case, 1985,
1987).

Notwithstanding the theory's promise, a final suggestion was that
there is one set of data for which the theory offers no simple or obvious
interpretation. These data have been gathered by contemporary theorists who favor a domain-specific view of development, and they indicate
that individual children may sometimes perform in an adult-like manner
on one particular class of tasks, while still performing in a child-like
fashion on all others. Such data have been reported when one or more
of the following conditions have been met: (a) The particular tasks on
which children's performance seems adult-like are ones that permit
them to apply a rich and extensive knowledge base (e.g., Chi & Koeske,
1983); (b) the children in question have had a particularly extensive
exposure to this task and, thus, time to acquire this knowledge base (Chi,

346

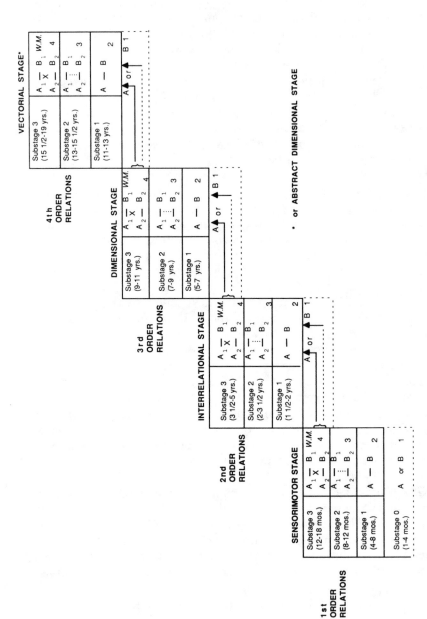

FIG. 19.1. Hypothesized structure of children's knowledge at different stages and sub-stages of development.

1978); and (c) the children are highly motivated, and have shown a talent for the domain of tasks in question from an early age (Feldman, 1986).

If taken at their face value, such data would appear to violate the notion of a cross-domain upper limit, to which all intellectual control structures are subject. There are also data that *support* the notion of an upper limit, however, and these appear anomalous when viewed from a domain-specific perspective. The data include results from studies on infants' earliest physical, numerical, and classificatory play, which appear to progress in a closely interlocked fashion (Langer, 1988). They also include data on toddler's linguistic, spatial, social, and numerical development, which show a similar linkage during the preschool years (Case, 1985; Case & Khanna, 1981). Finally, they include data on neo-Piagetian tests of working memory with numerical, verbal, and spatial content, which show a close correspondence during the years of early schooling (Case, 1985, chapter 12; Pascual-Leone, 1970, 1988). None of these data are easily explained from a modular or domain-specific perspective.

Given this pattern of reciprocal anomalies, the most obvious suggestion is that the truth must still lie somewhere in between, that there must be aspects to the developing human system that are general, as well as aspects that are specific, but that current theories still have not characterized these two aspects successfully within a single framework. The question that naturally arises, therefore, is how such a task might be accomplished. The answer that was proposed in chapter 3 was that a new program of research should be initiated, using methods that are likely to yield data of both the domain-specific and domain-general variety simultaneously.

It was with the goal of gathering such a data base that the present program of research was initiated. The first set of methods we used were ones traditionally employed by Piagetian and neo-Piagetian investigators. These included administering tests from a wide range of content domains to children at several different age levels, including tests of high-level thinking and tests of more basic "capacities" (in particular, working memory and processing speed), and utilizing an analytic framework that transcended any particular domain, and that would be sensitive to any cross-domain parallels in development that might be found. The second set of methods were ones that have been used more frequently by modular or domain-specific theorists. These included assessing children's cognitive competences in domains that are known to depend rather heavily on specific experiential and/or neurological substrates, designing the tests in such a fashion that children would be able to take advantage of whatever domain-specific knowledge they had acquired in these areas in their everyday lives, selecting subject populations with a wide range of life experiences and abilities, and analyzing the data in a fashion that would highlight domain-specific individual differences within age groups, not just domain-general differences across them.

As this dual faceted program of research got underway, an interesting pattern began to emerge in the data. Because the pattern appeared to be in accord with both of the two classically contrasting positions simultaneously, we decided to explore it further.

CROSS TASK GENERALITY AND SPECIFICITY IN THE DEVELOPMENT OF CHILDREN'S QUANTITATIVE STRUCTURES

The first domain in which the dual pattern became apparent was that of children's quantitative reasoning. The starting point for our work in this domain was a series of studies using Siegler's (1978) version of Inhelder and Piaget's (1958) balance beam. On this task, it was already known that children go through the following developmental progression: At 4 years of age, they can predict which side of a beam will go down when one side is piled high with weights and the other side has almost none (Liu, 1981; Marini, 1984). At 6 years of age, they can predict which side of a beam will go down when all strong visual cues are removed, and a stack of washers is placed on one side that differs by only one unit from the stack on the other (Marini, 1984; Siegler, 1978). At 8, they can predict which side will go down when two stacks of washers are identical in height, but placed at slightly different distances from the fulcrum (Marini, 1984; Siegler, 1978). Finally, at 10 years of age, they can predict which side will go down in a situation where weight and distance are set in conflict and the only cue as to which side will go down is which variable exhibits the greater numerical contrast (Marini, 1984). As is indicated in Table 19.1, the control structures underlying this progression can be characterized as proceeding through a sequence of four levels, from pre-dimensional, to uni-dimensional, to bi-dimensional, and finally to integrated bi-dimensional thought (Case, 1985).

Given that this sort of detailed analysis had already been conducted, what Marini (chapter 4) set out to do in our first set of studies was to test the generality of this progression across tasks with different surface content. To do so, he designed a set of tasks that could be solved by control structures that were formally identical to those in Table 19.1. On one task, children were asked which of two children would be more satisfied with the number of marbles received (as opposed to the number they hoped for). On another, they were asked to judge the

TABLE 19.1

4 years

PROBLEM SITUATION	OBJECTIVE
• Balance beam with an object on each arm.	• Determine which side will go down.

STRATEGY

1. Look at each side. Predict that the one which looks *heavy* will go down, the *light* one up.

6 years

PROBLEM SITUATION	OBJECTIVES
• Balance with stack of objects on each arm.	• Predict which side will do down.
• Each stack composed of a number of identical units.	• Determine which side has larger number of units.

STRATEGY

1. Count each set of units; note which side has the bigger number.
2. Pick side with bigger number as the one which will weigh more (and therefore go down).

8 years

PROBLEM SITUATION	OBJECTIVES
• Balance beam with stack of objects on each side.	• Predict side which will go down.
• Each object stack composed of a number identical units.	• Determine side with greater number of objects.
• Each object at a specifiable distance from fulcrum.	• Determine side with weight at greater distance.

STRATEGY

1. Count each set of weights; note which side has greater number.
2. Repeat 1 for distance pegs.
3. If the weights are about equal, predict that the side with the greater distance will go down. Otherwise predict that the side with greater weight will go down.

10 years

PROBLEM SITUATION	OBJECTIVES
• Balance beam with stack of weights at various distances.	• Predict which side will go down.
• Action of weight and distance in opposite directions.	• Determine whether weight or distance has a greater effect.
• Each weight stack composed of equal amounts.	• Determine relative number of weights on each side.
• Each distance composed of number of equal units.	• Determine relative distance on each side.

STRATEGY
1. Count each distance; note size
   as well as direction of difference.
2. Repeat step 1 for weight.
3. Compare the magnitude of the
   results in steps 1 and 2. Notice
   which is bigger.
4. Focus on dimension of greater
   difference. Pick side with higher
   value as one which will go
   down.

relative size of shadows cast on a screen by sticks of varying lengths and distances (see Siegler, 1978; Inhelder & Piaget, 1958). Two other tasks that were designed in the same format were DeMerssman's (1976) version of Damon's (1973) Distributive Justice task, and Noelting's Juice Mixing task (Noelting, 1982). For each of these tasks, test items were constructed to fall into one of four categories: (a) *predimensional problems:* ones for which a very large difference existed on the more salient independent variable, and no difference was present on the less salient variable; (b) *unidimensional problems:* ones for which a very small difference existed on the more salient independent variable, and no difference was present on the less salient variable; (c) *bidimensional problems:* ones for which no difference existed on the more salient independent variable, and only a small difference on the less salient variable; and (d) *integrated bidimensional problems:* ones for which a small difference existed on each variable, and the two variables acted in opposite directions.

The pattern of results under these conditions was strikingly simple. The pre-specified sequence of control structures was clearly evident across all the various tasks. Moreover, although there was some cross-task variability in the level of performance of individual children, the average age at which each level in the hierarchy was attained was identical across all the tasks as well. In fact, the cross-task parallel was so close that we began to wonder whether the reason might lie in the constrained conditions under which we were assessing the children, rather than in their ability to construct similar control structures, in different situations, at certain pre-specified points in their development.

In order to explore this possibility, Sandieson and I decided to examine children's performance under testing conditions that were more variable. The tasks we set the children all involved questions about time or money, but they varied widely in format, familiarity, content, presentation, and response mode. Under these conditions, a modest amount of developmental variability appeared as a function of task format and context, but there was still considerable consistency, especially in children's conceptual representation of the various tasks. This consistency appeared to be maintained across tasks that differed considerably in their computational complexity, and hence in their working memory requirements. As long as tasks with a high computational demand could be conceptualized in a simple fashion, many children seemed to find some way around the working memory load that they entailed. When a high computational load was accompanied by a high conceptual load, however, one could virtually guarantee that such short cuts would not be found, and that the task would not be solved until relatively late in children's development (Case & Sandieson, 1987).

To determine the relative power of the conceptual and nonconceptual factors, Griffin conducted a reanalysis of our data. For this purpose, she first formed sets of tasks that could be characterized as having two orthogonal requirements: a conceptual requirement that varied across four levels, from predimensional, to unidimensional, to bidimensional, to integrated bidimensional thought, and a "task" factor, which allowed tasks to vary in their wording, perceptual display, response format, and computational complexity. As predicted, there was an extremely strong developmental effect with regard to the general conceptual factor, and a much more modest effect due to specific task factors (Griffin et al., chapter 5).

At about the same time as we were gathering these data, Capodilupo (1985) began the study of musical sight-reading that was reported in chapter 6. Capidolupo's study had originally been conceived as one in which the working memory demand of various musical sight-reading tasks would be varied in a purely computational manner: for example, by requiring subjects to play two notes rather than one, or to attend to rhythm and pitch simultaneously, rather than to just one or the other. Although significant effects due to these factors did emerge, children often managed to circumvent the computational obstacles they encountered. For example, they might locate one note on the piano keyboard and hold their thumb over it, then return to the musical score, locate the second note on the keyboard, and play it simultaneously with the first. In effect, this strategy transfers the working memory load from the mind to the fingers. Thus, the strategy can be executed by children whose working memory is quite low.

When increased computational complexity was accompanied by increased *representational* complexity, however, this sort of memory-saving solution was almost never observed. In fact, even with training that was carefully designed to minimize students' representational difficulties—using principles drawn both from the literature on musical cognition and the literature on instructional design—the developmental norms remained identical to those that were obtained in our earlier investigations. Predimensional sight-reading tasks were mastered by 4-year-olds, unidimensional tasks by 6-year-olds, bidimensional tasks by 8-year-olds, and integrated bidimensional tasks by 10-year-olds.

Table 19.2 summarizes the data across these various tasks and studies. Obviously, the classification of tasks by conceptual level did not eliminate all performance variability from one task to the next. However, unlike the case where tasks are classified merely by the general function they require (e.g., "decentering"), or by the logical concept with which they deal (e.g., conservation), the new classification did contain the variability to a very modest range.

Because children's performance seemed to be most strongly related to the representational complexity of the tasks relative to their age, the most obvious way to explain the data was to suggest that, at each successive developmental level, children possess a more complex general conceptual representation of their quantitative world, and that this general representation enables them to assemble a variety of more specific executive control structures to meet the requirements of particular tasks. The term *central conceptual structure* was coined to refer to such a structure, and was defined as a network of semantic nodes and relations that plays a central role in mediating children's performance, across a broad range of tasks (though not all), and that also plays a central role in their development.

In order to explore the role of such structures in children's development, we decided to conduct a training study. Our first step in designing such a study was to describe the various conceptual elements and relations that children appeared to understand at one particular developmental level in greater detail. For this purpose, we chose to use the sort of "network" representation that is common in contemporary cognitive science and to concentrate on the unidimensional thought that is typical of 6-year-olds in our culture. The set of concepts and relations that we hypothesized as underlying this sort of thought, using this sort of representation, is illustrated in Figure 19.2. With this sort of specification in hand, our next step was to find a group of children who were at the approximate age where this sort of thought first emerges, but who as yet showed no evidence of it. Next, we developed a curriculum that would expose these children to the opportunity to assemble all the various elements of the hypothesized conceptual structure into a configuration that Piaget would have referred to as "a coherent whole." Finally, we assembled all the various measures reported in chapters 4 to 6, and presented them as pre- and posttests.

In the two studies reported in the present volume (Case & Sandieson, chapter 7) and in two follow-up studies (Griffin, Case & Capodilupo, in press) the results from this four-step process were essentially the same.

TABLE 19.2

Percentage of children in four age groups attaining each of four conceptual levels (0, 1, 2, 3) on six different tests of numerical cognition

Age (years)	Conceptual Level	Juice Mixing 1 (Chapter 4)	Balance Beam (Chapter 4)	Projection of Shadows (Chapter 4)	Birthday Party 2 (Chapter 4)	Distributive Justice (Chapter 4)	Money (Chapter 5)	Time (Chapter 5)	Musical Sight-Reading (Chapter 6)
10	3	60	55	60	70	75	82	67	80
	2	73	95	85	100	100	98	96	90
	1	100	100	100	100	100	100	100	100
	0	100	100	100	100	100	100	100	100
8	3	33	25	20	20	25	40	20	30
	2	74	65	55	70	75	78	69	60
	1	100	100	100	100	100	100	100	80
	0	100	100	100	100	100	100	100	100
6	3	4	0	0	.5	0	0	0	10
	2	29	5	5	15	5	11	8	10
	1	96	95	95	80	95	80	69	80
	0	100	100	100	100	100	93	84	100
4	3	—	0	0	0	0	0	0	0
	2	—	0	0	0	0	0	0	0
	1	—	15	20	25	30	20	27	0
	0	—	95	100	85	80	78	76	100

Task

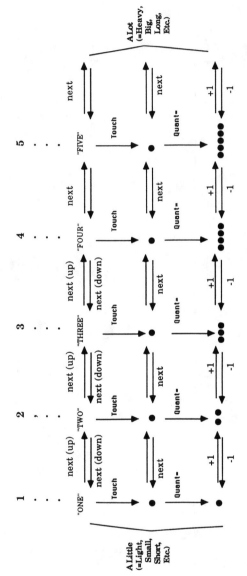

FIG. 19.2. Cognitive structure underlying 6-year-old's numerical understanding (Dotted lines indicate "optional" (i.e., non-universal) notational knowledge).

Before our intervention, the majority of children who were exposed to the curriculum appeared to be functioning at a predimensional level on all of our measures. After our intervention, the majority of children appeared to be functioning at a unidimensional level across all the tasks, even though the training never once introduced any of the physical dimensions whose understanding the tasks involved (e.g., time, music), nor any of the cultural artifacts that are used in the tasks for representing them (e.g., clocks or musical scores). A control group included in each study showed no such gain.

The conclusion to which we were led by the training studies was that it is a mistake to see children as assembling executive control structures for each separate task in complete isolation from those for each other task, subject only to an upper bound on their processing capacity. Rather, it seemed more appropriate to view children as assembling a central conceptual structure that is applicable to a broad range of tasks, then utilizing this central structure, more or less successfully, as a guide for assembling the particular executive control structures that each new task may require.

At first glance, this shift in conceptualization might appear to be a rather small one. We began with a theory that referred to middle childhood as the "dimensional stage," and that suggested that children move from unidimensional to bidimensional to integrated bidimensional thought during this time period. We then designed a series of tasks that require these different forms of thought and found strong evidence that the tasks are passed in the order and at the rate predicted. Finally, we trained children in one of these forms of thought, and showed that their performance took on a new character, across the full range of tasks that we had developed.

Although the change in conceptualization might appear to be small, it is important to realize that, in postulating a central conceptual structure of the sort illustrated in Figure 19.2, we had actually made two rather large alterations in our original position. The most obvious shift was in the hypothesized locus of generality in children's performance: from the size of their working memory to a conceptual structure that they assembled *within* that memory. The other change was that the locus of generality had been moved from one that could easily be seen as constraining performance across *any* set of tasks, to one that was necessarily restricted to a particular task domain, in this case, the domain of number knowledge.

As it happens, the domain of number knowledge is one that modular theorists have frequently cited as a good example of mental modularity. Human beings are evidently born with a specific predisposition to attend to this dimension (Starkey, Spelke, & Gelman, 1983). In addition, the knowledge that they attain in this domain remains relatively confined, both neurologically and psychologically, to the area of functioning that Gardner (1983) has referred to as logico-mathematical. In expanding our view of children's control structures, then, so that these structures included a conceptual as well as an executive component, and in modeling the conceptual component in the fashion that we had, we had also been moving our theory in the direction of a more modular position.

Having moved our initial theory in the direction of a more modular position, the question we had to face was how far to continue in this direction. Should conceptual change across domains be seen as sharing certain very general characteristics, and as taking place at a similar rate—in which case one could infer the action of a common *central* constraint—or should each domain be seen as having its own unique sort of conceptual structure, which develops in its own unique fashion and at its own unique rate? To address these questions, we turned our attention to the domain of social cognition.

CROSS-TASK GENERALITY AND SPECIFICITY IN THE DEVELOPMENT OF CHILDREN'S SOCIAL STRUCTURES

At the outset, our work on the development of children's social cognition did not have the same advantage as our work on the development of children's logico-mathematical cognition. We did not have the same sort of crisply defined tasks and measurement techniques that Siegler (1978) had provided us with his work on the balance beam. Nor did we have a very well articulated sense of how children's social control structures might develop beyond the age of about 4 years (Case, 1985). What we did have, however, was Nelson's analysis of children's understanding of social scripts (Nelson, 1978; Nelson & Gruendel, 1981), and Schank and Abelson's (1977) analysis of the episodic structure that such scripts normally entail. Thus, what Goldberg-Reitman (chapter 8) decided to do was to design a set of cartoon tasks that would embody familiar scripts of the sort Schank and Abelson had analyzed and then investigate children's understanding of them. The particular scripts she created involved the four standard parental functions cited in the sociological literature: protection, physical care, emotional nurturance, and instruction.

The developmental progression on these tasks turned out to be the same for each function: By the age of 4 (if not before), children understood what sort of maternal response would follow any particular initiating event, and could explain why this response would occur by referring to the relevant aspect of the preceding event. By 6, children appeared capable of integrating an explicit evaluation of the mother's internal state (especially her desires) with a similarly explicit evaluation of the external events depicted in the cartoon sequence. Finally by the age of 10, they could envision multiple courses of action that a mother might take, and could cite her specific motive or desire for each. They also appeared capable of integrating these various specific motives under a more general rubric, such as "caring."

As Goldberg-Reitman pointed out, these data were directly parallel to those reported by Nelson and her colleagues, in which children move from thinking in terms of behavioral scripts (at 4 years) to plans (at 6 years) to roles (at 10 years). In addition, they seemed parallel to the classic data on moral development reported by Kohlberg (1958), in which children move from a stage where their primary concern is with the behavioral consequences of their actions (4 years), to one where their primary concern is with other people's judgments of their actions (6 to 8 years), to one where their primary concern is in fulfilling a clearly defined set of social obligations. Finally, the data appear similar to those reported by Fischer et al (1984), in which children progress from a stage where they can imitate a "behavioral role" (4 years), to one where they can imitate a "true" role (6 years), to one where they can imitate multiple interacting roles simultaneously (10 years). In all of these situations, children proceed from a stage where they do not analyze novel behavioral sequences in terms of the underlying motives, feelings, or judgments they entail (4 years), to a stage where they first consider one such internal state (6 years), then two (8 years), and then two or more in an integrated fashion (10 years). It thus seemed that children might be developing a central conceptual structure in the social domain that was unique to that area in its specific elements and relations, but exhibited the same general progression in form as children's central conceptual structure in the domain of number.

Further evidence in support of this suggestion was gathered by Bruchkowsky, in her studies on children's empathy (chapter 9). In one experiment, Bruchkowsky showed that children's ability to answer the questions about a film clip, in a modified empathy paradigm, followed a similar conceptual and temporal progression to the one hypothesized by Goldberg-Reitman, during the same age range. In another, she showed that the emergence of these structures was preceded, in the preschool years, by a less complex progression, whose form was also similar to that revealed on logico-mathematical tasks.

At about the same time that Goldberg-Reitman was studying children's understanding of their mothers' role, McKeough (chapter 10) began her study of children's narrative. The pattern she discovered was as follows: At the age of 4, children tell simple stories that entail a sequence of temporally and causally related events, of the sort they encounter recurrently in their everyday lives. At 6, they tell stories that tend to center around a problem. At 8, they tell stories that center around a problem and a series of further complications, often ones that foil attempts to solve the original problem. Finally at 10, they tell stories in which their account of the major and minor problems is well planned in advance, and integrated at the end. At each stage, one can see the working memory requirements increase, in a predictable fashion.

When these data were first gathered, none of us saw any direct relationship between Goldberg-Reitman's or Bruchkowsky's data and those reported by McKeough. On further reflection, however, McKeough concluded that the three sets of data all do depend on a common set of conceptual attainments. In generating a story that centers around a problem, children move from a purely behavioral analysis to an analysis that considers the inner dilemma of the protagonist (Stein & Glenn, 1979). Similarly, in telling stories where one or more failed attempts to deal with this problem are recounted (an 8-year-old attainment) children "decenter" from a focus on a single inner state change (i.e., bad feeling to good feeling) and envision multiple state changes of this nature. Finally, in generating a well integrated plot and subplot (a 10-year-old accomplishment) children integrate two sequences of events, each tied to a set of inner state changes. Although a great deal of specific knowledge is involved in crafting each sort of narrative, then, it seems quite possible that there is a more general conceptual requirement as well.

A similar conclusion was reached by Griffin (chapter 11) in her study of children's "intrapersonal intelligence." Griffin's specific interest was the growth of children's understanding of "intentionality": the sort of stance that implies an affective or judgmental stance toward a proposition (Brentano, 1960). What she discovered was that children's understanding of intentionality—as indicated by their understanding of judgment and feeling words—also appeared to follow a pattern similar to the one reported by Goldberg-Reitman. At 4, children explain a feeling or a judgment by reference to an external behavior episode. They also localize the source of their feelings or judgments in the external, behavioral world. At 6, there is a shift toward explaining a feeling or a judgment by reference to an external behavior episode *and* an internal state that accompanies it. Their own feelings and judgments are now localized inside themselves, as well. Finally, at 8, they can take account of multiple behavioral episodes and the internal states and/or judgments that accompany them. Certain feelings that inherently involve two internal states can also be successfully identified for the first time.

The overall percentage of subjects performing at each level in our four studies on social cognition is indicated in Table 19.3. As may be seen, the general pattern is similar to the one reported for children's numerical cognition in Table 19.2. While there is some variability from task to task, this variability is by and large contained to a two-year interval. Thus, the overall pattern is essentially the same: At 4 years of age, children function in a fashion that could be called pre-intentional. At 6, they function in a fashion that could be called uni-intentional. At 8, they function in a fashion that could be called bi-intentional. At 10 they function in a fashion that could be called integrated bi-intentional.

Once these data were in hand, the most obvious way to explain them was to postulate the existence of a second central conceptual structure, one that had the same general sort of form as the one we had already explored for children's numerical cognition, but with different content. Accordingly, McKeough (chapter 12) decided to do a training study, in which she gave the social cognitive tests designed by Goldberg-Reitman, Bruchkowsky, and Griffin, to a group of 4 1/2-year-old children who were being trained to generate stories that were more characteristic of 6-year-olds. She also added a test to her battery that had been designed by Astington (1985), on the development of mental state verbs.

As was indicated in chapter 12, the majority of children in the control group performed at the pre-intentional level on the Story Telling task, after the instruction period. By contrast, the majority of children in the experimental group performed at the uni-intentional level, both on the Story Telling tasks and on the other social measures. This result has since been replicated on more than one occasion, in the context of

TABLE 19.3

Percentage of children in three age groups attaining each of three conceptual levels (0, 1, 2) on five different tests of social cognition

Age (years)	Conceptual Level	Task			
		Mother's Role (Chapter 8)	Empathy (Chapter 9)	Narrative Structure (Chapter 10)	Internal States (Chapter 11)
8–10	2*	90	68	75	90
	1	100	88	100	100
	0	100	100	100	100
6	2	10	30	10	22
	1*	81	58	90	80
	0	100	100	100	100
4	2	0	0	0	2
	1	20	26	5	22
	0*	89	53	75	75

*Predicted Level of Performance for age group.

studies with a pretest/posttest design and a variety of other controls (e.g., Case & McKeough, 1990). The conclusions that we draw from these data are as follows: First, the executive control structures children assemble for dealing with a broad range of specific social situations depend on the existence of a central conceptual structure that they have constructed for modeling social interaction. Second, children's central conceptual structures in this domain bear a certain resemblance—both in their form and in the timing of their emergence—to those in the domain of number. Finally, these commonalities suggest that both structures may be subject to a common set of constraints, for example, in speed of processing or in working memory.

CROSS-TASK GENERALITY AND SPECIFICITY IN THE DEVELOPMENT OF CHILDREN'S SPATIAL STRUCTURES

With the notion of a central conceptual structure in hand, and with examples of trainable structures available from both the social and numerical domains, it became possible to view the data from other domains in a similar light. In her study of children's art (chapter 13), Dennis had already demonstrated an interesting developmental progression. Four-year-olds appear to organize their figures on a page without reference to the relationship of these figures to each other in the real world. By the age of 6, they appear to be able to take inter-object relations into account, and thus to draw a coherent "scene" in which the figures are arranged with respect to a single spatial axis or "ground line." By the age of 8, two such ground lines can be used: one to signify a set of foreground spatial relationships, and one to signify a set of background relationships. Finally, by the age of 10, these two sets of relationships can be integrated with each other, often by the provision of a continuous middle ground. In and of themselves, the data on children's drawing do not indicate any necessity for moving from the general system theory in chapter 2 to a theory that includes some provision for conceptual structures of a more modular nature. In conjunction with the data from the previous two sections, however, they do open up this sort of possibility, because they highlight a network of conceptual relations that is unique to the spatial domain in its content, but general in its form and in its age of emergence.

This possibility was given further support by the study of children's motor development that was reported in chapter 14. What Reid demonstrated in this study was a recursive re-structuring on motor tasks that had a similar general nature to that documented by Dennis. At the age of 6, children for the first time showed evidence of being able to conceptualize a "mental corridor" or "axis" in three-dimensional space. Then, between the ages of 6 and 10, they progressed from a substage where they were capable of thinking in terms of a single spatial axis to one where they were capable of thinking of two such spatial axes, to one where they were capable of thinking about two or more such axes in an integrated fashion. This progression appeared across a broad range of motor tasks, including those that involved both fine and gross motor coordination. The progression also appeared to be related to the development of children's spatial working memory, and to the manner in which they represent space in their drawings. Finally, there also appeared to be a parallel progression at lower stages as well, but one that involved spatial axes of a more elementary nature.

The three conclusions that the spatial data suggest, then, are similar to those suggested by the studies on social cognition: A limited number of central conceptual structures may underlie children's development across a wide range of tasks in the spatial domain.[1] These structures may change in a fashion, and at a rate, that is directly parallel to the change in children's quantitative and social structures. And all three sorts of structure may well be constrained by some more general set of developments, such as changes in speed of processing or working memory.

INDIVIDUAL AND GROUP DIFFERENCES IN THE EXTENT OF CROSS-DOMAIN GENERALITY

As was mentioned at the beginning of this chapter, the data that have been gathered by modular theorists have shown a wide range of intraindividual variability. As was also mentioned, they have revealed a pattern that is of particular theoretical significance, one in which an individual child performs at an age-appropriate level in most domains, but at an adult level in the domain of his greatest interest and/or experience (Chi & Koeske, 1983; Feldman, 1986). Of all the possible developmental outcomes, this one seems hardest to square with the notion of a systemwide "upper bound," to which all children's various conceptual structures are subject.

The specific tasks that were developed in the first three sections included tests of the sort that have been used by modular theorists: that is, those that encourage children to draw on their everyday knowledge base in formulating a response, and those in which children receive considerable specific instruction. The question that naturally arose,

---

[1]For recent evidence on is point, see Case et al, 1990.

therefore, was whether the cross-domain equivalences that had been discovered at the group level in our studies would be maintained at the individual level, when tasks from several different domains were administered to the same subjects, and the performance of individual children was examined.

In chapter 15, four different studies of this sort were reported, comparing children's levels of performance on tasks drawn from varying combinations of domains. The pattern across these four studies was extremely coherent. In neither study where only two measures were administered did any child ever show a "split" in his or her level of conceptual reasoning that exceeded two substages, and the great majority of differences were confined to one substage. In the study where multiple measures were administered in one domain, the percentage of individual children showing an asynchrony in performance of one substage was greatly reduced, and no two-substage splits were reported. Finally in the study where several measures were administered in each of two domains, the percentage of subjects showing a split of even one substage fell to less than 2%. Moreover, these splits, when they did occur, tended to involve underperformance, not overperformance, in a particular domain. Taken at face value, then, these data suggest that wide differences in children's performance are more likely to be the result of different specific items of task knowledge than different levels of development across an entire conceptual system.

In chapter 16, Crammond raised the issue of the "typicality" of subjects in the studies that had been conducted to that point, pointing out that even a small number of subjects with a wide discrepancy in functioning across conceptual domains could be problematic for the neo-Piagetian position, and that the selection procedure that had been used was one that was likely to decrease the likelihood that such subjects would be included in the samples. In her own work, Crammond examined the development of children with diagnosed difficulties in one particular area of scholastic functioning to see if their general developmental profiles would be different from those of other children. She focused on these groups following a suggestion in the literature that math-disabled children may have a disability in their working memory for spatial versus verbal relations, while reading-disabled children may show the reverse pattern (L.S. Siegel & Linder, 1984), that is, that these disadvantages could be domain-specific in their nature. In fact, however, this was not the pattern that she found. Rather she found a very broad deficit for both groups that was general to the entire working memory system. Rather than challenging the notion of a system-wide upper limit on children's functioning, then, Crammond's data added further support to it.

The population studied by Porath in chapter 17 had the potential to challenge the notion of a system-wide upper bound much more seriously, because the children were selected for an asymmetrical *talent* rather than a disability. Like asymmetrically disabled children, asymmetrically gifted children are quite rare. Thus, they could easily have been missed in earlier studies. Accordingly, Porath decided to do a study in which she carefully selected two groups of such children, one verbally gifted and one spatially gifted. She also decided to compare these groups to others of average IQ and to a group of generally-gifted children, using a broad battery of measures.

As might have been expected, no evidence was found that the control children performed at a different developmental level from one particular domain to the next. Children of average IQ tended to function at the same general conceptual level across domains, and generally gifted children appeared to excel only in tasks where some form of improvement in performance via rapid learning was possible. Interestingly, asymmetrically gifted populations did not appear to show much specificity of functioning, either. Each group did contain a modestly elevated number of children who were one substage ahead in their conceptual development in the particular area of their giftedness. Moreover, as domain-specific theory would predict, these conceptual advances appeared to be a direct product of greater affective investment (and hence experience) in the domain of exceptionality. A similar interpretation seemed applicable to two case studies of child prodigies. These children are even more rare in the general population (Porath estimated their frequency as 1 in 10,000 or less), yet their basic pattern of general conceptual development appears to be little different. That is, they appear to show only a modest—one substage—general conceptual elevation in the area of their specific talent. While the data do show an asymmetry in development, then, they do not show the sort of asymmetry that one might have expected from the literature. Strikingly absent is the sort of pattern in which a child is functioning at an adult level in one domain, but a child-like level in all others.

In spite of these data, Porath had the distinct impression that the asymmetrically gifted children she studied *were* functioning at a much higher level in their domain of giftedness than in any other. Thus, she persisted with her investigation, and rescored her data using more specific measures of achievement. Here she found what she had originally been looking for. Both the asymmetrically gifted children, and the two child prodigies for whom retrospective data were available, showed levels of specific attainment in their domain of exceptionality that approached or exceeded normal adult levels, whereas their performance in other domains remained childlike. The very real possibility exists, then, that the sort of data originally cited as being problematic for neo-Piagetian theory by modular theorists were also of this more particular nature. That is not to say that they are in any less need of explanation. However, it *is* to say that they do not challenge the proposition advanced in the present volume, namely, that children's central conceptual structures develop at approximately the same rate across different domains in response to the action of system-wide biological constraints and/or potentiators.

The final study (chapter 18) was included in order to counteract any possible impression that central conceptual structures depend *exclusively* on biological potentiators for their development. In the experiment conducted by Fiati, a subculture was studied in which relatively little value was placed on high-level numerical structures, and no instructional support was provided for their development. In contrast to other groups in the same general cultural and linguistic milieu, this group showed a highly asymmetrical profile of development in adulthood. Although social and spatial cognition appeared to reach normal adult levels, numerical cognition did not advance beyond the level often found at the age of 6 years in Western groups, namely, unidimensional thought. Furthermore, working memory for numbers also failed to develop beyond the 6-year-old level (i.e., two units).

In the face of these cross-cultural data, the point that has been made repeatedly by developmentalists in the sociohistoric tradition (e.g., Bruner, 1964; Cole & Bruner, 1971; Cole & Scribner, 1974; Lave, 1988; Vygotsky, 1962) deserves reiteration: Development cannot be understood without studying the cultural milieu into which children are born, and the social and symbolic supports that this context provides for the development of particular central conceptual structures. This is true even when the structures are ones for representing domains as basic as space, number, and social interaction, domains to which, by biological nature, the human infant is innately pre-attuned.

TOWARD A THEORY OF INTELLECTUAL
DEVELOPMENT THAT OCCUPIES A
MIDDLE GROUND ON THE
GENERALITY/SPECIFICITY ISSUE

It was not our intention in the present program of research to present a new theory of the mind or its development. Rather, our goal was to gather a new set of data that might lay the foundation for a such a theory, by combining the research methods of those who have favored a domain-specific view of intellectual development with those who have favored a more general or systemic view. This having been said, however, we did end up proposing a new construct, namely the *central conceptual structure*. And, perhaps predictably, this construct possessed properties that were previously associated only with a modular or general-systemic view. A question that naturally arises, therefore, is what a general theory of development might look like, in which the construct whose role we have attempted to elucidate in the present volume plays a central role.

Although many approaches might be taken to answering this question, one possible way to address it is to specify the elements from the various developmental "schools of thought" that are compatible with the new construct, and that could profitably be retained and integrated in a new general theory. Such a description is offered below.[2]

Elements from Contemporary Modular and/or "Neo-Nativist" Theory

1. *Children's cognitive processes may be parsed into a set of basic categories or "domains of functioning."*** The three domains that were investigated most directly in the present program of research were the numerical, social, and spatial. However, the full set very probably include all the classical domains identified by psychometric investigations, such as verbal, numerical, and spatial functioning, as well as the additional domains that have been proposed more recently by differential theorists, such as social, motor, and musical functioning (Gardner, 1983).[3]

2. *The origin of these domains lies in the modular structure of the human nervous system,** in the evolutionary history of the human organism, and the modular structure of the cortex to which this history has given rise* (Fodor, 1982; Gardner, 1983). This modular structure insures that stimulation of relevance to each of these categories is processed by its own distinctive neurological system (Gardner, 1983; Luria, 1973), that infants respond to stimulation in each category in a different and distinctive fashion (Bower, 1972), and that the cognitive operations that generate these responses are organized into coherent and distinctive system as well (Spelke, 1988).

3. *The conceptual systems or "theories" that children construct reflect this modular structure.** Although children are capable of constructing con-

---

[2]In this description, propositions that received some form of direct empirical support in our own data are indicated with a double asterix (**). Propositions that are congruent with these propositions, but depend for their empirical support on data that have been gathered elsewhere, are indicated with a single asterix (*).

[3]Causal analysis is another domain that appears to be independent, and that should perhaps be added to this list (see Demetriou & Efklides, 1988). For a developmental account of children's musical composition that is consistent with the present view, see Capodilupo (1990).

ceptual systems that transcend any of the modules described, many of the most important developmental structures build directly on one of the early modular systems, and continue to reflect its distinctive properties (Carey, 1985; Gelman & Carey, 1991). In the present volume, for example, the content of the social structures that were studied was quite different from the content of the numerical structures that was studied. It also appeared to be subject to different sorts of influence.

4. *In the course of development, children's conceptual systems are periodically re-worked, in either a major or a minor fashion*** (Carey, 1985). In the present volume, the major re-workings all tended to occur at about the age of 5 or 6. The minor re-workings tended to occur at 7 to 8 and 9 to 10.

5. *At the heart of any conceptual system is a core set of elements, that may be characterized as a central conceptual structure"*.** This proposition is the only one in this group that does not derive directly from contemporary modular theory, but that appears to be congruent with this theory: At the heart of children's conceptual systems is a core set of elements, that play a key role in determining the nature of the theories that they construct, and the explanations for any local set of phenomena that they fashion. The present volume was largely devoted to identifying these core structures and to exploring their developmental significance.

Elements from Contemporary Domain-Specific and/or Neo-Associationist Theory

1. *Central conceptual structures may be represented as semantic networks***, that is, as a set of nodes and relations between them (Chi, 1988). In the present volume, such representations were developed for children's early numerical and social structures, and were illustrated in Fig. 19.2 (p. 356). Similar representations for children's spatial structures have been presented elsewhere (Case et al, 1990).

2. *Domain-specific experience is necessary for the development of such semantic networks.** Both the content of the nodes, and the content of the relations among them, are subject to influence by the child's experience in the particular domain in question (Chi, 1988; Chi & Koeske, 1983). Indeed, without such experience, developmental change in the structures is impossible. In the present volume, the necessity of domain-specific experience was demonstrated by the performance of the control groups (who were missing this experience) in the training studies that were reported in chapters 7 and 11. The sufficiency of

such experience—once certain general constraints had been met—was demonstrated by the performance of the treatment groups.

3. *Associative as Well as Semantic Aspects of this Experience are Important.*** The strength of relationships among nodes is just as important as the nature of these relationships, and is also influenced by children's experience, via the standard laws of practice and association[4] (Pascual-Leone, 1970; Rumelhart & McClelland, 1987). The importance of such factors was demonstrated in the present volume by the large amount of practice that proved necessary in the training studies in order to "consolidate" the structure that was trained. Consolidation is a concept that can only be given meaning within some sort of associative framework.

4. *Cognitive strategies are strongly influenced by the presence of these structures.*** The cognitive strategies that children employ at any age or stage are strongly influenced by the nature of their central conceptual structures (Chi, 1988). This influence was demonstrated in the present volume by the spontaneous change in the strategies that children employed, after training, on the transfer tasks (see chapters 7 and 11).

Elements from Contemporary Sociocultural or "Contextual" Theory

1. *Culturally specific experience plays an increasing role with age, in shaping the content of children's central conceptual structures.*** With age, the experience that is relevant to the formation of central conceptual structures becomes less universal, and more highly dependent on technologies and bodies of knowledge that are unique to the culture in which they were developed (Cole & Scribner, 1974; Vygotsky, 1962). This proposition has received extensive support in the sociocultural literature (e.g., Cole, Gay, Glick, & Sharp, 1971), and was demonstrated in the present volume by the results reported in chapter 18.

2. *Social institutions such as schooling, play an increasingly important role with age in providing this experience,*** and thus in determining the pattern, rate, and cross-domain profile of children's cognitive functioning. This fact was also demonstrated in the cross-cultural study, by the performance of the unschooled groups.

---

[4]The variable in the present volume that seems most likely to be affected by practice is the extent to which any central conceptual structure is "consolidated," and can function as a unit in higher integrations. Automaticity of access (and hence speed of processing) might be another variable that is influenced by practice.

3. *One of the most important functions of schools is to familiarize children with the culture's symbol systems and the concepts and conventions underlying their use.* Certain central conceptual structures, such as those that are involved in understanding number or perspective drawing, are clearly dependent on such systems if they are to develop to higher levels. Once introduced, they function as independent "tools of thought," which can be applied in a large number of situations but have no direct relationship to the situations in which they were acquired (Bruner, 1964; Gardner, in press; Goodman, 1976).

4. *Central conceptual structures can continue to develop, both in content and level, as a culture and its symbol system themselves continue to evolve.** To the extent that a culture continues to evolve and to create new knowledge and artifacts, the central conceptual structures and strategies that it depends on will continue to evolve as well. Intellectual development, thus, has no fixed endpoint, and schooling constitutes a potential vehicle for bringing children into contact with a broad range of possible developmental outcomes.

Elements from Contemporary Neo-Piagetian Theory

1. *Children's central conceptual structures in different domains are subject to common general developmental constraints.*** Notwithstanding the fact that they entail different (module-specific) operations, and are dependent on different sorts of (culturally delivered) forms of experience, all central conceptual structures are subject to a common set of general developmental constraints. The existence of these system-wide constraints was demonstrated in the present research project by the common general form exhibited by central conceptual structures in different domains and by the common age-related constraints to which they were subject.

2. *These constraints operate on various aspects of the executive and/or working memory system.*** One of the psychological systems through which these constraints have their effect, though not necessarily the only one, is the executive system, the system responsible for dealing with novel information, storing it for brief periods of time, accessing other information that may be relevant, and making decisions that permit some form of coherent action. Tests that index the functioning of this system thus correlate with tests of structural proficiency, and are subject to identical numerical limits.

3. *These constraints are likely to have some sort of biological basis.** A wide variety of forms of evidence have been presented for this proposition elsewhere.[5] In the present volume, however, no direct evidence of this sort was presented. The only pieces of evidence that might

be indirectly relevant were that the measures of working memory showed a rapid increase, in synchrony, at about 5 years of age, and that no other discernable change took place concurrently in the children's environment.[6]

4. *The pattern of development that results from the operation of these constraints is hierarchical and recursive,*** The nature and timing of this pattern was illustrated in Fig. 19.1. Note that the major reworkings of children's conceptual structures proposed by modular theorists are most likely to occur *across* the stages that are indicated in the figure, and to result from the coordination of qualitatively different sorts of unit (A vs B). The more minor reworkings are likely to occur *within* stages, and to result from the coordination of similar units (A_1-B_1; A_2-B_2).

Foundational Elements from Classical Piagetian Theory

Finally, it should be noted that the foregoing sets of propositions presuppose a more general set of propositions, which were first proposed by Piaget and his predecessors (e.g., Baldwin, 1894/1968). These include:

1. *The importance of constructivity for the formation of central conceptual structures.* Regardless of the domain to which it applies, or the cultural experience on which it is dependent, any cognitive structure that entails genuine conceptual understanding must be actively constructed by the child.

2. *The importance of differentiation and coordination as developmental mechanisms.* New conceptual structures are formed by the hierarchical differentiation and coordination of existing structures.

---

[5]For example, it has been shown that the constraints to which the executive system is subject change rapidly during the years of biological maturation (as does the speed with which the executive system can access information from other systems); that the constraints then stay constant for several decades, even when new knowledge structures are being formed at a rapid rate; and that they then change again (becoming more severe) in middle and old age. It is also known that many aspects of executive functioning depend on the intact functioning of the frontal lobes, that these lobes show strong biologically related changes during the years of biological maturation and decline, and that measures of cortical functioning in these areas are correlated with measures of working memory (see Case, in press; Diamond, 1990; Goldman-Rakic, 1989; Pascual-Leone, 1989; Stuss, in press). Finally, it is known that practice has little impact, per se, on measures of speed or working memory, once a developmental asymptote has been reached.

[6]In the school systems where we worked, the children did not enter school at this age, for example (4 is the mandatory age of entry into kindergarten), nor did any change take place in the nature of their schooling (6 is the age of first exposure to formal instruction).

3. *Qualitative shifts entailed by structural re-working.* When a major re-working in children's general cognitive structures takes place, children become capable, at least potentially, of analyzing their experience in any domain in a qualitatively different fashion. As a consequence, external events that previously had little effect on them may suddenly begin to exert a major influence.

4. *Universal sequence of structural levels: from concrete to abstract.* The content of children's cognitive structures may vary from task to task, or from culture to culture. The rate of development may also vary across different contexts within or across cultures. What is universal, however, is the progression from simple sensorimotor structures to representational structures of increasing complexity, abstractness, and power.

As I have already mentioned, the one construct in the above set of postulates that is genuinely new, and that serves to give some coherence to what would otherwise be four or five rather disparate and unconnected sets of propositions, is the notion of a central conceptual structure. Interestingly, the feature that allows the construct to play this sort of unifying role is that it bears a strong resemblance to one notion from each of the different theoretical systems that it may potentially help to integrate. The modular notion to which the notion of a central conceptual structure bears a resemblance is the naive "theory"; the neo-connectionist notion it resembles is the "knowledge network"; the relevant sociocultural notion is the "interpretative frame"; the neo-Piagetian notion to which it bears a resemblance is the "executive control structure"; and finally, the parallel classic Piagetian notion is the "operational structure."

Because the notion of a central conceptual structure bears a resemblance to each one of these previous constructs, it can be substituted for them without doing great violence to the other propositions with which each notion is normally associated. At the same time, however, because the notion is also *different* from each one of these constructs, it permits the five sets of propositions to be brought together in a manner that would otherwise not be possible. In effect, then, the construct occupies a sort of semantic middle ground, around which the various propositions mentioned above may be arrayed and unified. For the reader with an historical interest, the features that the construct shares (and does not share) with each of its precursors are indicated in Table 19.4. The developmental assertions have been made regarding the construct are compared with those that have been advanced for other constructs in Table 19.5.

TABLE 19.4
Notion of Central Conceptual Structure Compared to Constructs from
other Theoretical Systems

A Central Conceptual Structure is				
A Coherent System of Mental Elements	Comprised of Conceptual Nodes and Relations	Which Represent Core Elements of a "Domain of Knowledge"	Which are Used to Interpret Novel Situations or Tasks in These Domains	Other Constructs Possessing similar Features
√	X	X	√	Operational Structure (Piaget, 1950)
√	√	*	√	Naive Theory (Wiser & Carey, 1982)
√	√	*	√	Local Knowledge Network (Chi, 1988)
√	X	X	X	Executive Control Structure (Case, 1985)
√	√	*	√	Interpretive Frame (Bruner, 1964)

*Not clear whether core elements are distinguished from more peripheral elements.

DIRECTIONS FOR FUTURE RESEARCH

Given that the notion of a central conceptual structure may be capable of playing some sort of unifying role in the field of cognitive development, the most obvious direction for further research is to explore the new possibilities that the construct opens up, and to conduct further work aimed at the development of a more tightly integrated and coherent theoretical system. This general enterprise is likely to be facilitated if the following general tasks are pursued.

Central Conceptual Structures in Other Domains

The first and most obvious task is to identify a broader array of central conceptual structures. If the general theory is correct, then structures should exist that are similar in their general form to those illustrated, but have content that is drawn from one of the other basic domains that have been identified by modular theorists. As this work progresses, it should become possible to answer certain additional questions, such as:

• Is it necessary to use different forms of modeling in different domains (e.g., analogical versus digital) in order to capture the

TABLE 19.5
Developmental Hypotheses Regarding Central Conceptual Structures
Compared to Those Regarding Other Theoretical Constructs

	Central Conceptual Structures are . . .				
	Reorganized Periodically in the Course of Development	By Differentiation and Coordination of Elements	Which is Facilitated by System-Wide Changes in Operative Capacity	As Well As Acquisition of Symbols and Symbolic Systems of Culture	With Concomilant Changes in Children's Task-Specific Cognitive Strategies
Operative Structures	√	√	√	X	√
Naive Theories	√	X	X	√	√
Local Knowledge Networks	√	**	X	√	√
Executive Control Structures	√	√	√	√	√

**Sometimes (see Chi, 1988 in press).

content of children's central conceptual structures with precision and accuracy? (c.f. Lautrey, DeRibaupierre, & Rieben, 1988).

- How many domains constitutes the optimal number to postulate in order to do justice to the full set of data on children's development?
- Is it better to model conceptual and procedural aspects of these structures within a single system, or to model them separately?
- How should one conceive of the interaction of these two components?
- Can one specify, a priori, what sorts of tasks in a domain will require the mediation of a central conceptual structure, and what sorts can be handled by more specific mechanisms?

Central Conceptual Structures at Other Stages

A second task is to identify the central conceptual structures at earlier and later stages of development than those studied in the present volume. This seems particularly important at the higher age levels, where the Piagetian empirical legacy is least strong, and where the role of cultural and "disciplinary" knowledge structures, as well as formal "notational systems" (Gardner, in press) is likely to be strongest.

*Trans-Domain Parallels in Central Conceptual Structures and
Their Implications*

A third line of work that seems necessary is to explore the parallels
that exist across structures, and the factors that are responsible for
producing these parallels. The further questions that this line of inquiry
will open up include:

- Can "deep" conceptual or executive structures which have identifiable system-wide semantic content, be isolated?
- Can the psychological and/or neurological prerequisites for the
cross-domain parallels that are observed be identified?

Educational Implications of Modifying Children's Central Conceptual Structures

- Do central conceptual structures constitute prerequisites for profit-
ing from certain kinds of existing school curricula?
- If so, should they be taught directly to children who do not already
possess them, prior to the teaching of the subject matter in question?
- Are certain levels of structure not attained, unless special provision
is made for experience that permits children to develop their
informal understanding, and integrate it with a more formal understanding (perhaps one that is rooted in a particular symbolic
system)?

Clinical Implications of Modifying Children's Central Conceptual Structures

- Is it the case that dysfunctional pathways of socio-emotional development are at least partly rooted in dysfunctional variants of
central conceptual structures?
- Should the goal of clinical work and therapeutic intervention be
the identification of such structures and the facilitation of their
reworking?

TOWARD A MULTI-LEVEL VIEW OF THE HUMAN
MIND AND ITS ADAPTIVE CAPABILITIES

At the beginning of this volume, and repeatedly throughout it, I have
returned to the classic question of whether the human mind should be
viewed as a general system or a modular device. Each time I have done
so, I have suggested that the current issue is not which of these two polar
positions is correct, but rather what sort of intermediate position does
greatest justice to the data that are currently available. With the data

from this research program now in hand, with the notion of a central conceptual structure explicated, and with the general outline of a more unified developmental theory sketched out, it is this question to which I would like to return.

In the context of neo-Piagetian theory, developmental changes in children's intellectual competence are seen as stemming from two general sources: *local change,* that is, changes in the knowledge relating to a specific task, or the perceptual and social context in which that task is normally encountered, and *general change,* including change in the capacity of the organism to process information, and the style with which it selects and integrates that information.

In the context of modular and/or domain-specific theory, changes in children's competence are seen as resulting from two general sources as well. The first is essentially the same as the one postulated in neo-Piagetian theory: changes in task-specific or context-specific knowledge. However, the second source is an *intermediate change:* a change in the structure of the child's knowledge about an entire domain of tasks. This latter change is seen as stemming either from a maturational change in the module that controls the subject's response to tasks in this domain, or from the re-working of a theory whose boundaries are co-incident with those of a module. In either case, the notion that domain-specific changes in the structure of children's knowledge are a function of general systemic changes is explicitly rejected.

The data that were gathered in this research project provide an equal degree of support—or non-support—for both positions. They confirm the importance of the sorts of change that each theory mentions, thus supporting its positive claims. However, they also confirm the importance of the factor that each theory omits, thus refuting any negative claims, whether implied or explicit. Because the operation of both sorts of change (i.e., general and intermediate) were clearly evident in the present data, the view of the human mind that is supported is one of a multi-level system, whose structures and processes can vary in their degree of applicability, along a continuum from specific through intermediate (module-wide) through to general-systemic. The corresponding view of human development is one in which changes take place at all levels, in a recursive and interactive fashion, according to a process that depends on both biological and cultural/experiential factors.

This multi-level view of the human mind is not unique to the present research program. It is not even unique to developmental psychology. In the current psychometric literature, for example, after a protracted debate between general-factor theorists such as Spearman (1904, 1927) and local-factor theorists such as Thurstone (1938) or Guilford (1976), a unified view is emerging, one which has important similarities with the one proposed in the present volume (Carroll, 1976; Carroll, et al., 1984; Gustaffson, 1984; Snow et al., 1984). Interestingly, the historical progression by which this view has been reached appears to be similar as well, in the sense that it has included a period in which a variety of alternative "middle ground" positions have been proposed and evaluated: some tilted more in the general direction (e.g., Vernon, 1965) and some tilted more toward modularly (Cattell, 1976; Horn, 1971).

It is too early to tell whether the currently favored unifying model in psychometrics will achieve a broad degree of acceptance. However, the dialectical process at work in the field does at least suggest that a unifying model of this sort is desirable, and that a consensus on its outlines may ultimately be possible. For obvious reasons, a consensus that spans the two disciplines and integrates the differential and developmental approaches, would have even more to recommend it. Such a model would have to grapple with a set of deep-rooted differences across the two fields in the conception of intelligence, and of its general, intermediate, and specific aspects. However, such an enterprise is not without precedent (see, for example, Gardner, 1983; Demetriou & Efklides, 1988, 1990; Pascual-Leone & Goodman, 1979; Sternberg, 1984). As a long-term goal, I believe it remains worthy of continued effort.

EPILOGUE AND CONCLUSION

The present program of research was based on an historical analysis that yielded two general conclusions. The first was that there had been a dialectical progression in the field of intellectual development, from theories that were overly general, monolithic, and endogenous (Baldwin, 1894/1968; Piaget, 1950), to theories that were overly specific, atomistic, and exogenous (Klahr & Wallace, 1976; Siegler, 1986), to theories that occupied a middle position between these two extremes. The second was that a tension could still be identified between those middle positions that leaned in the direction of generality and those that leaned in the direction of domain-specificity or modularity. It was further suggested that, in order to resolve this tension, it might be necessary to synthesize the sorts of research methods that had previously been reserved for one of these two positions or the other.

That was the rationale for the program of research that was undertaken in the present volume. What this research revealed, perhaps predictably, was a conjoint pattern of data in which regularities were present at both the modular and the systemic level. In order to explain this pattern, a set of central conceptual structures was postulated. Each of these structures was hypothesized to represent a core set of semantic relations and to be module-wide in its domain of applicability. However, each structure was also hypothesized to be subject to system-wide constraints on its construction and application. The semantic *content* of such structures, particularly at upper age levels, appears to be dependent on the culture, its symbolic systems, and the institutions within which these systems are acquired and/or utilized. By contrast, the general *constraints* to which the structures are subject appear to be more dependent on a set of systemic factors of a biological and/or neurological sort. In effect, then, central conceptual structures appear to constitute a kind of pivotal point, where the forces of biology and culture meet, and around which children's understanding of their world can coalesce.

If this view of development turns out to be a useful one, even in the short run, there will be an interesting irony for historians of the field to contemplate. Although the first post-Piagetian theories were designed with the intention of striking a balance between general-systems and task-specific perspectives, they were not entirely successful, because they sacrificed too much from the original Piagetian system that was their legacy. In postulating a system in which specific concepts, skills, and control structures were assembled by the child, unconstrained by any developmental factor other than general M-power or working memory, neo-Piagetian theorists sacrificed the notion of an operational structure, which had been one of the most important and original of Piaget's contributions. Similarly, in suggesting that the only source of generality in children's thinking was in the form of module-specific theories (Carey, 1985) or domain-specific knowledge networks (Chi, 1983), the neo-nativist theorists also sacrificed too much from the original Piagetian system; in particular, they eliminated the notion of a system-wide change in operative level or capacity.

Because the construct each group of theorists sacrificed was the one the other group maintained and developed, and because both constructs appear to have some merit, what we have attempted to do in the present volume is to lay the groundwork for a synthesis, in which both constructs are refined, reworked, and integrated. The broad outline of one such synthesis was sketched in the present chapter. Hopefully, other contemporary developmentalists will find this outline useful, and either join in the effort of developing it further, or use in as a foil in developing a unified theoretical position of their own.

References

Adams, J. A. (1971). A closed-loop theory of motor learning. *Journal of Motor Behavior, 3,* 111–149.

Ainsworth, M. D. S., Blehar, M. C., Waters, E., and Wall, S. (1978). *Patterns of attachment: A psychological study of the strange situation.* Hillsdale, NJ: Lawrence Erlbaum Associates.

Ames, L. (1937). The sequential patterns of prone progressions in the human infant. *Genetic Psychology Monographs, 19,* 411–460.

Ammons, R. B., & Ammons, C. H. (1962). *Quick Test.* Missoula, MT.: Psychological Test Specialists.

Anderson, J. R. (1983). *The architecture of cognition.* Cambridge: Harvard University Press.

Applebee, A. N. (1978). *The child's concept of story.* Chicago: University of Chicago Press.

Astington, J. W. (1985). *Children's understanding of promising.* Unpublished doctoral dissertation. Ontario Institute for Studies in Education, University of Toronto.

Astington, J. W., Olson, D., & Harris, P. (Eds.). (1989). *The child's theory of mind.* New York: Cambridge University Press.

Baddeley, A. D. (1986). *Working memory.* Oxford: Clarendon.

Baldwin, J. M. (1968). *The development of the child and of the race.* New York: Augustus M. Kelley. (Original work published 1894).

Bamberger, J. (1973). Learning to think musically. *Music Educator's Journal, 59*(7), 5–57.

Bamberger, J. (1978). Intuitive and formal musical knowing: Parables of cognitive dissonance. In S. S. Madeja (Ed.), *The arts, cognition, and basic skills* (pp. 173–209). St. Louis, MO: Cemrel Inc.

Bartlett, F. C. (1932). *Remembering.* London: Cambridge University Press.

Barden, R. C., Garber, J., Duncan, F. W., & Masters, J. C. (1980). Children's consensual knowledge about the experiential determinants of Emotion. *Journal of Personality and Social Psychology, 40,* 750–760.

Bassok, M., & Holyoak, K. J. (1989). Inter-domain transfer between isomorphic topics in algebra and physics. *Journal of Experimental Psychology: Learning, Memory, and Cognition, 15,* 153–166.

Bates, E. (1976). *Language and context.* New York: Academic.

Bauer, R. A. (1977). Memory, processes in children with learning disabilities: Evidence for deficient rehearsal. *Journal of Experimental Child Psychology, 24,* 415–430.

Bauer, R. A. (1979). Memory acquisition, category clustering in learning disabled children. *Journal of Experimental Child Psychology, 27,* 365–383.

Bauer, R. A. (1982). Information processing as a way of understanding and diagnosing learning disabilities. *Topics in Learning and Learning Disabilities, 2,* 33–45.

Bauer, R. H., & Emhert, J. (1984). Information processing in reading disabled and non-disabled children. *Journal of Experimental Child Psychology, 37,* 271–281.

Bayley, N. (1935). The development of motor abilities during the first three years. *Society for Research in Child Development Monographs, 1,* 1–26.

de Beaugrande, R. (1982). A story of grammars and a grammar of stories. *Journal of Pragmatics, 6,* 383–422.

Beilin, H. (1971a). Developmental stages and developmental processes. In D. R. Green, M. P. Ford, & G. B. Flammer (Eds.), *Measurement and Piaget* (pp. 172–196). New York: McGraw-Hill.

Beilin, H. (1971b). The training and acquisition of logical operations. In M. F. Rosskopf, L. P. Steffe, & S. Taback (Eds.), *Piagetian cognitive-developmental research and mathematical education* (pp. 81–124). Washington, DC: National Council of Teachers of Mathematics.

Belmont, J. M., & Butterfield, E. C. (1971). What the development of short term memory is. *Human Development, 14,* 236–248.

Bereiter, C. (1983). Story grammar as knowledge. *The Behavioral and Brain Sciences, 4,* 593–594.

Bereiter, C., & Scardamalia, M. (1985). Cognitive coping strategies and the problem of "inert" knowledge. In S. Chipman, J. W. Segal, & R. Glasser (Eds.), *Thinking and learning skills: Current research and open questions* (Vol. 2, pp. 38–65). Hillsdale, NJ: Lawrence Erlbaum Associates.

Bernstein, N. (1967). *The coordination and regulation of movements.* London: Pergamon.

Berry, J. W. (1976). *Human ecology and cognitive style.* New York: Wiley.

Biggs, J., & Collis, K. (1982). *Evaluating the quality of learning: The SOLO taxonomy.* New York: Academic.

Borke, H. (1971). Interpersonal perception of young children: Egocentrism or empathy? *Developmental Psychology, 5,* 663–669.

Borke, H. (1973). The development of empathy in Chinese and American children between three and six years of age: A cross-cultural study. *Developmental Psychology, 9,* 102–108.

Bower, G. H., Black, J. B., & Turner, T. J. (1979). Scripts in memory for texts. *Cognitive Psychology, 11,* 177–220.

Bower, T. G. R. (1974). *Development in infancy*. San Francisco: W. H. Freeman.

Bowlby, J. (1969). *Attachment and loss* (Vol. 1). London: Hogarth.

Brainerd, C. J. (1978). The stage question in cognitive-developmental theory. *The Behavioral and Brain Sciences, 1,* 173–182.

Brekke, B., Johnson, L., Williams, J. D., & Morrison, E. (1976). Conservation of weight with the gifted. *The Journal of Genetic Psychology, 129,* 179–184.

Brentano, F. (1960). The distinction between mental and physical phenomena. In R. M. Chisholm (Ed.), *Realism and the background of phenomenology* (pp. 39–61). New York: The Free Press.

Bretherton, I., Fritz, J., Zahn-Waxler, C., & Ridgeway, D. (1986). Learning to talk about emotions: A functionalist perspective. *Child Development, 57,* 529–548.

Broughton, J. M. (1984). Not beyond formal operations but beyond Piaget. In M. L. Commons, F. A. Richards, & C. Armon (Eds.), *Beyond formal operations* (pp. 395–412). New York: Praeger.

Brown, A. L. (1973). Conservation of number and continuous quantity in normal, bright, and retarded children. *Child Development, 44,* 376–379.

Brown, A. L. (1974). The role of strategic behavior in retardate memory. In N. R. Ellis (Ed.), *International review of research in mental retardation*. New York: Academic Press.

Brown, A. L. (1975). The development of memory: Knowing, knowing about knowing, and knowing how to know. In H. W. Reese (Ed.), *Advances in child development and behavior* (Vol. 10, pp. 104–152). New York: Academic.

Brown, A. L., Bransford, J. D., Ferrara, R. A., & Campione, J. C. (1983). Learning, remembering, and understanding. In J. H. Flavell & E. M. Markman (Eds.), *Carmichael's manual of child psychology* (Vol. 1, pp. 77–166). New York: Wiley.

Brown, A. L. & Campione, J. C. (1984). Three faces of transfer: Implications for early competence, individual differences and instruction. In M. Lamb, A. L. Brown, & B. Rogoff (Eds.), *Advances in developmental psychology* (Vol. 3, pp. 143–192). Hillsdale, NJ: Lawrence Erlbaum Associates.

Brown, J. S., Collins, A., & Duguid, P. (1989). Situated cognition and the culture of learning. *Educational Researcher, 18,* 32–42.

Bruchkowsky, M. M. (1984). *The development of empathy in early childhood*. Unpublished master's thesis. University of Toronto, Ontario Institute for Studies in Education, Toronto.

Bruchkowsky, M. M. (1989). *Affect and cognition in the development of empathy in middle childhood*. Unpublished doctoral thesis. University of Toronto, Ontario Institute for Studies in Education, Toronto.

Bruner, J. S. (1964). The course of cognitive growth. *American Psychologist, 19,* 1–15.

Bruner, J. S. (1986). *Actual minds, possible worlds*. Cambridge, MA: Harvard University Press.

Bryant, B. K. (1982). An index of empathy for children and adolescents. *Child Development, 53,* 413–425.

Bryant, P., & Trabasso, T. (1971). Transitive inferences and memory in young children. *Nature, 232,* 456–458.

Campione, J. C., Brown, A. L., Ferrara, R. A., & Bryant, N. R. (1984). The zone of proximal development: Implications for individual differences and learning. In B. Rogoff & J. V. Wertsch (Eds.), *New directions for child development: No. 23. Children's learning in the "zone of proximal development"* (pp. 77–91). San Francisco: Jossey-Bass.

Capodilupo, A. M. (1985). *Sight reading of musical notation: A neo-Piagetian investigation.* Unpublished master's thesis. University of Toronto, Ontario Institute for Studies in Education, Toronto.

Capodilupo, A. M. (1990). *Cognitive development in music: A neo-structural investigation of normally-achieving and reading disabled children.* Unpublished doctoral dissertation, University of Toronto, Ontario Institute for Studies in Education, Toronto.

Carey, S. (1985). *Conceptual change in childhood.* Cambridge, MA: MIT Press.

Carey, S. (1988). Reorganization of knowledge in the course of acquisition. In S. Strauss (Ed.), *Ontogeny, phylogeny, and historical development* (pp. 1–27). New York: Ablex.

Cary, S. & Gelman, R. (1991). *The epigenesis of mind: Essays on biology and knowledge.* Hillsdale, NJ: Lawrence Erlbaum Associates.

Carraher, T. D. (1985). Mathematics in the streets and schools. *British Journal of Developmental Psychology, 3,* 21–29.

Carroll, N. B. (1976). Psychometric tests as cognitive tasks: A new "Structure of Intellect". In L. B. Resnick (Ed.), *The nature of intelligence.* Hillsdale, NJ: Lawrence Erlbaum Associates.

Carroll, J. B., Kohlberg, L., & DeVries, R. (1984). Psychometric and Piagetian intelligences: Toward resolution of controversy. *Intelligence, 8,* 67–91.

Carter, K. R. (1985). Cognitive development of intellectually gifted: A Piagetian perspective. *Roeper Review, 7,* 180–184.

Case, R. (1970). *Information processing, social class, and instruction: A developmental investigation.* Unpublished doctoral dissertation, University of Toronto, Ontario Institute for Studies in Education, Toronto.

Case, R. (1972a). Learning and development: A neo-Piagetian interpretation. *Human Development, 15,* 339–358.

Case, R. (1972b). Validation of a neo-Piagetian capacity construct. *Journal of Experimental Child Psychology, 14,* 287–302.

Case, R. (1974). Structures and strictures: Some functional limitations on the course of cognitive growth. *Cognitive Psychology, 6,* 544–573.

Case, R. (1975). Social class differences in intellectual development: A neo-Piagetian investigation. *Canadian Journal of Behavioral Science, 7,* 78–95.

Case, R. (1978). A developmentally based theory and technology of instruction. *Review of Educational Research, 48,* 439–463.

Case, R. (1978). Intellectual development from birth to adulthood: A neo-Piagetian investigation. In R. S. Siegler (Ed.), *Children's thinking: What develops?* (pp. 109–150). Hillsdale, NJ: Lawrence Erlbaum Associates.

Case, R. (1985). *Intellectual development: Birth to adulthood.* New York: Academic.

Case, R. (1987). The structure and process of intellectual development. *International Journal of Psychology, 22,* 571–607.

Case, R. (1988). Neo-Piagetian theory: Retrospect and prospect. In A. Demetriou (Ed.), *The neo-Piagetian theories of cognitive development: Towards an integration* (pp. 267–287). Amsterdam: North-Holland (Elsevier).

Case, R. (in press). The role of frontal lobe maturation in the regulation of human development. *Brain & Cognition.*

Case, R., & Globerson, T. (1974). Field independence and mental capacity. *Child Development, 45,* 772–778.

Case, R., & Griffin, S. (1989). Child cognitive development: The role of central conceptual structure in the development of scientific and social thought. In C. A. Hauert (Ed.), *Advances in psychology: Developmental psychology* (pp. 193–230). Amsterdam: North-Holland (Elsevier).

Case, R., & Hayward, S. (1984). *Understanding causality in the sensorimotor period: The infant balance beam test.* University of Toronto (OISE), Toronto.

Case, R., Hayward, S., Lewis, M., & Hurst, P. (1987). Toward a neo-Piagetian theory of cognitive and emotional development. *Developmental Review, 8,* 35.

Case, R., & Khanna, F. (1981). The missing links: Stages in children's progression from sensorimotor to logical thought. In K. W. Fischer (Ed.), *New directions for child development* (Vol. 12, pp. 21–32). San Francisco: Jossey-Bass.

Case, R., & Kurland, M. (1978). *Construction and validation of a new test of children's M-space.* Unpublished manuscript, University of Toronto, Ontario Institute for Studies in Education, Toronto.

Case, R., Kurland, M., & Goldberg, J. (1982). Operational efficiency and the growth of short term memory. *Journal of Experimental Child Psychology, 33,* 386–404.

Case, R., Marini, Z., McKeough, A., Dennis, S., & Goldberg, J. (1986). Horizontal structure in middle childhood: Cross-domain parallels in the course of cognitive growth. In I. Levin (Ed.), *Stage and structure: Reopening the debate* (pp. 1–39). Norwood, NJ: Ablex.

Case, R., & McKeough, A. (1990). Schooling and the development of central conceptual structures. *International Journal of Education, 13,* 835–855.

Case, R., McKeough, A., Okamoto, Y., Barany, D., Berg, R., Bleiker, C., Garrett, N. B., Henderson, B., & Krohn, C. (1990, December). *The role of central conceptual structures in the development of children's numerical, literary, and spatial thought.* Year 1 Report submitted to Spencer Foundation.

Case, R., Okamoto, Y., Henderson, B., & McKeough, A. (in press). The role of central conceptual structures in the development of children's quantitative and social thought. In W. Edelstein & R. Case (Eds.) *The new structuralism in cognitive development theory and research.* Basel: S. Karger.

Case, R., Okamoto, Y., Henderson, B., & McKeough, A. (in press). The role of central conceptual structures in the development of children's quantitative and social thought. In W. Edelstein & R. Case (Eds.) *Challenges and constraints of constructivism.* Basel: S. Garger.

Case, R., & Sandieson, R. (1987, April). *General developmental constraints on the acquisition of special procedures (and vice versa).* Paper presented at the meeting of the American Educational Research Association, Baltimore, MD.

Case, R., & Sandieson, R. (1988). A developmental approach to the identification and teaching of central conceptual structures in the middle grades. In J.

Hiebert & M. Behr (Eds.), *Research agenda in mathematics education: Number concepts and operations in the middle grades* (pp. 236–270). Hillsdale, NJ: Lawrence Erlbaum Associates.

Case, R., Sandieson, R., & Dennis, S. (1986). Two cognitive developmental approaches to the design of remedial instruction. *Cognitive Development, 1,* 293–333.

Case, R., & Threadgill-Sowder, J. (1990). The development of computational estimation: A neo-Piagetian analysis. *Cognition and Instruction, 7,* 79–104.

Cattell, R. B. (1971). *Abilities: Their structure, growth, and action.* Boston, MA: Houghton Mifflin.

Cecci, S. J. (1989). On domain specificity . . . more or less: General and specific constraints on cognitive development. *Merrill-Palmer Quarterly, 35,* 131–142.

Chandler, M. J. (1977). Social cognition: a selective review of current research. In W. F. Overton & J. M. Gallagher (Eds.), *Knowledge and development* (pp. 93–147). New York: Plenum.

Chandler, M. J., & Boyes, M. (1982). Social-cognitive development. In B. Wolman (Ed.), *Handbook of developmental psychology* (pp. 387–402). Englewood Cliffs, NJ: Prentice-Hall.

Chandler, M. J., & Greenspan, S. (1972). Ersatz egocentrism: A reply to H. Borke. *Developmental Psychology, 7,* 104–106.

Chi, M. T. H. (1976). Short-term memory limitations in children: Capacity or processing deficits? *Memory & Cognition, 23,* 266–281.

Chi, M. T. H. (1977). Age differences in the speed of processing: A critique. *Developmental Psychology, 13,* 543–544.

Chi, M. T. H. (1978). Knowledge structures and memory development. In R. Siegler (Ed.), *Children's thinking: What develops?* (pp. 73–96). Hillsdale, NJ: Lawrence Erlbaum Associates.

Chi, M. T. H. (1981). Knowledge development and memory performance. In M. Friedman, J. P. Das, & N. O'Connor (Eds.) *Intelligence and learning* (pp. 221–236). New York: Plenum.

Chi, M. T. H. (1983). Knowledge-derived categorization in young children. In D. R. Rogers & J. A. Sloboda (Eds.), *The acquisition of symbolic skills* (pp. 327–334). New York: Plenum.

Chi, M. T. H. (1985). Interactive roles of knowledge and strategies in the development of organized sorting and recall. In S. Chipman, J. Segal, & R. Glaser (Eds.), *Thinking and Learning skills: Current research and open questions, 2,* 457–485. Hillsdale, NJ: Lawrence Erlbaum Associates.

Chi, M. T. H. (1988). Children's lack of access and knowledge reorganization: An example from the concept of animism. In M. Perlmutter & F. E. Weinert (Eds.), *Memory development: Universal changes and individual differences* (pp. 169–194). Hillsdale, NJ: Lawrence Erlbaum.

Chi, M. T. H., & Koeske, R. (1983). Network representation of a child's dinosaur knowledge. *Developmental Psychology, 19,* 29–39.

Chi, M. T. H., & Rees, E. (1983). A learning framework for development. *Contributions to Human Development, 9,* 71–107.

Chomsky, C. (1970). The acquisition of syntax in children from 5 to 10. Cambridge: MIT Press.

Chomsky, N. (1957). *Syntactic structures.* The Hague: Mouton.

Clark, A. B. (1897). Some observations on children's drawings. *Educational Review, 13,* 76–82.

Clark, E. (1973). What's in a word? In T. E. Moore (Ed.), *Cognitive development and the acquisition of language* (pp. 65–110). New York: Academic.

Clement, D. C. (1978, November). *Children's understanding of school roles and school people.* Paper presented at the American Anthropological Association Meeting, Los Angeles, CA.

Cohen, R. L. (1982). Individual differences in short-term memory. *International Review of Research in Mental Retardation, 11,* 43–77.

Cohen, R. L., & Netley, C. (1981). Short-term memory deficits in reading disabled children, in the absence of the opportunity for rehearsal strategies. *Intelligence, 5,* 69–76.

Cole, M., & Bruner, J. S. (1971). Cultural differences and inferences about psychological process. *American Psychologist, 26,* 867–876.

Cole, M., Gay, J., Glick, J. A., & Sharp, D. (1971). *The cultural context of learning and thinking.* New York: Basic Books.

Cole, M., & Scribner, S. (1974). *Culture and thought.* New York: Wiley.

Cooke, E. (1885, January). Art teaching and child nature. *London Journal of Education* (pp. 462–465).

Cormier, S. M. (1987). The structural processes underlying transfer. In S. M. Cormier & J. D. Hagman (Eds.), *Transfer of learning: Contemporary research and application* (pp. 152–181). New York: Academic.

Damon, W. (1973). *The child's conception of justice as related to logical thought.* Unpublished doctoral dissertation. University of California, Berkeley.

Damon, W. (1977). *The social world of the child.* San Francisco: Jossey-Bass.

Daneman, M., & Carpenter, P. (1980). Individual differences in working memory and reading. *Journal of Verbal Learning and Verbal Behavior, 19,* 450–466.

Daneman, M., & Case, R. (1981). Syntactic form, semantic complexity, and short-term memory: Influences on children's acquisition of new linguistic structures. *Developmental Psychology, 17,* 367–378.

Dasen, P. (1972). Cross-cultural Piagetian research: A summary. *Journal of Cross-Cultural Psychology, 17,* 367–378.

Davies, J. B. (1978). *The psychology of music.* London: Hutchinson.

DeMersseman, S. L. (1976). *A developmental investigation of children's moral reasoning and behavior in hypothetical and practical situations.* Unpublished doctoral dissertation. University of California, Berkeley.

Demetriou, A., & Efklides, A. (1988). Experiential structuralism and neo-Piagetian theories: Toward an integrated model. In A. Demetriou (Ed.), *The neo-Piagetian theories of cognitive development: Toward an integration* (pp. 137–173). Amsterdam: North-Holland (Elsevier).

Demetriou, A., & Efklides, A. (1990). *Experiential structuralism: A framework for unifying cognitive developmental theories.* Unpublished manuscript.

Demetriou, A., Shayer, M., & Pervez, M. (1988). The structure and scaling of concrete operational thought: Three studies in four countries. *Genetic, Social, and General Psychology Monographs, 114,* 307–376.

Denckla, M., & Rudel, R. (1976). Rapid automatized naming (R.A.N.): Dyslexia differentiated from other learning disabilities. *Neuropsychologia, 14,* 471–479.

Dennis, S. (1981). *Developmentally based instruction: How low memory demand, contextual meaningfulness, and concrete objects influence the learning of proportionality.* Unpublished master's thesis, University of Toronto, Ontario Institute for Studies in Education, Toronto.

Dennis, S. (1987). *The development of children's drawing: A neo-structuralist approach.* Unpublished doctoral dissertation, University of Toronto, Ontario Institute for Studies in Education, Toronto.

DeRibaupierre, A., & Rieben, L. (1985). Étude du functionement operatoire: Quelques problèmes méthodologiques [A study of operational functioning: Several methodological problems]. *Bulletin de Psychologie, 38,* 841–852.

Diamond, A. (1991). Neuropsychological insights into the meaning of object concept development. In S. Carey & R. Gelman (Eds.) *The epigenesis of mind; Essays on biology and knowledge* (pp. 67–110). Hillsdale, NJ: Lawrence Erlbaum Associates.

van Dijk, T., & Kintsch, W. (1983). *Strategies of discourse comprehension.* New York: Academic.

Doctor, E. A., & Coltheart, M. (1980). Children's use of phonological encoding when reading for meaning. *Memory & Cognition, 8,* 195–209.

Dunn, L., & Dunn, L., (1981). Peabody Picture Vocabulary Test—Revised. Circle Pines, Minn: American Guidance Service.

Eisner, E. W. (1991). *The enlightened eye.* New York: Macmillan.

Ekman, P., & Friesen, W. (1975). *Unmasking the face.* Englewood Cliffs, NJ: Prentice-Hall.

Elkind, D. (1961). Children's discovery of the conservation of mass, weight, and volume. *Journal of Genetic Psychology, 98,* 219–227.

Elkind, D. (1976). *Child development and education: A Piagetian perspective.* New York: Oxford University Press.

Ellis, N. C. (1981). Visual and name coding in dyslexic children. *Psychological Research, 43,* 201–218.

Ellis, N. C., & Miles, T. R. (1978). Visual information processing in dyslexic children. In M. M. Gruneberg, P. E. Morris, & R. N. Sykes (Eds.), *Practical aspects of memory* (pp. 561–569). London: Academic.

Eng, H. (1931). *The psychology of children's drawings.* London: Routledge.

Feigl, H. (1958). *The "mental" and the "physical."* Minneapolis: University of Minnesota Press.

Feldman, D. H. (1986). *Nature's gambit: Child prodigies and the development of human potential.* New York: Basic Books.

Ferrara, R. A., Brown, A. L. & Campione, J. C. (1986). Children's learning and transfer rules of inductive reasoning: Studies in proximal development. *Child Development, 57,* 1087–1099.

Feschbach, N. D., & Roe, K. (1968). Empathy in six- and seven-year-olds. *Child Development, 39,* 133–145.

Fiati, T. A. (1987). *Environmental and educational influences on cognitive development in Ghana: A neo-Piagetian investigation.* Unpublished doctoral dissertation, Ontario Institute for Studies in Education, University of Toronto, Toronto.

Field, D. (1987). A review of preschool conservation training: An analysis of analyses. *Developmental Review, 7,* 210–251.

Fischer, K. W. (1980). A theory of cognitive development: The control and construction of hierarchies of skills. *Psychological Review, 87,* 477–531.

Fischer, K. W., & Canfield, R. L. (1986). The ambiguity of stage and structure in behavior: Person and environment in the development of psychological structure. In I. Levin (Ed.), *Stage and structure: Reopening the debate* (pp. 246–267). New York: Plenum.

Fischer, K. W., & Ferrar, M. J. (1988). Generalizations about generalization: How a theory of skill development explains both generality and specificity. In A. Demetriou (Ed.), *The neo-Piagetian theories of cognitive development: Toward an integration* (pp. 103–137). Amsterdam: North-Holland (Elsevier).

Fischer, K. W., Hand, H. H., Watson, M. W., VanParys, M. M., & Tucker, J. L. (1984). Putting the child into socialization: The development of social categories in preschool children. In L. Katz (Ed.), *Current topics in early childhood education* (Vol. 5, pp. 27–72). Norwood, NJ: Ablex.

Fischer, K. W., & Pipp, S. L. (1984). Processes of cognitive development: Optimal level and skill acquisition. In R. J. Sternberg (Ed.), *Mechanisms of cognitive development* (pp. 45–80). New York: W. H. Freeman.

Fischer, K. W., & Silvern, L. (1985). Stages and individual differences in cognitive development. *Annual Review of Psychology, 36,* 613–648.

Fitts, P. M. (1954). The information capacity of the human motor system in controlling the amplitude of movement. *Journal of Experimental Psychology, 47,* 381–391.

Fitzpatrick, C. J. (1985). Children's development out of event-bound conceptions of their emotions. In I. Fast (Ed.), *Event theory: An integration of Piaget and Freud* (pp. 79–110). Hillsdale, NJ: Lawrence Erlbaum Associates.

Flavell, J. H. (1963). *The developmental psychology of Jean Piaget.* Princeton, NJ: Van Nostrand.

Flavell, J. H. (1968). *The development of role-taking and communication skills in children.* New York: Wiley.

Flavell, J. H. (1971). Stage-related properties of cognitive development. *Cognitive Psychology, 2,* 421–453.

Flavell, J. H. (1974). The development of inferences about others. In W. T. Mischel (Ed.), *Understanding other persons* (pp. 66–117). Oxford: Basil, Blackwell.

Flavell, J. H. (1977). *Cognitive development.* Englewood Cliffs, NJ: Prentice-Hall.

Flavell, J. H. (1982). On cognitive development. *Child Development, 53,* 1–11.

Flavell, J. H., Bolkin, P. T., Fry, L. C., Wright, J. W., & Jarvis, P. E. (1968). *The development of role-taking and communication skills in children.* New York: Wiley.

Flavell, J. H., Shipstead, S. G., & Croft, K. (1978). Young children's knowledge about visual perception: Hiding objects from others. *Child Development, 49,* 1208–1211.

Flavell, J. H., & Wohlwill, J. F. (1969). Formal and functional aspects of cognitive development. In D. Elkind & J. H. Flavell (Eds.), *Studies in cognitive development: Essays in honor of Jean Piaget.* New York: Oxford University Press.

Fletcher, J. M. (1985). Memory for verbal and nonverbal stimuli in learning disability subgroups: Analysis by selective reminding. *Journal of Experimental Child Psychology, 40,* 244–255.

Fodor, J. (1982). *The modularity of mind.* Cambridge, MA: MIT Press.

Freeman, N. H. (1972). Process and product in children's drawing. *Perception, 1,* 21–33.

Furman, I. (1981). *The development of problem solving strategies: A neo-Piagetian analysis of children's performance on a balance task.* Unpublished doctoral dissertation. University of California, Berkeley.

Furth, H. G. (1980). *The world of grown-ups: Children's conception of society.* New York: Elsevier.

Gagné, R. M. (1968). Contributions of learning to human development. *Psychological Review, 75,* 177–191.

Gardner, H. (1980). *Artful scribbles.* New York: Basic Books.

Gardner, H. (1983). *Frames of mind: The theory of multiple intelligences.* New York: Basic Books.

Gardner, H. (in press). *The unschooled mind.* New York: Basic Books.

Gelman, R. (1969). Conservation acquisition: A problem of learning to attend to relevant attributes. *Journal of Experimental Child Psychology, 7,* 167–187.

Gelman, R. (1972). The nature and development of early number concepts. In H. W. Reese (Ed.), *Advances in child development and behavior* (Vol. 7, pp. 115–168). New York: Academic.

Gelman, R. (1978a). Cognitive development. *Annual Review of Psychology, 29,* 297–332.

Gelman, R. (1978b). Counting in the preschooler: What does and what does not develop? In R. Siegler (Ed.), *Children's thinking: What develops?* (pp. 213–242). Hillsdale, NJ: Lawrence Erlbaum Associates.

Gelman, R., & Gallistel, C. R. (1978). *The young child's understanding of number.* New York: Harvard University Press.

Gentner, D. (1975). Evidence for the psychological reality of semantic components: The verbs of possession. In D. A. Norman, D. E. Rumelhart, & The LNR Research Group (Eds.), *Explorations in cognition* (pp. 211–247). San Francisco: Freeman.

Gesell, A., Halverson, H., Thompson, H., Ilg, F., Castner, B., Ames, L., & Amatruda, C. (1940). *The first five years of life.* New York: Harper & Brothers.

Ginsburg, H., & Opper, S. (1969). *Piaget's theory of intellectual development.* Englewood Cliffs, NJ: Prentice-Hall.

Glaser, R. (1976). Cognitive psychology and instructional design. In D. Klahr (Ed.), *Cognition and instruction* (pp. 303–316). Hillsdale, NJ: Lawrence Erlbaum Associates.

Glick, M. L., & Holyoak, K. J. (1987). The cognitive basis of knowledge transfer. In S. M. Cormier & J. D. Hagman (Eds.), *Transfer of learning: Contemporary research and application* (pp. 9–46). New York: Academic.

Globerson, T. (1985). Field dependence/independence and mental capacity: A developmental approach. *Developmental Review, 5,* 261–273.

Glucksberg, S., Krauss, R. M., & Higgins, R. (1975). The development of referential communication skills. In F. D. Horowitz (Ed.), *Review of child development research* (Vol. 4, pp. 305–345). Chicago, IL: University of Chicago Press.

Gnepp, J. (1985, April). *Children's use of person-specific information in predicting and explaining emotions.* Paper presented at the meeting of the Society for Research in Child Development, Toronto, Ontario, Canada.

Goldberg-Reitman, J. (1984). *Young girls' understanding of their mother's role: A developmental investigation.* Unpublished doctoral dissertation, University of Toronto, Ontario Institute for Studies in Education, Toronto.

Goldman-Rakic, J. (1989, August). *Cellular and circuit basis of working memory in prefrontal cortex of nonhuman primates.* Paper presented for Netherlands Institute for Brain Research, Intermission Summer School, Amsterdam, The Netherlands.

Goodenough, F. L. (1926). *Measurement of intelligence by drawings.* Chicago: World Book Company.

Goodman, N. (1976). *Languages of Art: An approach to a theory of symbols.* Indianapolis: Hackett Publishing.

Goodnow, J. J., & Bethon, G. (1966). Piaget's tasks: The effects of schooling and intelligence. *Child Development, 37,* 573–582.

Gould, M. E. (1984, May). *Children's recognition and resolution of ambiguity in making affective judgments.* Paper presented at the meeting of the Midwestern Psychological Association, Chicago, IL.

Graves, D. H. (1983). *Writing: Teachers and children at work.* London: Heinmann Educational Books.

Griffin, S. A. (1985). *Intentional learning: A construct to guide research efforts towards a fuller understanding of developmental and individual differences in children's learning behavior.* Unpublished manuscript, The Ontario Institute for Studies in Education, Toronto.

Griffin, S. A. (1988, December). *Children's understanding of pride and embarrassment.* Paper presented at the conference on Shame and Related Self-Conscious Emotions, sponsored by the Sloan and MacArthur Foundations, Asilomar, CA.

Griffin, S. A., Case, R., & Capodilupo, S. (in press). Teaching for understanding: The importance of central conceptual structures in the elementary school mathematics curriculum. In A. Strauss (Ed.), *Educational environments.* Norwood, NJ: Ablex.

Guilford, J. P. (1967). *The nature of human intelligence.* New York: McGraw-Hill.

Gustafsson, J. E. (1984). A unifying model for the structure of intellectual abilities. *Intelligence, 8,* 179–203.

Halford, G. S. (1980). Toward a redefinition of cognitive developmental stages. In J. Kirby & J. B. Biggs (Eds.), *Cognition, development, and instruction* (pp. 103–137). New York: Academic.

Halford, G. S. (1982). *The development of thought.* Hillsdale, NJ: Lawrence Erlbaum Associates.

Halford, G. S. (1988). A structure mapping approach to cognitive development. In A. Demetriou (Ed.), *The neo-Piagetian theories of cognitive development: Towards an integration.* Amsterdam: North-Holland (Elsevier).

Halford, G. S. (1989). Reflections on 25 years of Piagetian cognitive developmental psychology, 1963–1988. *Human Development, 32,* 325–357.

Halverson, H. M. (1931). An experimental study of prehension in infants by means of systematic cinema records. *Genetic Psychology Monographs, 10,* 107–285.

Hammill, D. D., & Larsen, S. C. (1983). *The test of written language.* Austin, TX: Pro-ed.

Harris, D. B. (1963). *Children's drawings as measures of intellectual maturity.* New York: Harcourt, Brace & World.

Harter, S. (1982). A cognitive-developmental approach to children's use of affect and trait labels. In F. Serafica (Ed.), *Social cognition and social relations in context* (pp. 27–61). New York: Guilford.

Harter, S. (1983). Children's understanding of multiple emotions: A cognitive developmental approach. In W. F. Overton (Ed.), *The relationship between social and cognitive development* (pp. 147–194). Hillsdale, NJ: Lawrence Erlbaum Associates.

Higgins, E. T. (1989). Continuities and discontinuities in self-regulatory processes: A developmental theory relating self and affect. *Journal of Personality, 57,* 407–444.

Hildebrandt, C. (1987). Structural developmental research in music: Conservation and representation. In J. C. Peery, I. W. Peery, & T. W. Draper (Eds.), *Music and child development* (pp. 80–95). New York: Springer-Verlag.

Hoffman, M. L. (1982). The measurement of empathy. In C. E. Izard (Ed.), *Measuring emotions in infants and children* (pp. 67–110). Cambridge: Cambridge University Press.

Hoppe-Graffe, S. (1989, July). *The process of development as construction: Evidence from pretend play.* Paper presented at the biennial meeting of the International Society for the Study of Behavioral Developments. Jyväskylä, Finland.

Horn, J. L. (1976). Human Abilities: A review of research and theory in the early 1970's. *Annual Review of Psychology, 27,* 437–485.

Hughes, R., Jr., Tingle, B. A., & Swain, D. B. (1981). Development of empathic understanding in children. *Child Development, 52,* 122–128.

Hulme, C., Thomson, N., Muir, C., & Lawrence, A. (1984). Speech rate and the development of short-term memory span. *Journal of Experimental Child Psychology, 38,* 241–251.

Inhelder, B., & Piaget, J. (1958). *The growth of logical thinking from childhood to adolescence.* New York: Basic Books.

Inhelder, B., Sinclair, H., & Bovet, M. (1974). *Learning and the development of cognition.* Cambridge, MA: Harvard University Press.

Izard, C. E., & Dougherty, L. M. (1980). *A system for identifying affect expressions by holistic judgments (Affex).* Newark: Instructional Resources Center, University of Delaware.

Izard, C. E. (1984). *Approaches to a developmental research on emotion-cognition relationships.* Unpublished manuscript, University of Delaware, Newark.

Jackson, N. E., & Butterfield, E. C. (1986). A conception of giftedness designed to promote research. In R. J. Sternberg & J. E. Davidson (Eds.), *Conceptions of giftedness* (pp. 151–181). Cambridge, England: Cambridge University Press.

Jacobson, M. G., & Robinson, A. (1987, April). *A comparison of the formal reasoning abilities of intellectually gifted and nongifted children.* Paper presented at the annual meeting of the American Educational Research Association, Washington, DC.

Jastak, K. F., & Jastak, S. R. (1978). *Wide Range Achievement Test.* Wilmington, DE: Jastak Associates.

Johnson, C., & Wellman, H. (1982). Children's developing conceptions of the mind and brain. *Child Development, 53,* 222–234.

Johnson, J., Fabian, V., & Pascual-Leone, J. (1989). Quantitative hardware stages that constrain language development. *Human Development, 32,* 245–271.

Jorm, A. (1983). Specific reading retardation and working memory: A review. *British Journal of Psychology, 74,* 311–342.

Kaiser, H. F. & Caffry, J. (1965). Alpha factor analysis. *Psychometrika, 50,* 1–14.

Karp, S. A., & Konstadt, N. I. (1963). *Children's Embedded Figures Test.* New York: Cognitive Tests.

Katz, R. B., Shankweiler, D., & Liberman, I. Y. (1981). Memory for item order and phonetic recoding in the beginning reader. *Journal of Experimental Child Psychology, 32,* 474–484.

Keating, D. P. (1975). Precocious cognitive development at the level of formal operations. *Child Development, 46,* 276–280.

Keating, D. P. (1980). Thinking processes in adolescence. In J. Adelson (Ed.), *Handbook of adolescent psychology* (pp. 211–246). New York: Wiley.

Keele, S. W. (1968). Movement control in skilled motor performance. *Psychological Bulletin, 70,* 387–403.

Keele, S. W., & Posner, M. I. (1968). Processing of visual feedback in rapid movements. *Journal of Experimental Psychology, 77,* 155–158.

Keele, S. W., & Summers, J. J. (1976). The structure of motor programs. In G. E. Stelmach (Ed.), *Motor control: Issues and trends* (pp. 109–121). New York: Academic.

Keil, F. C. (1981). Constraints on knowledge and cognitive development. *Psychological Review, 88,* 197–227.

Keil, F. C. (1986). On the structure-dependent nature of stages of cognitive development. In I. Levin (Ed.), *Stage and structure: Reopening the debate* (pp. 144–163). Norwood, NJ: Ablex.

Kellogg, R. (1967). *The psychology of children's art.* San Diego: CRM (Random House).

Kernberg, O. F. (1976). *Object relations theory and clinical psychoanalysis.* New York: Aranson.

Khanna, F. B. (1985). *Vertical and horizontal structure in the cognitive development of preschool children.* Unpublished doctoral dissertation, University of Toronto, Ontario Institute for Studies in Education, Toronto.

Klahr, D. (1989). Information-processing approaches. *Annals of Child Development, 6,* 133–185.

Klahr, D., & Wallace, J. G. (1976). *Cognitive development: An information-processing view.* Hillsdale, NJ: Lawrence Erlbaum Associates.

Kohlberg, L. (1958). *The development of modes of moral reasoning and choice in years ten to sixteen.* Unpublished doctoral dissertation, University of Chicago, Chicago.

Kohlberg, L. (1969). Stage and sequence. The cognitive-developmental approach to socialization. In D. Goslin (Ed.), *Handbook of socialization theory and research* (pp. 347–480). New York: Rand McNally.

Kohlberg, L. (1976). Moral stages and moralization. In T. Lickona (Ed.), *Moral development and behavior* (pp. 31–53). New York: Holt, Rinehart & Winston.

Kopp, C., & Brownell, C. (Eds.) (1991). The development of the self. Special issue of *Developmental Review, 12.*

Kuhn, D. (1983). On the dual executive and its significance in the development of developmental psychology. In D. Kuhn & J. A. Meachum (Eds.), *On the development of developmental psychology* (pp. 81–110). New York: Karger.

Kurland, D. M. (1981). *The effect of massive practice on children's operational efficiency and short term memory.* Unpublished doctoral dissertation, University of Toronto, Ontario Institute for Studies in Education, Toronto.

Lakatos, I. (1962). Falsification and the methathodology of scientific research programmes. In I. Lakatos & A. Musgrave (Eds.), *Criticism and the growth of knowledge* (pp. 91–196). New York: Cambridge University Press.

Langer, J. (1988). A note on the comparative psychology of mental development. In S. Strauss (Ed.), *Ontogeny, phylogeny, and historical development* (pp. 68–85). Norwood, NJ: Ablex.

Larkin, J. H. (1983). The role of problem representation in physics. In D. Gentner & A. L. Stevens (Eds.), *Mental models* (pp. 75–98). Hillsdale, NJ: Lawrence Erlbaum Associates.

Laurendeau, M., & Pinard, A. (1970). *Development of the concept of space in the child.* New York: International University Press.

Lautrey, J., DeRibaupierre, A., & Rieben, L. (1987). Operational development and individual differences. In E. DeCorte, H. Lodewigrs, R. Parmentier & P. Span (Eds.), *Learning and Instruction* (pp. 19–30). Oxford, England: Lewen University Press & Pergamon Press.

Lave, J. (1988). *Cognition in practice: Mind, mathematics, and culture in everyday life.* Cambridge, MA: Cambridge University Press.

Levin, I. (1986). *Stage and structure: Reopening the debate.* Norwood, NJ: Ablex.

Lewis, M., & Feiring, C. (1979). *The child's social network: social object, social functions, and their relationship.* In M. Lewis & L. Rosenblum (eds.) *The child and its family: the genesis of behavior* (Vol 2). New York: Plenum.

Lewis, M., & Starr, M. (1979). Developmental continuity. In J. Osofsky (Ed.), *Handbook of infant development* (pp. 653–670). New York: Wiley.

Liberman, I. Y., Mann, V. A., Shankweiler, D., & Werfelman, M. (1982). Children's memory of recurring linguistic and nonlinguistic material in relation to reading ability. *Cortex, 18,* 367–375.

Liu, P. (1981). *An investigation of the relationship between qualitative and quantitative advances in the cognitive development of preschool children.* Unpublished doctoral dissertation, University of Toronto, Ontario Institute for Studies in Education, Toronto.

Loban, W. D. (1963). *The language of elementary school children.* Champaign, IL: National Council of Teachers of English.

Loban, W. D. (1966). *Language ability: Grades seven, eight, and nine* (Cooperative Research Monograph No. 18). Washington, DC: U.S. Department of Health, Education, and Welfare, Office of Education.

Lorsbach, T. C., & Gray, J. W. (1986). Item identification speed and memory span performance in learning disabled children. *Contemporary educational psychology, 11,* 68–78.

Lovell, K., & Shields, J. B. (1967). Some aspects of a study of the gifted child. *British Journal of Educational Psychology, 37,* 201–209.

Lowenfeld, V., & Brittain, W. (1970). *Creative and mental growth*. New York: Macmillian.

Lunzer, E. A. (1965). Problems of formal reasoning in test situations. *Monographs of the Society for Research in Child Development, 30* (2, Whole No. 100), 19–46.

Luquet, G. H. (1913). *Les dessins d' un enfant* [A child's drawings]. Paris: Alcan.

Luquet, G. H. (1927). *Le dessin enfantin* [Children's drawing]. Paris: Alcan.

Luria, A. R. (1973). *The working brain*. London: Penguin Press.

Mandler, J. M. (1982). Recent research on story grammars. In J. F. Leny & W. Kintsch (Eds.), *Language and comprehensions* (pp. 207–218). Amsterdam: North-Holland.

Mann, V. A. (1986). Why some children encounter reading problems: The contributions of difficulties with language processing and phonological sophistication to early reading disability. In J. K. Torgesen & B. Y. L. Wong (Eds.), *Psychological and educational perspectives on learning disabilities* (pp. 133–159). New York: Academic.

Mann, V. A., Liberman, I. Y., & Shankweiler, D. (1980). Children's memory for sentences and word strings in relation to reading ability. *Memory & Cognition, 8*, 329–335.

Marini, Z. A. (1984). *The development of social and physical cognition in childhood and adolescence*. Unpublished doctoral dissertation, University of Toronto, Ontario Institute for Studies in Education, Toronto.

Marini, Z. A., & Case, R. (1989). Parallels in the development of preschoolers' knowledge about their physical and social worlds. *Merrill-Palmer Quarterly, 35*, 63–88.

McCaskill, C. A., & Wellman, B. L. (1938). A study of common motor achievements at the preschool ages. *Child Development, 9*, 141–150.

McClelland, J. L. (1989). *Parallel distributed processing: Implications for cognition and development* (Tech. Rep.). Pittsburgh, PA: Dept. of Psychology, Carnegie Mellon University.

McGraw, M. B. (1940). Neuromuscular development of the human infant as exemplified in the achievement of erect locomotion. *Journal of Pediatrics, 17*, 747–771.

McGraw, M. B. (1941). Neural maturation as exemplified in the reaching-prehensile behavior of the human infant. *Journal of Psychology, 11*, 127–141.

McKeough, A. (1982). *The development of complexity in children's narrative*. Unpublished master's thesis, University of Toronto, Ontario Institute for Studies in Education, Toronto.

McKeough, A. (1986). *Developmental stages in children's narrative*. Unpublished doctoral dissertation, University of Toronto, Ontario Institute for Studies in Education, Toronto.

McLaughlin, G. H. (1963). Psycho–logic: A possible alternative to Piaget's formulation. *British Journal of Educational Psychology, 33*, 61–67.

Meltzoff, A. N. (1981). Imitation, intermodal coordination and representation in early infancy. In G. Butterworth (Ed.), *Infancy and epistemology* (pp. 85–114). Brighton, England: Harvester.

Mitchell, B. F. (1977). *Children's motor responses to precision KR: A neo-Piagetian interpretation*. Unpublished doctoral dissertation, The Florida State University, College of Education, Tallahassee.

Monsell, S. (1982). Components of working memory underlying verbal skills: A "distributed capacities" view. In H. Bouma & D. G. Bouwhuis (Eds.), *Attention and performance X: Control of language processes* (pp. 327–350). Hillsdale, NJ: Lawrence Erlbaum Associates.

Morra, S., Moizo, C., & Scopesi, A. M. (1988). Working memory (or the M-operator) and the planning of children's drawing. *Journal of Experimental Child Psychology, 46*, 41–73.

Mounoud, P. (1982). Revolutionary periods in early development. In T. G. Bever (Ed.), *Regressions in mental development: Basic phenomena and theories* (pp. 119–131). Hillsdale, NJ: Lawrence Erlbaum Associates.

Mounoud, P. (1986). Similarities between developmental sequences at different age periods. In I. Levin (Ed.), *Stage and structure: Reopening the debate* (pp. 40–58). Norwood, NJ: Ablex.

Mounoud, P., & Bower, T. G. R. (1974). Conservation of weight in infants. *Cognition, 3*, 29–40.

Nelson, K. (1978). How children represent knowledge of their world in and out of language: A preliminary report. In R. S. Siegler (Ed.), *Children's thinking: What develops?* (pp. 255–274). Hillsdale, NJ: Lawrence Erlbaum Associates.

Nelson, K. (1981). Social cognition in a script framework. In J. H. Flavell & L. Ross (Eds.), *Social cognitive development: Frontiers and possible futures* (pp. 97–118). Cambridge, England: Cambridge University Press.

Nelson, K., & Gruendel, J. (1981). Generalized event representations: Basic building blocks of cognitive development. In M. E. Lamb & A. L. Brown (Eds.), *Advances in developmental psychology.* (Vol 1). Hillsdale, NJ: Lawrence Erlbaum Associates.

Newell, A., Shaw, J. C., & Simon, H. A. (1958). Elements of a theory of human problem solving. *Psychological Review, 65*, 151–166.

Newell, A., & Simon, H. (1972). *Human problem solving.* Englewood Cliffs, NJ: Prentice-Hall.

Noelting, G. (1980a). The development of proportional reasoning and the ratio concept, I. *Educational Studies in Mathematics, 11*, 217–253.

Noelting, G. (1980b). The development of proportional reasoning and the ratio concept, II. *Educational Studies in Mathematics, 11*, 331–363.

Noelting, G. (1982). Le développement cognitif et le mécanisms de l'équilibration [Cognitive development and the mechanisms of equilibration]. Chicoutimi, Quebec: Gaëtan Morin.

Olson, D. R. (1970). *Cognitive development: The child's acquisition of diagonality.* New York: Academic.

Olson, D. R. (1980). *The social foundations of language and thought.* New York: Norton.

Olson, D. R. (1988). On the origin of beliefs and other intentional states in children. In J. Astington, M. Harris, & D. Olson (Eds.), *Developing theories of mind.* (pp. 414–427) Cambridge, England: Cambridge University Press.

Olson, D. R., & Bialystok, E. (1983). *Spatial cognition.* Hillsdale, NJ: Lawrence Erlbaum.

Overton, W. F. (1983). World views and their influence on psychological theory and research. In H. W. Reese (Ed.), *Advances in child development and behavior* (Vol. 18, pp. 191–226). New York: Academic.

Pascual-Leone, J. (1969). *Cognitive development and cognitive style.* Unpublished doctoral dissertation, University of Geneva, Geneva.

Pascual-Leone, J. (1970). A mathematical model for the transition rule in Piaget's development stages. *Acta Psychologica, 32,* 301–345.

Pascual-Leone, J. (1976). A view of cognition from a formalist's perspective. In K. F. Riegel & J. Meacham, (Eds.), *The developing individual in a changing world* (pp. 89–100). The Hague: Mouton.

Pascual-Leone, J. (1988). Organismic processes for neo-Piagetian theories: A dialectical causal account of cognitive development. In A. Demetriou (Ed.), *The neo-Piagetian theories of cognitive development: Toward an integration* (pp. 25–65). Amsterdam: North-Holland (Elsevier).

Pascual-Leone, J., & Goodman, D. (1979). Intelligence and experience: A neo-Piagetian approach. *Instructional Science, 8,* 301–367.

Pascual-Leone, J., & Smith, J. (1969). The encoding and decoding of symbols by children: A new experimental paradigm and a neo-Piagetian model. *Journal of Experimental Child Psychology, 8,* 328–355.

Perfetti, C. A., & Lesgold, A. M. (1977). Discourse comprehension and sources of individual differences. In M. A. Just & P. A. Carpenter (Eds.), *Cognitive processes in comprehension* (pp. 141–183). New York: Wiley.

Perkins, D. N., & Salomon, G. (1987). Transfer and teaching thinking. In D. N. Perkins, J. Lochhead, & J. C. Bishop (Eds.), *Thinking: The second international conference* (pp. 285–303). Hillsdale, NJ: Lawrence Erlbaum Associates.

Peterson, C., & McCabe, A. (1983). *Developmental psycholinguistics: Three ways of looking at child's narrative.* New York: Plenum.

Piaget, J. (1950). *The psychology of intelligence.* London: Routledge & Kegan Paul.

Piaget, J. (1970). Piaget's theory. In P. H. Mussen (Ed). *Carmichael's Handbook of Child Development* (pp. 703–732). New York: Wiley.

Piaget, J. (1972). Intellectual evolution from adolescence to adulthood. *Human Development, 15,* 1–12.

Piaget, J. Development and learning. In R. E. Ripple & V. N. Rockcastle (Eds.), *Piaget rediscovered.* Ithaca, NY: Cornell University Press.

Piaget, J., & Inhelder, R. (1956). *The child's conception of space.* London: Routledge & Kegan Paul.

Piaget, J., & Inhelder, B. (1974). *The child's conception of quantities.* London: Routledge & Kegan Paul.

Pinard, A. (1975). Note sur la compatibilité des notions de stade et de décalage dans la theorie de Piaget [Note on the compatability of notions of stage and décalage in Piaget's theory]. *Canadian Psychological Review, 16,* 255–261.

Pinard, A., & Laurendeau, M. (1969). Stage in Piaget's cognitive developmental theory: Exegesis of a concept. In D. Elkind & J. H. Flavell (Eds.), *Studies in cognitive development* (pp. 121–170). London: Oxford University Press.

Porath, M. (1988). *The intellectual development of gifted children: A neo-Piagetian analysis.* Unpublished doctoral dissertation, University of Toronto, Toronto.

Pressley, M. (1982). Elaboration and memory development. *Child Development, 53,* 296–309.

Propp, V. (1968). *The morphology of the folktale.* Austin, TX: University of Texas Press. (Original work published 1922)

Raven, J. C. (1962). *Colored progressive matrices.* New York: Psychological Corp.

Raven, J. C., Court, J. H., & Raven, J. (1983). *Standard progressive matrices manual.* London: H. K. Lewis.

Reid, D. T. (1987). *Motor development in children: A test of the vertical structure hypothesis.* Unpublished doctoral dissertation, University of Toronto, Ontario Institute for Studies in Education, Toronto.

Reiss, J. A., & Cunningham, J. G. (1988, March). *The development of affective state understanding in two- and three-year-olds.* Paper presented at the Conference on Human Development, Charleston, SC.

Resnick, L. B. (1976). Task analysis in instructional design: Some cases from mathematics. In D. Klahr (Ed.), *Cognition and instruction* (pp. 51–80). Hillsdale, NJ: Lawrence Erlbaum Associates.

Rich, S. (1979). *The development of information processing speed and span in normal and retarded children.* Unpublished master's thesis, University of Toronto, Ontario Institute for Studies in Education, Toronto.

Rich, S. (1982). *Cognitive restructuring in children: The prediction of intelligence and learning.* Unpublished doctoral dissertation, Ontario Institute for Studies in Education, University of Toronto.

Rogoff, B. (1989). The joint socialization of development by young children and adults. In A. Gellatly, D. Rogers & J. Sloboda (Eds.), *Cognition and social worlds* (pp. 57–82). Oxford: Clarendon.

Rosenblatt, E., Gardner, H., & Winner, E. (1985, April). *Story understanding beyond grammar: Sensitivity to compositional principles specific to stories.* Paper presented at the biennial meeting of the Society for Research in Child Development, Toronto, Canada.

Rourke, B. P., & Strang, J. D. (1978a). Neuropsychological significance of variations in academic performance: Motor, psychomotor, and tactile perception abilities. *Journal of Pediatric Psychology, 3,* 212–225.

Rourke, B. P., & Strang, J. D. (1978b). Neuropsychological significance of variations in patterns of academic performance: Verbal and visual spatial abilities. *Journal of Abnormal Child Psychology, 6,* 121–133.

Rukavina, I. (1985). *The development of cognitive and affective aspects of empathy.* Unpublished master's thesis, University of Toronto, Ontario Institute for Studies in Education, Toronto.

Rumelhart, D. E. (1975). Notes on a schema. In D. G. Bobrow & A. Collins (Eds.), *Representation and understanding: Studies in cognitive science* (pp. 211–236). New York: Academic.

Rumelhart, D. E., & McClelland, J. L. (1987). Learning the past tenses of English verbs: Implicit rules or parallel distributed processing? In B. MacWhinney (Ed.), *Mechanisms of language acquisition* (pp. 195–248). Hillsdale, NJ: Lawrence Erlbaum Associates.

Rushton, J. P., Brainerd, C. J., & Pressley, M. (1983). Behavioral development and construct validity: The principle of aggregation. *Psychological Bulletin, 94,* 18–38.

Salame, P., & Baddeley, A. (1982). Disruption of short-term memory by unattended speech: Implications for the structure of working memory. *Journal of Verbal Learning and Verbal Behavior, 21,* 150–164.

Sattler, J. M. (1982). *Assessment of children's intelligence and special abilities.* Boston: Allyn & Bacon.

Saxe, G. B., Guberman, S. R., & Gearhart, M. (1987). Social processes in early number development. *Monographs of the Society for Research in Child Development, 52* (Serial No. 216).

Scardamalia, M. (1974). Some performance aspects of two formal operational tasks. In G. I. Lubin, J. F. Magery, & M. K. Poulsen (Eds.), *Piagetian theory in the helping professions: Proceedings of the Fourth Interdisciplinary Seminar* (pp. 19–27). Los Angeles: University of Southern California.

Schank, R. C., & Abelson, R. P. (1977). *Scripts, plans, goals, and understanding: An inquiry into human knowledge structure.* Hillsdale, NJ: Lawrence Erlbaum Associates.

Schmidt, R. A. (1975). A schema theory of discrete motor skill learning. *Psychological Review, 82,* 225–260.

Scott, A. D. (1983). Evaluation of motor control. In C. A. Trombly (Ed.), *Occupational therapy for physical dysfunction* (2d ed., pp. 46–58). Baltimore, MD: Williams & Wilkins.

Searle, J. R. (1983). *Intentionality.* Cambridge, England: Cambridge University Press.

Segalowitz, S. J. (1988). Brain lateralization in children: Developmental implications. In D. L. Molfese & S. J. Segalowitz (Eds.), *Brain Lateralization in Children.* New York: Guilford.

Segalowitz, S. J., Wagner, W. J., & Menna, R. (in press). Lateral versus frontal ERP predictors of reading skills. *Brain and cognition.*

Selman, R. L. (1980). *The growth of interpersonal understanding: Developmental and clinical analyses.* New York: Academic.

Selman, R. L., & Byrne, D. F. (1974). A structural developmental analysis of levels of role-taking in middle childhood. *Child Development, 45,* 803–806.

Serafine, M. L. (1980). *Detecting musical thought: A set of tasks for children.* Unpublished manuscript, Yale University, New Haven, CT.

Serafine, M. L. (1981). Musical timbre imagery in young children. *Journal of Genetic Psychology, 139,* 97–108.

Serafine, M. L. (1983). Cognition in music. *Cognition, 14,* 119–183.

Shallice, T., & Warrington, E. K. (1970). Independent functioning of verbal memory stores: A neuropsychological study. *Quarterly Journal of Experimental Psychology, 22,* 261–273.

Shankweiler, D., & Crain, S. (1986). Language mechanisms and reading disorder: A modular approach. *Cognition, 24,* 139–168.

Shatz, M., & Gelman, R. (1973). The development of communication skills: Modification in the speech of young children as a function of listener. *Monographs of the Society for Research in Child Development, 38,* 1–38.

Shayer, M., Kuchemann, D. E., & Wylam, H. (1976). The distribution of Piagetian stages of thinking in British middle and secondary school children. *British Journal of Educational Psychology, 46,* 164–173.

Shirley, M. M. (1931). *The first two years: A study of twenty-five babies. Postural and locomotor development.* Westport, CT: Greenwood.

Sigel, I. E. (1969). The Piagetian system and the world of education. In D. Elkind & J. H. Flavell (Eds.), *Studies in cognitive development: Essays in honor of Jean Piaget* (pp. 465–490). New York: Oxford University Press.

Siegel, L. S. (1968). The development of the ability to process information. *Journal of Experimental Child Psychology, 6,* 308–383.

Siegel, L. S., & Heaven, R. K. (1986). Categorization of learning disabilities. In S. J. Ceci (Ed.), *Handbook of cognitive, social and neurophysiological aspects of learning disabilities* (pp. 95–121). Hillsdale, NJ: Lawrence Erlbaum Associates.

Siegel, L. S., & Linder, B. (1984). Short-term memory processes in children with reading and arithmetic learning disabilities. *Developmental Psychology, 20,* 200–207.

Siegel, S. (1956). *Nonparametric statistics for the behavioral sciences.* York, PA: McGraw-Hill.

Siegler, R. S. (1976). Three aspects of cognitive development. *Cognitive Psychology, 8,* 481–520.

Siegler, R. S. (1978). The origins of scientific reasoning. In R. S. Siegler (Ed.), *Children's thinking: What develops?* (pp. 109–150). Hillsdale, NJ: Lawrence Erlbaum Associates.

Siegler, R. S., & Robinson, M. (1982). The development of numerical understanding. In H. W. Reese & L. P. Lipsitt (Eds.), *Advances in child development and behavior, 16,* 241–312. New York: Academic.

Sifft, J. M. (1978). *An application of neo-Piagetian theory to motor development.* Unpublished master's thesis, University of Wyoming, Laramie.

Simon, H. A. (1972). Complexity and the representation of patterned sequences of symbols. *Psychological Review, 79,* 369–382.

Simon, D. P., & Simon, H. A. (1978). Individual differences in solving physics problems. In R. S. Siegler (Ed.), *Children's thinking: What develops?* (pp. 324–348). Hillsdale, NJ: Lawrence Erlbaum Associates.

Skinner, B. F. (1950). Are theories of learning necessary? *Psychological Bulletin, 57,* 193–261.

Slobin, D. I. (1973). Cognitive prerequisites for the development of grammar. In C. A. Ferguson & D. I. Slobin (Eds.), *Studies of child language development* (pp. 175–276). New York: Holt.

Sloboda, J. A. (1974). The eye-hand span: An approach to the study of sight reading. *Psychology of Music, 2(2),* 4–10.

Sloboda, J. A. (1976a). The effect of item position on the likelihood of identification by inference in prose and music reading. *Canadian Journal of Psychology, 30,* 228–238.

Sloboda, J. A. (1976b). Visual perception of musical notation: Registering pitch symbols in memory. *Quarterly Journal of Experimental Psychology, 28,* 1–16.

Sloboda, J. A. (1977). Phrase units as determinants of visual processing in music reading. *British Journal of Psychology, 68,* 117–124.

Sloboda, J. A. (1978). The psychology of music reading. *Psychology of Music, 6(2),* 3–20.

Snow, R. E., Kyllonen, P. C., and Marshalek, B. (1984). The topography of ability and learning correlations. In R. Sternberg (Ed.), *Advances in the Psychology of Intelligence*. (pp. 47–103). Hillsdale, NJ: Lawrence Erlbaum Associates.

Spearman, C. (1904). "General Intelligence": Objectively determined and measured. *American Journal of Psychology, 15*, 201–292.

Spearman, C. (1927). *The abilities of man*. New York: MacMillan.

Spelke, E. S. (1988). Where perceiving ends and thinking begins: The apprehension of objects in infancy. In A. Yonas (Ed.), *Perceptual development in infancy: Minnesota symposia in child psychology* (pp. 197–234). Hillsdale, NJ: Lawrence Erlbaum Associates.

Spring, C., & Capps, C. (1974). Encoding speed, rehearsal, and a probed recall of dyslexic boys. *Journal of Educational Psychology, 66*, 780–786.

Spring, C. (1976). Encoding speed and memory span in dyslexic children. *Journal of Special Education, 10*, 35–40.

Spring, C., & Perry, L. (1983). Naming speed and serial recall in poor and adequate readers. *Contemporary Educational Psychology, 8*, 141–145.

Sroufe, A. L. (1979). Socioemotional development. In J. Osofsky (Ed.), *Handbook of infant development* (pp. 462–516). New York: Wiley.

Stanovich, K. E. (1986). Cognitive processes and the reading problems of learning disabled children: Evaluating the assumption of specificity. In J. K. Torgesen & B. Y. L. Wong (Eds.), *Psychological and educational perspectives on learning disabilities* (pp. 87–131). New York: Academic.

Starkey, P. D., & Cooper, R. G. (1980). Perception of numbers of human infants. *Science, 210*, 1033–1035.

Starkey, P. D., Spelke, E. S., & Gelman, R. (1983). Detection of intermodal numerical correspondence by human infants. *Science, 222*, 179–181.

Stein, N. L., & Glenn, C. G. (1979). An analysis of story comprehension in elementary school children. In R. Friedle (Ed.), *Discourse process: Multidisciplinary perspectives* (Vol. 2, pp. 53–120). Norwood, NJ: Ablex.

Stern, D. N. (1985). *The interpersonal world of the infant: A view from psychoanalysis and developmental psychology*. New York: Basic.

Sternberg, R. J. (1984). Mechanisms of cognitive development: A componential approach. In R. J. Sternberg (Ed.), *Mechanisms of cognitive development*. San Francisco: Freeman.

Sternberg, R. J. (1989). Domain generality versus domain specificity: The life and impending death of a false dichotomy. *Merrill-Palmer Quarterly, 35*, 115–131.

Sternberg, R. J., & Davidson, J. D. (1985). Cognitive development in the gifted and talented. In F. D. Horowitz & M. O'Brien (Eds.), *The gifted and talented: Developmental perspectives* (pp. 37–74). Washington, DC: American Psychological Association.

Stigler, J. W., & Perry, M. (1988). Mathematics learning in Japanese, Chinese, and American classrooms. In G. B. Saxe & M. Gearhatt (eds.) *Children's mathematics. New Directions for Child Development, 41*, 27–54.

Strang, J. D., & Rourke, B. P. (1983). Concept-formation/nonverbal reasoning abilities of children who exhibit specific academic problems with arithmetic. *Journal of Clinical Child Psychology, 12*, 33–39.

Strayer, J. (1983, April). *Affective and cognitive components of children's empathy.*

Paper presented at the meeting of the Society for Research in Child Development, Detroit.

Strayer, J. (1987, April). *Relation of different empathy measures to different prosocial behaviors.* Paper presented at the annual meeting of the Society for Research in Child Development, Baltimore, MD.

Stuss, D. T., (in press). Biological and psychological development of frontal executive functions. *Brain and cognition.*

Sugarman, S. (1982). *Children's categorization.* Hillsdale, NJ: Lawrence Erlbaum Associates.

Sundberg, J., & Lindblom, B. (1976). Generative theories in language and music descriptions. *Cognition, 4,* 99–122.

Swanson, H. L. (1978). Verbal encoding effects on the visual short-term memory of learning disabled and normal readers. *Journal of Educational Psychology, 70,* 539–544.

Swanson, H. L. (1983). A study of nonstrategic linguistic coding in visual recall of learning disabled readers. *Journal of Learning Disabilities, 16,* 209–216.

Swanson, H. L. (1984). Semantic and visual memory codes in learning disabled readers. *Journal of Experimental Child Psychology, 37,* 124–140.

Terman, L. M., & Merrill, M. A. (1973). *Stanford-Binet intelligence scale: Manual for the third revision Form L-M.* Chicago: The Riverside Publishing Company.

Thatcher, R. W. (in press). Maturation of the human frontal lobes: physiological evidence for staging. *Developmental neuropsychology.*

Thomas, J., & Bender, P. (1977). A developmental explanation for children's motor behaviour: A neo-Piagetian interpretation. *Journal of Motor Behaviour, 9,* 81–93.

Thurston, L. L. (1938). Primary mental abilities. *Psychometric Monographs,* No. 1.

Todor, J. (1975). Age differences in integration of components of motor tasks. *Perceptual and Motor Skills, 41,* 211–215.

Todor, J. (1979). Developmental differences in motor task integration: a test of Pascual-Leone's theory of constructive operators. *Journal of Experimental Child Psychology, 28,* 314–322.

Torgesen, J. K. (1977). Memorization processes in reading-disabled children. *Journal of Educational Psychology, 69,* 571–578.

Torgesen, J. K. (1985). Memory processes in learning disabled children. *Journal of Learning Disabilities, 18,* 350–357.

Torgesen, J. K., & Houck, G. (1980). Processing deficiencies in learning disabled children who perform poorly on the digit span task. *Journal of Educational Psychology, 72,* 141–160.

Toussaint, N. A. (1974). An analysis of synchrony between concrete operational tasks in terms of structural and performance demands. *Child Development, 45,* 922–1001.

Turiel, E. (1975). The development of social concepts. In D. DePalma & J. Foley (Eds.), *Moral development* (pp. 7–37). Hillsdale, NJ: Lawrence Erlbaum Associates.

Turiel, E. (1978). The development of concepts of social structure: Social convention. In J. Glick & K. A. Clarke-Steward (Eds.), *The Development of Social Understanding* (Vol. 1, pp. 25–107). New York: Gardner.

Vaughan, G. M., & Corballis, M. C. (1969). Beyond tests of significance: Estimating strength of effects in selected ANOVA designs. *Psychological Bulletin, 72,* 204–313.

Van de Koppel, J. M. H., & Van Helfteren, A. M. (1982). *The African Embedded Figures Test.* Tilburg, The Netherlands: Tilburg University.

Vernon, P. E. (1965). Ability factors and environmental influences. *American Psychologist, 20,* 723–733.

Vygotsky, L. S. (1962). *Thought and language.* Cambridge, MA: MIT Press. (Original work published 1934) E. Hanfmann, G. Vaker, translators.

Warrington, E. K., & Shallice, T. (1972). Neuropsychological evidence of visual storage in short term memory tasks. *Quarterly Journal of Experimental Psychology, 24,* 30–40.

Webb, R. A. (1974). Concrete and formal operations in very bright 6- to 11-year-olds. *Human Development, 17,* 292–300.

Weininger, O. (1986). *The Differential Diagnostic Technique: A visual motor projective test. Research and clinical use.* Springfield, IL: Charles C. Thomas.

Wechsler, D. (1967). *Wechsler Preschool and Primary Scale of Intelligence.* Palo Alto, CA: Psychological Corporation.

Wechsler, D. (1970). *Wechsler Intelligence Scale for Children* (Revised). Stanford: Psychological Corporation.

Wechsler, D. (1974). *Wechsler Intelligence Scale for Children* (Revised). New York: The Psychological Corporation.

Wilkensky, R. (1983). Story grammars versus story points. *The Behavioral and Brain Sciences, 4,* 577–591.

Wilson, E. O. (1975). *Sociobiology: The new synthesis.* Cambridge, MA: Belknap Press, Harvard University.

Wiser, M. (1988). The differentiation of heat and temperature: History of science and novice-expert shift. In S. Strauss (Ed.), *Ontogeny, phylogeny, and historical development* (pp. 28–48). Norwood, NJ: Ablex.

Wiser, M., & Carey, S. (1982). When heat and temperature were one. In D. Gentner & A. L. Stevens (Eds.), *Mental models* (pp. 267–297). Hillsdale, NJ: Lawrence Erlbaum Associates.

Witkin, H. A., Dyk, R. B., Faterson, H. F., Goodenough, D. R., & Karp, S. A. (1962). *Psychological differentiation.* New York: Wiley.

Wolf, T. (1976). A cognitive model of musical sight reading. *Journal of Psycholinguistic Research, 2,* 143–171.

Woodcock, R. W. (1973). *Woodcock Reading Mastery Tests.* Circle Pines, MN: American Guidance Service.

Author Index

Subject Index